The Register of the Company
of Pastors of Geneva
in the Time of Calvin

The Register of the Company of Pastors of Geneva in the Time of Calvin

Edited and Translated by
PHILIP EDGCUMBE HUGHES

Wipf & Stock
PUBLISHERS
Eugene, Oregon

Wipf and Stock Publishers
199 West 8th Avenue, Suite 3
Eugene, Oregon 97401

The Register of the Company of Pastors of Geneva in the Time of Calvin
By Hughes, Philip E.
Copyright©1966 Wm. B. Eerdmans Publishing Co.
ISBN: 1-59244-486-5
Publication date 1/23/2004
Previously published by Wm. B. Eerdmans Publishing Co., 1966

CONTENTS

Introduction   3

1541

   ECCLESIASTICAL ORDINANCES   35
      FOUR ORDERS IN THE CHURCH
      The duty of pastors   36
      The examination of pastors
      To whom it belongs to institute pastors
      The election of pastors
      Fixing a day of the week for assembling   37
      What is to be done when there are differences
         over doctrine   38
      Ministerial discipline
         Vices which are intolerable in a pastor
         Vices which can be endured provided they are
            rebuked   39
      Fixing a day of censure every three months   40
      The frequency, place, and time of preaching
      Appointment of five pastors and three coadjutors
      THE SECOND ORDER, WHICH WE HAVE CALLED TEACHERS
      Establishment of a college   41
      THE THIRD ORDER, WHICH IS THAT OF ELDERS, WHO
         ARE CALLED "COMMIS", OR THOSE DELEGATED
         BY THE SEIGNEURY TO THE CONSISTORY
      The manner of their election   42
      THE FOURTH ORDER OF ECCLESIASTICAL GOVERNMENT,
         NAMELY, DEACONS
      The hospital   43
      CONCERNING THE SACRAMENTS   44
      Baptism
      The supper
      CONCERNING MARRIAGE   45

VI   Contents

      INTRODUCTION OF HYMNS
      CONCERNING BURIAL
      THE VISITATION OF THE SICK   46
      THE VISITATION OF PRISONERS
      THE ORDER TO BE MAINTAINED IN THE CASE OF ADULTS
          FOR PRESERVING DISCIPLINE IN THE CHURCH   47
      The appointment of a day for the Consistory
      The persons whom the elders or delegates (commis)
          ought to admonish   48

1546

THE REGISTER   53

      ORDINANCES FOR COUNTRY PARISHES
      CONCERNING SERMONS   54
      CATECHISM
      PENALTIES
      BY WHOM FINES ARE TO BE EXACTED   55
      CONCERNING BAPTISM
      CONCERNING THE SUPPER   56
      CONCERNING THE TIME FOR ASSEMBLING IN CHURCH
      FAULTS WHICH CONTRAVENE THE REFORMATION APART
          FROM THOSE MENTIONED ABOVE
      Superstitions
      Blasphemies   57
      Contradiction of the Word
      Drunkenness
      Songs and dances   58
      Usury
      Disturbances
      Ill-will
      Games
      Fornication
      CONCERNING THE ELECTION OF GUARDS   59
      SENDING DELINQUENTS BEFORE THE CONSISTORY

1547

      MEMORANDUM FOR THE BRETHREN WHO ARE BEING SENT
          TO THE CHAPTER WHICH IS TO BE HELD AT GEX BY
          THE DELEGATES (COMMIS) OF THE SEIGNEURS OF
          BERNE ON THURSDAY 9 JUNE   60
      LETTER TO NEUCHATEL   64

Contents   VII

LETTERS FROM THE PRESBYTERY OF MORGES ON BEHALF OF LOUIS TREPPEREAU AND ANTOINE SAUNIER, MINISTERS	65
PETITION OF ADAM FUMEE AND MICHELLE MILLONE	68
THE CASE OF PIERRE BOUCHERON AND MARGUERITE DES BORDES	68
CALVIN SUBDUES AN UPROAR	70
EXTRACT FROM THE ORDINANCE OF MESSIEURS CONCERNING THE GIVING OF NAMES IN BAPTISM	71
MARRIAGE ORDINANCES ISSUED BY AUTHORITY OF MESSIEURS	72
Which persons may not marry without permission	
Persons who may marry without permission	73
For what reasons a promise may be rescinded	74
Promises are to be made simply	
Concerning the period of fulfilling a marriage after the making of a promise	
Concerning banns and engagements	75
Concerning the celebration of a marriage	
Concerning the communal dwelling of the husband with the wife	76
Concerning the degrees of consanguinity which prevent marriage	
Concerning the degrees of affinity	
For what reasons a marriage shall be declared null and void	77
For what reasons a marriage can be rescinded	

1548

VISITATION OF THE PARISHES	82
REQUEST FOR DIVORCE BY FRANCOIS FAVRE	84
TESTIMONIAL FOR MONSIEUR ANTOINE	85

1549

COPY OF A LETTER SENT BY THE MINISTERS OF THE CHURCH AT MONTBELIARD TO THE PASTORS OF THE CHURCH IN GENEVA, LAUSANNE, NEUCHATEL, AND ELSEWHERE THROUGHOUT THE DOMINION OF THE SEIGNEURS OF BERNE	87
THE REPLY TO THE ABOVE LETTER	88
NEGLIGENCE OVER REFORMATION REPROVED	90
THE AFFAIR OF M. PHILIPPE DE ECCLESIA	92
CONCERNING PIERRE TOUSSAIN OF MONTBELIARD	93

Copy of a letter from Pierre Toussain, pastor of the church at Montbeliard, to Calvin, Farel, Viret, and their colleagues
Second letter ... 95
To the letters above we replied in the following way ... 96
LETTER FROM THE COMPANY SENT TO A SYNOD OF MINISTERS, BOTH FRENCH AND GERMAN SPEAKING, OF THE STATE OF BERNE, HELD ON 19 MARCH 1549 ... 100
ARTICLES CONCERNING THE SACRAMENTS ... 101
CONTINUATION OF THE CASE OF M. PHILIPPE DE ECCLESIA ... 105
TESTIMONIAL FOR JEAN DE LA BARRE ... 108
M. PHILIPPE DE ECCLESIA AGAIN
CHARGES AGAINST M. JEAN FERRON ... 109
ORDINANCE OF MESSIEURS FORBIDDING GIRLS GUILTY OF FORNICATION TO WEAR THE VIRGIN'S HAT ... 112
ELECTION OF JEAN FABRI AS PASTOR ... 113
A MUTUAL AGREEMENT CONCERNING THE SACRAMENTS BETWEEN THE MINISTERS OF THE CHURCH IN ZURICH AND JOHN CALVIN, MINISTER OF THE CHURCH IN GENEVA, NOW PUBLISHED BY ITS AUTHORS ... 115
Heads of agreement ... 117
The whole spiritual government of the Church leads us to Christ
True knowledge of the sacraments comes from the knowledge of Christ
The nature of the knowledge of Christ
Christ our Priest and King
How Christ communicates Himself to us ... 118
Spiritual communion
The purposes of the sacraments
Thanksgiving ... 119
Distinction between the signs and the things signified
The promise in particular is to be regarded in the sacraments
The elements not to be gazed on ... 120
The sacraments effect nothing by themselves
God uses them as instruments, but in such a way that all the power is His
How the sacraments confirm
Not all who partake of a sacrament partake of the reality ... 121

Contents IX

    The sacraments do not confer grace
    The gifts of God are offered to all, but
      only believers appropriate them
    Believers before and apart from the use of
      the sacraments also partake of Christ
    Grace is not bound to the action of the
      sacraments, but the benefit of them is
      sometimes received after the action   122
    The idea of a local presence must be put away
    Explanation of the words of the Lord's supper,
      "This is my body"
    Concerning the eating of Christ's Body   123
    Against transubstantiation and other follies
    The body of Christ is locally in heaven
    Christ not to be worshipped in the bread
REPLY FROM ZURICH TO CALVIN'S LETTER OF
  1 AUGUST 1549   124

1550

FURTHER VISITATIONS   128
LETTERS TO DURAND AND NINAUX
ABROGATION OF FESTIVALS   130

1551

ALLIANCE BETWEEN BERNE AND GENEVA RENEWED   131
COMMOTION IN THE CITY
INTRUSION OF TWO HERETICS   132
JEROME BOLSEC REPRIMANDED
COMPLAINTS AGAINST M. PHILIPPE DE ECCLESIA   133
LETTER FROM CALVIN IN THE NAME OF THE COMPANY
  TO THE PRESBYTERY OF NEUCHATEL
LETTER CONCERNING THE SCANDALOUS CONDUCT OF SIMON
  GOLAND, PASTOR OF THE PRESBYTERY OF TERNIER   134
TESTIMONIAL FOR MATHIEU ISSOTIER   136
THE TRIAL OF JEROME BOLSEC   137
  PETITION FROM BOLSEC TO MESSIEURS   139
  COPIES OF LETTERS WRITTEN TO THE COUNCIL ON
    BEHALF OF BOLSEC BY JACQUES DE BOURGOGNE OF
    VEIGY   140
  ARTICLES WHICH WE HAVE EXTRACTED FROM THE
    OPINIONS HELD BY ONE CALLED MAITRE JEROME THIS
    16TH DAY OF OCTOBER 1551   142
  QUESTIONS FOR JEROME BOLSEC   145

BOLSEC'S REPLY	146
THE REPLIES GIVEN BY THE MINISTERS OF THE WORD OF GOD TO THE ANSWERS WRITTEN BY MAITRE JEROME BOLSEC	153
ARTICLES PROPOSED BY JEROME BOLSEC TO MAITRE JEAN CALVIN	163
CALVIN'S REPLY	166
COPY OF THE ARTICLES PRESENTED TO MESSIEURS BY THE MINISTERS FOR BOLSEC'S INTERROGATION	167
CORRESPONDENCE CONCERNING THE BOLSEC AFFAIR	169
I. Copy of a circular letter addressed by the Company of Pastors to the Swiss churches	
II. Reply from the ministers of Basle	172
III. Letters from Simon Sulzer to Calvin	175
IV. Reply from the ministers of Zurich	177
V. Reply from M. Farel and the ministers of Neuchâtel	180
VI. Letter from Oswald Myconius of Basle	184
DECISION ON THE TROUBLE CAUSED BY BOLSEC	186

1552

BANISHMENT OF M. JEAN DE SAINT-ANDRE FROM BERNESE TERRITORY	187
DIFFICULTIES OVER APPOINTMENT TO JUSSY	188
VISITATION OF PARISHES	190
LETTER FROM FIVE STUDENTS IN PRISON IN LYON	191
ANTONIO BARGIO AND HIS WIFE ELIZABETH	192
LETTER FROM AN UNKNOWN LADY PERSECUTED BY HER HUSBAND BECAUSE OF HER FAITH	193
REPLY TO THE PRECEDING LETTER	196
THE QUESTION OF PUBLIC PENITENCE	198
CRITICISM OF CALVIN'S INSTITUTES	200
PHILIPPE DE ECCLESIA ARRAIGNED	201
TESTIMONIAL GIVEN TO M. BERNARD ARNAIL, DOCTOR OF MEDICINE	206
DEATH OF LOUIS COUGNIER AND APPOINTMENT OF JEAN MACAR TO RUSSIN	207

1553

CERTAIN ARRANGEMENTS FOR PREACHING	209
ARTICLES PRESENTED TO MESSIEURS AGAINST PHILIPPE DE ECCLESIA	
LETTER FROM LAUSANNE CONCERNING FABRI AND VITALIS	211

Contents XI

LETTER FROM TREPPEREAU EXCUSING HIMSELF FOR LEAVING HIS PARISH	212
LETTER FROM LAUSANNE REQUESTING A TEACHER FOR THEIR COLLEGE	213
REPLY TO THE PRECEDING LETTER	214
LETTER FROM THE FRENCH CHURCH IN STRASBOURG CONCERNING TROUBLE-MAKERS NAMED TAPETIER AND NICAISE	215
REPLY TO THE PRECEDING LETTER	216
REPLY CONCERNING THE DIFFICULTIES BETWEEN FABRI AND VITALIS, SENT TO MESSIEURS OF LAUSANNE	218
NICOLAS COLLADON APPOINTED TO VANDOEUVRES IN PLACE OF DE ECCLESIA	220
FRANCOIS BOURGOIN REQUESTS A CHANGE OF PARISH	
LETTER TO THE COMPANY FROM MACAR, WHO WAS IN BERNE	221
FONCENEX	222
THE TRAL OF MICHAEL SERVETUS	223
THE THEOLOGICAL DISPUTE	
OPINIONS OR PROPOSITIONS TAKEN FROM THE BOOKS OF MICHAEL SERVETUS	224
THE REPLY OF MICHAEL SERVETUS TO THE ARTICLES OF JOHN CALVIN	
A BRIEF REFUTATION OF THE ERRORS AND IMPIETIES OF MICHAEL SERVETUS	225
PHILIBERT BERTHELIER	285
CONCERNING THE ORDER OF THE CONSISTORY	286
LETTER FROM THE COMPANY OF PASTORS OF GENEVA TO THE BELIEVERS OF CERTAIN ISLANDS IN FRANCE	289
DEATH OF SERVETUS	290
AUTHORITY OF THE CONSISTORY	291
OBJECTIONS TO FAREL'S PREACHING	292
PHILIBERT BERTHELIER	293

1554

FRANCOIS BERTHELIER	294
PHILIBERT BERTHELIER	
RAYMOND CHAUVET ARRESTED AT DRAILLANS	295
A LIBELLOUS BOOK HANDED TO MESSIEURS	
ANDRE VULLIOD BANISHED	296
RAYMOND CHAUVET RELEASED	
JEAN DE MONTLIARD APPOINTED TO DRAILLANS	297

M. ANDRE LE COUR APPOINTED TO CELIGNY	
TESTIMONIAL FOR JEAN DE PIOTAY, SURGEON	
A SCOTSMAN	
JOURNEY OF JEAN FABRI TO BERNE	298
LETTER FROM THE PASTORS OF GENEVA TO THEIR EXCELLENCIES OF BERNE	299
LETTER FROM THE PASTORS OF GENEVA TO THEIR COLLEAGUES OF BERNE	301

1555

THE CONSISTORY'S AUTHORITY CONFIRMED	305
RAYMOND CHAUVET SENT TO BERNE	
CALVIN AND CHAUVET GO TO BERNE	306
ANSWER TO THE ACCUSATIONS MADE AGAINST THE MINISTERS OF GENEVA	307
CALVIN AND CHAUVET VISIT BERNE AGAIN	
JEAN VERNOU AND JEAN LAUVERGEAT	308
M. JACQUES L'ANGLOIS SENT TO POITIERS	
TESTIMONIAL FOR JEAN THIERSAULT	
CHAUVET AND MACAR GO TO BERNE	309
TUMULT IN GENEVA	
LABORIER AND TRIGALET FOR PIEDMONT	
RETURN OF MACAR FROM BERNE	310
IMPRISONMENT OF VERNOU, LABORIER, AND TRIGALET	
D'AIREBAUDOUZE APPOINTED TO JUSSY	
MATTEO GRIBALDI REPRIMANDED	311
TESTIMONIAL FOR NICOLAS PASTEUR	
LETTER FROM LABORIER, VERNOU, TRIGALET, AND OTHERS IMPRISONED AT CHAMBERY TO THE COMPANY OF PASTORS OF GENEVA	

1556

DEATH OF ABEL POUPIN	314
DEPOSITION OF JEAN FABRI	
VISITATIONS IN THE CITY	315
CLAUDE BADUEL	
PIERRE DUC	316
LOUIS ENOCH	
PRESENTATION OF MACAR AND ENOCH	
PRESENTATION OF BADUEL	
JEAN VIGNAULX SENT TO PIEDMONT	
THE CONSISTORY PERMITTED TO ADMINISTER THE OATH	317

Contents   XIII

    BOINVILLE
    MINISTERS SENT TO BRAZIL
    VISIT OF CALVIN TO FRANKFURT   318
    MARTIN DE ARGUES SENT TO BOURGES
    JEAN LAUVERGEAT SENT TO PIEDMONT
    ORDINANCES CONCERNING BLASPHEMY AND ADULTERY
    ALBERT SENT TO PIEDMONT   319

1557

    DISCUSSIONS AUTHORIZED   320
    JEAN CHAMBELI SENT TO PIEDMONT
    MATHIEU GRANDJEAN APPOINTED SCHOOLMASTER AT THE
        HOSPITAL
    A MARRIAGE DISSOLVED BECAUSE OF TOO GREAT
        INEQUALITY OF AGE   321
    SCHOOLMASTERS IN THE VILLAGES
    JEAN GERARD SENT TO BLOIS
    SYNDICS
    DE CHERPONT APPOINTED SCHOOLMASTER AT NEUCHATEL
    VISITATIONS   322
    M. GASPARD SENT TO PARIS
    JEAN D'ESPOIR ASSIGNED TO ROUEN
    JEAN DE PONVERS ASSIGNED TO THE ISLAND OF
        NOIRMOUTIER
    DEATH OF SAINT ANDRE
    CLAUDE CHEVALIER ASSIGNED TO POITIERS   323
    ANTOINE BACHELAR ASSIGNED TO LYON
    MARTIN TACHARD AND GIOFFREDO VARAGLI SENT
        TO PIEDMONT
    EVRARD APPOINTED TO ANVERS
    MONSIEUR DE LA GARDE APPOINTED TO ANDUZE   324
    ANTOINE VIVES APPOINTED TO ISSOUDUN
    ELECTION OF NEW MINISTERS
    CHARLES MAUBUE APPOINTED SCHOOLMASTER
        OF THE HOSPITAL   326
    DE MONTLIARD APPOINTED TO CELIGNY AND
        NICOLAS PETIT TO DRAILLANS
    COLLADON, DE COLLONGES, AND DU PONT PRESENTED
        IN GENEVA   327
    MATHIEU GRANDJEAN PRESENTED IN RUSSIN
    CLAUDE BADUEL PRESENTED AT VANDEOUVRES
    ARRANGEMENTS IN GENEVA
    ANDRE LE COUR PRESENTED AT CHANSY AND CARTIGNY 328

DE SAULES GOES TO PARIS
TENSION BETWEEN GENEVA AND BERNE
LE GAY APPOINTED TO BEARN
PASQUIER BACNOT APPOINTED TO PIEDMONT ... 329
CLAUDE BOISSIERE ASSIGNED TO AIX
FRANCOIS LE GAY FOR BEARN
LETTER FROM NICOLAS DES GALLARS, IN PARIS, TO HIS GENEVAN COLLEAGUES
LETTER FROM CALVIN TO DES GALLARS ... 331
LETTER FROM THE COMPANY OF PASTORS TO THE CHURCH IN PARIS ... 333
DEATH OF MATHIEU MALESIER ... 336
D'ESPOIR APPOINTED TO BOSSEY

1558

JEAN MACAR APPOINTED TO PARIS ... 337
CLAUDE BOISSIERE APPOINTED TO SAINTES
JACQUES ROUVIERES AND LANCELOT D'ALBEAU APPOINTED TO TOURS
MINISTERS' SALARIES INCREASED ... 338
APPOINTMENTS TO ISSOUDUN, BOURGES, BLOIS, AND ROMORANTIN
MARTIN TACHARD APPOINTED TO PRAGELAT
CHARLES DU PLESSIS APPOINTED TO TOURS
AMBROISE FAGET APPOINTED TO ORLEANS ... 339
REVOLT OF NICOLAS PETIT
JEAN MACAR BROUGHT BACK FROM PARIS
APPOINTMENTS TO LYON AND POITIERS ... 340
LUCAS HOBE APPOINTED TO SAINT-JEAN-D'ANGELY
MINISTERS' SALARIES CONVERTED TO MONEY
JACQUES CHRISTIANI APPOINTED TO ISSOUDUN
CHAMBELI APPOINTED TO LE HARVE DE GRACE ... 341
APPOINTMENTS TO GUYENNE
OTHER APPOINTMENTS
THEODORE DE BEZE CALLED TO THE MINISTRY

1559

PIERRE VIRET INVITED TO GENEVA ... 342
DEATH OF JACQUES BERNARD
DEATH OF CLAUDE DU PONT ... 343
THEODORE DE BEZE CONFIRMED AS MINISTER
APPOINTMENT OF JEAN MERLIN

Contents   XV

APPOINTMENTS TO THE COLLEGE	
APPOINTMENTS TO PARISHES	344
LETTER FROM CALVIN TO AN UNKNOWN WOMAN	
SUMMARY OF THE CONFESSION OF FAITH OF THE STUDENTS OF THE ACADEMY OF GENEVA	345
APPOINTMENTS TO FRANCE	347
FURTHER APPOINTMENTS	
DEATH OF LANCELOT D'ALBEAU, MARTYR	348
DEATH OF JEAN RANDON	

1560

VARIOUS APPOINTMENTS	349
THEODORE DE BEZE IN GASCOGNE	
DEATH OF JEAN TAGAUT	
CLAUDE DUMOULIN APPOINTED TO FONTENAY	
DEATH OF JEAN BALDIN AND APPOINTMENT OF GASPARD CARMEL IN HIS PLACE	350
VARIOUS APPOINTMENTS	
DEATH OF GASPARD CARMEL, FAREL'S NEPHEW, AND APPOINTMENT OF CHARLES MAUBUE TO MOENS	
CLAUDE BADUEL APPOINTED PROFESSOR	
DEATH OF JEAN MACAR	351
MONSIEUR D'ANDUZE RETURNS TO GENEVA AND JEAN PINAULT GOES TO JUSSY	
JEAN BOULIER APPOINTED TO VANDOEUVRES	

1561

VARIOUS APPOINTMENTS	352

1562

FURTHER APPOINTMENTS	354
CHURCHMEN FROM LYON ADMONISHED	355
DE BEZE AND FRANCE	
FURTHER APPOINTMENTS	356
FRICTION AMONG THE PASTORS	
ADVICE OFFERED TO CERTAIN BRETHREN	357

1563

VARIOUS APPOINTMENTS	360

1564

THE YEAR OF CALVIN'S DEATH	362
ANTOINE CHEVALIER AND CAEN	365
ARRANGEMENTS FOLLOWING CALVIN'S DEATH	
REQUEST FROM JERSEY	366
RETURN OF JEAN-RAYMOND MERLIN	367
APPOINTMENT OF JEAN TREMBLEY	
OUTBREAK OF PLAGUE IN GENEVA	
PUNISHMENT OF GASPARD ROCCA	371
COMPLAINT AGAINST THE COUNCIL	
DISMISSAL OF MERLIN	
APPOINTMENT OF CHARLES PERROT AND JEAN-FRANCOIS SALVART	372
CHARGES AGAINST AN UNNAMED PERSON	373
DEATH OF MATURIN CORDIER	374

The Register of the Company
of Pastors of Geneva
in the Time of Calvin

INTRODUCTION

It was only late in 1546, more than ten years after Calvin's first arrival in their city, that the pastors of the Genevan church started to keep a register of their affairs and transactions. Those ten years had seen not only Calvin's coming in 1536, but also his expulsion in 1538 and his return in 1541, now to remain and lead the Reformation in Geneva for the remaining twenty-three years of his life. Unfortunately, the register was not as faithfully kept as one would have wished. It seems to have been written up somewhat spasmodically, with the result that there are numerous gaps and omissions, sometimes at points where we should very much like to have more information. Had the secretaries of the Company of Pastors been aware that what they were writing up was to become a historic document, they would doubtless have left us a fuller and more detailed record. As it is, however, it provides only a partial account of the doings and deliberations of the Company of Pastors in Calvin's time. Fortunately, there are other sources of information by which the record can be supplemented and filled out. But in itself the Register of the Company of Pastors is, none the less, a document the importance of which it would be difficult to exaggerate. The publication of its text makes available an indispensable work of reference for all serious students of Calvin and the city which adopted him.[1]

It is a popular fantasy that the Frenchman John Calvin descended on Geneva as a religious tyrant whose aim was to dominate and subdue the unwilling populace of this city of no more than moderate importance and size. (It numbered some 20,000 souls in his day, which is comparable to the population of a large city parish of our day.) The fact is that nothing was further from his mind than to remain and make his home in this

---

[1] The original manuscript of *The Register of the Company of Pastors* is in the State Archives of the city of Geneva, together with a wealth of other material of the greatest interest and value. There are also important documents and *Calviniana* in the possession of the University of Geneva.

3

place, and nothing was further from his desires than to be involved in the tensions, conflicts, and harassments of public life which are the lot of the religious leader, and which were especially so in those troubled times of transition. The height of Calvin's ambition was to lead a life of scholarly retirement devoting himself to the literary tasks which he felt he had been called to fulfil. Prior to his fortuitous (as it seemed) arrival in Geneva, William Farel and Peter Viret, in fulfilment of the desire of both Council and people, had already made a start with the preaching of the Reformed faith and the establishing of evangelical worship there. It was not, therefore, to a hostile scene that he came.

Calvin describes (in the preface of his commentary on the book of Psalms) how, after his experience of a sudden conversion, being retiring (*subrusticus*) by nature, he had set his heart on an obscure and leisurely existence congenial to a man with scholarly objectives. He was actually on his way to Strasbourg, intent on finding the desired seclusion there, when the fateful encounter with Farel in Geneva took place — and even his going by way of Geneva, where he designed to spend no more than a single night, was fortuitous, in that, because of the recurrence of hostilities between Francis I and Charles V, the direct road from Paris to Strasbourg was blocked, making it necessary for him to travel by a circuitous route. So he arrived in Geneva, a bird of passage, incognito and unannounced. But someone recognized him and betrayed his presence to Farel — and that, virtually, was the end of his well-laid plans for a peaceful and detached existence. Farel lost no time: "Learning that my heart was set on a sheltered life of private studies, and finding that he gained nothing by his entreaties, he proceeded to utter an imprecation that God would curse my leisure if I should withhold my help when the necessity was so great," Calvin writes. His resistance was broken, however unwillingly; he abandoned his cherished purpose and his journey; but his naturally timid and reticent disposition caused him to stipulate that he would not place himself under obligation to assume any particular office in the church.

In this young man, then twenty-seven years old, the fiery Farel discerned the master spirit that was needed if the building of the edifice of the Reformation was to be successfully carried through in Geneva. Recoiling, as we have seen, from any position of prominence, John Calvin commenced his career in the city with the humble title of *Lecteur en la sainte Ecriture en l'église de Genève*, which indicates that his personal wishes were respected to the extent that he was allowed to occupy the post of teacher, certainly less conspicuous than that of pastor. But it was not long — and for a man of his magisterial abilities it could not have been long — before he was compelled by circumstances of controversy in the city to display his exceptional qualities of mind and personality and also to add to his teaching commitments the responsibility of public preaching. This first period of two years would have been taxing enough for the most imperious of spirits: how much more for a man like Calvin who had no taste for public affairs and still longed for the solitude of the scholar's sanctuary. That he was impelled by no ambition or psychological urge to play the part of a dictator is shown by his own admission (in the same preface): "I was not animated by such greatness of mind as not to rejoice more than was seemly when certain commotions caused me to be expelled from Geneva". It was a dispute with the civil authorities, involving the right of the pastors to speak freely from their pulpits and to act freely in the administration or otherwise of the sacrament that led to the banishment of Calvin, Farel, and Viret from Geneva on 23 April 1538.

For Calvin at any rate, it was an occasion for rejoicing to the extent that it seemed that the moment had now come when he could with a good conscience withdraw from the public scene and devote himself in tranquillity to his literary pursuits. But it was not to be even now; for on his arrival in Strasbourg and the announcement of his intention not to accept appointment to any official post in the church there, his friend Martin Bucer threatened him with divine judgment, somewhat after the manner of Farel two years previously, holding before him the admonitory example of the prophet Jonah. Far more reluctantly did he respond subsequently to the call to return to Geneva. In going back he was governed, not by personal inclination, but by his sense of duty and his love for the Church of Christ in Geneva: "The welfare of this church lay so near to my heart", he says again, "that for its sake I would not have hesitated to lay down my life; nevertheless my timidity suggested to me many reasons for excusing myself from again voluntarily taking on my shoulders so heavy a burden. At length, however, a solemn and conscientious regard to my duty prevailed with me to return to the flock from which I had been torn: but with what grief, tears, and misgivings I did this the Lord is my best witness".

Calvin's banishment from Geneva lasted two and a half years. As the *Guillermins* (a title formed from Farel's Christian name, Guillaume) established themselves and some degree of peace and order was restored to the Genevan scene, a situation appropriate to the reinstatement of Calvin came into being. An official delegation was despatched from the city to entreat the Reformer to return. This was in October 1540. Farel added his voice to the solicitations; but Calvin replied to him: "I would prefer a hundred other deaths to this cross on which I would have to die a thousand times each day". "As often as I think how unhappy I was at Geneva", he wrote again to his friend, "I tremble in my innermost being when mention is made of my return. . . . I know well that wherever I go I must always expect to meet with suffering, and that, if I will live for Christ, life must be a conflict. But when I think to what tortures my conscience was exposed, to what agonies I was subjected, and how I suffered the loss of all rest and quiet, I must pray you to forgive me if I dread that place as destructive of peace and safety". And the following year: "If I had the choice I would do anything rather than what you wish, Farel. But as I am not left to my own choice, I bring my heart as a sacrifice and offering to the Lord". Understandably, too, Bucer was eager to keep Calvin with him in Strasbourg, and the civil authorities there were unwilling to release him until persuaded by insistent letters from Zürich and Basle as well as Geneva, which urged the necessity of Calvin's presence for the well-being of both church and state in Geneva. Neuchâtel, incidentally, had proved adamant in refusing to release Farel. And so Calvin (and Strasbourg) yielded at length to this unwelcome pressure. On 13 September 1541 he entered the city of Geneva again, never now to abandon it. His advent was greeted with scenes of joy and with every mark of civic honour. The populace spontaneously demonstrated their contrition for having allowed him to be driven from their midst.

But Calvin's return was in no sense that of the triumphant potentate. At no time did he attempt to usurp the authority of the civil magistrate, though it was only to be expected that a mind as powerful as his would leave its stamp not only on the church but also on the state; nor is it surprising, taking into account also his legal training and knowledge, that his counsel was repeatedly sought by the secular authorities — but always on such occasions his services were given in his capacity as a private person and without regard to his ecclesiastical status. Indeed, the whole structure of society as conceived in Calvin's mind was based on the distinction between church and state as two separate powers whose spheres of authority were clearly defined, the former wielding the spiritual sword in the faithful proclamation of the Word of God, and the latter the secular sword in the maintaining of good and just government and the punishment of offenders

INTRODUCTION

against the statutory laws; and both being subject to the supreme authority of Almighty God. At the same time, while each power was regarded as having an autonomy of function, the relationship envisaged was one of harmony in which church and state cooperated fruitfully with each other to the glory of God. In practice, however, it was not always easy to agree on the precise line of demarcation that should be drawn between the two jurisdictions, with the result that conflicts — for example, the dispute (of which more will be said later) as to whether the right of excommunication belonged to those who wielded the spiritual sword or to those who wielded the secular sword.

Concrete regulations concerning the functions of the church in Geneva and its relationship to the state were embodied in the Ecclesiastical Ordinances which were officially adopted and promulgated by the General Council on 20 November 1541, and which are prefixed to the Register of the Company of Pastors.[2] The preamble of this important document declared that there was need for "a certain rule and method of living by which each estate attends to the duty of its office", and that accordingly it had been deemed "advisable that the spiritual government of the kind which our Lord demonstrated and instituted by His Word should be set out in good order so that it might be established and observed among us". Of special significance is the concluding proviso which was added to the Ordinances to reassure the magistracy that there was no intention that the church should encroach on its domain:

> All this is to be done in such a way that the ministers have no civil jurisdiction and wield only the spiritual sword of the Word of God, as St. Paul commands them, and that there is no derogation by this Consistory from the authority of the seigneury or the magistracy; but the civil power shall continue in its entirety. And in cases where there is need to administer some punishment or to restrain the parties, the ministers together with the Consistory, having heard the parties and administered such reprimands and admonishments as are desirable, shall report the whole matter to the Council, which thereupon shall take steps to set things in order and pass judgment according to the requirements of the case.

The following July the form of oath to be required of all ministers on their admission to the pastoral office was approved by the Council. The minister had to swear that he would serve God faithfully, would observe the Ecclesiastical Ordinances, would maintain the honour and welfare of the city and its

---

[2] See pp. 35ff. below.

rulers, and would obey the laws and the magistracy of the republic, without prejudice to the liberty which belonged to him in the work of teaching as God had commanded and in fulfilling the various duties of his office.

The Ecclesiastical Ordinances defined four orders as having been instituted by Christ for the government of His Church: namely, pastors, teachers, elders, and deacons. The pastors, to whom alone the public ministry of Word and sacraments was entrusted, were to be elected to their office only after a searching test of their ability in theology and homiletics and an investigation to establish the blamelessness of their lives. Those so elected were to be presented to the Council, with whom it rested to ratify the ministers' choice; and, finally, the common consent of the members of the church was obtained by presenting the candidates to the people in public preaching. Their induction was to follow a ceremony of swearing in before the Council. These provisions immediately show how closely church and state were linked together in the Reformed perspective. This bond was further emphasized by the arrangement that any dispute over a doctrinal issue which the ministers were unable to resolve among themselves was to be referred to the civil authorities for judgment. Again, decisions of the ministers concerning the discipline of any of their number found guilty of delinquency were to be referred to the Council, to whom the right was reserved of ratifying or otherwise the punishment proposed.

The collaboration of church with state was made even more intimate by the regulations governing the appointment of the order of elders, who were the official ecclesiastical delegates of the civil power. Two were to be elected from the Little Council, four from the Council of Sixty, and six from the Council of Two Hundred, men of good character and reputation, who together with the Company of Pastors constituted the Consistory. The primary function of the elders was the supervision of the morals and discipline of the citizenry in their relationship to the church.

Of the remaining two orders, the teachers, as their name implies, were to be responsible for the education and Christian instruction of the people, especially the young, and one of the objectives in the establishment of a college was to ensure that future generations might not lack persons adequately trained and equipped both for the ministry of the church and for the government of the state. The fourth order, that of deacons, was charged with the care of and the administration of charity to the poor, the sick, and the aged, for whom suitable institutions were provided. Begging, accordingly, was declared an offence.

But the marriage between church and state in Geneva, however ideal in theory, was not one of uninterrupted harmony in day to day experience. Personality of genius though he was, there is plenty of evidence to demonstrate the falsity of the fashionable assertion that it was Calvin who always called the tune and tyrannically governed the life of the Genevan republic. Indeed, the civil power did not show any noticeable disposition to relinquish its authority or submissively to place itself under the control either of the church as a whole or of Calvin in particular. Calvin's years in Geneva were years of struggle rather than domination. To recognize this fact is not to minimize the extent to which a great mind was able over the years to impress its vision on the course of events and on the moulding of a community. Calvin's achievement — and it was in all essentials *his* — was truly phenomenal; it rested, however, not on dictatorial imposition, but on the logic of the scriptural principles which he sought to elucidate and apply. This alone explains the enduring nature of his achievement.

It should not be forgotten that when Calvin first came to Geneva, and was unwillingly held there by Farel, the city had already committed itself to the Reformation. Already, before his arrival, the state had not only overthrown the papal hegemony and outlawed the celebration of the mass, but had also pronounced strict penalties against libertinism and made church attendance obligatory on pain of a fine (measures of which Calvin is commonly said to have been the initiator by those who caricature him as a misanthropic kill-joy). All along, in jealously guarding what it considered its prerogatives, the state sought to have the last word and to exercise the power of veto. Matters even of faith no less than of worship had ordinarily to be submitted to the Council for approval and ratification. Thus in 1537 we find the Council sanctioning the confession of faith that Farel had prepared, issuing statutes concerning the administration of baptism and holy communion, and assuming to itself the right of pronouncing judgment in matrimonial cases after consultation with the ministers. In the same year the Council authorized the holding of a public conference with the Anabaptists, determined the length and conditions of its duration, and then decreed the banishment of all Anabaptists and forbade Farel to engage in such discussions in future without the Council's permission. It was criticism from the city's pulpits of unjustified interference in the ecclesiastical sphere which, in 1538, led to the attempt by the Council to impose a ban on preaching and thereafter to the expulsion of Calvin and his colleagues from Geneva.

But there is no evidence to suggest that during Calvin's absence from the city-state the people found themselves able to relax under a more indulgent régime. They were not granted any greater freedom of person or of opinion; the simple reason being that it was the duly appointed Council, not a fictitious tyrant named Calvin, that had ruled the republic hitherto and that continued to rule it. Why should the Council be expected to alter the regulations which it itself had passed? Accordingly, during the years of Calvin's banishment we see the magistracy maintaining a stern surveillance over the lives of the inhabitants, insisting on attendance at church and at holy communion, rigorously opposing all forms of papistry, and imposing a strict censorship on the publications of the printing-houses. It is absurd, therefore, to speak as though the expulsion of Calvin was symptomatic of the state's lack of sympathy with the Reformation and of a longing for less exacting standards of religion and morality. Nor did the recall of Calvin indicate any fundamental change in the state of affairs. It has been suggested, for instance, that the Consistory was instituted as an instrument of domination and as such presented a threat to the authority of the Council. But the facts do not support such a view and in any case, as Calvin himself wrote to the ministers of Zürich, the Consistory was formed "for the purpose of regulating the morals of the place, and had no civil jurisdiction, but only the right of reproof in accordance with the Word of God, the most severe sentence in its power being that of excommunication".

It was precisely over the right of excommunication that a protracted dispute developed, a dispute that illustrates with particular clarity the tenacity with which the civil power clung to what it had decided were its own prerogatives, even in the face of the most persistent pressure from the church. As a chronicle of this dispute the Register of the Company of Pastors is a contemporary document of special interest. Calvin, as we have seen, considered that the right of excommunication belonged to the Company of Pastors, in accordance with his understanding of the Ecclesiastical Ordinances. The Council, however, interpreted the situation otherwise. Ordinarily, in ecclesiastical matters, it rested with the Council to pronounce and impose the penalty for any infraction of the regulations. But the ministry claimed that excommunication was an exception to this rule, and, on the face of it, the Ordinances would seem to indicate plainly enough that excommunication was a discipline within their jurisdiction. Recalcitrant persons who persistently refused to heed the admonitions addressed to them were to be "forbidden the communion of the supper" or "separated from the church" and denounced to the Council, the ban evidently being imposed by the Consistory and the denunciation that followed being intended both for the information of the Council and also so that the Council might take any further disciplinary action that might be deemed necessary under the civil law.[3] The members of the Council doubtless argued that the terms of the concluding proviso of the Ecclesiastical Ordinances (already quoted above) justified their interpretation of things, and they may also have been swayed by the consideration that Zwingli and Bullinger in Zürich, and leaders in other Reformed centres in Switzerland had shown themselves content to leave the machinery of excommunication in the hands of the magistracy, judging that the church was sufficiently safeguarded by the Christian policy to which their states had committed themselves.

In March 1543, some fifteen months after the promulgation of the Ecclesiastical Ordinances, it is recorded in the Council's Register that the question as to whether or not the Consistory should have the power of banning those incapacitated from receiving communion was discussed in the Council of Sixty, and that "it was resolved that the Consistory should have neither jurisdiction nor power to ban from the supper, but only to admonish and then to report to the Council, so that the Seigneury might pass judgment on the delinquents according to their deserts". Anyone, therefore, from whom the pastors might withhold the sacrament was tempted to feel that an appeal to the Council might be to his advantage. In September 1548, for example, the Council attended to a complaint made by a man named Amar and ruled that the ministers possessed the right "only of admonition and not of excommunication"; and in December of the same year the Council countermanded the pastors by authorizing Guichard Roux to receive the sacrament. Again, in February 1553, we find the pastors objecting before the Council that the Consistory was being treated contemptuously by a number of people who were saying that excommunication was not a function of this body, and demanding that the Consistory should be treated with greater respect.

This whole dispute came to a head over the case of Philibert Berthelier, whom the Consistory had banned from communion in 1551. Two days before Christmas in 1552 the Council sought to bring about that those who had been excommunicated should be restored to the fellowship of the holy table, including Berthelier. But the rebelliousness of spirit which Berthelier displayed was,

[3] See pp. 48f. below.

it seemed, so unmistakable, that even the Council was convinced of his unworthiness and supported the ban that had been placed on him.[4] Subsequently however, the Council reversed their attitude and, without consulting with the Consistory, told Berthelier that he could consider himself free to receive communion. Not surprisingly, this action evoked the strongest protestations from the ministers, "who unanimously declared that they could not admit this man, or others like him, to the supper until the Consistory had evidence of his repentance, and had absolved him". They also objected that the Ecclesiastical Ordinances made it clear that the right of excommunication belonged to the Consistory and not to the Council. Calvin, moreover, voiced a public protest from the pulpit. On 7 September 1553 the city ministers, apart from Calvin, presented themselves before the Council and protested that the Council was unlawfully demanding that they should break their oath of obedience to the Council's own ordinances. The Council in turn retorted that it had no intention of violating the regulations it had imposed. The following day the ministers presented a written plea to the Council in which they maintained not only that the right of excommunication was plainly assigned to the pastors in the Ecclesiastical Ordinances, but also that the added requirement that persons thus banned should be reported to the Council did not indicate that the Council had a power of veto over the Consistory's decisions, but that the Council should take suitable steps to deal with any who might show themselves refractory and scornful of spiritual discipline. It was then, such persons being a scandal to society, that the state should exercise the power of the sword with which it had been entrusted. Otherwise the dignity and authority with which the Consistory was vested would be brought into contempt, and might better be abolished altogether.[5]

On 21 December the Council ruled that, because of his continued intransigence, Philibert Berthelier should not be readmitted to communion. His brother François was also excommunicated because of the outrageous accusations he had made against the ministers in the presence of the Council. But the controversy dragged on for another full year before it was finally resolved. At a session of the Council of Sixty and the Council of Two Hundred held on 24 January 1555 Calvin, who was accompanied by the other ministers of the city, addressed the assembly and then the first syndic, Amblard Corne announced that it had been resolved

[4] See p. 205 below.
[5] See pp. 286ff. below.

that "the Consistory should retain its status and exercise its accustomed authority, in accordance with the Word of God and the Ordinances previously passed".[6] It might have been thought that so imprecise a statement would be less than satisfactory and open to interpretation either way; but evidently its context was one which conceded to the pastors the right which they had claimed all along in this dispute.

Another matter that was to prove a source of friction between church and state concerned the dismissal of ministers who had been found guilty of offences which were regarded as incapacitating them for the pastoral office. In such cases there was no dispute as to where the final authority lay: the Ecclesiastical Ordinances made it quite plain that the pronouncing of the sentence of deposition belonged to the Council.[7] The problem arose when the Council showed itself unwilling to accede to the pastors' request for the removal of one of their number whom they judged unworthy to continue as a fellow pastor. Philippe de Ecclesia was arraigned before the ministers of the Genevan church on 15 February 1549 and admitted at least in part, the justness of the charge that he had been guilty of teaching certain errors and absurdities. A fraternal reprimand was administered to him and he was barred from speaking at the meetings of the Congregation until the next day of censures. This action was the culmination of frequent warnings that had been given him in the past. De Ecclesia expressed his acceptance of the decision of the brethren, and his plea that the discipline imposed on him might not be made public was granted. He was admonished also himself not to disclose what had taken place in the Congregation and to avoid the company of evil living and dissolute persons.[8] De Ecclesia, however, failed to honour this agreement and shortly after was recalled for uttering further calumnies against his fellow ministers and their doctrine and for revealing what had taken place at the time of his previous arraignment. His answers to the accusations, which he denied, were inconsistent and hypocritical, and because of his intransigence and bad faith it was resolved that he should be deposed from the ministry and that the Council should be informed accordingly. When summoned before the Council de Ecclesia denied every accusation and countercharged the Company of Pastors with fabricating a case against him. The response of the Council was a request

[6] See pp. 305 below.
[7] See p. 39 below.
[8] See pp. 92f. below.

to the ministers to pardon him and restore him to his place among them.

Understandably, the ministers felt this decision to be outrageous and seriously damaging to the dignity of their office, and they informed the Council that they were unable to reconsider their judgment concerning de Ecclesia's unsuitability to continue in the pastoral office. But the Council was no less obdurate and repeated its instruction that he was to be reinstated. On receiving a further remonstrance, the Council, while acknowledging that de Ecclesia's conduct had been reprehensible, undertook to administer a severe reprimand, warning him that if he appeared before it again there would be no further leniency. At the same time it persisted in its demand that the ministers should restore him. With this demand the Company now complied, though unwillingly and contrary to their convictions, declaring that responsibility for any harm resulting to the church rested on the shoulders of the Council.[9]

De Ecclesia continued to be a thorn in the side of the Company of Pastors. On 13 April 1549, just a week after the Council's ruling, he was made to withdraw from the Congregation, being told that, until such time as there was evidence of a change of heart on his part, he would not be permitted to preach in the Congregation when it would ordinarily have been his turn to do so. This action was justified on the grounds that the pastors had explained to the Council that they would tolerate an evil which they were prevented from removing: they would accept de Ecclesia as a minister conforming to the Council's ruling, but they were unable to welcome him as a brother.[10] De Ecclesia next appears in the Register of the Company of Pastors in August 1551 when his brothers-in-law complained to the Congregation about his objectionable behaviour to his wife, their sister, and to their family in general. This *contretemps* seems to have been satisfactorily settled by the Congregation and a reconciliation effected between the parties concerned.[11]

Nearly a year later, in March 1552, de Ecclesia was the cause of further trouble. As Jean de Saint-André had been expelled by the Bernese from Jussy (a parish which came under the jurisdiction of Geneva), the Council ordered the Company to proceed to the appointment of a minister in his place. Accordingly, it was resolved to move de Ecclesia from Vandoeuvres to Jussy.

---

[9] See pp. 105ff. below.
[10] See pp. 108f. below.
[11] See p. 133 below.

(Perhaps it was felt that he would be less trouble at a comparative distance from Geneva and in Bernese territory.) De Ecclesia, however, would not agree to the proposed change and voiced his objections to the scheme (as he had a right to do). These the Company found unsubstantial. On the matter being brought to the attention of the Council, the latter ruled that de Ecclesia should remain in the parish of Vandoeuvres and that the ministers should choose someone else for Jussy. This was another slap in the face for the Company of Pastors. But the Council brushed aside their protests, threatening that it would elect a man for Jussy if they refused to do so. And this it proceeded to do when the pastors made it plain that they could not conscientiously act otherwise than they had already done. So the Council nominated François Bourgoin to Jussy. This called forth a further protest from the ministers that the regulations of the Ecclesiastical Ordinances were being violated. But the Council was not to be moved. Bourgoin, for his part, declared that under the circumstances he could not acquiesce in the proposed arrangement. But the Council remained adamant, even when the pastors offered a compromise involving the allocation to Jussy of Jean Fabri (who had stated his willingness to go there). In the meantime, however, while these and other protests were flying to and fro, new accusations were brought against de Ecclesia to the effect that he had been engaging in acts of usury, which necessitated the Council to set up an investigation. It was also reported that de Ecclesia had been a companion of Jerome Bolsec (whose case had been recently concluded and who had been banished from the city) and that he had proclaimed from the pulpit that the body of Christ is ubiquitous.[12]

Consequently, in November of that same year (1552) de Ecclesia was arraigned before the Council. The ministers from the city and country parishes were also present. The accused man had no defence to offer to the charges of usury and disloyalty and accordingly was censured and condemned by the Council. Yet, even now, the pastors were requested to pardon him again and to let him continue in his position as a member of their Company. They had every justification for finding this an amazing request, even though the condition was added that de Ecclesia should acknowledge his fault and ask for forgiveness. Their rejoinder was that he had given ample proof of the sort of man he was and that it was vain to expect a change of heart in him now. On 16 December, their day of censures, the ministers

---

[12] See pp. 187ff. below.

in Congregation further cross-examined de Ecclesia and then reported to the Council that they had found no evidence of a repentant spirit in him, that therefore the condition imposed for his restoration had not been fulfilled, and that they were unable to accept him as one of their number. De Ecclesia made counter-protests before the Council. A week later the Council ordered the Company of Pastors to be reconciled to de Ecclesia. The ministers in turn objected that they could not conscientiously consent to this. The situation was not improved by the Council's simultaneous demand that persons who had been banned from communion should be reinstated forthwith. On 6 January 1553 the Consistory assembled, together with a number of special delegates from the Council, to give de Ecclesia yet another hearing. He "offered the same excuses as on previous occasions, speaking of reconciliation and protesting that he wished us no harm and that all should be forgiven, without in any way acknowledging his faults or showing signs of repentance". It was the unanimous judgment of the meeting that he had failed to satisfy the condition imposed by the Council, and the following week, on 27 January, the Council sentenced de Ecclesia to be deposed from his office as a minister of the Genevan church.[13]

This affair took place in the mid-course of Calvin's career in Geneva. It would be difficult to imagine an occasion better suited for the display of the tyrannical powers which some have supposed Calvin wielded. But it affords no evidence of the manifestation by him of any kind of authoritarianism. On the contrary, the de Ecclesia case indicates as clearly as anything could that, although conflicts between church and state were not unknown in Geneva, the state, so far from being cowed by some horrific kind of ecclesiastical domination, had no hesitation in withstanding the will of either the single person of Calvin or the united body of the pastors. It also testifies to the respect which the Reformers had for the authority of the state, even at those times when they found themselves unable to approve of its rulings. As Professor Basil Hall has written:

> Those who wish to focus denigration of Calvin and what he stood for on his supposed cruelty and dictatorial powers fail to come to grips with two major facts. First, if Calvin was a cruel man how did he attract so many, so varied, and so warmly attached friends and associates who speak of his sensitiveness and his charm? The evidence is plain for all to read in the course of his vast correspondence. Secondly, if Calvin had dictatorial control over Genevan

[13] See pp. 201ff., 209ff. below.

affairs, how is it that the records of Geneva show him plainly to have been the servant of its Council which on many occasions rejected out of hand Calvin's wishes for the religious life of Geneva, and was always master in Genevan affairs? A reading of Calvin's farewell speech to the ministers of Geneva made shortly before he died should resolve doubt upon this point. To call Calvin the 'dictator of a theocracy' is, in view of the evidence, mere phrase-making prejudice. Calvin in Geneva had less power either in theory or in practice than had Archbishop Whitgift in England, and less again than had Archbishop Laud, for he had neither the authority of their office nor the consistent and powerful political support which they received.[14]

The Register of the Company of Pastors affords an abundance of evidence to corroborate this judgment. A revealing incident, not recorded in the Register, took place on 24 September 1548, when Calvin, none other, was summoned to appear before the Council in order to give an explanation of the contents of a letter from him to Viret in which he had made certain critical remarks concerning the city of Geneva and its government, and which had been intercepted and brought to the attention of the Council. Calvin offered his apologies and requested that what he had said might be taken in good part. On 18 October the Council announced that no further action would be taken, but admonished Calvin to be more mindful of his duty in the future!

Finally, in this respect, it would seem that far too many people are ignorant of the significant fact that Calvin was not granted even the elementary privilege of bourgeois status in the republic of Geneva until the year 1559 — that is, twenty-three years after his arrival in the city and only some five years before his death; and further, and consequently, that he had no vote until that year in the conduct of civic affairs. Such unconcern for even the humblest public status and recognition hardly comports with the image of a man who was, supposedly, ambitious for absolute power and domineering in his attitude to other mortals.

But, someone is sure to ask, what about the burning of Servetus? Does not that incident show Calvin in the role of an intolerant tyrant? The short answer to this question is that it was the custom of that age to burn heretics, and Calvin, in so far as he approved of what was done, was conforming to that custom (except that, as we shall see, he desired for Servetus a death less painful than burning). To say this is not to condone what was done to Servetus; but it is important to remember that Calvin belonged to the

---

[14] "The Calvin Legend," in *The Churchman*, London, Vol. 73, No. 3, September 1959, pp. 124f.

sixteenth, not the twentieth, century and that the toleration which Protestantism takes so much for granted today, though it is a fruit of the Reformation, was not immediately comprehended by those pioneers of evangelical freedom. It should be remembered, too, that the middle years of the sixteenth century were years of the greatest peril for the Reformation movement which was then still in its formative stage, and that Calvin in Geneva (like his fellow Reformers in other places) was intent on protecting his church from forces that threatened to destroy the edifice which was being constructed with such laboriousness. Accordingly, there was an exceptional sensitiveness to the peril of giving free rein to the disseminators of false teaching. In any case, it needs to be emphasized that Servetus was not burnt by Calvin, who had no authority to pronounce, or even to vote for, any such sentence. The death penalty was imposed by the civil authorities, and would have been imposed by them even if there had been no such person as Calvin in Geneva.

To describe this one instance of a man who was put to death in Calvin's Geneva, then, specifically as an example of *protestant*, or, more narrowly, *Calvinistic*, intolerance is nonsense. Servetus had been taken prisoner in the city of Vienne where, by the practice of flagrant duplicity, he had for years enjoyed the hospitality and the patronage of the papal archbishop; but he had managed to escape from custody before being brought to trial. He was tried *in absentia*, however, and sentence was passed that, once apprehended, he was to be burnt alive by a slow fire until his body had been reduced to ashes, and his books with him. Meanwhile the city of Vienne contented itself with burning an effigy of him together with his writings. This was the pattern of procedure that could have been expected in any city in which he was apprehended, whatever its religious affiliation. By papist and protestant alike Servetus was execrated as the most detestable of heretics, and it is one of the quirks of history that he was put to death in a protestant rather than a papal community. Such evidence as is available suggests that Servetus had made his way to Geneva in the expectation that the anti-Calvin party which was then in power, would take his part and see that he came to no harm — indeed, his temerity was such that he may well have hoped to supplant Calvin as religious leader in that city. On Sunday 13 August 1553 he was bold enough to mingle with the worshippers in La Madeleine when Calvin himself was preaching, and, on being recognized, was immediately arrested by a civic official on a charge of heresy. And so the whole sorry tale of the trial unfolded. Servetus alternated between arrogance and plaintiveness, according as he felt things were going well or badly for him. He was championed by the rebellious Philibert Berthelier, around whom the controversy over excommunication was raging at that very time. But both the vanity and the violence of his opinions left him in the end a self-convicted man.

That the life of a man of so many-sided an intellect and so remarkable in his capacities should be extinguished in such a horrible manner was beyond all dispute tragic. The brilliance, it is true, was offset by a deep gulf of darkness in his character. And this duplicity was his undoing. He was like an animal which, impelled by presumption, is caught in a trap which it has knowingly entered. The theological interchange in the Servetus affair is carefully recorded in the Register of the Company of Pastors.[15] There was an element of personal tragedy for Calvin, too; for this was not the first time that he and Servetus had had dealings with each other. Years earlier, when they were both in Paris as young men known by reputation to each other, a meeting had been negotiated between them. Because of his evangelical convictions Calvin had to move with the greatest circumspection, and the possibility was there that Servetus might be a decoy to bring about his capture. None the less, he kept the appointment and waited for a long time at the agreed rendezvous, for he had hopes of gaining Servetus for the evangelical cause. But Servetus failed to put in an appearance. In later years Calvin wrote: "I was even ready to risk my life to win him to our Lord, if possible". Had this meeting taken place, the subsequent situation might have been very different. While Calvin expected and approved of the death sentence for so incorrigible a heretic, yet, as he said in a letter sent to Farel on 20 August 1553, it was his wish that some less cruel form of execution than burning might be permitted. This hope was to be disappointed. On 27 October 1553 sentence was publicly pronounced and Servetus was led off to the stake and burnt to death.

And so the deed was done. It was but a single drop in the ocean of savage tortures and persecutions and deaths that adherents of the Reformation were suffering in those days when it had become customary to hunt and destroy men like brutes. News was constantly reaching Geneva of fresh atrocities perpetrated against evangelical Christians; fugitives from persecution were constantly pouring into Geneva and finding shelter and succour there (which gave rise to the main complaint of the anti-Calvin

---

[15] See pp. 223ff. below.

faction whose policy was Geneva for Genevans, and who bitterly opposed this influx of foreigners); and dedicated men were constantly being sent out from Geneva to imperil their lives by taking the message of the Gospel into hostile territory. These were times of violence and insecurity. Protestants were condemned as heretics by papists, and Servetus was condemned as a heretic by both protestants and papists.

The sentence in the Servetus case was decreed by the anti-Calvin party then in power in Geneva. Calvin concurred with its justness. But first there had been consultation with the churches of Zürich, Schaffhausen, Basle, and Berne — Geneva's fellow-Reformed churches in Switzerland — and all (including Berne, which, as the Register shows time and again, was not the friendliest and most co-operative of neighbours to Geneva, or Calvin) demanded that Servetus should be punished with the utmost rigour of the law. On 8 September Farel wrote from Neuchâtel to Calvin that, as the apostle Paul had said that he did not wish to escape death if he deserved it,[16] so he had often expressed his willingness to die if he had taught anything contrary to the doctrine of the Gospel, and, indeed, would consider himself worthy of the worst possible torture if he had turned anyone from the faith and teaching of Jesus Christ. "In fact", Farel added, "I cannot demand for others anything else than what I demand for myself". This, as Doumergue has observed, throws light on the psychology of the men of the sixteenth century. The following year, on 14 October, Melanchthon, who was as gentle as Farel was fiery, wrote to Calvin: "Now and in the generations to come the Church owes and will owe you gratitude. I maintain that your magistrates have acted justly in executing this blasphemer following a lawful trial".

Melanchthon, like Farel, was Calvin's friend; but even Bolsec, whose antipathy to Calvin needs no comment, expressed his full approval of what had been done, and this despite the fact that he himself had been condemned and banished from Geneva some time previously. In a letter to Cardinal de Tournon he described Servetus as a "foul and monstrous heretic" who was "altogether wicked and unworthy to share the company of men", and declared his wish that "all persons of this kind should be exterminated and the Church of our Lord thoroughly purged of such vermin". In view of what he had experienced in Geneva and his attitude to Calvin, it might have been expected that Bolsec would be predisposed to take the side of Servetus. His judgment

---

[16] The allusion is to Acts 25:16.

INTRODUCTION

affords further and striking confirmation of the judgment of that age.

Bolsec's trial and banishment had taken place two years before the Servetus affair. The theological dispute with him is fully recorded in the pages of the Register of the Company of Pastors,[17] and it throws some interesting light on the question of the tolerance of Calvin and his contemporaries. The matter under debate was the doctrine of predestination and its implications — a matter in which it would be felt today that there is room for difference of opinion and emphasis. But, once again, the state of affairs in the church of Geneva must be given due weight. Virtually surrounded as the small city-state was by hostile forces, while Geneva itself was the scene of deep spiritual struggle, Calvin was intent on establishing a strong integrity of doctrine so that the Reformation might be secured for the generations to come. What he believed to be at stake was nothing less than the truth of the sovereignty of God, which was the key-stone of the whole Reformed system. Moreover, Bolsec's attack amounted to an affirmation of a certain adequacy of man in the realization of salvation, which in effect was little different from the semipelagian teaching of the Roman Catholic church. And it must be added that Bolsec, now pursuing the somewhat dubious career of a theologian-cum-physician of sorts, had previously been a monk, and, understandably, ex-monks were treated with a measure of healthy suspicion until the sincerity of their professed change of heart had been sufficiently tested.

On 8 March 1551 Jerome Bolsec was summoned before the Consistory because of the wild denunciations he had been uttering against the doctrine of predestination, and his opinions were rebutted by Calvin in a friendly and gentle manner. The attempt to curb his slanders was unsuccessful, however, and he was cited again on 15 May and sternly reprimanded.[18] He appeared for the third time before the pastors at their Congregation held on 16 October of the same year and made a frontal assault on their doctrine, declaring that their God was a tyrannical idol like the pagan deity Jupiter, that their teaching was heretical, and that it was false to affirm that Augustine had maintained the doctrine of election — indeed, he asserted that this doctrine had been invented by the Italian scholar Lorenzo Valla during the preceding century! Calvin, who was not present at the commencement of the meeting, had come in unperceived and taken a place among the

[17] See pp. 137ff. below.
[18] See pp. 132f. below.

listeners. No sooner had Bolsec finished speaking than he stood up and treated the company to a characteristically brilliant display of intellectual virtuosity. In an oration that lasted an hour he refuted Bolsec point by point, quoting numerous passages from Scripture and from Augustine with such fluency that it seemed as though he had just that moment come from studying them. Thus, as on so many other occasions, Calvin's phenomenal memory was used with crushing effect. A state official who was present took Bolsec into custody.

It would be difficult for anyone to deny the violent and scandalous nature of the slanders which Bolsec continued to utter even while he was in prison. As usual, Calvin staunchly expounded and defended the Reformed doctrine; but it seems that he would have been pleased to call off this particular dispute — perhaps because so much of Bolsec's assault was on him personally, and Calvin was never much interested in self-defence. In response to the counter-charges levelled against him by Bolsec, he complains, *inter alia*, that Bolsec had passed over in silence the fact that he (Calvin) had besought the Council even with tears that the matter might be dropped.[19] This, surely, should be the last nail in the coffin of the calumny that there was no mild and forgiving side to Calvin's nature: it is simply not true that he hungrily demanded the destruction of any person who might be so rash as to disagree with him. The civil authorities disregarded his request, however, and required the trial to be carried through to its conclusion.

Transcripts of the theological interchange between Bolsec and the pastors were sent by order of the Council to the other chief centres of the Reformation in Switzerland, so that Geneva might have the benefit of their judgment before a final decision in this affair was announced. The replies received are of considerable interest.[20] The letter from Basle, dated 21 November 1551, deplores the trouble which Bolsec had caused in the Genevan church and indignantly disavows a claim made by him that the church of Basle held opinions similar to his own. The response is cautiously worded, however, especially in that the assertion of a double predestination is avoided: "Those whom God draws believe; those whom He does not draw do not believe. . . . This only we say: what takes place is plain enough; but why it takes place is due to a hidden cause which God alone knows. Nor is it for us to inquire

[19] See p. 167 below.
[20] They are included, with the exception of that from Berne, in the Register, pp. 169ff. below.

into this cause. But this much is certain: that they (those who are not drawn) rejected the Word which was preached to them because it was contrary to their inclinations. . . . It is better that we should start from faith rather than from the foreknowledge of God or from predestination and election, . . . for in this way our teaching is not bound up with doubtful questions by which it could be side-tracked. . . . You see, then, our simplicity with regard to this question, which is the most difficult and intricate in religion".

In thanking the pastors of Basle for their prompt reply — the transcript and covering letter had been sent to the different churches on 14 November — Calvin expressed a measure of disappointment over the indecisive manner in which they had written. By contrast, however, the letter from Zürich, which was dated 27 November, was openly critical, and, emanating from that quarter, must have come as a shock to Calvin. A letter from him to Farel dated 8 December expressed his sense of disappointment at the attitude of Bullinger and his colleagues, from whom he had anticipated the fullest support. It is true that the ministers of Zürich declared their great grief at the news of the problems with which the church in Geneva was confronted and their admiration for the work which Calvin and his fellow-pastors were doing in that city. But it was their hope that a reconciliation between Bolsec and the Genevan pastors might be negotiated. And they did not scruple to introduce a reproving note: "In your judgment Jerome has conducted his case in an intemperate manner; but, our brothers, we look for moderation in you also, for you seem in your letter . . . to be extremely severe". That letter had described Bolsec as pestilential, rash, irresponsible and impostrous (surely with some justification) and had expressed the desire that the church of Geneva might be rid of him, "but in such a way that he does not become injurious to our neighbours".[21] It may be that this was taken to imply a penalty more drastic than was intended. The Zürich pastors even stated that they had no wish "to tighten the chains of a captive man, unknown to us, as we have not been appointed his judges". In explaining their own view of the doctrine in dispute, they took care to add that "the fact that the reprobate do not believe the Word of God, but wickedly live in opposition to God, ought to be attributed to them, not to God, who justly and condignly condemns those whom He condemns, since it is in man, not in God, that sin inheres".

[21] See p. 170 below.

Farel and the ministers of Neuchâtel (though they were not among those to whom the transcript of the Bolsec debate was officially sent) wrote supporting the Genevan pastors up to the hilt. In a vituperative denunciation of Bolsec they likened him to Judas Iscariot. They commended their colleagues in Geneva for having dealt with this matter wisely, and expressed the belief that all good men would approve what they had done.[22] If the reaction from Neuchâtel was as expected, so also, no doubt, was the reaction from Berne (which is not included in the Register). The latter was as distant and unfavourable as the former was warm and approving. It was an opportunity not to be missed by those in Berne who regarded the republic of Geneva with such jealous rivalry. They admonished their neighbours to be careful not to treat those who are in error with too great severity. They reminded them that the doctrine of predestination had been an embarrassment to excellent men and that it was not milk for children but meat for the mature. Moreover, they did not consider Bolsec to be so black as he had been painted, and so they wished him to be treated with leniency as a brother and fellow-Christian and by the arts of persuasion to be brought to a better frame of mind. All this sounds admirable — until one remembers that subsequently the Bernese ran this same man Bolsec out of their territory when he sought asylum there. And there is even more irony, if possible, in the fact that, in 1558, Valentin Gentilis was induced by Calvin with the use of persuasion to retract his anti-trinitarian views but was later arrested by the Bernese and burnt to death in their city.[23]

Bolsec, in fact, was not even an inhabitant of Geneva. The situation is well summed up by Calvin himself in a letter he wrote to Bullinger following the somewhat unsympathetic response from Zürich. He found it incomprehensible that Bullinger and his colleagues should have wished to afford protection to a man who had seditiously stirred up trouble in a peaceful church, who had tried to split their ranks with disastrous discord, and who, without the slightest provocation, had publicly charged them with all sorts of infamies. The expulsion from Geneva of this agitator and charlatan, who in any case did not belong there, seems a reasonable enough action under the circumstances. Jerome Bolsec was to become the most vicious and unscrupulous inventor of slanders against Calvin's good name.

But the church in Geneva was far from being preoccupied with

---

[22] See pp. 180ff. below.
[23] The text of the reply from Berne is given in *Calvini Opera*, VIII, pp. 238ff.

its own troubles and problems. No church was less open to the charge of introversion than this church. This is something to which the Register of the Company of Pastors bears clear testimony. In Geneva, as we have already remarked, the most sustained opposition to Calvin came, not from persons who were out of sympathy with the Reformation, but from the "Geneva for the Genevans" party who resented the policy of welcoming into the city large numbers of refugees from the persecutions that were raging against adherents of the Reformed faith in France and elsewhere. Geneva, indeed, became the most famous haven for evangelical fugitives of the day. No doubt this steady influx from abroad posed problems of administration and accommodation in the small republic — and there were inevitably some undesirable individuals who slipped in under false colours. But these considerations did not stifle the magnaminity which held out the hand of hospitality to those who were destitute and in distress.

Calvin's Geneva, however, was something more than a haven of refuge for the afflicted: it was also a school, in which, with the aid of regular lectures and daily sermons, the people were instructed and built up to be strong in the Christian faith. Even more significantly, it was a school of missions: it was open not only to receive fugitives but also to send out witnesses who would spread the teaching of the Reformation far and wide. Geneva, indeed, received only to give. It was a dynamic centre of missionary concern and activity, an axis from which the light of the Good News radiated forth through the testimony of those who, after thorough preparation in this "school", were sent forth in the service of Jesus Christ.

The record in the Register of this missionary activity is impressive, even though it is incomplete and undramatic in its presentation. Here is irrefutable proof of the falsity of the too common conclusion that Calvinism is incompatible with evangelism and spells death to all missionary enterprise. The Register gives the names of 88 men who were sent out from Geneva as bearers of the Gospel between the years 1555, when it was first considered safe for their names to be recorded, and 1562, when the wars of religion commenced in France and it became expedient once again to cease minuting the names of such men, most of whom went into French territory. Since the Reformation was a new dawn of the Gospel after centuries of comparative darkness in Europe, it was not (with one exception) to the heathen overseas but to the mission-field of Europe, and in the main of France, that these men were despatched.

In certain respects, Geneva was strategically placed as a launching-ground for these enterprises, being situated at the tip of the southwestern section of Switzerland which juts into the heart of France and is also near to the northern territory of Italy. But it would be hard to exaggerate the extremely hazardous nature of the assignment undertaken by those who sallied forth from Geneva as missionaries. The unbridled hostility to the Reformation meant that the utmost secrecy had to be observed in sending out these evangelical emissaries. Ordinary prudence dictated that their identity should customarily be concealed by the assumption of pseudonyms (hence the occurrence at times in the Register of more than one name for the same person: for example, "Jean Gérard, otherwise called du Gay", "Guy Moranges, alias la Garde", "Jean Boulier, called de la Roche").[24] Their lines of infiltration were along perilous paths through the mountains, where they were dependent on friendly cottagers for food and hiding in case of necessity. Nor did the danger end when they arrived at their various destinations, for there too the utmost caution had to be observed lest they should be discovered and apprehended with all the dire consequences that would be involved. Where a congregation was mustered, services were conducted in a private home behind locked doors or in the shadows of a wooded hillside. There were times when, as much for the sake of the work as for his own safety, it became advisable for a missionary-pastor to leave a place because his activities were becoming suspect and his identity was no longer well concealed (he was becoming, as the Register puts it, *"trop découvert"*).[25] It is against this sort of background that the letter of 12 October 1553 from the Company of Pastors in Geneva, addressed, without the mention of names, "to the believers of certain islands in France", and pseudonymously signed "Charles d'Espeville" (a cover-name sometimes used by Calvin), must be understood.[26]

As previously remarked, the Register names 88 such men who were sent out from Geneva between 1555 and 1562; but there were many more who are not mentioned in these annals. In 1561, for example, which appears to have been the peak year for this missionary activity, the despatch of only twelve men is recorded; whereas evidence from other sources indicates that in that year alone no less than 142 — nearly twelve times twelve —

---

[24] See pp. 321, 338, 351 below.
[25] Cf. p. 323 below.
[26] See pp. 289f. below.

men ventured forth in their respective missions.[27] This concern on the part of Geneva for the spiritual benefit of others in foreign territories was the opposite of self-centred: indeed, Geneva was willing, in times of urgent demand, to deprive itself of pastors whom it needed for itself rather than to withhold men who could go out to establish an evangelical ministry elsewhere.

Nor was it unusual for Reformed missionaries to be arrested, persecuted, and put to death. Thus, for example, the Register for 17 June 1555 records the receipt of a letter from three men, Jean Vernou, Antoine Laborier, and Jean Trigalet, who had been arrested and imprisoned at Chambéry while *en route* to Piedmont in Italy as missionaries.[28] They never regained their freedom, but suffered martyrdom in the same place. Experiences of this kind, however, deplorable though they were, did not have the effect of inhibiting the sending out of more men along the same and similar perilous routes. On 16 August 1557, to take another incident mentioned in the Register, Nicolas des Gallars, himself a Frenchman of noble birth and one of Calvin's right-hand men, set out from Geneva in order to serve the cause in Paris, where peril lurked for professors of the Reformed faith around every street corner. On the way his companion was seized and put to death, but des Gallars managed to escape and reach his destination. Not long after his arrival enemy forces suddenly descended on his congregation and threw some two hundred of them, including many of high birth, into custody, as he tells in a letter of 7 September 1557.[29] Again, in 1559 there is the somewhat terse entry: "Maître Lancelot d'Albeau was appointed to Valence, where, after faithfully preaching the Gospel, he was seized by his enemies and sealed the doctrine of the truth with his blood and his death".[30]

Another laconic but exceptionally interesting minute concerns the sending of two ministers, Pierre Richer and Guillaume Charretier, to Brazil in August 1556.[31] The Huguenot leader, Admiral Coligny, had been induced to believe that a colony of Protestant emigrants might be formed in South America, where they would be free from persecution, and able to establish their own culture and to evangelize the heathen natives. Accordingly a group of

[27] For a careful study of this whole situation see Robert M. Kingdon, *Geneva and the Coming of the Wars of Religion in France, 1555-1563*, Geneva, 1956.
[28] See pp. 311ff. below.
[29] See pp. 329f. below.
[30] See p. 348 below.
[31] See p. 317 below.

Reformed colonists was sent out to the islands which the French had taken off the coast of Brazil, and Richer and Charretier were appointed by the Genevan church as chaplains to the Reformed group and missionaries to the South American Indians. The governor of the colony, Villegagnon, betrayed Coligny's trust in him, however. He turned against the Calvinists in this expedition, throwing four of them to a watery grave in the sea because of the faith they confessed, and causing the rest to seek safety by returning to their homeland, which, ironically, they had left in order to enjoy freedom to express and practise their faith without being hated and hunted like animals. But, abortive though this excursion proved to be, it testifies strikingly to the far-reaching vision which Calvin and the church in Geneva had of their missionary task.

Calvin's Geneva was also outward looking in its attitude to evangelical churches in other places. Proof of this is found, for instance, in the drawing up of the *Consensus Tigurinus* (or Zürich Agreement), the text of which is given in the Register.[32] Calvin was particularly eager to achieve a theological harmony of the Reformed churches, and not least in respect of eucharistic doctrine, both because of the central evangelical importance of right belief at this point and also because it had proved a focus of some contention, especially with the German churches. It was on 1 August 1549 that Calvin sent a letter and twenty-four articles or heads of agreement concerning the sacraments in general and the holy communion in particular to the pastors and teachers of the church of Zürich for their approval. These articles were the outcome of a previous visit to Zürich by Calvin and Farel for the purpose of consultation over these matters. The response from Zürich was enthusiastic and the *Consensus* was adopted also by the church of Neuchâtel.

A few months earlier, in fact, a sort of prototype or prior draft of the *Consensus Tigurinus* had been sent by the Genevan Company of Pastors to the pastors of the church of Berne. The text of the twenty articles comprising this document, together with the covering letter, is also recorded in the Register.[33] Moves of this kind are indicative of Calvin's deep concern for doctrinal unity, particularly since the terms of the *Consensus Tigurinus* do not represent his personal sacramental views in the fulness of their emphasis: in the interests of harmony he was willing to

---

[32] See pp. 115ff. below.
[33] See pp. 101ff. below.

moderate his own position, though not, of course, to compromise his convictions.

The extent of Calvin's influence throughout Europe is sufficiently well known: from far and wide his advice and help were eagerly sought by a great variety of persons. By way of illustration of his wider ecumenical outlook I wish only to mention here the correspondence that passed between him and Archbishop Cranmer in 1552 concerning the latter's grand project for the convening of an international congress of Reformed churchmen. "As nothing tends more injuriously to the separation of the churches than heresies and disputes respecting the doctrine of religion", wrote Cranmer on 20 March 1552, "so nothing tends more effectually to unite the churches of God, and more powerfully to defend the fold of Christ, than the pure teaching of the Gospel and harmony of doctrine. Therefore I have often wished, and still continue to do so, that learned and godly men, who are eminent for erudition and judgment, might meet together in some place of safety, where, by taking counsel together and comparing their respective opinions, they might handle all the heads of ecclesiastical doctrine and hand down to posterity, under the weight of their authority, some work not only upon the subjects themselves but upon the forms of expressing them". To this Calvin replied that it was his wish too "that grave and learned men from the principal churches might meet together at a place appointed and, after diligent consideration of each article of the faith, hand down to posterity a definite form of doctrine according to their united opinion". He observed that it was "to be reckoned among the greatest evils of our time that the churches are so estranged from each other that scarcely the common intercourse of society has place among them, much less that holy communion of the members of Christ which all persons profess with their lips, though few sincerely honour it with their practice". He added the famous comment that, if he could be of any service, he would not shrink from crossing ten seas, should that be necessary, for the purpose of attending such a gathering.[34]

Cranmer's project was never achieved. With the death of Edward VI and the accession to the throne of "Bloody" Mary he and many of his fellow-Reformers in England suffered martyrdom, while numerous others found refuge in Reformed circles on the Continent, including the church of Geneva. The glorious reign of Elizabeth I, however, saw the restoration of the Reformed worship

---

[34] Thomas Cranmer, *Works* (Parker Society edition), Vol. II, Cambridge, 1846, pp. 431ff.

of the Book of Common Prayer. Not long after she had become queen a request was sent — in April 1560 — to Geneva by the Bishop of London (Edmund Grindal) for the sending of a good man to serve as minister of the French Protestant congregation in London, which was now being established again. The man chosen for this assignment was Calvin's close friend and lieutenant Nicolas des Gallars. The fact of his despatch is cursorily mentioned in the Register of 1560;[35] but the sparing of so valuable a pastor is a measure of the importance which Calvin attached not only to the French congregation in London but also to the Church of England, in whose affairs des Gallars might be expected to play a not insignificant part, as had been the case with his predecessors in the post. It was, in short, a measure of Calvin's ecumenical perspective.

Enough has been said, I trust, to give some idea of the wealth of interesting material that is to be found in the Register of the Company of Pastors, much of it now published for the first time. The perusal of the Register enables us, as it were, to listen in to some of the most significant deliberations of the Company of Pastors, to obtain an insight into the doctrinal and ecclesiastical problems with which Calvin and his colleagues had to contend, and to gain an intimate glimpse of the Reformed microcosm that was Geneva in the middle years of the sixteenth century. By no means least, we are shown that Calvin's Geneva was not an introspective hothouse of pietism, not merely a haven and place of refuge for those in distress (as so many seem to regard the church of our twentieth century), but especially a dynamic centre of evangelism and Christian instruction — "the most perfect school of Christ which has been seen on earth since the days of the apostles", as John Knox described it — where good men were built up in the faith in order that, at whatever peril to themselves, they might launch out from that haven into the storms beyond and minister the life-giving message to others.

* * * * *

This translation follows on the publication in Geneva (Librairie Droz) of the original text under the title *Registres de la Compagnie des Pasteurs de Genève au Temps de Calvin*, Tome I, 1546-1553, edited by Jean-François Bergier (1964), Tome II, 1553-1564, edited by Robert M. Kingdon in collaboration with Jean-François Bergier and Alain Dufour (1962). A wealth of bibliographical information will be found in the annotations included in these volumes. The

---

[35] See p. 350 below.

language of the *Register* varies between French and Latin. There are some places where the meaning is obscure, but every effort has been made to give a clear and faithful rendering of the original.

I wish to express my gratitude to the anonymous patron of Reformed studies through whose generosity this whole project was made possible, and to my friend the Rev. J. Marcellus Kik, under whose direction it has been brought to completion; and I acknowledge my indebtedness to Professor Jean-François Bergier, of the University of Geneva, and M. Gustave Vaucher, State Archivist in Geneva, who, in personal consultation during my visits to Geneva and also by correspondence, have given me much valuable assistance and at the same time the privilege of their friendship.

PHILIP EDGCUMBE HUGHES

Ecclesiastical Ordinances

1541

20 November 1541

ECCLESIASTICAL ORDINANCES[1]

In the Name of Almighty God, we the Syndics, the Little and Great Council, assembled with our people at the sound of the trumpet and the great bell, in accordance with our ancient customs, having considered that it is a thing worthy of commendation above all else that the doctrine of the holy Gospel of our Lord should be carefully preserved in its purity and the Christian Church properly maintained, that the young should be faithfully instructed for the future, and the hospital well administered for the succour of the poor, which cannot be done unless there is a certain rule and method of living by which each estate attends to the duty of its office: for this reason it has seemed to us advisable that the spiritual government of the kind which our Lord demonstrated and instituted by His Word should be set out in good order so that it may be established and observed among us. And accordingly we have made it a fixed rule to observe and maintain in our city and territory the ecclesiastical polity which follows, since we see that it is taken from the Gospel of Jesus Christ.

FOUR ORDERS IN THE CHURCH

Firstly, there are four official orders which our Lord instituted for the government of His Church: firstly, pastors; secondly, teachers; thirdly, elders, otherwise called the Seigneury's delegates (*com-*

---

[1] The Ecclesiastical Ordinances, the foundation of the whole organization and discipline of the church of Geneva, were promulged by the General Council on 20 November 1541, scarcely more than two months after Calvin's return to Geneva (13 September). Although it was only in 1546 that the Register of the Company of Pastors was commenced, the secretary was careful to place this basic text at the head of the volume. His transcription is the only contemporary copy in existence today.

mis); and, fourthly, deacons. If, then, we wish to have the Church well ordered and maintained in its entirety, we must observe this form of government.

The duty of pastors

With regard to pastors, whom Scripture also sometimes calls overseers, elders, and ministers, their office is to proclaim the Word of God for the purpose of instructing, admonishing, exhorting, and reproving, both in public and in private, to administer the sacraments, and to exercise fraternal discipline together with the elders or delegates (*commis*).

To the end that nothing disorderly should be done in the Church, no man ought to undertake this office without vocation, in connection with which three things should be considered: firstly, the examination, which is the most important; secondly, to whom it belongs to institute ministers; and, thirdly, what ceremony or mode of action may best be observed in inducting them to this office.

The examination of pastors

The examination consists of two parts, the first of which concerns doctrine, to ascertain whether he who is to be ordained has a good and sound knowledge of Scripture, and then whether he is a fit and proper person to communicate it to the people in an edifying manner.

Moreover, in order to avoid all danger of some false belief being held by the one who is to be received, he will be required to declare that he accepts and adheres to the doctrine approved in the Church. To ascertain whether he is fit to teach, it will be necessary to proceed by way of interrogation and by privately hearing him expound the teaching of the Lord.

The second part concerns his life, namely, whether he is of good morals and has always conducted himself without reproach. The rule of procedure to which we should adhere is very well shown by St. Paul.

To whom it belongs to institute pastors

In this connection it will be advisable to follow the order of the ancient Church, seeing that it is but the putting into practice of what we are shown in Scripture.

The election of pastors

In the first place, the ministers shall elect the one whom it is proposed to appoint, after having given due notice to the Seigneury.

Thereafter he is to be presented to the Council. And if he is found worthy the Council is to welcome and receive him in such a manner as it shall deem to be expedient, giving him their commendation in order, finally, to present him to the people in preaching, so that he may be received with the common consent of the company of the faithful. If he should be found unworthy and shown to be such by legitimate proofs, it will be necessary to proceed to a new election in order to choose another candidate.

As for the manner of inducting him, since the ceremonies of former times have been changed into numerous superstitions by reason of the infirmity of the times, it will suffice that a declaration explaining the office to which he is being ordained should be made by one of the ministers, and then that prayers and intercessions should be offered to the end that the Lord may grant him grace to acquit himself faithfully in it.[2]

After he has been elected he is to be sworn in by the Seigneury. There shall be a prescribed form of this oath appropriate to what is required in a minister, and the form to be used is to be inserted.

Moreover, just as it is necessary to examine ministers carefully when one wishes to elect them, so also it is necessary to have a good system whereby to hold them to their duty.

Fixing a day of the week for assembling

Firstly, in order that all ministers may maintain purity and agreement of doctrine among themselves, it will be expedient for them to meet together on one particular day of the week for discussion of the Scriptures, and no one shall be exempted from this without legitimate excuse. Any man who is negligent over this is to be reprimanded.[3]

As for those who preach in the villages under the jurisdiction of the Seigneury, our ministers of the city should exhort them to attend whenever they are able. In the event of absence for a whole

---

[2] The original draft of this paragraph is of interest. That it had to be altered, mention of the imposition of hands being omitted, is indicative of the problems with which the Reformers were faced as they sought to shape an acceptable form of ecclesiastical order. The original draft (subsequently struck out) read as follows: "As for the manner of inducting him, the practice of the imposition of hands is approved — a ceremony which was observed by the apostles and then in the ancient Church — provided that it is used without the superstition and without offense. But, because there has been a great deal of superstition in former times, and it may be the occasion of scandal, the practice may be omitted because of the infirmity of the times." For the content of the oath mentioned in the next paragraph, see Introduction, pp. 7f. above.

[3] This weekly gathering of ministers was known as the Congregation.

month, however, this is to be treated as gross negligence, except in the case of illness or some other legitimate hindrance.

What is to be done when there are differences over doctrine

If any difference over doctrine should arise, the ministers are to meet together to discuss the matter. Then, if need be, they shall invite the elders delegated by the Seigneury to help in settling the dispute. Finally, if through the obstinacy of one of the parties they cannot reach amicable agreement, the case shall be referred to the magistrate for resolution.

Ministerial discipline

In order to obviate all scandals of conduct it will be needful to have a form of discipline for ministers, as set out below, to which all are to submit themselves. This will help to ensure that the minister is treated with respect and the Word of God is not brought into dishonour and scorn by the evil fame of ministers. Moreover, as discipline will be imposed on him who merits it, so also there will be need to suppress slanders and false reports that may unjustly be uttered against those who are innocent.

But first of all it must be noted that there are crimes which are altogether intolerable in a minister and faults which may be endured provided that a fraternal admonition is offered.

Vices which are intolerable in a pastor

Heresy
Schism
Rebellion against ecclesiastical order
Blasphemy which is open and deserving of civil punishment
Simony and all corruption by bribes
Intrigues for usurping another's position
Leaving one's church without lawful permission and genuine vocation
Treachery
Perjury
Fornication
Larceny
Drunkenness
Assault punishable by the laws
Usury
Games forbidden by the laws and of a scandalous nature
Dancing and similar dissoluteness

Offences bearing civil infamy
Offences which in another would merit separation from the Church

Vices which can be endured provided they are rebuked

Strange methods of treating Scripture which result in scandal
Curiosity in searching out vain questions
The advancing of some doctrine or manner of conduct not accepted in the Church
Negligence in studying and especially in reading the Holy Scriptures
Negligence in reproving vices related to flattery
Negligence in performing all the duties of one's office
Buffoonery
Deceitfulness
Defamation
Dissolute language
Rashness
Evil scheming
Avarice and niggardliness
Uncontrolled anger
Brawling and quarrelling
Dissoluteness unbecoming a minister, whether in clothing or in conduct or in any other way

With regard to offences which ought under no circumstances to be tolerated, if they are civil offences, that is to say, those which are punishable by the laws, and any minister is guilty of them, the Seigneury shall take the matter in hand and, over and above the ordinary punishment customarily imposed on others, shall punish him by deposing him from his office.

With regard to other offences of which the first investigation belongs to the ecclesiastical Consistory, the delegates (*commis*) or elders together with the ministers shall attend to them. And if anyone is convicted of them they shall report it to the Council, with their decision and judgment — but in such a way that the final judgment concerning the punishment shall always be reserved to the Seigneury.

With regard to lesser vices which should be corrected by simple admonition, the procedure shall be according to the order of necessity, in such a way that in the last resort cases shall be brought before the Church for judgment.

Fixing a day of censure every three months

For the effective maintenance of this discipline, every three months the ministers are to give special attention to see whether there is anything open to criticism among themselves, so that, as is right, it may be remedied.

The frequency, place, and time of preaching

On Sundays there shall be a sermon at daybreak in St. Pierre and St. Gervais, and at the customary hour in St. Pierre, La Madeleine, and St. Gervais.

At noon the catechism, that is to say, instruction of little children, shall be conducted in all three churches, namely, St. Pierre, La Madeleine, and St. Gervais; and also at three o'clock in all three parishes.

In sending children to catechism and receiving the sacraments, the boundaries of the parishes should as far as possible be observed: thus St. Gervais shall comprise what it had in the past, and similarly La Madeleine, and St. Pierre what belonged formerly to St. Germain, Ste. Croix, Notre Dame la Neuve, and St. Légier.

On work-days, in addition to the two customary sermons, there shall be preaching in St. Pierre three times a week, namely, on Monday, Wednesday, and Friday, and the bells are to be rung for these sermons, one after the other, at an hour such that they can be finished before one is started elsewhere. If there should be any extraordinary service for the necessity of the times, the order of Sunday shall be observed.

Appointment of five pastors and three coadjutors

For the purpose of maintaining these and other duties proper to the ministry, there will be need of five ministers and three coadjutors. The latter, who will also be ministers, will assist and collaborate as necessity requires.

THE SECOND ORDER, WHICH WE HAVE CALLED TEACHERS

The proper office of teachers is to instruct the faithful in sound doctrine in order that the purity of the Gospel may not be corrupted either by ignorance or by false opinions. At the same time, as things are disposed today, we comprehend in this title the aids and instruments for preserving the doctrine of God and ensuring that the Church is not desolated through the fault of pastors and ministers. And so, to use a more intelligible word, we shall call it the order of the schools. The degree nearest to the ministry and most closely associated with the government of the Church is the teaching of theology, the scope of which includes both Old and New Testaments.

Establishment of a college

But since it is possible to profit from such teaching only if in the first place there is instruction in the languages and humanities, and since also there is need to raise up seed for the future so that the Church is not left desolate to our children, it will be necessary to build a college for the purpose of instructing them, with a view to preparing them both for the ministry and for the civil government.

First of all it will be necessary to allocate a place both for the giving of lessons and for the housing of children and others who wish to benefit, to have a learned and experienced man in charge both of the house and of the studies who himself can also teach, and to engage and hire him with the provision that under his charge he shall have teachers both of languages and of dialectic, if possible. Again, there will be need of young men for teaching the little children, which we wish and order to be done.

All such persons shall be subject to ecclesiastical discipline, like the ministers.

There is to be no other school in the city for little children, but the girls shall have their school separate, as has been the case hitherto.

None is to be accepted unless he has been approved by the ministers, after having first notified the Seigneury, and then in turn he is to be presented to the Council with their recommendation, as a safeguard against abuses. Moreover, the examination should be conducted in the presence of two members of the Little Council.

THE THIRD ORDER, WHICH IS THAT OF ELDERS, WHO ARE CALLED "COMMIS," OR THOSE DELEGATED BY THE SEIGNEURY TO THE CONSISTORY

Their office is to watch over the life of each person, to admonish in a friendly manner those whom they see to be at fault and leading a disorderly life, and when necessary to report them to the Company, who will be authorized to administer fraternal discipline and to do so in association with the elders.

As this church is now placed, it will be desirable to elect two from the Little Council, four from the Council of Sixty, and six from the Council of Two Hundred, good-living and honourable men, without reproach and beyond all suspicion, above all who fear God and possess the gift of spiritual prudence; and their election should be such that there will be some of them in each quarter of the city, so that they may attend to all that we wish to be done.

The manner of their election

Accordingly we have decided that the manner of their election should be as follows: the Little Council shall consult with a view to nominating the most suitable and competent men that can be found; and, in order to effect this, it shall summon the ministers for the purpose of conferring with them; and then they shall present those on whom they have agreed to the Council of Two Hundred for their approval. If they are approved and found worthy, they shall take a special oath, the form of which shall be drafted as for the ministers. And at the end of the year after their election by the Council they shall present themselves to the Seigneury so that it may be decided whether they should be retained or replaced, though, so long as they are fulfilling their duties faithfully, it will be inexpedient to replace them frequently without good cause.

THE FOURTH ORDER OF ECCLESIASTICAL GOVERNMENT, NAMELY, DEACONS

There were always two kinds of deacons in the early Church. The one kind was deputed to receive, dispense, and keep the goods for the poor, not only daily alms, but also possessions, revenues, and pensions; the other kind to care for and remember the sick and administer the allowance for the poor, a custom which we still retain at present. And in order to avoid confusion, since we have stewards and hospitallers, one of the four stewards of the hospital shall be the receiver of all its bounty and shall be adequately paid so that he may the better fulfil his office.

The number of four stewards is to remain as it has been, one of whom shall have charge of the income, as has been said, both in order that the dispensation may be made regularly and on time, and also that those who wish to make some charitable gift may be assured that the bounty will not be employed otherwise than according to their intention. And if the revenue is insufficient, or if an unusual necessity should occur, the Seigneury shall sanction an adjustment according to the needs of the situation.

The election of both stewards and hospitallers shall be conducted as for the elders and delegates (*commis*) to the Consistory; and in electing them the rule which St. Paul lays down for deacons (I Tim. 3, Titus 1) shall be followed.

Regarding the office and authority of the stewards, we confirm the articles which we have already prescribed for them, provided that in matters of urgency and where postponement would be dangerous, especially when there is no serious difficulty and no question of great expense, they should not be compelled always to call a meeting, but that one or two should have power to make reasonable arrangements in the absence of the others.

The hospital

It will be necessary to take every care that the communal hospital is well maintained and that its amenities are available both for the sick and for the aged who are unable to work. The same applies to widows, orphaned children, and other poor persons. These, however, are to be placed in a wing of the building apart and separate from the others.

Again, the succour of the poor who are scattered through the city shall be derived from this source, according as the stewards shall order it.

Again, besides the hospice for wayfarers, which must be maintained, there should be some separate hospitality for those who are seen to be deserving of special charity. And for this purpose a room shall be set aside to receive those whom the stewards shall recommend, and shall be reserved to this use.

Furthermore, the hospitallers must control their own families in an honourable and godly manner, seeing that they have to govern a house dedicated to God.

The ministers and the delegates (*commis*) or elders together with one of the syndics of the Seigneury are for their part to take care to inquire whether there is any fault or deficiency of conduct, so that they may request and admonish the Seigneury to put it in order. And for this purpose every three months several from their Company shall, together with the stewards, carry out a visitation to the hospital in order to ascertain whether everything is well regulated.

It will be necessary also, both for the poor in the hospital and for those in the city who have not the means for assisting themselves, that a physician and a surgeon should be specially appointed at the city's expense, who, while practising in the city, shall be charged with the care of the hospital and with the visitation of other poor persons.

As for the plague-hospital, it is to be kept entirely separate, and especially in the event of the city being visited by this scourge of God.

Moreover, in order to prevent mendicancy, which is contrary to good administration, it will be necessary for the Seigneury to appoint certain of its officers to remove any who persist in begging, when the people come out from church. And if any are offensive or recalcitrant they are to bring them before one of the syndics. Similarly at other times the district officials (*dizeniers*) are to take care that the prohibition against begging is properly observed.

CONCERNING THE SACRAMENTS

Baptism

Baptism is not to take place except at the hour of preaching and it shall be administered solely by the ministers or coadjutors. The names of the children together with the names of their parents are to be recorded. If any illegitimate child is found, the magistracy is to be informed.[4]

Strangers are not to be accepted as godparents but only Christian persons who are also members of our own communion, since others are not capable of promising the Church to instruct the children as they should.

The supper

Since the supper was instituted by our Lord for our frequent use, and since also it was so observed in the ancient Church until the devil overturned everything, setting up the mass in its place, to celebrate it so seldom is a fault requiring correction. For the present, however, we have decided and ordered that it should be administered four times a year, namely, at Christmas, Easter, Whitsun, and on the first Sunday of September in the autumn.

The ministers shall distribute the bread in orderly fashion and with reverence, and none other is to give the cup except the delegates (*commis*) or deacons together with the ministers, and for this purpose there shall not be a large number of vessels.

The tables shall be near the pulpit so that the mystery can be better and more easily expounded near the tables.

It shall be celebrated only in church at the most suitable time.

On the Sunday before its celebration an announcement shall be made that no child is to come to it before having made profession of faith in accordance with what is taught in the catechism.

---

[4] The original draft included a clause, subsequently struck out, requiring the font to be near the pulpit, so that "the mystery and use of baptism" might be better recited in the hearing of all.

And all strangers and newcomers are also to be exhorted to present themselves first in church so that they may be instructed, if that should be necessary, and thus that none should approach to his own condemnation.

CONCERNING MARRIAGE

After the calling of the customary banns the espousals shall be performed when the parties request it, whether on Sundays or on work-days, provided that it is done only at the beginning of public worship. On a day when the supper is celebrated it will be desirable to abstain for honour of the sacrament.

Regarding disputes in matrimonial cases, since this is not a spiritual matter but mixed up with civil law, it shall remain a matter for the Seigneury. Nevertheless we have advised that the duty of hearing the parties should be left to the Consistory, so that they may report their decision to the Council for it to pass judgment. Suitable ordinances are being drawn up which will be followed henceforth.

INTRODUCTION OF HYMNS[5]

It will be desirable to introduce hymns in order the better to incite the people to prayer and to the praise of God.

To begin with, the little children shall be taught, and then in course of time the whole church will be able to follow.

CONCERNING BURIAL

The dead are to be buried decently in the place appointed. We

---

[5] By *chants ecclésiastiques* ("ecclesiastical songs"), which we have here rendered as "hymns", metrical versions of the Psalms are doubtless intended. Calvin regarded music as one of the best, if not the best, of God's gifts to man for his enjoyment. As a young man Calvin had had aspirations as a writer of poetry. In 1539, while in Strasbourg, he had compiled a "book of music" containing metrical versions of a number of Psalms – five of them from his own pen – together with the Apostles' Creed and another Psalm in prose, which were set to music for use in public worship. The other metrical Psalms in the book were the compositions of the French poet Clément Marot. Calvin, however, did not persevere with the writing of verse. For one thing, he recognized in Marot a superior ability and was content to encourage him to develop his talent to the glory of God. The singing of Marot's Psalms, in fact, exercised a not unimportant influence on the progress of the Reformation, particularly in France.

In the Register, this brief section on singing in public worship comes between the two preceding paragraphs. It has seemed advantageous, by a slight transposition, to bring these two paragraphs on marriage together.

leave the question of the funeral procession and those who accompany it to the discretion of each individual.

We have further decided and ordered that undertakers should be under oath to the Seigneury to prevent all superstitions contrary to the Word of God, to avoid arranging funerals at an unsuitable hour, and to report it if anyone should die suddenly, so that all possible unseemliness may be obviated.

Again, they are not to arrange a funeral less than twelve hours or more than twenty-four hours after death.

THE VISITATION OF THE SICK

Because many are negligent to console themselves in God with His Word when they find themselves in necessity through illness, and consequently many die without any admonition or teaching, which is then more than ever salutary for man, for this reason we have decided and ordered[6] that no one is to remain three full days confined to bed without seeing that the minister is notified, and that, when any wish a minister to come, they shall take care to call him at a convenient hour, so as not to distract him from that office in which he and his colleagues serve the Church in common. It is to remove all excuses that we have resolved on this course, and especially we enjoin that relations, friends, and guardians are not to wait until the man is at the point of death, since in this extremity consolations are for the most part of little avail.

THE VISITATION OF PRISONERS

We have further ordered[7] that on a certain day of the week there shall be an address to those in prison for the purpose of admonishing and exhorting them; and two members of the Council shall be deputed to be present lest any fraud should be committed. And if there is anyone in irons whom it is not desirable to bring out, a minister may, with the approval of the Council, be allowed to enter in order to console him in person, as above. For when one waits until condemned prisoners are to be led away to death they are often so overwhelmed with horror that they are unable to receive or understand anything. And the day appointed for doing this is Saturday, after dinner.

[6] The original draft read: "It is agreed that Messieurs should order and make public. . . ." This gives some indication of the latent conflict between the Company, who wished themselves to promulge the ordinances, and the Council, who demanded the entire responsibility, even though retaining Calvin's proposals in all essential points.

[7] The original draft read: It is agreed that Messieurs should order . . ." (see preceding note).

THE ORDER TO BE OBSERVED WITH LITTLE CHILDREN

At noon on Sundays all citizens and inhabitants shall take or send their children to catechism, of which we have spoken above.

A particular form of instruction is to be composed for them and, besides the teaching which is to be given them, they are to be questioned about what has been said to see whether it has been well understood and remembered.

When a child has been sufficiently instructed to pass on from the catechism, he shall solemnly recite the sum of what is contained in it, and he shall do this as a profession of his Christianity in the presence of the church.

Before this has been done, no child is to be admitted as a communicant to the supper, and parents are to be cautioned not to bring them before the time, for it is very perilous both for the children and for their fathers to present them without good and sufficient instruction, which is the purpose of prescribing this order.

That there may be no misbehaviour, it is ordered that when the children go to school they shall assemble there before twelve o'clock and that the instructors shall keep them in good order in each parish.

Furthermore, their fathers are to send them or see that they are taken; and so that there may be a minimum of confusion the distinction between the parishes is, as far as possible, to be observed in this connection, as has been said above concerning the sacraments.

Those who contravene this order shall be called before the Company of elders or delegates (*commis*). And if they are unwilling to comply with good counsel the matter shall be reported to the Seigneury.

For the purpose of observing who are performing their duty and who not, the above-mentioned delegates (*commis*) shall keep a watchful eye.

THE ORDER TO BE MAINTAINED IN THE CASE OF ADULTS FOR PRESERVING DISCIPLINE IN THE CHURCH

The Appointment of a Day for the Consistory

The delegates (*commis*) shall assemble once a week together with the ministers, namely, on Thursdays, to see whether there is any disorder in the Church and to consult together concerning remedies when necessary.

Since they have no authority or jurisdiction to coerce, we have decided to give them one of our officers for the purpose of summoning those to whom they wish to give some admonishment.

If through contempt anyone should refuse to appear, it is their duty to inform the Council so that remedial steps may be taken.

The Persons Whom the Elders of Delegates (Commis) Ought to Adminish and How They Ought to Proceed

If anyone speaks critically against the received doctrine, he shall be summoned for the purpose of reasoning with him. If he is amenable he shall be dismissed without scandal or disgrace. But if he is stubborn he shall be admonished for a number of times until it becomes apparent that there is need of greater severity, and then he shall be forbidden the communion of the supper and denounced to the magistrate.[8]

If anyone is negligent to come to church in such a way that a serious contempt of the communion of Christians is apparent, or if anyone shows himself to be scornful of ecclesiastical order, he shall be admonished, and if he responds with obedience he shall be amicably dismissed. But if he persists, going from bad to worse, after he has been admonished three times, he shall be separated from the Church and denounced to the Seigneury.

As for correcting such faults as may be in the life of each person, one must proceed according to the order which our Lord has commanded.

This requires that secret vices should be rebuked in secret and that no one should take his neighbour before the Church to accuse him of some fault which is neither notorious nor scandalous, except after finding him rebellious.

Furthermore, those who mock at the specific admonitions of their neighbour shall be admonished afresh by the Church, and if they are willing neither to see reason nor to acknowledge their fault once they have been convicted of it, they shall be made to abstain from the supper until such time as they return to a better disposition.

As for those notorious and public vices which the Church cannot condone, if they are faults which deserve admonishment only, it shall be the duty of the elders or delegates (*commis*) to summon those who have offended, to remonstrate with them amicably to the end that they may mend their ways, and if amendment is ap-

---

[8] This clause and several of those that follow gave occasion several years later (in September 1553) for an animated dispute between the Company of Pastors and the Council concerning the right of excommunication from the Lord's supper (see pp. 285ff. below).

parent to trouble them no further. If they persist in their evil ways they shall be admonished anew. But if at length they fail to profit they shall be denounced as despisers of God and be made to abstain from the supper until such time as a change becomes apparent in their lives.

As for those crimes which deserve not only verbal rebuke but correction with punishment, if anyone should fall into them he shall, in accordance with the requirements of the case, be commanded to abstain for a period from the supper in order that he may humble himself before God and come to a better acknowledgment of his fault.

If through contumacy or rebelliousness such a person attempts to intrude himself contrary to the prohibition, it shall be the duty of the minister to send him away, seeing that it is not lawful for him to receive communion.

Nevertheless, all this is to be so moderated that no severity should have the effect of overwhelming the offender, but rather that the disciplines imposed should act as medicines to bring sinners back to our Lord.

All this is to be done in such a way that the ministers have no civil jurisdiction and wield only the spiritual sword of the Word of God, as St. Paul commands them [Cf. Rom. 13:1ff.], and that there is no derogation by this Consistory from the authority of the Seigneury or the magistracy; but the civil power shall continue in its entirety. And in cases where there is need to administer some punishment or to restrain the parties, the ministers together with the Consistory having heard the parties and administered such reprimands and admonishments as are desirable, shall report the whole matter to the Council, which thereupon shall take steps to set things in order and pass judgment according to the requirements of the case.

This system shall apply not only to the city but also to the villages under the jurisdiction of the Seigneury.

The Register

1546

17 December 1546

THE REGISTER

On Friday 17 December 1546 it was decided by us ministers of this church of Geneva, assembled in general congregation, that it would henceforth be useful to put into writing the deliberations, decisions, and ordinances, and other matters worthy of mention, concerning the state and government of the church, for use as time and place might require. And it was resolved that for this purpose one of the ministers should keep the Register.

ORDINANCES FOR COUNTRY PARISHES

On the same day certain ordinances were proposed and approved concerning the reformation of the parishes in the villages. And it was agreed that these should be presented to Messieurs, since it was through their decision and command that they were drafted. Subsequently they were passed and promulgated by them in the Council on 3 February 1547. And thereafter they were presented to the Two Hundred in the following form.[1]

---

[1] These "Ordinances concerning the polity of the churches under the Seigneury of Geneva which are thought to be useful, submitting everything to the discretion of Messieurs" (the original title, which is, however, omitted in the Register of the Company of Pastors) were intended to complete the Ecclesiastical Ordinances of 1541 by adding certain rules appropriate to the life of the country churches. The application of the general ordinances of 1541 in a setting very different as regards customs and mental outlook from that of the urban population had raised numerous difficulties. It was for this reason that, between 17 December 1546 and 3 February 1547, the Company drew up the regulations that follow. They were not formally adopted by the Council of Two Hundred until 17 May.

Concerning Sermons

1. All the members of each household shall attend church on Sundays, unless it is necessary to leave someone behind to look after children or livestock, under penalty of 3 sous.

2. If on a weekday there is a service ordered by good authority, those who are able to attend and have no legitimate excuse are to attend; at least one member of each household shall be present, under penalty as above.

3. Those who have servants or maids shall take them or send them, so that they may not live like beasts without instruction.

4. Everyone is to be present at the service when worship commences, under penalty as above, except for a legitimate reason.

5. During the sermon everyone shall listen attentively and there shall be no unseemly or scandalous behaviour.

6. No one shall leave the church until the prayer has been offered at the end of the sermon, under penalty as above, unless there is legitimate excuse.

Catechism

Because each preacher has two parishes the catechism shall be held in each parish every fortnight, and those who have children shall send them with the rest of the household who have not been present at the sermon as above.[2]

Penalties

1. Those who fail to fulfil their duty of attendance regarding either themselves or their families shall be warned by the guards.

2. If after warning they continue defaulting, they shall be liable to a fine of three groats for each time, of which one third shall be allocated to the guards and the other two thirds to the poor of the parish and shall be placed in the church plate to be distributed according to necessity, as stated above.

3. If any arrive after the sermon has begun, they shall be warned, and if after warning has been given they do not mend their ways, for each fault they shall be liable to a fine of three sous, which shall be allocated as above.

---

[2] In the two other copies of these particular ordinances which are preserved in the State Archives of Geneva another clause, omitted in the Company's Register, is included at this point, namely: "The same audience shall observe decent and orderly behaviour for the catechism, just as is required for the sermon."

4. If anyone shall be the cause of unseemly or scandalous conduct during the service, he shall be sent before the Consistory for them to decide what action shall be taken, in accordance with the gravity of the offence: thus, if it is a case of levity there shall be a suitable verbal reprimand; if it is found that it was done through malice, contempt, or rebelliousness, the offender shall be sent before Messieurs to be suitably punished.

By Whom Fines Are to be Exacted

1. The châtelain of the locality shall, on the report of the ministers and guards, compel delinquents to pay the fines they have incurred when they are unwilling to pay them spontaneously. Legitimate excuses shall, however, be accepted, but this shall be done without the appearance of a legal process.

2. If there should be any so rebellious that the penalties mentioned above do not cause them to mend their ways, they shall be sent before the Consistory with a report requesting that Messieurs may punish them in accordance with the seriousness of their obstinacy.

3. Fathers shall be held responsible for their children, and if there is any fault the penalty shall in the first place be exacted from them.

Concerning Baptism

1. Baptism shall be administered on any day of the week provided it takes place at the same time as the sermon. The ministers, moreover, shall admonish the people to link it with the catechism.

2. The children to be baptized shall be brought in when the catechism or the sermon begins.

3. Their fathers shall be present unless there is some legitimate excuse, particulars of which shall be communicated to the Consistory.

4. No godparent shall be accepted as sponsor for a child unless he is of an age to make the requisite promise, being at least fifteen years old, of the same confession with us, and has been duly instructed.

5. As for the names given, the ordinances of Messieurs shall be observed, both for avoiding superstition and idolatry and for removing from the Church all that is foolish and unseemly.[3]

---

[3] Cf. pp. 71f. below.

6. If midwives usurp the office of baptizing they shall be reprimanded or punished according to the seriousness of the offence, and the act shall be held as null and void since permission to perform it has not been given to them, under penalty of being placed for three days on bread and water and a fine of three sous; and all who consent to it and do not report it shall be subject to the same penalty.

Concerning the Supper

1. No one shall be admitted to the supper unless he has first made confession of his faith, that is to say, has declared before the minister that he wishes to live according to the Reformation of the Gospel and knows the creed, the Lord's prayer, and the commandments of God.

2. Those who wish to receive the supper shall be present at the beginning of the preaching service, and any who come at the end are not to be admitted.

3. Other impediments shall be made known to the Consistory for it to take action in accordance with what is ordered.

4. Communicants shall remain to the end of the service, unless there is legitimate excuse, which shall be notified as above.

Concerning the Time for Assembling in Church

Churches are to be kept closed for the remainder of the time so that none may enter them outside the appointed hours for superstitious purposes; and if anyone should be found practising any particular superstition in or near a church he shall be reprimanded; and if there should be any superstition which he is unwilling to abandon he shall be punished for it.

Faults Which Contravene the Reformation Apart From Those Mentioned Above

Superstitions

1. Those who are found in possession of paternosters or images for the purpose of worshipping them shall be sent before the Consistory, and, besides the discipline which shall be imposed on them, they shall be sent before Messieurs.

2. Those who have been on pilgrimages or similar journeys.

3. Those who observe the Romish festivals or fasts shall only be reprimanded, unless they remain obstinately rebellious.

4. Those who have attended the mass shall, besides being reprimanded, be summoned before Messieurs.

5. For this offence Messieurs shall decide whether to punish them by imprisonment or by special fines, according to their discretion.

6. In the case of a fine they shall allocate some small part of it to the guards if the offence has been brought to light through their diligence.

Blasphemies

1. Any person who swears or blasphemes by the body or blood of our Lord, or in some similar way, shall have to kiss the ground on the first occasion; for the second there shall be a penalty of five sous; and for the last he shall be placed in the stocks for one hour.

2. Any person who curses or denies God or his baptism shall on the first occasion be placed on bread and water for nine days; and for the second and third occasions he shall be punished with a more rigorous physical punishment, at the discretion of Messieurs.

Contradiction of the Word

1. If any persons contradict the Word of God they shall be summoned before the Consistory for reprimand or they shall be sent before Messieurs to receive punishment in accordance with the seriousness of the case.

2. If the contradiction or rebellion involves scandal which demands a more prompt remedy, the châtelain shall take action for preserving the honour of God, of the magistrate, and of the minister.

Drunkenness

1. People are not to invite one another to excessive drinking, under penalty of three sous.

2. Taverns are to be closed during public worship, under penalty of three sous payable by the tavern-keeper; and anyone then entering a tavern shall pay the same amount.

3. If anyone is found drunk he shall pay three sous on the first occasion and shall be summoned before the Consistory; on the second occasion he shall pay the sum of five sous; and on the third he shall be fined ten sous and be put in prison.

4. No one shall take part in "Royaumes",[4] under penalty of ten sous.

Songs and dances

Anyone who sings indecent, dissolute, or outrageous songs or dances the fling or some similar dance shall be imprisoned for three days and shall then be sent before the Consistory.

Usury

No one shall lend money for usury or profit at a rate in excess of five per cent under penalty of the confiscation of the capital and condemnation to pay a fine as imposed according to the seriousness of the case.

Disturbances

1. No one shall stir up rowdy scenes or altercations, under penalty of being punished according to the seriousness of the case.
2. If anyone causes sedition or an assembly for making or sustaining contentions he shall be more rigorously punished in accordance with his deserts.

Ill-will

If there is ill-will or an altercation between any, the minister shall call the guards and shall endeavour, as is his duty, to bring the parties concerned to agreement, and if he is unable to achieve this the matter shall be brought before the Consistory.

Games

No one shall play dissolute games or any game for gold or silver or excessive stakes, under penalty of five sous and the forfeiture of the money staked.

Fornication

1. Any who are found practising fornication, if they are an unmarried man and an unmarried woman, shall be imprisoned

---

[4] "Royaumes" were banquets at which in earlier times the festival of Kings was celebrated; then banquets in general. The opposition, inspired by Calvin, of the Genevan authorities to luxurious living in the sixteenth century tended to set restraints on superfluous expenditure, whether for the table or for one's dress. This is one of its first manifestations. But the "grandes ordonnances somptuaires" were not published until later, from 1558 on.

for six days on bread and water and shall pay sixty sous into public funds.

2. If it is a case of adultery, that is to say, that one or the other is married, they shall be imprisoned for nine days on bread and water and pay into public funds a sum at the discretion of Messieurs, according to the greater seriousness of the offence.

3. Those who are engaged to be married shall not live together as man and wife until the marriage has been solemnized in church, otherwise they shall be punished as fornicators.

Concerning the Election of Guards

The châtelain shall assemble the healthiest and best of the parishioners (after having admonished them) for the election of guards,[5] who are to be good God-fearing men. Then they shall send the guards elected to the Consistory to be admonished concerning their duties; and from there they shall be sent before Messieurs to take the oath.

Sending Delinquents Before the Consistory

On the decision of the minister and his guards or of one of them the châtelain, or in his absence one of the assistants, shall send delinquents before the Consistory.

On 16 May 1547 these ordinances were read and then approved and passed, and it was further announced that of the penalties imposed for offences one third should be allocated to the parish guards, one third to the châtelain and administrator, and the remaining third to the poor of the parish and district.

By command of the syndics and Council of Geneva.

---

[5] The reference is to parochial guards charged with securing the observance of the present ordinances.

1547

[3 June 1547]

MEMORANDUM FOR THE BRETHREN WHO ARE BEING SENT TO THE CHAPTER WHICH IS TO BE HELD AT GEX BY THE DELEGATES (COMMIS) OF THE SEIGNEURS OF BERNE[1] ON THURSDAY 9 JUNE

The purpose of this memorandum is to show that it is not without cause that we are sending these brethren to report to those who have been deputed by the Seigneurs of Berne.

In the first place, inasmuch as we are all members of the one Church of God we ought to have communication with each other.

Again, the fact that we are neighbours implies that there can be neither good nor evil on the one side which is not felt by the other.

Likewise the civil bond which exists between our two cities gives us so much the greater access.

In addition, we wish to declare that we have always delighted to be of service to the Bernese churches according to our ability, and that we are as ready as ever.

Thus we hope that they will willingly approve what concern for the Church of God and a desire to discharge our duty to them have impelled us to do.

And, although they have adequate wisdom to judge what needs

---

[1] Gex and its territory, at the gates of Geneva, had belonged to the Bernese states since the conquest of 1536. The reference here is to the assemblies, held at irregular intervals, which the pastors of presbytery attended, and also a number of important laymen: bailiffs, local seigneurs, etc. The chapters were presided over by envoys sent from Berne who carried out a sort of inspection. Such a visitation took place in the spring of 1547, when Sulzer and the knights Graffenried and Steiger were present.

to be done, yet when it is a question of the honour of God and the edification of His Church diligence cannot be superfluous.

Moreover, we are at present constrained by a necessity greater than we would wish, in that there are many scandals in our neighbourhood which we see and cannot overlook, in consequence of which the Word of God is held in great contempt and, what is worse, the Gospel is quite commonly blasphemed.

Concerning these scandals, we for our part are well aware who are the cause of them. But since our brethren from Berne are here to remedy them we pray them to investigate them carefully, hoping that they will find out more than we are able to tell them here.[2]

At all events, we pray them to consider that as there have always been in the Church of God ministers whose only desire has been to have a good time and not to be bound by any restraint or discipline, so the same is likely to be the case in our day. Moreover, we wish them to discern between those who hold the honour of God in esteem and desire that everything should proceed in good order and those others who want to live in unrestrained license, causing the people to stumble because of their dissolute lives rather than edifying them by their doctrine.

We trust that they will take steps against the negligence of those who show no care for the charge which they hold and who preach only as a formality and as seldom as they can, involving themselves in profane affairs rather than in the duties of their office.

Again, we trust that they will take steps against those who, instead of being watchful over the flock in the parish to which they are appointed, do nothing but gad about hither and thither after their pleasures, and instead of living peacefully in their homes will always be found in some tavern, spending more on themselves than they have for sustaining their whole family, and indulging in all sorts of misbehaviour.

Again, there are those who are unrestrained in their participation in dissolute games and dances, and who, instead of conducting themselves in an honourable manner befitting the office of ministers, resemble common soldiers rather than ministers, both in their behaviour and in their clothing.

Again, there are those who beat and ill-treat their wives, and even

---

[2] The Company is protesting against the welcome which had been given in the territory of Gex to certain pastors from Geneva who had been deposed because of misconduct and compelled to leave the city, namely, Champereau, de la Mare, and some others.

are not free from strong suspicion of adultery, having at least a bad reputation for it, to the great prejudice of the Word of God.

Again, there are those who have little heart or zeal for maintaining the Reformation of the Gospel, and for reproving and correcting superstitions repugnant to it, and who even are more familiar with the papists than with those who faithfully follow the path of the Gospel.

Again, it is a great disgrace and scandal for ministers to molest and devour each other by having recourse to law-suits, especially when it is remembered that Messieurs of Berne have provided them with their own order of procedure, and that matters that ought to be brought before the Congregation are dragged into the courts — such matters as concern the office of the dean and officials of the presbytery, in accordance with the statutes which have been passed. These men even boast and babble jokingly in the taverns of their law-suits and litigations, in such a way that all modest persons feel ashamed.

We therefore pray them to examine carefully all these and similar matters which demand to be remedied; and if they find it a tiresome and annoying duty they should consider that it is no small thing to purge the Church of God of all disorders and scandals, and, moreover, that, inasmuch as ministers ought to be an example to all the people, they should take great care that ruin does not come from their side.

And we bring all this to their attention because of the love which we should bear towards them in our Lord, and indeed do bear towards them, in such a way that we likewise are ready to receive the admonitions which they shall offer us, if there should be anything to criticize in us.

Passed by the congregation of the brethren assembled on Friday 3 June 1547.

Jehan Calvin

Abelus Poupinus[3]	Philippe de Ecclesia[11]
Françoys Bourgoin[4]	Loys Gougnye[12]
Jacques Bernard[5]	J. de Sainct Andrey[13]
Loys Treppreau[6]	Nicolas des Gallars[14]
Malisier[7] Peyrier[8]	M. Cop[15]
Jo. Ferronius[9]	N. Petit[16]
Raymond Chauvet[10]	Jehan Baldin[17]

[3] Abel Poupin was a pastor in Geneva from 1545 to 1547 and from 1548 to 1556.

⁴ François Bourgoin, Sire d'Aignon, was at first a canon at Nevers and subsequently a pastor in Geneva from 1545 to 1561, and in France from 1561 to 1565.

⁵ Jacques Bernard, a member of an ancient Genevan family, had been a priest and was one of the first supporters of the Reformation in his city.

⁶ Louis Treppereau, a native of Artois, had sought refuge in Geneva, and was admitted as a "coadjutor" of the pastors in 1542. He was soon placed in charge of the rural parish of Céligny, with the oversight also of the village of Crans, in the canton of Vaud (which then came under Bernese control). In 1553, when difficulties arose between Geneva and Berne and the latter forbade Genevan pastors to preach in their territory, Treppereau left the service of the Seigneury and was placed by the Bernese in charge of the church of Crans, which he had served until his departure from Céligny (cf. below pp. 212f.). This action displeased Calvin, who had regarded Treppereau as his protégé. Treppereau was later appointed to Lausanne, where he ministered for some twenty years.

⁷ Mathieu Malesier was pastor of the hospital in 1544. In 1545 he went to Bossey, and later on returned to Geneva.

⁸ Jean Périer, of Montauban, was pastor at Mérindol. He sought refuge in Geneva, and ministered at Neydens before returning to Mérindol in 1561.

⁹ Jean Ferron, of Poitiers, had been a pastor in Geneva since 1544; but he was deposed in 1549 (cf. elow, pp. 109ff.).

¹⁰ Raymond Chauvet, one of Calvin's most eminent colleagues, was a pastor in Geneva from 1545 to 1570.

¹¹ Philippe de Ecclesia was appointed a pastor in Geneva in 1542, and in 1544 was moved to Vandoeuvres. He was in trouble with the Company of Pastors in 1549 (see below, pp. 92f., 105ff., 201ff.).

¹² Louis Cougnier was pastor at Russin from 1544 until his death at the end of 1552.

¹³ Jean de Saint-André was appointed to Moëns as pastor in 1544, to Jussy in 1548, and from 1552 until his death in 1557 served as a pastor in Geneva. During this latter period he was secretary of the Company of Pastors.

¹⁴ Nicolas des Gallars, Sire de Saules, was born in 1520 and was appointed a pastor in Geneva in 1544. The greater part of his ministry was carried out in his native land, and he became one of the leaders of the church in France, especially after the Colloquy of Poissy. For a short period, from 1563 to 1564, he was minister of the French congregation in London (cf. below, p. 350).

¹⁵ Michel Cop, who was born in Basle about 1501, was a pastor in Geneva from 1545 until his death in 1566. He was the younger brother of Nicolas Cop, who was Rector of the University of Paris in 1533 and a great friend of Calvin.

¹⁶ Nicolas Petit, originally from the neighbourhood of Paris, sought refuge in Geneva, where he was admitted to the ministry. He served as pastor at Chancy from 1544 to 1557 and thereafter at Draillans until his death in 1578.

¹⁷ Jean Baldin, of St. Romain-du-Gard, was pastor at Jussy, and then at Moëns and Genthod until his death in 1560.

[15 April 1547]

LETTER TO NEUCHATEL

To the faithful servants and pastors of Christ in the church at Neuchâtel, both in the city and in the country, our beloved brethren and colleagues:

Because our brother Helias[19] who dwells among you wrote that a woman had betrothed herself to him on condition that, before the marriage was solemnized, he should certify to you by proper testimonies that he was not bound by any other marriage bond, at his request we appointed two from our college to inquire into this matter. After investigation, they reported to us as follows: that six men and one woman of acknowledged repute declared with one voice that Helias was known to them in La Rochelle when he was a priest in the church first of St. Nicholas and afterwards of St. Bartholomew, that he lived honourably among men without any whisper of fornication, that he never publicly had a wife there, and that there was never any rumour of a private or secret marriage known to them. Accordingly, they hold him to be a man free from any marriage tie. We wished this to be testified to you lest we should fail in our duty to our brother. Farewell, reverend brethren in the Lord.
Geneva, 15 April 1547

Ministers of the church in Geneva

The following are the names of the witnesses:

Stephanus Longavillanus	Renatus Ravalletus
Guillelmus Germanus	Hugo Graverius
Petrus Ponsellus	Ludovica Billota
Joannes Ballotus	

[18] In the Register this letter is placed after the two that immediately follow; but both because it antedates them and also because as placed in the Register it interrupts the documents relating to the Treppereau — Saunier affair I have ventured to transpose it to this position. P. E. H.

[19] Little is known about this person Helias. From this letter it is evident that he had come originally from La Rochelle where he had been a priest. Calvin had already recommended him to Farel in a letter dated 4 July 1546, in which he designates him as *Helias Lemoricus cognomine, natione Rupellensis* (*Calvini Opera*, XII, col. 356). Apparently Helias was already at Neuchâtel at this time. He became a pastor in the territory of Neuchâtel, and seems to have had the confidence of Calvin, who on several occasions entrusted him with messages for his colleagues (cf. *Calvini Opera*, XIII, col. 409; XVII, col. 325). His death would seem to have taken place in 1561, since at the end of that year the question of appointing a successor to him arose (cf. *Calvini Opera*, XIX, col. 149).

[3 May 1547]

LETTERS FROM THE PRESBYTERY OF MORGES ON BEHALF OF LOUIS TREPPEREAU AND ANTOINE SAUNIER, MINISTERS

To our very dear brethren, the learned and godly pastors of the church of Geneva:

Grace to you and peace from God our Father through Christ our Lord and Saviour be multiplied. Beloved brethren, Antoine Saunier,[20] who is uncommonly dear to us because he is pressed and as it were oppressed on every side by troubles, has asked us, meeting together in the Spirit of the Lord in Aubonne this third day of May 1547, that we should do our utmost to console him, at least in some measure. He suggests that it would be most convenient if, with the consent of us who as your and his brethren have assembled here, he were permitted to withdraw from the church at Rolle[21] which is in his charge, by an arrangement whereby we permit Louis Treppereau, our brother who was appointed by you to the churches of Céligny[22] and Crans,[23] to take his place in the church at Rolle, while he takes over from Louis in the churches of Céligny and Crans. Unitedly we have given serious consideration to his petition and in our judgment the reasons supporting it are not slight. This rightly moves and inclines us to assent to it. We have therefore consented and granted what he has requested, as we are authorized to do. We

---

[20] Antoine Saunier, a native of Dauphiné, was one of the prime movers in the Reformation in French Switzerland. When he was pastor at Perroy in the canton of Vaud, he had acquired the estate of Bossey (where the Institute of Ecumenical Studies is now situated). The exchange recommended by the classis of Morges would have enabled him to be nearby, as his estate was in the neighbourhood of the parish of Céligny. Later on Saunier was compelled to sell his estate in order to pay his debts. Regarding the approach of Saunier and his colleagues, see the letter from Viret to Calvin (Lausanne, 10 May 1547) and Calvin's reply (Geneva, 16 May 1547) in *Calvini Opera*, III, coll. 520-522.

[21] The borough of Rolle came under the parish of Parroy, both before and after the Reformation (up till 1621). The pastors of the presbytery of Morges designate the post occupied by Saunier by the name of Rolle here, doubtless because this locality was now clearly more important than the modest viticultural and rural village of Parroy, and perhaps also because Saunier was actually living there.

[22] Although an enclave in the canton of Vaud, situated between Coppet and Nyon, the village and territory of Céligny came under the Seigneury of Geneva.

[23] The village of Crans was within the canton of Vaud, but in accordance with its ecclesiastical statute it came under the Genevan parish of Céligny (cf. note 6, p. 63 above).

approach you with confidence regarding this concession of ours, commending to you the case of our brother who has made the request, for he is widely known for the heavy and indeed unremitting labour undertaken and endured by him for the sake of the Word of Jesus Christ, and not least is he known to us because of his truly Christian and entirely blameless manner of life among us. We sign in the name of all the brethren assembled:

Johannes Morandus,[24] *dean*[25]

P. Masuerius,[26] *juratus*   Renatus Perrotellus,[28] *juratus*
Guillielmus Pomerius,[27] *juratus* Michael Silvanus,[29] *juratus*

[3 May 1547]

To the Pastors and Brethren in the Church in Geneva, Beloved in the Lord and Distinguished for Their Piety and Prudent Solicitude:

To the pastors of the church in Geneva, famed for their piety and learning, grace and peace through Jesus Christ. Louis Treppereau the minister of the church in Céligny under your charge, beloved brethren, has complained before us, assembled in the Lord, concerning our brother Jean Morand that, again before us assembled in the same Lord, he asserted that our brother Trep-

---

[24] Jean Morand was, like Calvin, a native of Picardy. He had been vicar of the Bishop of Amiens, but when he was condemned by the faculty of theology of Paris because of his "heretical" opinions he withdrew, in 1537, to Geneva, whence he was recommended to Messieurs of Berne. He was appointed pastor at Cully and in 1538 was elected dean of the presbytery of Lausanne. Some months later he was recalled to Geneva by the Council to occupy one of the posts left vacant through the departure of Calvin and his colleagues. This phase of his ministry was not very happy, however, and he seized the opportunity of returning to the canton of Vaud to be installed at Nyon, where he remained until 1552. Thereafter trace of him is lost.

[25] The church of the canton of Vaud comprised four presbyteries (Lausanne-Vevey, Morges, Payerne, and Yverdon), each of which had at its head a dean and four "jurés". Morand, pastor at Nyon, was dean of his presbytery — the presbytery of Morges.

[26] Pierre Masuyer had been pastor at Cossonay since 1536. He was a friend of Viret and an adherent of Calvinist teaching.

[27] Guillaume Pommier is known to have been minister at Vufflens in 1555.

[28] René Perrotel, of Anjou, had formerly been a Franciscan friar. In which parish he was serving at this time (1547) is not known. In 1561 he was appointed to Orbe.

[29] Michael Sylvius, or du Bois, is known to have been appointed minister at St. Prex and Etoy in 1537.

pereau wished (as he had heard) to join our presbytery, which, he says, has brought him into undeserved suspicion among you. From this he desires to be set free. We also desire this — indeed our other brother Morand also asks that we should give him a free and true testimony concerning this matter. We solemnly declare that among those things which our brother Morand proposed, by virtue of his office, respecting Louis we heard no such thing as that about which Louis complains, and Morand himself has openly declared that Treppereau never requested any such thing from him. That you might be assured of our affection we have desired the names of our brethren to be subscribed as witnesses on this third day of May 1547.

>Renatus Perrotellus, *juratus*
>Gullielmus Pomerius, *juratus*
>P. Masuerius, *juratus*
>Michael Sylvanus, *juratus*

[6 May 1547]

On 6 May 1547 the brethren of both town and country being assembled in their congregation, the letters here attached[30] were presented to them and read, and they deliberated over them after having caused Maître Louis Treppereau, who was personally involved, to go out, and also after having heard Maître Antoine Saunier, who made strong representations in favour of bringing about the exchange mentioned in these letters. When, however, they had given careful consideration to the whole matter and had diligently examined all that had been written and proposed, the brethren failed to find the reasons alleged by Saunier sufficient to justify his leaving his church and moving to another; for the principal reason which he alleged was the convenience of his property which was situated near Céligny. And as for the scandal which he alleged might result if he were pressed by his creditors, it was considered that he could remedy this by selling or disposing of the property in question — indeed it would be much better were all this to perish rather than that still greater scandal should result from initiating such changes for the sake of private interests. It was also considered that because of his ability Saunier was needed by the church at Rolle where he was established and to which he was better suited than Maître Louis. It was therefore

---

[30] The reference is to the two preceding letters.

decided that things should remain as they were. This done, such admonitions were offered to Maître Louis as were then decided by the brethren.

[20 October 1547]

PETITION OF ADAM FUMEE AND MICHELLE DE MILLONE

On 20 October 1547 the ministerial brethren of the city were assembled at the request of a nobleman Adam Fumée[31] and Mlle. Michelle de Millone, who revealed that a marriage had been contracted between them in the presence of honest persons, but that they had no certificate or testimonial of it, and that it had not been performed in public. They declared that it was their earnest desire that it should now be publicly contracted and approved in the Church of God, but that there were certain very weighty reasons against making it known, and that if it were known their friends and close relations might be in great danger. He therefore requested the brethren to stand witness for him before the Seigneurs of this city that Michelle de Millone had been kept by him as his wife, as he still wished to keep her, and that she should be acknowledged as such. He also asked that the Seigneury should give him a certificate and testimonial which he could use in case of necessity, until such time as the matter could be made public with greater freedom. In consenting to this the brethren resolved that M. Calvin and M. Abel[32] should approach Messieurs to make this request and declaration, as agreed by the brethren.

[1 November 1547]

THE CASE OF PIERRE BOUCHERON AND
MARGUERITE DES BORDES

On Tuesday the first day of November in the same year a man named Pierre Boucheron[33] declared before the ministerial brethren of the city that, having left the habit of a Jacobin, he had contracted a marriage with a woman named Marguerite des Bordes, a

[31] Adam Fumée, called du Mont, a former abbot of La Couture du Mans, the brother of Antoine Fumée, was a member of the Council of parliament. He was a correspondent of Calvin's and a supporter — though a somewhat flexible one — of the Reformation.

[32] That is, Abel Poupin (see note 3, p. 62 above).

[33] Pierre Boucheron has not been further identified.

native of Paris, with the consent of her father whose name was
Pierre des Bordes, a boatman and fishmonger living in the Rue
Saint Honoré in Paris; that the marriage was solemnized in the
parish of Saint Germain de L'Auxerrois at the mass at about ten
or eleven o'clock in the morning towards the end of the month
of July last; but that he had not revealed to Marguerite that he
had previously been a Jacobin until several days later when they
were travelling from Paris to this city, and that Marguerite whom
he had taken and married as his wife felt some scruples about
this in her conscience. It was his desire that she should be reassured and consoled, and also that their marriage should be
accorded approval so that there should remain no scandal to the
Church of our Lord. Thereupon Pierre was questioned concerning his association with Marguerite and the means by which he
had entered into this marriage. He replied that in order to be
far away from the university, where there are Jacobins by whom
he would be recognized, he went to live in the house of Marguerite, and there fell ill; that after having been carefully nursed by
her and restored to health he made a proposal of marriage, to
which she consented, and also her father; and that it was solemnized as has been described.

Pierre was then caused to withdraw and Marguerite was called
in and questioned regarding this same matter. She was found to
be in agreement concerning the fact of the marriage, but alleged
that at the time she was unaware that Pierre had been a Jacobin
and that on learning of it she had been troubled in her conscience,
but that after she had learnt the reasons she was happier about it
than had previously been the case. It was explained to her that
the vows in question were monastic vows, and that it was the
commandment of God that all who cannot contain themselves
should marry, but that for her part it was necessary that she should
declare whether she felt able to live with Pierre as her husband
with a clear conscience. She replied in the affirmative that such
was her resolve. She was then asked to withdraw.

While they were outside the brethren conferred together. Then
by common consent both of them were recalled and told that the
beginning of this marriage had not been good, since what is not
done in faith is not done with a clear conscience and is contrary
to God, and that it was not right to proceed in this way, but since
they intended to live together and had been united they should
agree to do so in good conscience and to live together in seemly
union. It was decided that the brethren who knew them in Paris
should try to obtain attestation of their marriage in order to avoid
all scandal and to meet their request. In the meantime they were

to take care to live in such a manner that the Church might be edified.

And because Pierre had mentioned to some of the brethren that he had undertaken to make a journey to Lyons he was admonished to make suitable provision for his wife, so that she might not be exposed to danger.

[12 December 1547]

CALVIN SUBDUES AN UPROAR

On Monday 12 December 1547 it was decided by the brethren to present themselves before Messieurs for the purpose of objecting strongly to the insolence, debauchery, dissoluteness, and hostility which were leading church and city to ruin;[34] and this was done on the same day. It was further resolved that similar action should be taken by us at the next meeting of the Council of Two Hundred which was held on the Friday following, namely, the 16th day of the same month. On this day we left the Congregation sooner than was customary.

This was done not without great blessing from God, for when we arrived at the public hall, where the Two Hundred were assembled, a variety of disputes had already arisen and the minds of nearly all were so inflamed that they were not far from insurrection. Indeed, a most atrocious shedding of blood would have followed had not the Lord intervened. When he heard the alarming clamour and uproar Calvin rushed ahead into the midst of the tumult which was now quite out of hand, and the others followed him. Nearly all were so agitated and enraged that it was impossible to hear any one voice clearly. But after a little while calm was restored and the Two Hundred were brought to order. Presenting ourselves to them, we used the same exhortations as we had used before the Council previously, but on this occasion when insurrection was threatened, everything was handled by Calvin much more forcefully.

[34] The reference is to the disturbance occasioned in Geneva by the affair of Ami Perrin whose first trial had just terminated in his acquittal, while the trial of Meigret dragged on. The population of Geneva was seriously divided and inflamed, and heated incidents broke out on 16 December, as described in the immediately following account in the Register. Calvin, who went in person into the midst of the tumult hoping to pacify the seething assembly, has given us his own description in a letter to Viret dated 17 December (*Calvini Opera*, XII, coll. 632f.). See note 31, p. 107 below for further comments on Perrin and his fortunes as leader of the "libertines" in Geneva.

1547

EXTRACT FROM THE ORDINANCE OF MESSIEURS CONCERNING THE GIVING OF NAMES IN BAPTISM[35]

In the first place it is forbidden to give the names of idols which once prevailed in the land, because superstition could again be aroused by them, and also because they would be a memorial to the idolatry from which it has pleased God by His grace to deliver the land — names such as *Suaire*,[36] *Claude*,[37] *Mama*,[38] and others, and also names by which kings are called, both because it is an abuse and also because there has been false confidence in them.

Likewise the names of offices, because they belong only to those to whom the charge was entrusted and who were called of God — such as *Baptiste*,[39] *Ange*,[40] *Evangéliste*,[41] and other such names.

Likewise names belonging to God alone or to our Lord Jesus Christ — such as *Dieu le Fils*,[42] *Esprit*,[43] *Emmanuel, Sauveur*,[44] *Jésus*.

Likewise inept names to which some absurdity attaches and which could lead to mockery — such as *Toussaint*,[45] *Croix*,[46] *Dimanche*,[47] *Typhaine*,[48] *Sepulchre, Noël*,[49] *Pasques*,[50] *Pentecoste*, and also *Chrétien*,[51] because it is common to all.

Likewise double names and others which are ill-sounding, such as *Gonin, Mermet, Sermet, Allemand*.

[35] Here the Register of the Company of Pastors gives the official text of an ordinance issued by the Council of Geneva on 22 November 1546. It was an ordinance for which Calvin had pressed, but it came into being only after three months of vigorous discussion provoked by a dispute over a child which the father wished to name Claude and the pastors Abraham (cf. *Calvini Opera*, X, coll. 49f.).
[36] *Suaire* = "shroud".
[37] *Claude* was a name that had been popular in Geneva because of devotion to St. Claude, bishop of Basançon and patron of the neighboring abbey of St. Claude, which attracted numerous pilgrims.
[38] *Mama* for Mary mother of Jesus.
[39] *Baptiste* = John the Baptist.
[40] *Ange* = "angel".
[41] *Evangéliste* = "evangelist".
[42] *Dieu le Fils* = "God the Son".
[43] *Esprit* = "(Holy) Spirit".
[44] *Sauveur* = "Saviour".
[45] *Toussaint* = "All Saints".
[46] *Croix* = "Cross".
[47] *Dimanche* = "Sunday".
[48] *Typhaine* = "Epiphany".
[49] *Noël* = Christmas".
[50] *Pasques* = "Passover", "Easter".
[51] *Chrétien* = "Christian".

Likewise corrupted names, such as *Tyvan* and *Tevette* instead of *Etienne*[52] and *Monet* instead of *Simon*.

MARRIAGE ORDINANCES ISSUED BY AUTHORITY OF MESSIEURS[53]

Which Persons May Not Marry Without Permission

1. In the case of young people who have not previously been married none, whether male or female, their father being still alive, shall have authority to contract a marriage without the permission of their father unless they have reached the legal age, namely twenty years for a man and eighteen for a woman;[54] and if after having passed that age they have requested their fathers or caused them to be requested, to consent to their marriage, and their fathers have offered no objection, it shall be lawful for them to be married without the authority of their fathers.

2. The same regulation shall be observed by wards who are under the authority of trustees or guardians, though foster-mothers or guardians shall not consent to the marriage of their charge without consulting one of the relations, if there are any.

3. In the case of two young people who have contracted a marriage of their own impulse foolishly or frivolously, they shall be punished and chastened, and the marriage shall be rescinded at the request of those in charge of them.

4. If anyone, whether man or woman, is found to be guilty of subornation or of inciting them to such a marriage, those responsible shall be punished with three days on bread and water and shall implore the mercy of the court.

5. Those who are found to have collaborated in such a marriage as witnesses shall also be punished with one day's imprisonment on bread and water.

---

[52] *Etienne* = "Stephen".

[53] An earlier list of marriage ordinances, drafted under Calvin's inspiration and revised by him, has been published in *Calvini Opera*, X, coll. 33-44. It is dated 10 November 1545, and the set of ordinances given here derives from it. These ordinances are not dated, but their position here in the Register indicates that they cannot have been later than the year 1547. Actually, it seems that these ordinances were not promulgated by the Council, since the pastors, with Calvin at their head, raised the matter again in January 1550, and again in May 1551. The text as it stands here was, however, incorporated in the Ecclesiastical Ordinances of 1561.

[54] The draft of 1545 prescribed an age of twenty-four years for the man and twenty for the woman.

6. No one shall bring about a clandestine exchange of promises, conditional or otherwise, between young unmarried persons; but there shall be at least two witnesses. Otherwise everything shall be null and void.

7. In the case of children who marry without the consent of father or mother at the age when they are permitted to do so, as above, if it is known to the court that they have acted lawfully while their fathers have been negligent or excessively strict, the fathers shall be compelled to assign them a dowry or to grant them such portion and position as would have been the case had they consented to the marriage.

8. No father shall compel his children to enter into a marriage which he favours without their good will and consent, but the son or daughter who is unwilling to accept the partner whom the father has chosen may be excused, while always observing a modest and reverent spirit, without the imposition of any punishment by the father for such a refusal. The same shall be observed in the case of those who are under guardians.

9. Fathers or guardians shall not cause their children or wards to contract a marriage before they are of an age to confirm it. If, however, it should come about that a child having refused to marry in accordance with the father's wish, should afterwards choose a marriage which is not so much to his profit and advantage, then, because of rebellion or disrespect, the father shall during his lifetime be under no obligation to give him anything.

Persons Who May Marry Without Permission

10. Those who have already been married once, whether men or women, even though their fathers are still alive shall none the less be at liberty to contract a marriage, provided they have reached the age mentioned above, namely twenty years for a man and eighteen for a woman, and have been emancipated, that is to say, have left the home of their father and have kept house separately, though it is more fitting that they should always let themselves be governed by the advice of their fathers.

11. All promises of marriage should be made honourably and in the fear of God and in no way dissolutely or frivolously, as when merely touching glasses when drinking together without first having made a sober proposal, and those who do otherwise shall be punished; but at the request of one of the parties, claiming to have been taken by surprise, the marriage shall be rescinded.

12. If anyone brings a party before the courts alleging promise of marriage, unless there are two witnesses who are persons of good reputation, the oath shall be administered to the defendant who, on denying the charge, shall be absolved.

For What Reasons a Promise May Be Rescinded

1. Once it is clear that a promise has been made between competent persons the marriage may not be rescinded, with three exceptions: namely, when it is shown by adequate proof that a girl who was taken to be a virgin is not so, or when one of the parties suffers from a contagious and incurable disease.[55]

2. A marriage shall not be prevented from fulfilment through failure to provide a dowry or money or outfit, inasmuch as this is only an accessory matter.

Promises Are To Be Made Simply

While it is lawful when discussing or negotiating marriage to add conditions or to reserve consent, yet when it comes to making the promise it is to be pure and simple, and a proposal which is subject to conditions is not to be taken for a promise of marriage.

Concerning the Period of Fulfilling a Marriage After the Making of a Promise

1. After a promise has been made, marriage is not to be deferred more than six weeks, otherwise the parties shall be summoned before the Consistory and reproved; and if they fail to obey they shall then be sent before the Council so that they may be compelled to celebrate it.

2. If there should be any objection, the minister shall send the objector before the Consistory at its next meeting and admonish him to cite the accused party there. Nobody, however, shall be admitted as an objector unless he is a citizen or is otherwise known or has someone who knows him with him, so that the suffering of defamation or injustice by an honourable girl may be avoided.

---

[55] Though this clause speaks of three exceptions, only two are given. The third was, in fact, given in sequence in the draft of 1545, namely, the case of a man who, having promised marriage, left the city. But, a little further on, the text of the Register makes provision for this situation in the case of a man — or a woman — who is already married. No doubt this is the reason why provision for this kind of situation is omitted here.

3. In the event of the objector not putting in an appearance on the day appointed for hearing the case, the banns and the marriage shall be proceeded with as though no impediment had been alleged.

4. For the avoiding of all deceptions which might be perpetrated in this connection, no stranger coming from a distant country shall be permitted to marry unless he possesses good and reliable testimony, either through letters or from good and trustworthy persons, that he has not been married elsewhere and also respecting the integrity of his character. The same procedure shall be observed in the case of girls or women.

Concerning Banns and Engagements

1. The banns are to be published for three Sundays in church before the marriage takes place, having first obtained the signature of the first Syndic attesting that the parties are known — on the understanding, however, that the marriage may take place on the third publication and that if one of the parties should belong to another parish there should also be satisfactory attestation from that place.

2. During the engagement the parties are not to live together as man and wife up to the time when the marriage has been solemnized in church in a Christian manner. If any are found to have done the contrary, they shall be punished by imprisonment for three days on bread and water and summoned before the Consistory to be reprimanded for their misbehaviour.

Concerning the Celebration of a Marriage

1. At the time when they are to be wedded the parties shall come modestly to church, without drummers and fiddlers, maintaining the decorum and gravity befitting to Christians, and this shall be done before the bell has stopped ringing so that the solemnization of the marriage may take place before the sermon. If they are negligent or arrive late they shall be sent back.

2. It shall be lawful to celebrate marriages on any day of the week: on work-days at the service which the parties prefer and on Sundays at the service held early in the morning or at three in the afternoon, with the exception of the days when the supper is celebrated, in order that then there may be no distraction and all may be better disposed to receive the sacrament.

Concerning the Communal Dwelling of the Husband With His Wife

The husband is to have his wife with him living in the same house and maintaining one communal home. If it should happen that one leaves the other to live in separation, they shall be summoned so that they may be reproved and compelled to return to each other.

Concerning the Degrees of Consanguinity Which Prevent Marriage

1. No marriage may be contracted in a direct line, that is to say, of a father to his daughter or a mother to her son and all other descendants in sequence, inasmuch as this contravenes the propriety of nature and is forbidden both by the law of God and by the civil laws.

2. Similarly, the marriage of an uncle to his niece or great-niece, of an aunt to her nephew or great-nephew, and so on in sequence, inasmuch as the uncle represents the father and the aunt is in the place of the mother.

3. Similarly, between brother and sister, whether children of the same father and mother or of one of them.

4. With regard to the other degrees, while marriage is forbidden neither by the law of God nor by the civil law of the Romans, nevertheless for the avoidance of scandal (since for a long time it has not been customary), and for fear lest the Word of God should be blasphemed by the ignorant, marriage should not be contracted between first cousins until such time as we give a different ruling. There shall be no impediment to the other degrees.

Concerning the Degrees of Affinity

1. No man shall take as wife his son's or his grandson's widow, and no woman shall take as husband her daughter's or granddaughter's husband, and so on with other relations in a direct line.

2. No man shall take his wife's daughter or granddaughter, and so on.

3. So also a woman may not take her husband's son or grandson and so on.

4. Similarly, no man shall take the divorced wife of his nephew or great-nephew, and no woman shall take her niece's or great-niece's husband.

5. No man shall take the widow of his brother and no woman shall take him who was her sister's husband.

6. When it has come to notice that a man has committed adultery with another man's wife he may not take her in marriage because of the scandal and the dangers connected with it.

If a husband is not living in harmony with his wife, but they wrangle and dispute with each other, they shall be summoned before the Consistory so that they may be admonished to live in peace and unity, and each of them shall be reproved for their faults, according to the seriousness of the case.

If it is known that a husband ill-treats his wife by beating and tormenting her or that he is threatening to do her some injury, and it is known that he is a man whose temper is uncontrolled, he shall be sent before the Council so that he may be expressly forbidden to beat her under pain of certain punishment.

For What Reasons a Marriage Shall Be Declared Null and Void

1. If a woman should complain that the man who has taken her in marriage is physically impotent, being unable to consummate the marriage, and this is found to be true by confession or investigation, the marriage shall be declared null and void, the woman declared free, and the man forbidden to misuse any woman again.

2. Similarly, if a man complains that he cannot have intercourse with his wife because of some defect in her body and she is unwilling to have it put right, after the truth of the case has been established the marriage shall be declared null and void.

For What Reasons a Marriage Can Be Rescinded

If a husband accuses his wife of adultery and he proves it by sufficient witnesses or evidences and demands to be separated by divorce, it shall be granted, and thereafter he shall be able to marry again if he so wishes. Moreover, while he should be exhorted to pardon his wife, yet one has no right to compel him to do so against his will.

Although in ancient times the right of the wife was not equal with that of the husband where divorce was concerned, yet since, as the Apostle says, the obligation is mutual and reciprocal regarding the intercourse of the bed, and since in this the wife is no more subject to the husband than the husband to the wife, if a man is convicted of adultery and his wife demands to be separated from him, this shall be granted to her also, provided it proves impossible by good counsel to reconcile them to each other. If, however, the wife should fall into adultery through the evident fault of the husband, or the husband through the fault of the wife, in such a way that they are both to blame, or if there should be proof of some fraud perpetrated with a view to obtaining a divorce, then they shall not be permitted to demand it.

If a husband who has gone on a journey for business or for some other reason, and who is not debauched or alienated from his wife, fails to return after a long time, and it is not known what has happened to him, so that it may reasonably be conjectured that he is dead, his wife shall not be permitted to remarry until after the lapse of ten years from the day of his departure, unless there are reliable testimonies to his death, on hearing which she may be granted permission. Again the permission to remarry after ten years shall be withheld if there is any suspicion, either through news or through evidences, that the husband has been held prisoner or has been hindered by some other mishap, in which case the woman shall live in widowhood.

If through debauchery or some other evil disposition a husband goes away and abandons his place of residence, the wife shall make careful inquiry to ascertain the place to which he has withdrawn; and when she knows she shall come and request letters empowering her to recall him or otherwise to compel him to perform his obligations, or at least to notify him that he is to return to the marital home, under pain of proceedings being taken against him in his absence. Once this has been done, and there is no way of compelling him to return, the procedure shall be followed, in accordance with the warning given him, whereby he shall be publicly named in church on three Sundays at fortnightly intervals, such that the period shall be one of six weeks. The same shall be done three times in the court of the lieutenant. If he fails to put in an appearance, notification shall be given to two or three of his closest friends or relations, if he has any. And his wife shall appear before the Consistory when next it meets, in order to request a separation. This shall be granted to her, and she shall then be sent before Messieurs so that a judicial order may be made, and so that the man who has been so rebellious may be permanently banished. If he should put in an appearance, they are to be reconciled harmoniously and in the fear of God.

If any man makes a habit of deserting his wife for wandering abroad, on the second occasion he shall be punished with imprisonment on bread and water, and he shall be warned with stern threats that he is not to do the same again; on the third occasion he shall be treated with greater severity; and if there is no amendment the wife shall be granted a ruling to the effect that she is no longer bound to such a husband who keeps neither faith nor company with her.

If a husband who is debauched has deserted his wife without his wife having given him any occasion for doing so or being in any way to blame for it, and this is duly confirmed through the testimony of neighbours and relatives, and the wife comes to complain and seek redress, she shall be admonished to make careful inquiry to discover what has become of him and his nearest kinsmen or friends, if he has any, shall be summoned in order to obtain information from them. The wife, however, if she is unable to discover where he is, shall wait until the completion of one year, committing herself to God; and when the year is up she shall be able to come before the Consistory. If it is then ascertained that she needs to be married, she shall be exhorted and sent to the Council to swear on oath that she does not know where her husband has withdrawn to, and the same shall be required of his nearest kinsmen and friends. After this the public announcements previously mentioned shall be proceeded with so that liberty may be given to the woman to remarry. If the absent husband should return thereafter, he shall be punished in an appropriate manner.

If a wife leaves her husband and goes off to another place, and the husband comes to request a divorce and freedom to remarry, inquiry shall be made to see whether she is in a place from which she can be recalled or at least notified that she is to appear in order to reply to her husband's petition; and the husband shall be assisted with letters and other documents for doing this. When this has been done, the public announcements mentioned above shall be made, after having first called her nearest kinsmen and friends in order to admonish them to persuade her to return, if they can. If she appears within the prescribed period and the husband rejects her through suspicion that she has misconducted herself and because for a wife to abandon her husband in this way is too scandalous a matter, an attempt shall be made to effect a reconciliation and the husband shall be exhorted to pardon her fault. If, however, he persists in making an issue of this, inquiries shall be made from the place where she has been concerning the company she has kept and how she has behaved herself, and if no clear evidence or proof is found to convict her of having been disloyal to her marriage, the husband shall be compelled to be reconciled to her. In the event of her being charged with a very emphatic presumption of having committed adultery or of having kept bad and suspect company and of not having conducted herself honourably as a good woman, the husband's petition shall be heard and he shall be granted what reason dictates. If she does not appear within the prescribed period, the same procedure shall be followed against her as against the husband in a parallel case.

If[56] after having become engaged to a girl or woman a man goes off to another country and the girl or woman comes to make a complaint about it, requesting to be released from her promise in view of the other's disloyalty, inquiries shall be made to discover whether he has done this for some honest purpose and with her knowledge or through debauchery and because he has no wish to fulfil the marriage. If it is found that he has no apparent justification and that he has acted through bad faith, inquiries shall be made concerning the place to which he has withdrawn and if possible he shall be notified that he must come by a certain date to perform what he has promised.

If, after having been notified, he fails to appear, it shall be publicly announced in church for three Sundays that he has to appear, in such a way that there shall always be an interval between two announcements so that the whole period shall be one of six weeks. If he does not appear within this period, the girl or woman shall be declared free and he shall be banished for disloyalty. If he does appear, he shall be compelled to celebrate the marriage on the earliest possible day. If it is not known to which country he has gone and the girl or woman, together with his closest friends, shall swear that they are ignorant of it, the same public announcements shall be made as if he had been notified, with a view to setting her free.

If he had some just reason and had told her of it beforehand, the girl or woman shall wait for the space of one year before being permitted to proceed against him in his absence, and meanwhile the girl or woman shall do her utmost, both through her own efforts and through those of his friends, to induce him to return. If after the lapse of a year he does not return, then the public announcements shall be made in the manner described above.

The same shall be observed against a girl or woman, excepting that the man shall not be compelled to wait one year, even if she acted with his knowledge and consent, unless he had agreed that she should undertake a journey which required so long an absence.

If a girl who is duly bound by a promise is fraudulently trans-

---

[56] This and the four following paragraphs do not appear in the draft of 1545.

ported outside the territory so that the marriage cannot be fulfilled, inquiries shall be made to discover whether there is anyone in the city who has assisted in this deed, in order that he may be compelled to ensure that she returns, subject to such penalties as shall be decided; or, if she has trustees or guardians, they shall be enjoined to do everything possible to ensure that she returns.

If after his wife has deserted him a husband makes no complaint but keeps silent about it, or if a wife deserted by her husband dissimulates without saying a word about it, and this becomes known, the Consistory shall summon them in order to ascertain the facts of the case with a view to avoiding all scandals, because there could have been collusion, which is not to be tolerated, or even something much worse; and, having learnt the situation, steps shall be taken according to the means available to prevent the occurrence of voluntary divorces, that is to say, divorces arranged at the pleasure of the parties concerned without the authority of law. And married couples shall not be permitted to live apart from each other; but at the request of the husband the wife shall be compelled to follow him when he wishes to change his place of residence or when he is compelled by necessity to do so, provided that he is not a debauched man who is leading her astray and into an unknown territory; but it must be in a reasonable territory that he wishes to reside, and in an honourable position, so that he may live as a respectable man and keep a respectable household.

All matrimonial causes concerning personal relationships and not goods shall receive attention in the first instance in the Consistory where an amicable solution, if one can be found, shall be effected in the name of God. If it is necessary to pronounce some judicial sentence, the parties shall be sent to the Council with a statement of the decision of the Consistory so that the definitive sentence may be given.

1548

VISITATION OF THE PARISHES

In the month of[ ]¹ 1546 it was resolved by the brethren assembled in general congregation that thenceforward visitations should be made of all the parishes of this church of Geneva.² This also met with the approval of Messieurs, and order was given that two councillors should accompany the minister deputed³ for the visitation for the purpose of visiting the *châtelain*⁴ — the minister for his part to inquire concerning the doctrine and manner of life of the pastor of the place, and the councillors concerning the

---

¹ The date was 11 January (see next note).
² The ordinances of 1541 had already provided for periodic meetings of the pastors; but this was not enough to ensure that their parishes were functioning properly. In May 1544 Calvin appeared in person before the Council and pressed for the issuing of regulations concerning the visitation of parishes. But there was considerable delay before a scheme authorizing these visitations was approved. They were sanctioned by the pastors on 11 January 1546. (See *Calvini Opera*, X, coll. 45-48). A fortnight later, on 25 January, the scheme was presented to the Council and adopted. The reference here is to this "order of visitation of the country churches." The scheme operated in the following way: the Council appointed two of its members and the Company two pastors to carry out the visitation, the purpose of which was to determine the purity of the evangelical doctrine preached by the pastor whose parish was being visited and the quality of his preaching, which ought to be neither scandalous nor arcane; to promote regular attendance at public worship and the Christian way of life; to ascertain whether the pastor was fulfilling his other pastoral duties and leading an honourable life. The order also makes provision for the practical details of the visitation.
³ From this it seems that, contrary to the terms of the Order of Visitation, it was decided to appoint only one pastor for the visitation of each parish. This may well have been because the pastors in Geneva were not numerous and the heavy demands of their work made it difficult for them to spare two of their number for the purpose of visitation of the country parishes.
⁴ The *châtelain* was a local official of the Seigneury who administered the estates which came under its supervision. The office was generally held by a citizen. In effect, its administration was essentially fiscal.

manner of life of the *châtelain*. Messieurs Calvin, Abel,[5] and Ferron were delegated by the brethren, and Messieurs Chicand[6] and Chautemps[7] were deputed by the Council.

In the year 1547 Messieurs Calvin, Bourgoin, and des Gallars were deputed by the brethren to visit the parishes; but in this year no visitation was made because authorization could not be obtained from the first syndic[8] then in office, who seemed to have some reasons for deferring the visitations because of the prevailing state of affairs.

The brethren, however, when the year had gone by, were not satisfied and reproved the brethren deputed by them for insufficient diligence. Accordingly, for the following year, 1548, they re-elected and confirmed Messieurs Calvin, Bourgoin, and des Gallars for the conducting of these visits and admonished them to do their duty better.

On Sunday 15 July the visitations were commenced. And Messieurs Bourgoin, Chicand, and Chautemps went to Neydens[9] and on the same day also to Bossey.[10]

The following Sunday, the 22nd, des Gallars went with Messieurs Chicand and Chautemps to Céligny,[11] and on the same day also returned by way of Genthod.[12]

On Sunday 5 August the same year Monsieur Calvin went with the above-mentioned deputies to visit Satigny.[13]

[5] That is, Abel Poupin.

[6] Antoine Chicand was one of the most prominent figures in Genevan politics during the second quarter of the sixteenth century and one of the architects of independence and of the Reformation in Geneva. He was elected a councillor in 1530 and was appointed syndic in 1531 and thereafter several more times. He died in 1554.

[7] Jean Chautemps was no less active in his support of the Reformation in Geneva, from the time when Farel first began to preach there. As a businessman he was astute and audacious and was among the first to encourage capitalist enterprise in Geneva, investing money in industrial activities entirely new to the city. At the same time he was a conscientious servant of the Seigneury, both by assisting in the administration of its goods and also by playing his part in the government as a councillor from 1542 onwards. He was syndic in 1556. His death took place in 1562.

[8] In the year 1547 the first syndic was Girardin de la Rive, another eminent magistrate of the young republic.

[9] The pastor at Neydens, in Haute Savoie, was Jean Périer.

[10] The pastor at Bossey, also in Haute Savoie, was Mathieu Malesier.

[11] The pastor at Céligny, a Genevan enclave in Vaudois territory, was Louis Treppereau.

[12] The pastor of Genthod, on the west bank of the Lake of Geneva, between Geneva and Versoix, was Jean Baldin.

[13] The pastor of Satigny, a Genevan village on the right bank of the Rhône, was Jacques Bernard.

On Sunday 12 August the Sire d'Aignon[14] visited Russin and Dardagny.[15]

On Sunday 19 August des Gallars visited Chancy and Cartigny.[16]

The following Sunday, the 26th, M. d'Aignon visited Jussy and Foncenex.[17]

On 2 September d'Aignon visited Vandoeuvres and Cologny.[18]

On 16 September des Gallars visited Moëns.[19]

These were the visitations completed for this year.

[30 October 1548]

REQUEST FOR DIVORCE BY FRANCOIS FAVRE

On Tuesday the penultimate day of October 1548 we ministers of the city were called before Messieurs to give advice concerning a divorce case involving François Favre[20] and his wife. Favre asked to be separated from his wife because she had numerous lawsuits and her properties were situated in Morges where he was unable to attend to them, and he had not taken her on this condition. Moreover, he confessed to having committed adultery, which his wife also objected against him in agreeing to the divorce. On this Monsieur Calvin began to give his opinion, affirming that adultery is sufficient cause for divorce from the wife's side as well as from the husband's; for although the husband has pre-

---

[14] The Sire d'Aignon was François Bourgoin.

[15] The pastor of Russin and Dardagny, which formed a single parish on the right bank of the Rhône, was Louis Cougnier.

[16] The pastor of Chancy and Cartigny, another single parish but on the left bank of the Rhône, was Nicolas Petit.

[17] The pastor of Jussy, an ancient episcopal seat, and Foncenex, a village of Haute Savoie situated today across the frontier, was Jean de Saint-André.

[18] The pastor of Vandoeuvres and Cologny, to the east of Geneva, was Philippe de Ecclesia.

[19] The pastor of Moëns, near Ferney, ancient territory of the cathedral chapter, was Jean Baldin.

[20] François Favre, a wealthy merchant draper, played an important political role in Geneva at the time of independence. His daughter Françoise married Ami Perrin who later led the opposition to the Calvinist movement. It is his third wife whom he now wishes to divorce. He died three years later, on 28 November 1551.

eminence over the wife, yet in this there is equality — St. Paul, I Cor. 7, "the husband has not power over his body, etc." It was necessary, moreover, to consider when this fornication or adultery had taken place, whether or not it was before the marriage was contracted, and if it was during the marriage, whether since the adulterous act the wife had consented to continue living with her husband, so that the fault was cancelled. And, again, Messieurs were urged to beware lest there should be any collusion between the parties, which would open the door for the dissolving of many marriages. It was pointed out, further, that the wife, who was an interested party had not brought an action, although she accused him of disgraceful conduct. Accordingly, Messieurs were unanimously exhorted to give careful attention to the outcome of this case. Thereupon we were dismissed.

On 8 November of the same year . . . .[21]

[13 November 1548]

TESTIMONIAL[22] FOR MONSIEUR ANTOINE,[23]

Ministers of the Genevan Church

Since this our brother has lived among us for a long time and has also taught the boys in the ptochotrophium[24] for almost six years, he has requested us to testify to the manner in which he has conducted himself during the whole of this period, lest good men should suspect that he comes to them without the commendation of a testimonial from this church. This we could not refuse him. We know him, then, to be a pious and God-fearing man. To those among whom he has moved he has given proof of his life. Nor has there been in his morals anything objectionable which would be unworthy of a Christian man. He has always been sedulous in his attendance at public worship. When he was placed in charge of the boys of our ptochotrophium not only did he fulfil his duties faithfully in that office, but he was also known as a worthy and upright man. He was not dismissed from this

[21] The rest of this paragraph is missing.
[22] The text of this testimonial has previously been published in *Calvini Opera*, XIII, col. 101.
[23] Named as "Magister Ant. Grenet" in the records of the hospital, on the occasion of his departure, 20 December 1548.
[24] The ptochotrophium was the hospice for the poor.

appointment, but relinquished the post of his own accord when he felt that there was little hope that certain lawsuits, which had arisen not through his own but through someone else's fault, would be easily settled. We, indeed, as far as we are able to judge, regard him not only as an honourable man but also as one so versed in the teaching of piety that, should any appointment be given him, it would be fulfilled with becoming faithfulness and diligence.

Geneva, The Ides of November[25] 1548

Joannes Calvinus, with the approval of the brethren

---

[25] 13 November.

1549

[10 January 1549]

COPY OF A LETTER SENT BY THE MINISTERS OF THE CHURCH AT MONTBELIARD[1] TO THE PASTORS OF THE CHURCH IN GENEVA, LAUSANNE, NEUCHATEL, AND ELSEWHERE THROUGHOUT THE DOMINION OF THE SEIGNEURS OF BERNE[2]

Most reverend brethren, you have doubtless learnt that several months ago an Interim[3] of the Emperor was received by our senior duke Ulrich, and that by his order it was commanded to be publicly observed here, with the result that the papal mass, festivals of the saints, superstition concerning food, and other such things were restored contrary to our will and desire. And, although in the meantime we had been ordered more than once not to say anything publicly against this new decree, and warned that, if anything untoward should happen to us as a result of our assem-

---

[1] The county of Montbéliard belonged to Duke Ulrich of Württemberg who had encouraged Farel's evangelical preaching from the beginning, as had also his brother, Count George, the administrator of the county. In 1542, however, Ulrich replaced the latter as administrator by his son, the young Duke Christopher, who encouraged the spread of Lutheranism in the territory and opposed the activity of the Reformer Toussain, Farel's friend and successor. Toussain was able to resume his work in 1546, after a short absence.

[2] The text of this letter has been published in *Calvini Opera*, XIII, coll. 152f.

[3] The Interim of Augsburg had been promulgated some months previously, on 15 May 1548, and was imposed on the majority of the Protestants of the Empire. Together with many other German princes, Duke Ulrich of Württemberg submitted, and his son Duke Christopher also, though not without protest. The Council of Montbéliard offered a more vigorous resistance. Between November 1548 and January 1549 the situation of the county regarding the application of the Interim was much confused. Uncertain what course to follow, the pastors consulted their colleagues in Strasbourg, Basle, and Geneva. This explains the present letter.

blies, our prince would be unable to help us, we proceeded by common consent (thanks be to Christ) to perform the duties of our office, determined to teach such things as pertain to the glory of the Lord and to the edification of our churches, in accordance with the Word of God. But at length these mandates, of which we are sending you a copy, were conveyed to us from the dukedom by our senior prince. And since we are unable under any circumstances to accept them, we daily expect nothing else than that we shall all be deprived of the ministry of the Word. And we debated among ourselves — certain of our brethren having proposed it — whether it would have been advisable for us to continue to assemble, even against the will of the magistrate, if that should be possible, as assuredly all of us here would gladly endure even unto death. Since, however, we saw that this could not be done and that such an attempt would not only be of no avail but would occasion manifest offence to our junior prince Christopher and his councillors and to the populace, who are at present not ill disposed toward us and our ministry, we at length decided, all other remedies having been tried in vain, to submit to this final and urgent mandate of our senior duke, as our chief magistrate, however impious it might be. We prefer to do this rather than stir up greater disturbances here by useless opposition, thereby rendering our ministry suspect to them and to many others. We wished to inform you of these things so that you might commend our churches and us ourselves to the Lord God in your holy prayers. Farewell. *Montbéliard, 10 January 1549*

*Your servants and brethren in the Lord,
the ministers of the presbytery of Montbéliard*

[16 January 1549]

THE REPLY TO THE ABOVE LETTER[4]

To the ministers of the church of Montbéliard, faithful servants of Christ, our most dear brothers and colleagues: Grace to you and peace from God our Father and the Lord Jesus Christ, most dear and cordially honoured brethren. At last what we have long feared has come to pass, that among you also Satan through his ministers should overthrow the order of the Church established by the Lord. Your letter, however, has brought this much of

---

[4] This reply is also given in *Calvini Opera*, XIII, coll. 155ff. It was first published by Beza in *Calvini Epistolae*, p. 82.

consolation, as far as such can be found in so extremely sad a matter, that from it we have learnt that you all stood firm in your office to the last. For, as you have solemnly testified, constancy in condemning those corruptions which were being introduced to defile the purity of sound doctrine was worthy of you as ministers of Christ. Now also, in that you have chosen exile rather than perfidious dissimulation, you have displayed a glorious proof of the sincerity of your faith. For when he who hitherto had shown hospitality to the Church of Christ in his dominion, and also had permitted you liberty to preach Christ, removes you from the office of teaching, to proceed further is in our judgment inexpedient, especially when it is apparent that there is no hope of progress, and the flock over which Christ had placed you as pastors no longer desires your services. For as he is a traitor who of his own will withdraws and deserts his post, so it is not for us to resist when we are compelled by force, unless it should be that the Church calls on us by name to undergo persecution; for then it is better to die a hundred times than to disappoint the prayers of those who were prepared to follow Christ. Your circumstances, however, are very different. For as long as you were pastors your application and attention to the flock were not deficient. Now, when zeal in perseverance will bring no benefit, and not even the sheep themselves, to whom your faith is bound, think that it would be of value to them for you to tend them further, you have clearly discharged your duty.

Let it remain, therefore, that you commend to Christ the oversight which was entrusted to you, so that He alone may rule by His Spirit now that there is no place for your work. Apart from this, we can well imagine with what grief you are oppressed, faced as you are with nothing but exile and poverty. But the chief grief is that occasioned by this disaster to the Church, which you have shown that you feel more deeply than your own. And we, indeed, are affected by your misfortunes, whether public or private, as is only right. Would that we might be allowed to stretch out our hand to you! Now it is left to us to exhort you to persevere to the end in this witness of Christian sincerity. However unhappy your condition, it will be more blessed than if you had retained a position and title from which the Son of God is banished. Soon, however, we shall see that He reigns in heaven in such a way that He wills to exercise His power on earth also. Meanwhile, since the moment of victory is not yet, we must prepare ourselves for warfare.

Farewell, beloved and most honourable brothers. May the Lord Jesus be with you, console you, and strengthen you in holy perseverance!
Geneva, 16 January 1549

> The ministers of the church of
> Geneva, brothers truly united to
> you in the Lord,
>
> Joannes Calvinus *in the name of all*

[*18 January 1549*]

NEGLIGENCE OVER REFORMATION REPROVED

The following is a copy of the document which was publicly read at the sermons and catechisms on Sunday, 18 January 1549,[5] by order of Messieurs[6]

Grace and peace from God the Father and from Jesus Christ His Son our Lord.

We, Syndics of the Council of Geneva, to all our dear, loyal, and well-beloved citizens, burghers, dwellers, and inhabitants of our city, greetings in our Lord. We give notice to you that, in view of the great misfortunes and disorders which are at present throughout the earth, and which are sure witnesses of the wrath of God against men and that His rod is exercised for the punishment of their ingratitude and the great iniquities which are daily committed in all states, and especially the despising of His holy Word and His ordinances; — recognizing, on the other hand, the singular grace which He accords us in His mercy, and that we must render account to Him of the people whom He has committed to our charge; in view also that the rules and statutes, which we have made and frequently published following the reformation that we have derived from the Gospel, are not being observed in accordance with our intention and desire, but indeed are rather despised, we do not wish to be ungrateful to God for His blessings, nor to be the cause of the blood of our subjects being required at our hands, as it certainly will be if through our

---

[5] There is an error in the date here, since 18 January 1549 fell on a Friday. The present proclamation must have been read on Sunday, 20 January, in conformity with a decision of the Council taken on Friday, 18 January.

[6] The text of this letter has been published in *Calvini Opera*, XIII, coll. 158ff.

fault and negligence God is dishonoured and His holy ordinances trampled under foot: — for this reason, following the example both of the good kings of the ancient Church and also of the Christian princes, rulers, and magistrates who have submitted themselves to the Word of God, and wishing to remedy such evils as far as we are able, according to the grace and authority which He has given us, we declare to all those mentioned above that we are much grieved and displeased that the holy ordinances and remonstrations which have been made to them through the Word of God, which is daily preached to them, have not been better observed, as would have been proper, and also that the rules made by us have not been better kept and put into practice. In this the magistrates and the ministers of the Word of God have been negligent and have not fulfilled the duty of their office by admonishing and reproving vices and setting a good example, as they are bound to do and their vocation demands.

In view, therefore, of the contempt and apathy shown by many, and virtually by all, in attending sermons and catechisms or instructions of children, and in consequence of the transgressions which are committed against the Word of God and our orders and edicts in conformity with it, concerning the abolition of papal ceremonies, idolatries, superstitions, blasphemies, sorceries, charms, drunkenness, gluttony, dances, improper songs, games, dissoluteness in clothing, fornication, usury, thieving, deceitfulness, and other such iniquities and scandals which are prevalent, by which the wrath of God is provoked and kindled — being sorrowful and displeased that God is not better feared and served, and desiring to take steps for setting these things in order, we declare that it is our intention to take matters in hand and to give every care and diligence that all, great and small, shall conform to a Christian manner of living. And we command each and every one of those mentioned above to cooperate faithfully in this, each one according to his status and ability, and all fathers of families to be diligent in instructing their children, their servants, and their maids, and in seeing that they come to sermons and catechisms. In particular, we command our officers to be vigilant in seeing to it that our rules and ordinances are observed without favour to great or small, and without fear of the present troubles, and that those who have a public charge should be the first to behave well and to set a good example to others and bring them to good order. We also command the preachers to perform their duty by being more careful and earnest than they have been to teach, to admonish, and to rebuke vices as they ought, inasmuch as each and every one of you love the honour of God and fear to offend Him, and inasmuch as you wish to escape our displeasure and severe punishment. And, so that there may be no plea of ignorance, it is our will and command that these presents be publicly read in church, the people having first been called together.

Made the 18th day of January 1549, and signed thus: by the command of my Seigneurs, Ruffi;[7] and sealed in red wax with the seal of the city.

[15 February 1549]

THE AFFAIR OF M. PHILIPPE DE ECCLESIA[8]

On Friday 15 February 1549 the brethren of both city and country, ministers of this church, were specially convened to consider the charge that Maître Philippe de Ecclesia had maintained in the meetings of the Congregation certain propositions which were not edifying and led to useless questions, often overthrowing and obscuring what had been clearly defined. In this connection a list had been made containing a number of ineptitudes and absurdities, and even erroneous teaching, which was read to him point by point. He acknowledged and confessed that he had uttered the most part of this, while he did not remember the rest. The brethren, however, insisted that he had uttered and held all the opinions recorded in the list. And because he had frequently been warned in the past to desist from such propositions and to speak in a more edifying manner, and had done nothing about it, but had persisted to the contrary the brethren agreed that he should be reprimanded for his rebelliousness and that he could not be excused for having contravened the order and discipline of the church. This ruling meant that the matter could be taken further if it were wished to proceed by the strict letter of the law and bring the case before Messieurs for action to be taken in accordance with the articles formulated for such a case. But as they wished to proceed by way of fraternal correction the brethren resolved among themselves that he should be warned not to speak in the Congregation at all, neither after someone else had expounded nor when his own turn came round to expound, until the next day

---

[7] Pierre Ruffi was secretary of the Council. He died soon afterwards, during that same year.

[8] See note 11, p. 63, on Philippe De Ecclesia.

of censures. (The reason for this was cited from St. Paul: that he who brings nothing of edification ought to keep silence in the church [I Cor. 14:26, 28] — how much more he who teaches false doctrine!) In the meantime they would test out the measure of his amendment and obedience. If he was unwilling to obey this ruling, the case would be taken before the Consistory for proceedings in accordance with the articles.

De Ecclesia was then recalled so that the brethren might announce their decision, and he accepted the discipline imposed on him, agreeing to desist from speaking in the Congregation. He begged that at least he might not be disgraced and that this sentence should not be made public. To this the brethren responded that the first who disclosed it would be treated as infamous and a perjuror. Each one consented to this. There was, therefore, no need to take the case further. Likewise he was warned by decision of the brethren not to keep company with suspect, evil living, and dissolute persons, and not to disclose what had been said in the Congregation.

On the same day, after this had been done, it was decided by the brethren that thenceforward any of the ministers who should speak after the expounder should also be severely censured if he should be in error; and this applied to the expounder also.[9]

[12 February 1549]

CONCERNING PIERRE TOUSSAIN OF MONTBELIARD

COPY OF A LETTER[10] FROM PIERRE TOUSSAIN, PASTOR OF THE CHURCH AT MONTBELIARD,[11] TO CALVIN, FARBEL, VIRET, AND THEIR COLLEAGUES

Most respected brethren, from the document which we now send you in the name of the prince and the brethren who are ministers of the Word here you will easily understand in what state our affairs are.[12] For I, vile and abject sinner though I am, would rather die than affirm anything which I know to be contrary

[9] For subsequent developments in the De Ecclesia affair see pp. 105ff., 133, 188ff., 201ff., 209ff. below.
[10] The text of this letter has been published in *Calvini Opera*, coll. 183f.
[11] Concerning Pierre Toussain, see note 1, p. 87 above.
[12] Cf. note 3, p. 87 above.

to the glory of the Lord. And although I see the enemies of the Gospel lying in wait for me on all sides, so that I cannot continue here any longer without great peril to my life (for the administrator of Besançon[13] has already written a letter to our prince demanding all but the death sentence for me as — so he writes — a breaker of the Emperor's commands); yet if godly and learned men judge that I can continue with a good conscience, and that to do so pertains to the glory of God I shall not be reluctant to lay down my life for my flock (if that should seem good to the Lord God). For Brenz[14] who was here for some time with the prince considers that I shall act in a manner unworthy of a servant of Christ if I do not make a stand in the position offered. We are also awaiting the opinion of the brethren in Strasbourg and Basle concerning this matter; and although I have no hope that the adversaries will tolerate me here for long or as the sole preacher, yet since we shall leave nothing unattempted, we shall be excused before the Lord God, and the prince, the people, and the Councillors will see that it is not through my fault that the ministry of the Word has not been preserved here. Farewell, most reverend brethren, whom I also pray to inform me privately: whether a minister or other person can in good conscience decide to have his infant children baptized;[15] and again, whether a minister when totally deprived of his ministry, and asked by the prince or the church nonetheless to stay on as long as the Lord permits, can do so with a good conscience. Farewell again in the Lord Jesus, and continue to help me with your holy prayers. I entreat the Lord God to preserve you to His holy Church.

Montbéliard, 12 February 1549

Yours in the Lord,

Petrus Tossanus

---

[13] The administrator of the Archbishopric of Besançon was François Bonvalot, abbot of Luxeuil and Saint-Vincent.

[14] Johann Brenz (1499-1570), the Lutheran Reformer of Swabia and Württemberg, had met and gained the support of Duke Ulrich at the Colloquy of Marburg in 1529. In 1548 his outspoken criticism of the Augsburg Interim resulted in his having to leave Württemberg, and he found refuge with Duke Christopher at Montbéliard. Archbishop Cranmer invited him to come to England, but he declined. Later, in 1553, he was appointed Provost of the Stiftskirche in Stuttgart.

[15] The sacramental ministry having been forbidden: presumably the question being whether this related to the eucharist only, or to baptism as well.

Second Letter[16]

Esteemed brethren, after I had written this letter to you, we became anxious about the messenger sent by us to Strasbourg, who was held up by floods; but at length he brought us the reply of our brother ministers of the Word there, a copy of which I am sending to you. And although our brother ministers in Basle have not yet sent their agreed opinion, yet certain of them and also Martin Cellarius[17] are of the opinion of the brethren in Strasbourg, and Count George of Württemberg[18] gives the same counsel.

Regarding the other ministers who have been deprived of the ministry of the Word by the senior duke's[19] councillors, the godly prince Christopher made provision for their stipends to be paid to them for six or eight months, permitting them to remain in their churches which meant that at least they might in some measure be of service to the flock by means of private teaching and consolation. For this reason I was not of the opinion that they should immediately desert their churches and betake themselves elsewhere, unnecessarily becoming a burden on others. I therefore wrote to the brethren in Strasbourg requesting that they would communicate to me privately their opinion on this matter. They have replied as follows: "All the colleagues unanimously decide that a minister who has been removed from public ministry ought, unless he is called to public office elsewhere, or he perceives that he can bear more fruit for the Lord elsewhere, to remain with his church even though he has been deprived, if he may lawfully do so, so that he may provide the ministry of the Word for the Lord's flock in private while it is not possible to do so publicly. The same reasons lead us to this judgment as we advanced concerning your public ministry of the Word, namely, that this ministry ought not to be withdrawn from your church, even though the ministry of the sacraments is forbidden you. For a faithful minister loves the Lord's flock and perseveres in his care of it to the end, etc."

---

[16] The text of this letter has been published in *Calvini Opera*, XIII, coll. 184f.

[17] Martinus Borrhaeus, known as Cellarius (1499-1569), taught the Old Testament for many years at Basle and was three times Rector of the university there.

[18] Count George was the brother of Duke Ulrich of Württemberg and had formerly been administrator of the county of Montbéliard (see note 1, p. 87 above).

[19] Duke Ulrich of Württemberg.

[19 February 1549]

TO THE LETTERS ABOVE WE REPLIED IN THE FOLLOWING WAY:[20]

Regarding the matter about which we have been consulted by Christ's faithful servant and our esteemed colleague Pierre Toussain, we resolved, after invoking God's Spirit, as is needful, that we should reply as follows:

In the first place we perceive that there are two reasons in particular which dispose Toussain to depart: firstly, because he has been deprived of the ministration of the sacraments, which is part of the ministry that has hitherto been operative in Montbéliard, he considers that he has been deposed from his office; secondly, because the rest of the brethren whom he had as colleagues in the same function have been dismissed, he is afraid lest by retaining the position of a teacher he should occasion offence to many, as though dissociating himself from those with whom he had a common calling, and many should interpret him to have been impelled by private reasons rather than by concern for the public good of the Church. When all the brethren together consulted last month as to how they ought to act we replied as follows: "As he is a traitor who of his own will withdraws and deserts his post, so it is not for us to resist when we are compelled by force, unless it should happen that the Church should call on us by name to undergo persecution . . . . Your circumstances, however, are very different. For as long as you were pastors your application and attention to the flock were not deficient. Now when zeal in perseverance will bring no advantage, and not even the sheep themselves, to whom your faith is bound, think that it would be of value to them for you to tend them further, you have clearly discharged your duty." If this exception is acknowledged, the first difficulty will be solved. For the services of Toussain are demanded both by the most illustrious prince Christopher and by the people themselves. As long, therefore, as he has a church to which he is able to be of use he does not seem to be acting rightly and in accordance with his duty if he deserts it. If he were retained on condition that, by some disgraceful pact, such as very many others have entered into, his freedom for teaching honestly and in sincerity should be restricted, it would be preferable to die a hundred times rather than to purchase the position of a teacher at so great a cost. But

---

[20] This letter was published by Beza in *Calvini Epistolae*, p. 317. It is also given in *Calvini Opera*, XIII, coll. 193ff.

now when complete liberty to confess Christ is permitted, there is no cause for him to remove himself. Moreover, in that he is deprived of some part of his ministry, although this is grievous to bear, yet his engagement to the Church is not for this reason entirely dissolved, inasmuch as he has not been completely deposed from his office. For although he is unable to fulfil the office of pastor in every respect, yet it is a great thing if he functions as a teacher. And since the sacraments are as it were accessory to the Word, once they have been removed to cast away the Word as well, of which they are distinguished parts, would be too absurd. And so our respected brethren the pastors of the church in Strasbourg wisely advise that the Church can for the time being be sustained by the Word, while it lacks the sacraments.

If Toussain and the church in Montbéliard had not been under duress, and the use of the sacraments had not hitherto been granted, he would eagerly have chosen to be appointed to the unrestricted office of teaching. In actual fact, he commenced his ministry there in this capacity and for some time held the role of teacher before he assumed the functions which belong to the pastoral office. Now that the power of darkness has prevailed to the extent that Satan's servants have snatched away what hitherto he held by the goodness of Christ, what remains for him except to return to his earlier career and to devote himself faithfully to the task of teaching and admonishing, until the Lord builds up again what has now collapsed? In former times, when saintly pastors were driven from their churches by the fury of tyrants, they still would visit them secretly, sometimes even dressed as soldiers, as Eusebius relates. This opportunity, therefore, which has been granted to Toussain should much less be rejected on the ground that he who previously was a pastor has now to show himself as a teacher; for he will be engaged in an occupation approved of God and beneficial to the Church, even though deprived of one half of his accustomed ministry. In this respect the prophets have set us an example, in that, when the temple was in ruins and the sacrificial rite for the time being snatched from them, they did not cease to fulfil the role of teachers. This, it is true, was something about which they complained: "How shall we sing the Lord's song in a strange land?" [Ps. 137:4]. Yet when they taught this song to the people they thereby undertook the office of teaching. Accordingly, when we are violently robbed of the use of the sacraments, the pastor, so far from leaving his post and turning his back on the duty of teaching, ought then most of all to devote himself to it and, if permitted, to redouble his zeal and application in teaching.

It is our judgment, therefore, that though Toussain is deprived of the ministry of the sacraments, yet, when the most illustrious prince offers him the position of a teacher and the people demand his services, his deposition is not of such a kind as to dissolve his obligation, but that he ought to occupy the office of a teacher so long as liberty is granted him to teach without compromise. Not only do we judge this to be expedient, but we believe it to be altogether necessary — unless it is by the calling of God, whom hitherto he has obeyed, that he wishes to withdraw himself. Because we are quite sure that he abhors such a course with all his heart, we are confident that he will without difficulty be induced to remain. Further, with regard to his fear lest wicked men should spread the slander that it is carefulness to be retained in office rather than zeal for building up the Church by which he is motivated, this is a suspicion which should as far as possible, be guarded against. But if the sanctity of a genuine vocation places him, as we believe, under obligation, then, whatever may be the opinion of men, he ought none the less to persevere with constancy in that which he knows is pleasing to God. We, indeed, have more than enough firsthand knowledge how great is the ingratitude of our age, though we realize that all God's servants have experienced this discomfort and heard well-doing evil spoken of. Our brother Toussain ought not therefore to expect that all will approve what he builds up with the greatest conscientiousness, though he does not shun even the peril of death. There will always be cowardly and worthless men who disguise the disgrace of their own slothfulness by misrepresenting him. Nor is it the case that by not rejecting the opportunity offered to him of building up the Church he will thereby dissociate himself from his brethren who are deprived of it; but rather the brethren should encourage him not culpably to allow what remains of the light to be extinguished. For it befits the servants of Christ that, the more they find their mouths to be stopped, the more they should by every means earnestly co-operate to the end that the pure doctrine of the Gospel may sound forth from the tongues of others and their own silence be as it were compensated for by the voice of others.

Now we pray God that, as we have faithfully advised our brother Toussain what we judge to be for the good of the Church, so He will strengthen his heart to endure bravely the conflicts which we perceive to lie before him. It does not surprise us if a godly man hesitates and is perplexed in circumstances so complicated. It does not surprise us either if he is agitated by a variety of thoughts in the present sudden scattering of the Church. It does not surprise us, finally, if, in the midst of the wickedness of the times and of the perverse and malign slanders of men, he is uncertain and undecided as he considers what he ought to do, while he desires to give satisfaction to all. Nor is it in any superficial manner that we congratulate him because he directs all his thoughts and energies to this one end, namely, that he may first be submissive to God, and then that he may expend his whole self for the Church. It is a singular gift of God that he neither desires nor looks for anything else than that which will contribute to the tranquillity of his conscience. Moreover, in that he mistrusts his own judgment and permits himself to be ruled by the counsels of his brethren, we admire, as is right, his pious modesty. And here, indeed, we have followed no other path than that which the Lord Himself commanded by His Spirit and His Word, inasmuch as we make it our starting-point that He should govern our minds and tongues. And the fruit of his modesty will not, we trust, bring regrets, since, being reassured of his vocation, he will be much better equipped to withstand all assaults of whatever kind, and, supported by the approval of the godly, he will be less vulnerable to the calumnies of wicked men. It will certainly be a source of satisfaction to the weak when they learn that it is through acquiescence in the counsels of his brethren that he stands firm in his own church. Moreover, apart from concern for the Church, we are influenced also by the conscientiousness of the most judicious prince whom we see to be so disposed that he omits nothing whereby at least some part of the kingdom of Christ may remain intact within his dominion. Since this heroic magnitude of mind has been given him from heaven, it is the duty of Toussain to co-operate with all his might. We also hope that it will shortly come to pass that by the blessing of God he may find some way through all obstacles to promote the progress of so glorious a project and at length be crowned with success.

Geneva, 19 February 1549

[13 March 1549]

LETTER FROM THE COMPANY SENT TO A SYNOD OF MINISTERS, BOTH FRENCH AND GERMAN SPEAKING, OF THE STATE OF BERNE, HELD ON 19 MARCH 1549[21]

To the pastors of the Church of Berne, from both city and country, esteemed and faithful servants of Christ, our honoured and beloved colleagues and brethren, now meeting together in Berne.

Because we offer for your perusal our opinion concerning the sacraments without having been asked to do so, the reason for this decision of ours must briefly be given you, although both as far as you are concerned and in a matter so appropriate, a long explanation seems unnecessary. When by its edict the illustrious Council calls you together for consultation on a variety of questions including the peace of the Church, the principal bond of which is agreement in pure doctrine, it is probable that there will be some discussion concerning the sacraments, since this is a matter which for a long time has exercised the Bernese church. Moreover, although we have had no request for an exposition of our doctrine, we judge that it belongs to our office spontaneously to make known to you what we all feel with one spirit and utter with one voice. For since it is the same Christ whom we both proclaim, the same Gospel which we profess, the same body of the Church of which we are members, and the same ministry, the fact that we are subjects of different dominions ought not to sunder the unity of our faith or to prevent so many bonds of sacred fellowship consecrated by the blessing of Christ from flourishing between us. The fact also that we are neighbours, which imposes an obligation between the children of this age, ought no less to weigh with us. Indeed, we are so much involved

---

[21] The original of this letter is preserved, with Calvin's autograph, "*omnium nomine*", in the Bürgerbibliothek of Berne. Johann Haller wrote on this letter: "*Genevensium epistola et declaratio de coena Domini ad synodum bernensem. Non autem fuit exhibita certas ob causas*". Haller evidently feared that to produce this letter and the accompanying articles at the synod would have the effect of creating new tension between the churches of Geneva and Berne, whereas by his conciliatory approach he had had some success in resolving the differences between them. The letter has been published in various places, including *Calvini Opera*, XII, coll. 216ff. Haller had been in Geneva during the previous month (February) following a "visitation" of the School in Lausanne. Calvin and his colleagues had welcomed him with great cordiality. There is no reason to suppose, however, that he had any hand in the composition of this letter.

with each other that our very geographical situation holds us as it were mutually bound together. Hence comes the federal association between our two cities.[22] Some men from our college are actually ministering in churches on Bernese territory,[23] just as on the other hand several of your men are in charge of churches within the dominion of Geneva. For these reasons it is in your interest no less than in ours that the form of doctrine which we follow should be made known to you. To say no more, by this means many sinister suspicions will at least be counteracted and malevolent men be deprived of substance for slander. We are quite confident that our good-will will be welcome not to you only but also to your most illustrious Council. It only remains for this document of ours to be received calmly and with equanimity. If this is the case, as we very much hope, we believe that there is nothing in it which you cannot readily embrace. Farewell, honoured and beloved colleagues. Long may the Lord Jesus preserve the Bernese republic in a flourishing state by His power; may He sustain the distinguished Council under whose auspices you are gathered; may He guide and bless your synod; and may He govern you with a spirit of wisdom, zeal, and rectitude to the promotion of the Church's edification!

[13 March 1549]

ARTICLES CONCERNING THE SACRAMENTS[24]

1. Since the Lord instituted the sacraments to the end that through them He might testify and pledge His grace to us, as they are true testimonies and seals of the grace of God, so they should truly exhibit to us that of which they are figures.

2. Furthermore, the truth of the sacraments is contained in Christ. But that this may the better be established, Christ Him-

---

[22] The reference is to the treaty which since 1526 had unified the citizenry of Berne and Geneva. During this present year (1549) negotiations were taking place for its renewal.

[23] In 1544, following a prolonged dispute between the governments of Berne and Geneva and resort to arbitration, Basle, acting as arbitrator, granted to the Genevans the rights of patronage and of nomination of pastors relating to the ancient possessions of the Genevan priory of Saint-Victor and those of the cathedral chapter situated in Bernese territory. These rights affected fourteen parishes in the bailiwicks of Gex, Ternier, and Thonon.

[24] The articles which follow were sent with the letter above. See note 21 above. They have been published in *Calvini Opera*, VII, coll. 716ff. (cf. the articles of the Consensus Tigurinus, pp. 115ff. below).

self is in the first place to be accounted as their substance or foundation, and then the fruit and force of His death, and whatever blessings proceed from Him.

3. This, therefore, is the object of the sacraments: first, that we should lay hold of Christ as the fount of all blessings; then that we should be reconciled to God by the benefit of His death; that we should be renewed in holiness of life by His Spirit; and, finally, that we should follow after righteousness and salvation.

4. Thus in baptism Christ Himself with His blood should be considered first of all, then the cleansing and newness of life which flow therefrom. In the supper His body crucified for us and His blood shed on the cross hold the first place, then the expiation of sins, the privilege of adoption, newness of life, and whatever things pertain to eternal life.

5. Therefore all who use the sacraments rightly and piously receive Christ, as He is offered to us there, together with His spiritual gifts. For in order that God may be true to His Word, it is necessary that whatever He signifies and promises should be fulfilled and performed by Him. And in order that the signification may be true it is necessary that the effect or the reality itself should correspond to the sign.

6. In saying, however, that through the sacraments we become participants of Christ and of His spiritual gifts, we have respect not to bare signs but rather to the promise which is annexed to them. To the extent, therefore, that our faith in the promise there set forth prevails, to that extent will the force and efficacy of which we speak display itself. Thus the material element of water or bread or wine in no way offers us Christ, nor does it make us partakers of His spiritual gifts; but it is the promise, whose function is to lead us to Christ by the direct road of faith, that ought rather to engage our attention.

7. Hence the error of the papists is overthrown, who gaze on the elements and attach the confidence of their salvation to them, since the sacraments separated from Christ are nothing other than empty displays. In them all, this message should clearly sound forth, that we must cling to Christ alone, and to nothing else, and that the grace of salvation must be sought from no other source.

8. Moreover, if any benefit is conferred on us through the sacraments, it is not because of any virtue of their own, even if you understand the promise of which they are signs. For it is God alone who acts by His Spirit. The fact that He makes use of the ministry of the sacraments does not mean that He infuses His own power into them, nor that He derogates in any degree

from the effectual working of His Spirit; but, having respect to the capacity of our ignorance, He provides them as aids, in such a way, however, that the whole power of action remains with Him alone.

9. Accordingly, as Paul instructs us that both he who plants and he who waters is nothing, but God alone who gives the increase [I Cor. 3:7], so also it must be said of the sacraments that they are nothing, since they will be without profit unless God effects all things in their entirety. They are indeed instruments by which the Lord efficaciously acts when He so pleases, but in such a way that the whole work of our salvation must be attributed to Him alone.

10. We therefore judge that it is Christ alone who truly baptizes inwardly, who makes us partakers of Himself in the supper, in other words who fulfils that of which the sacraments are figures, making use of these aids in such a way that the whole effect resides in His Spirit.

11. Thus the sacraments are sometimes called seals, and yet the Spirit alone is properly the seal, as also He is the initiator and perfecter of faith. For all these attributes of the sacraments sink into a position of inferiority, so that not even the least portion of our salvation may be transferred from its sole Author to mere creatures.

12. Furthermore, we carefully teach that God does not exert His power promiscuously in all who receive the sacraments, but only in the elect. For just as He enlightens with faith only those whom He has foreordained to life, so by the secret and special power of His Spirit He brings it about that to them alone the sacraments furnish what they offer.

13. By this teaching that fabrication of the sophists is overthrown which teaches that the sacraments of the new law confer grace on all who do not interpose the impediment of mortal sin.[25] For, apart from the fact that in the sacraments nothing is appropriated except by faith, it must also be maintained that the grace of God is least of all bound to them in such a way that whoever has the sign also possesses the reality. For the signs are administered equally to the reprobate with the elect, but the truth of the signs is known to the latter only.

14. It is indeed true that Christ together with His gifts is offered to all in common, and that the truth of God is not invali-

---

[25] Cf. Council of Trent, Session VII (3 March 1547), Canon 6, on the sacraments in general.

dated by the unbelief of men, but that the sacraments always retain their power; yet not all have the capacity for receiving it. Accordingly, on God's part there is nothing that changes, but where man is concerned each one receives according to the measure of his faith.

15. Moreover, as the use of the sacraments confers nothing more on unbelievers than if they were to abstain from them — indeed rather is fatal to them — so the truth of which they are figures is assured to believers even apart from their use. Thus in baptism Paul's sins were washed away, which had already been washed away previously. Thus also baptism was the bath of regeneration for Cornelius, although this had already been given by the Holy Spirit [Acts 9:18; 22:16; 10:47f.]. Thus in the supper Christ communicates Himself to us although He abides perpetually in us; but to the extent that faith is confirmed and increased by the sacraments, and the gifts of God are confirmed in us, to that extent also Christ in a manner increases in us and we in Him.

16. The benefit which we derive from the sacraments ought by no means to be restricted to the time when they are administered to us, as though the visible sign conveyed with itself the grace of God only at that moment when it is actually being proffered. For God sometimes regenerates in childhood or adolescence those who have been baptized in earliest infancy. Thus the benefit of baptism lies open to the whole course of life, because the promise which is contained in it is perpetually in force; and the use of the holy supper, which in the act itself benefits us too little because of our carelessness or sluggishness, afterwards produces its own fruit.

17. It is especially important that any idea of a local presence of Christ should be put away. For while the signs are here in the world seen by our eyes, and touched by our hands, Christ must be sought nowhere else than in heaven, and in no other way than with the mind and understanding of faith. It is therefore a perverse and impious superstition to enclose Him under the elements of this world.

18. In this way not only is the fiction of the papists concerning transubstantiation refuted, but also all gross figments which either detract from Christ's heavenly glory or are incompatible with the truth of His human nature. For we consider it no less absurd to locate Christ under the form of bread, or to conjoin Him with the bread, than for the bread to be transubstantiated into His body.

19. And lest there should be any ambiguity when we say that Christ is to be sought in heaven, this manner of speaking signifies and expresses the distance between places. For although properly speaking there is no place above the heavens, yet because the body of Christ, in that it bears the nature of a human body, is finite and is contained in heaven, it is necessarily as far distant from us in terms of separation between places as heaven is from earth.

20. If, then, it is not right for us to conjoin Christ with the bread and the wine, much less may we worship Him in the bread. For although the bread is offered to us as a symbol and pledge of the communion which we have with Christ, yet because it is a sign and not the reality itself, and does not have the reality included in itself, those who persuade themselves that Christ is to be adored in it make an idol of it.[26]

[March 1549]

CONTINUATION OF THE CASE OF M. PHILIPPE DE ECCLESIA[27]

Since the administering of the censure to Maître Philippe de Ecclesia as described above, regarding which he showed some sign of repentance, it has been disclosed on good evidence that he has not ceased to slander each of the ministers in particular and all in general together with their doctrine, complaining of the censure and of the prohibition which was placed on him. For this reason he was recalled to give an account of himself. He denied everything, confessing none the less certain subsidiary matters which he thought were not prejudicial to him. Further hearing was deferred to the next meeting of the Congregation at which all the brethren of both city and country were obliged to

---

[26] The copy of the letter and the twenty articles preserved in Berne carry the following signatures of Genevan pastors:

Joannes Calvinus	M. Malissianus
Abelus Poupinus	Joannes Pyrerius
Nicolaus Gallasius	A Sancto Andrea
Franciscus Bourgoinus	Joannes Baldinus
Michael Copus	Ludovicus Cogneus
Jacobus Bernadus	Nicolaus Parvus

Johann Haller's reply to the twenty articles of the Genevan pastors has been published in *Calvini Opera*, VII, coll. 723ff.

[27] Cf. pp. 92f. above. The account which follows provides quite the best source of information concerning this affair.

assemble, and he was then interrogated afresh. He persisted in his denials, but nevertheless was found to be inconsistent. After causing him to withdraw, the brethren, recognizing his hypocrisy, unanimously declared that in view of the fact that he had himself revealed what he had requested should be concealed, and that they had all agreed to be accounted as infamous and perjurors if they should reveal it, it was only right that he should be accounted as such. Moreover, he had showed himself to be rebellious against all correction and had only pretended to submit to it. And since he had not in fact accepted the correction imposed on him, but had continued in the false doctrine for which he had been reprimanded and clearly showed his intransigence, for these reasons they considered him unworthy to continue as a minister and resolved that the Company should be purged of him, and that this should be made known to Messieurs.

This decision was announced to Messieurs,[28] but Philippe who had been instructed to appear before them failed to do so. The case was therefore deferred to another day when he would be present. The charge was then recited anew in his presence,[29] and his defence was heard, in the course of which he denied everything that had been said, asserting in the presence of all the brethren who were there that the accusations had been invented, and for his part alleging a number of fabrications to the contrary and giving more proof of his impudence than hitherto. Accordingly the brethren felt themselves greatly outraged and were unable to endure being so insulted; for he even denied what had taken place at the previous censure and everything of which the brethren had knowledge. After we had withdrawn, Messieurs communicated to us through Monsieur the third syndic[30] that

---

[28] Calvin and his colleagues presented themselves before the Council on Tuesday 26 March for the purpose of taking up certain matters, but in particular the "scandalous" attitude of de Ecclesia.

[29] This was two days later, on Thursday 28 March. The Register of the Council shows that the charge preferred against de Ecclesia by Calvin and his colleagues contained the following accusations: that, though admonished on several occasions to desist from the utterance of his false and heretical opinions, so far from desisting he had become even worse; that once when summoned to defend himself before the Congregation he had failed to put in an appearance; that he mocked at the Company of Pastors, even pretending to expound Greek, a language which he did not understand, and propounding doctrines — such as that Jesus Christ must have suffered many times — which were plainly contrary to Holy Scripture.

[30] The third syndic at that time was Pierre Tissot. The election of the four syndics took place in February of each year. The order of the syndics (first, second, third, and fourth) depended in general on their age or their seniority in political experience, and at times also on particular considerations,

they desired us to pardon him and grant him full restoration. Thereupon we of the city replied that what had been done concerning Maître Philippe was known by the whole Congregation and that we could not announce a reversal of the decision without being derogatory to them.

Because of this the whole matter was referred to the next Congregation to which all the brethren were summoned. And they reaffirmed their previous decision that Maître Philippe should not be accepted as brother or minister in the Congregation. Thereupon they went at once into the presence of Messieurs, where this decision was again announced. In spite of this, however, Messieurs persisted in their desire that we should pardon him. We replied that there was no evidence of any repentance. They said that they would give him a severe reprimand and would summon Maître Philippe and inform him through the first syndic Ami Perrin[31] that Messieurs were well aware that he had practised serious deception and had behaved himself badly, that from now on he must mend his ways, that this would be the last warning, and that he would not be spared if he appeared before them again. None the less, Messieurs would reinstate him in the ministry and include him in the Company of Pastors. To this we replied that we would tolerate an evil which we could not remove, although we in no way approved of it, and we declared that if evil resulted from it the responsibility for it would be theirs before God and before men. And this took place on 6 April 1549.

---

such as personal prestige, special qualities, or party pressure. It was thanks to this last mentioned factor that Ami Perrin was appointed first syndic in this year 1549.

[31] Ami Perrin, one of the principal statesmen of the new Seigneury, is best known as the leader of the so-called "libertine" party who, in the name of the ancient Genevan traditions and the Swiss alliance, opposed the new political situation inspired by the Calvinists and favourable to the integration of the French refugees who had found a haven in Geneva. The issue was, in the main, a political one, involving questions of the relationship between Church and State and the boundaries of their respective jurisdictions in the administration of discipline to persons who at the same time were both citizens and churchmen (as the de Ecclesia affair indicates). Perrin had been a supporter of the Reformation in Geneva and, in fact, had voted against Calvin's exile. In 1547 he had been accused of treason, but his trial ended in his acquittal (cf. note, 34, p. 70), and now, less than two years later, he holds the office of the highest magistracy of the city. The struggle between the Perrinists, standing for the Old Genevans and their traditions, and the Calvinists, whose ranks included so many refugees from abroad, continued until 1555, when the Perrinist party was finally eliminated and Ami Perrin withdrew to the territory of Berne.

[13 April 1549]

TESTIMONIAL FOR JEAN DE LA BARRE[32]

The pastors and ministers of the church of Geneva to all Christ's godly servants and all who desire the spread of His kingdom, greeting.

Since this good man whose name is Jean de la Barre[33] has lived among us for about eight months, but now has not found a position in which he can maintain himself, and therefore is thinking of migrating to another vicinity where a better opportunity may be offered him, we ought not to deny his request that we should give him a testimonial regarding the manner of his conduct here. Although, indeed, his inner life cannot be open to us, yet as far as it is permitted to us to know we can testify that he has conducted himself honestly and piously, as becomes a Christian and God-fearing man. Nor do we doubt that he is impelled by proper zeal, and we also hope that in future he will continue in the same way in which he has started. Therefore wherever our testimonial is accepted, his life, which we at least have been able to observe, is free of suspicion.

From our assembly, 13 April 1549

Ioannes Calvinus, *in the name of the brethren*

[13 April 1549]

M. PHILIPPE DE ECCLESIA AGAIN

On the same day 13 April, which was a Friday,[34] when our general censures were due to be made prior to the festival of Easter, before proceeding to the censures the brethren wished to consider whether Maître Philippe ought to be present, and caused

---

[32] The text of this testimonial has been published in *Calvini Opera*, XIII, coll. 235.

[33] A Jean de la Barre is inscribed in the register of the inhabitants of Geneva, but this inscription is dated 17 December 1549, which is some eight months later than this testimonial announcing the impending departure from Geneva of the person of this name. Assuming it to be the same person, he may have returned to Geneva in December and been granted registration as a citizen, or it is possible that he may have changed his mind about leaving the city. The testimonial says that he was only "thinking" of migrating.

[34] This is an error, for 13 April 1549 fell on a Saturday. The date intended, therefore, must be the 12th.

him to withdraw. It was resolved that, in view of his obstinacy and his failure to show any sign of repentance, he ought not to be present either to censure or to be censured, for which in fact he was incapacitated, since on the occasion when we had declared before Messieurs that we would tolerate an evil which we could not remove we had also declared that we would tolerate him only in his ministry, but that we must withhold our approval until we saw some amendment in him. This done, he departed asking whether he should expound in the Congregation when his turn came. After deliberation, it was replied by unanimous consent that he was not to do so until he gave evidence of a change of heart.[35]

[April 1549]

CHARGES AGAINST M. JEAN FERRON[36]

On the same day we proceeded to the censures. When it came to the turn of Ferron the brethren were long in deliberation over him because on previous days of censure he had been accused of a number of frivolities, to some of which he had confessed, including dishonourable contacts with his female servants. And although the case had been brought before the Lieutenant[37] and also before Messieurs, yet it had not been established, since there were only single individuals as witnesses. There were, however, very strong presumptions, and in acquitting him Messieurs had admonished him to behave himself properly, etc. The scandal was great throughout the city and elsewhere, so much so that numbers were withdrawing from his preaching. For this reason the brethren agreed that it would be wise to move him and send him to another place outside the city. It was decided that he should be informed of this and then that we should take the matter before Messieurs.

[35] De Ecclesia was finally deposed from his post as pastor of Vandoeuvres in 1553 as the result of fresh accusations (see pp. 201ff. below).

[36] The affair of Jean Ferron, to which the Company devoted a large part of their deliberations during the spring and summer of 1549, had had its beginnings in March before the Council: on 5 March two servants had laid a complaint against the pastor of Saint Gervaise, an inquiry had been opened, and Calvin was informed of the situation so that he could give his advice. At first Ferron seemed submissive and offered his resignation. But at the end of the month he asked for a trial. After a fresh inquiry the Council did no more than administer a formal admonition. Cf. *Calvin Opera*, XXI, coll. 447ff.

[37] The Lieutenant was the magistrate charged with the drawing up of criminal proceedings.

After he had been suitably reprimanded he began to excuse and defend himself. And then he said that he had found no fellowship among us, that he knew whom it was intended to put in his place and that we had him all ready and that for more than four years this had been our intention. He also attacked our brother M. Calvin, saying that he was ill-disposed to him, that he was a vindictive person since if he had anything against a man he remained ill-disposed to him to the end, and that he liked to be flattered. Then he attacked one of the others, calling him smooth-tongued and insulting, and asserting that he was as good a man as Calvin or any of the others. Thereupon, transported with rage, he left the congregation and went off without returning.

The brethren now began to discuss his case anew, saying that a new situation required a new ruling and that this should be added to the declaration which was to be made before Messieurs, and also that they could no longer regard him as a brother.

On Monday the 15th day of the same month the brethren of both country and city assembled once more and resumed their deliberation concerning the offensive conduct of Jean Ferron. And M. Calvin requested that he might be informed by the brethren whether he had in any respect exceeded the charge which had been given him. Thereupon, after Ferron and Calvin had been caused to withdraw, it was unanimously agreed by the brethren that Calvin had fulfilled his duty and proceeded in accordance with their intention, that Ferron was in the wrong and had greatly offended the whole Company, and that they should be informed of this. As to the principle of the matter, Maître Guillaume Farel,[38] who had come on a visit to us, proposed that Ferron should be given the option of having the matter discussed by the neighboring churches of Lausanne and Neuchâtel, provided he was willing to abide by their judgment. This suggestion was adopted by the brethren and was put to Ferron, who was unwilling to accept it. Accordingly we were compelled to present ourselves before Messieurs and bring the affair to their attention. This was done with Ferron present. Messieurs then ordered that Ferron should go and live at Satigny in place of Maître Jacques Bernard and that Bernard should come to the city.

On Friday 3 May, when the brethren of both country and city were assembled, the case of Ferron was brought before them and the ruling of Messieurs was announced to the brethren who had been absent. Upon this, Ferron began to beg the brethren to leave him in his present post, putting forward certain reasons and

---

[38] Farel was pastor at Neuchâtel.

saying that he would himself resign his office, but that he wished to leave it with honour. After begging the brethren to consent to this he went out. The brethren were of the opinion, however, that it was not in their power to alter the resolution which they had already passed and still less the ruling of Messieurs, and that Ferron should be asked whether he was prepared to obey the decree of Messieurs or not. On being recalled, he replied that he could not do so and that both we and Messieurs had treated him unjustly.

On the Thursday before Whitsun, which was 6 June, we again presented ourselves before Messieurs in connection with this affair. They declared that in all that we had done in this affair we had proceeded properly, but that their hands were not bound in such a way that they could not permit Ferron to continue in his present position and place.

On Friday 30 August in the same year, which was the day of our censures, Ferron confessed of his own free will that in the absence of his wife he had sported with his chambermaid, touching her in certain places, but said that this was done for the purpose of testing whether she was a good girl, and that the girl had made several complaints about this and had gone away offended. Ferron acknowledged that our Lord wished to humiliate him and that he knew that the Lord was stronger than he, and he besought the brethren to follow His example in dealing with this affair. Having heard this appeal, the brethren resolved not to investigate the case further, but to summon the syndic of the Consistory together with certain assistants whom he could consult concerning this affair and then proceed in accordance with ecclesiastical order. The syndic in question notified Messieurs of this, and they forthwith took the investigation into their own hands. M. Calvin, M. Abel,[39] and M. Jacques Bernard then appeared before them on behalf of our Congregation and Ferron was summoned and gave an account similar to that which he had given at our Congregation. Thereupon, having heard what he had to say, Messieurs suspended him from the ministry while the case was more fully investigated, so that the scandal resulting from it might be avoided and also because the supper was to be celebrated the following Sunday.

On the following Thursday, which was 5 September, Ferron was summoned before Messieurs who confronted him with the girl. She proffered several other dishonourable charges against him. Accordingly Messieurs deposed him from the ministry. He re-

---

[39] That is, Abel Poupin (see note 3, p. 62).

quested testimonial letters and some assistance, making various complaints about his poverty. But these were refused him.

On the next day, the 7th[40] of the same month, Ferron presented himself before the brethren assembled in Congregation, declaring that he was sad at being separated from their Company, but that he wished to be one with them in doctrine and in charity, and requesting that they would kindly give him their advice since he had a good mind to go to France, but that if the brethren advised against this he would not go, for he wished to be obedient to what they would say. By unanimous consent the brethren replied to him that, so far as the unity and charity which he wished to have with us were concerned, this was quite in accordance with their desire, but that they were unable to advise him, seeing that he had not been governed by our advice when he was joined with us, and that now that he was separated, they did not see why he should be more likely to follow it — indeed that he was two-faced; for he had plans contrary to those he had mentioned to the brethren. He was then reproved for certain reports which he and his wife had spread through the city.

Ferron arose and when he had walked three or four steps he turned and asked that at the very least he might have some certificate from our Congregation, such as we might be willing to grant him. After discussing this request, the brethren declared that they could not grant him this.[41]

[28 July 1549]

ORDINANCE OF MESSIEURS FORBIDDING GIRLS GUILTY OF FORNICATION TO WEAR THE VIRGIN'S HAT

On Sunday 28 July, at the main service at 8 o'clock, an ordinance made by Messieurs was announced in St. Pierre ordering that girls who had not kept their honour should not henceforward present themselves in church for marriage with the hat which virgins are accustomed to wear, but that they should have their heads veiled; otherwise they could be sent away.

---

[40] This should be the 6th.
[41] This is the conclusion of the Ferron affair. It is not known what became of Ferron after this. Very probably he left Geneva.

[September 1549]

ELECTION OF JEAN FABRI AS PASTOR

On Monday the 9th day of the same month[42] the brethren of both city and country assembled for the purpose of proceeding to the election of a minister in Ferron's place; and on this occasion several reputable persons were proposed who would be able to serve in the Church of our Lord, but no decision was reached. It was resolved, however, that on the following Friday all should reassemble to make the election and that meanwhile each one should give thought to the matter and commend it in prayer to our Lord.

On Friday 13 September the brethren assembled again to make this election, and, after invocation of the name of God, all unanimously elected Maître Jean Fabri, native of [blank],[43] who had been minister of the Word of God in Lyon[44] and had conducted himself faithfully there. And, after having called Fabri in, the choice of the brethren was announced; he declared his acceptance, and a passage was given him to expound on the following day at noon. This passage was: "There are three that bear witness in heaven", I John 5.[45]

Afterwards the brethren were informed that Messieurs were unwilling for them to elect another minister in Ferron's place, on the grounds that the church could be well served by six pastors and that this number was adequate. Thereupon it was decided to postpone the election until they had appeared before Messieurs so that they could hear their objections and remonstrate with them. Monsieur Calvin was requested to do this, and it was felt it would be better for him to go on his own before any other method was tried. This he did on the following Monday, the 13th[46] day of the same month. Nothing was achieved, however. Calvin now

---

[42] The month of September. This follows immediately after the account of the Ferron affair. The preceding paragraph concerning the ordinance which was publicly announced on 28 July is written at the top of a page in the Register, interrupting the record of the proceedings with Ferron, which extended from 13 April to 6 September.

[43] Jean Fabri, or Favre, of Larche, Basses-Alpes, was a pastor in Geneva from 1547 to 1556. Three other persons named Fabri, natives of the same place, and no doubt related to Jean Fabri, settled in Geneva: Pierre, a shoemaker, on 18 October 1557; Antoine, a gunsmith, on 4 April 1558; and another Pierre, on 4 July 1558.

[44] Fabri had been in Lyon in 1547.

[45] The precise reference is I Jn. 5:7 — a verse which, because of the textual evidence now available, is acknowledged to be unoriginal.

[46] This should be the 16th.

preached a number of very animated sermons concerning the ministry and the service of the Church. And after having waited long enough the brethren resolved to present themselves again before Messieurs in order to object that they could not adequately fulfil their charges if the customary number of ministers in the city was not maintained. Accordingly they appeared together before Messieurs in Council on Monday 14 October 1549, and Calvin spoke in the name of all. On the same day the Council announced that, in view of the objections we had offered and the reasons given, we should proceed with the election.

On Friday 18 October, when the brethren of both city and country had assembled in Congregation, this order of the Council was announced. Thereupon Fabri was called in. On the same day, at the hour of noon, he expounded the passage which had been given him; and after he had finished his exposition the brethren, as was customary, told him what they found to criticize in it. On the next day, the 19th, the examination of Fabri on the articles of religion was commenced, and was continued all the following week. Meanwhile a passage was given him from St. John, chapter 5: "Verily, verily, I say unto you that he who hears my word, etc." [Jn. 5:24], on which to preach before the brethren on the following Friday, the 25th; and Messieurs were invited to send some members of their Council to hear the sermon so that they might report on it to the Council. Accordingly Messieurs the Syndics Tissot,[47] Vandel,[48] and Roset[49] were appointed and were present in our congregation to hear Fabri's sermon.

On Monday 28 October the brethren of the city appeared before Messieurs for the purpose of presenting Fabri and reporting on what they had learnt of him concerning both his life and his doctrine. The brethren were all present, moreover, to plead and remonstrate with Messieurs respecting an order which they had issued without having called or heard them, that thenceforward there should be a sermon daily in St. Pierre in the morning before daybreak, on the ground that this requirement would not be to the church's advantage and could not be fulfilled, and that only trouble and scandal would follow from it. But an offer was made

---

[47] Pierre Tissot, who was third syndic for that year, 1549, (see note 30 above), was a member of an old Genevan family. He had been a councillor since 1538, and served as syndic in 1544, 1549, and 1554, as Treasurer from 1541 to 1543, and as Lieutenant for the year 1553.

[48] Pierre Vandel was a Councillor and an attorney. Because of his association with Perrin he left the city and was condemned to death for contempt of court in 1555.

[49] Claude Roset, the father of the statesman and chronicler Michel Roset, was a Councillor and served as syndic on a number of occasions.

to have a sermon every Sunday in La Madeleine at eight o'clock, since there were so many people in St. Pierre that all were not able to hear. From this Messieurs would know that they did not wish to spare themselves where they saw that the edification of the church was involved.

Fabri was received as a minister of the church of Geneva and took the oath before Messieurs in the customary manner.

With regard to the other matter, it was ordered that the sermons should continue according to the accustomed scheme, except that the proposed should be given in La Madeleine in addition to the others, as had been suggested by the ministers.

[1 August 1549]

A MUTUAL AGREEMENT CONCERNING THE SACRAMENTS BETWEEN THE MINISTERS OF THE CHURCH IN ZURICH AND JOHN CALVIN, MINISTER OF THE CHURCH IN GENEVA, NOW PUBLISHED BY ITS AUTHORS[50]

I Cor. 1 [vs. 10]: Now I beseech you, brethren, by the name of our Lord Jesus Christ, that ye all speak the same thing, and that there be no divisions among you, but that ye be perfectly joined together in the same mind and in the same judgment.

John Calvin to the most distinguished men and faithful servants of Christ, the pastors and teachers of the church of Zürich, his very dear colleagues and respected brethren, greetings.

Although I confer with you rather frequently on the same subject, I do not think I need be afraid of seeming to be tiresome to you; for since we are of one mind what I do can only have your approval. As for the urgency of my insistence, the constant en-

---

[50] The agreement that follows is a copy of the *Consensus Tigurinus* (or Agreement of Zürich), that is, the theological concordat drawn up by Calvin and Bullinger in 1549, which unified the Reformation in Switzerland for the first time. It has the disadvantages of a compromise document, however, and, because of the concessions which were made for the sake of achieving agreement, it should not be taken as fully representative of Calvin's doctrine of the eucharist. But it is an important witness to Calvin's intense desire for the peace of the Church, especially where cardinal doctrinal issues were involved. Cf. also the articles on the sacraments sent to the church of Berne (pp. 101ff. above), of which the present articles are a repetition and an expansion. The text of the *Consensus Tigurinus* has been republished many times. It is given in *Calvini Opera*, VII, coll. 733ff. For English versions see *Calvin's Tracts*, translated by Henry Beveridge, Vol. II (Edinburgh, 1849), pp. 200ff.

treaties of excellent men impel me to it. I have already pointed out on a number of occasions that with slight enough cause, yet not without some excuse, many are offended because my teaching on the sacraments seems to differ from yours in some way unknown to me. They rightly respect your church which is adorned by so many remarkable gifts. They also have some deference for our church, and perhaps for me as an individual. They wish to be assisted by my writings in learning the doctrines of piety, provided that no appearance of dissension retards their progress. And since I considered that there would be no remedy better fitted to remove this stumbling-block than for us to confer together in a friendly manner and produce proof of our agreement, for this reason, as you know, I paid you a visit. Moreover, my venerable colleague William Farel (indefatigable soldier of Christ that he is), who at other times has been my leader and instigator, did not decline to accompany me as my companion. That we agree among ourselves we can indeed on both sides testify truly and faithfully, but because I have failed to persuade all of the true facts of the case it grieves me very much that those for whose peace of mind I would wish to show special consideration continue to be anxious or uncertain. Accordingly, as I said to begin with, I judge that I am doing nothing untimely in urging that some public testimony should be provided of the agreement that exists between us.

Now I have thought it worthwhile to summarize and arrange in order the main articles on which we conferred together, so that, if my plan receives your approval it will be possible for anyone to find tabulated as it were what was done and transacted between us. I am confident that you will bear me witness that in all that I have set down I have reproduced a reliable record of our discussions. Pious readers will perceive, I trust, that we — that is, Farel and I — have aimed, with a zeal equal to your own, at honest clarity free from all pretence and subtlety. At the same time I would like them to know that nothing is included which all our own colleagues who serve Christ under the jurisdiction of the republic of Geneva or in the territory of Neuchâtel, have not approved by their subscription.

Farewell, most excellent men and brethren truly and cordially esteemed by me. May the Lord continue to direct you by His Spirit, and bless your labours for the edification of His Church.

Geneva, 1 August 1549

HEADS OF AGREEMENT

The Whole Spiritual Government of the Church Leads Us to Christ:[51]

Since Christ is the end of the law and the knowledge of Him comprehends in itself the whole sum of the Gospel, there is no doubt that the whole spiritual government of the Church is intended to lead us to Christ, as it is through Him alone that man comes to God, who is the ultimate end of the life of blessedness. Therefore whoever deviates even in the slightest degree from this can never speak duly or appropriately of any ordinances of God.

True Knowledge of the Sacraments Comes from the Knowledge of Christ:

Since, moreover, the sacraments are appendages of the Gospel, he alone can fittingly and usefully discourse of their nature, virtue, function, and benefit who begins with Christ: and that not merely by bringing in the name of Christ in an incidental manner, but by truly grasping for what purpose He was given us by the Father and what blessings He has procured for us.

The Nature of the Knowledge of Christ:

It must therefore be held that Christ, while being the eternal Son of God, of the same essence and glory as the Father, assumed our flesh in order that He might communicate to us the process of adoption that which He possessed by nature, namely, that we might be the sons of God. This takes place when, having by the power of the Holy Spirit been engrafted into the body of Christ, we are first accounted righteous by the free imputation of righteousness and are then regenerated into a new life;[52] whereupon, as those who are formed again in the image of the Heavenly Father, we renounce the old man.

Christ Our Priest and King:

Thus Christ in His flesh is to be considered as our priest who made expiation for our sins by the unique sacrifice of His death, who by His obedience blotted out all our iniquities, who provided

---

[51] The headings to the respective articles do not appear in the original, but were written in the margin of the Register by the same hand that wrote the original text. Beza incorporated them in the editions he edited, and they have been retained ever since.

[52] The sequence here should be understood as logical rather than chronological.

a perfect righteousness for us, and who now intercedes for us so that access to God lies open for us. He is to be considered as the expiatory offering by which God has been reconciled to the world. He is to be considered as a brother who transformed us from miserable sons of Adam into blessed sons of God. He is to be considered as a restorer who by the power of His Spirit reforms whatever is vicious in us so that we may cease to live for the world and the flesh and God Himself may live in us. He is to be considered as a king who enriches us with every kind of blessing, who governs and protects us by His power, who equips us with spiritual weapons, who delivers us from all harm, who rules and directs us by the sceptre of His mouth. And He is to be so considered in order that He may raise us to Himself, the true God, and to the Father, until what has finally to take place is fulfilled, namely, that God should be all in all.

How Christ Communicates Himself to Us:[53]

Furthermore, in order that Christ may show Himself to us in this way and produce these effects in us, it is necessary that we should be made one with Him and grow together into His body. For He does not infuse His life into us unless He is our head "from whom the whole body, joined and knit together by every joint with which it is supplied, when each part is working properly, makes bodily growth and upbuilds itself in love" [Eph. 4:16].

Spiritual Communion:

We have spiritual communion with the Son of God when, dwelling in us by His Spirit, He makes all believers participants of all the blessings that reside in Him. In order to testify this, both the preaching of the Gospel was instituted and also the use of the sacraments entrusted to us, the sacraments, namely, of holy baptism and the holy supper.

The Purposes of the Sacraments:

The purposes of the sacraments are these: that they should be marks and badges of the Christian profession and fellowship or brotherhood, and that they should be incitements to thanksgiving

---

[53] This article was not part of the agreement as it was approved in Zürich in May. Calvin suggested its insertion in a letter which he wrote to Bullinger on 26 June (the text of which is given in *Calvini Opera*, XIII, coll. 305ff.), feeling that the transition from the previous article to the one that then followed was too abrupt.

and exercises of faith and godly living, indeed contracts binding us to this; but among the other purposes this is the principal one, that by means of the sacraments God may testify, represent, and seal His grace to us. For although they signify nothing else than what is announced by the Word itself, yet it is a great thing that as it were living images should be submitted to our eyes which are better calculated to impress our senses, leading them as it were into the reality, in that they call to our remembrance Christ's death for us and all its benefits, so that faith may be more fully exercised; and it is, further, a great thing that what has been uttered by the mouth of God should be confirmed and ratified as it were by seals.

Thanksgiving:

Since, moreover, the testimonies and seals of His grace which the Lord has given us are true, beyond doubt He truly furnishes inwardly by His Spirit that which the sacraments figure to our eyes and other senses: which is that we should possess Christ as the fount of all blessings, so that we may be reconciled to God by the benefit of His death and be renewed by the Spirit in holiness of living; in other words, that we may attain to righteousness and salvation; and at the same time that we may return thanks for these benefits formerly exhibited on the cross, which we appropriate by faith daily.

Distinction Between the Signs and the Things Signified:

Therefore, although we distinguish, as is right, between the signs and the things signified, yet we do not divorce the reality from the signs, since we acknowledge that all who by faith embrace the promises there offered receive Christ spiritually together with His spiritual gifts, while those who have long since been made partakers of Christ continue and renew that communion.

The Promise in Particular Is To Be Regarded in the Sacraments:

It is important for us to direct our attention not to bare signs, but rather to the promise which is annexed to them. To the extent, therefore, that our faith in the promise there offered prevails, to that extent will the virtue and efficacy of which we speak display itself. Thus the material element of water, bread, or wine by no means offers us Christ, nor does it make us participants of His spiritual gifts: but it is the promise, whose function is to lead us to Christ by the direct road of faith that ought rather to engage our attention; and it is this faith which makes us partakers of Christ.

The Elements Not To Be Gazed On:

Accordingly the error is overthrown of those who gaze on the elements and attach the confidence of their salvation to them, since the sacraments separated from Christ are nothing but empty displays. In them all, this message should clearly sound forth, that we must cling to Christ alone and to nothing else, and that the grace of salvation must be sought from no other source.

The Sacraments Effect Nothing by Themselves:

Furthermore if any benefit is conferred on us through the sacraments, it is not because of any virtue of their own, even though you understand the promise of which they are signs. For it is God alone who acts by His Spirit. The fact that He makes use of the ministry of the sacraments does not mean that He infuses His own power into them, nor that He derogates in any degree from the effectual working of His Spirit; but, having respect to the capacity of our ignorance, He provides them as aids; in such a way, however, that the whole power of action remains with Him alone.

God Uses Them as Instruments, But in Such a Way That All the Power Is His:

Accordingly, as Paul instructs us that both he who plants and he who waters is nothing, but God alone who gives the increase [I Cor. 3:7], so also it must be said of the sacraments that they are nothing, since they will be without profit unless God effects all things in their entirety. They are indeed instruments by which God acts efficaciously when He so pleases, but in such a way that the whole work of our salvation must be attributed to Him alone. We conclude, therefore, that it is Christ alone who truly baptizes inwardly and who makes us partakers of Himself in the supper, in other words, who fulfils that of which the sacraments are figures, and that He makes use of these aids in such a way that the whole effect resides in His Spirit.

How the Sacraments Confirm:

Thus the sacraments are sometimes called seals and are said to nourish, confirm, and promote faith; and yet the Spirit alone is properly the seal, and is also the initiator and perfecter of faith. For all these attributes of the sacraments sink into a position of inferiority, so that not even the least portion of our salvation may be transferred from its sole Author to creatures or to elements.

Not All Who Partake of a Sacrament Partake also of the Reality:

Furthermore we carefully teach that God does not exert His power promiscuously in all who receive the sacraments, but only in the elect. For just as He enlightens with faith only those whom He has foreordained to life, so also by the secret power of His Spirit He causes them to appropriate what the sacraments offer.

The Sacraments Do Not Confer Grace:

By this teaching that fabrication of the sophists is overthrown which teaches that the sacraments of the new law confer grace on all who do not interpose the impediment of mortal sin.[54] For, apart from the fact that in the sacraments nothing is appropriated except by faith, it must also be maintained that the grace of God is least of all bound to them in such a way that whoever has the sign also possesses the reality. For the signs are administered to the reprobate equally with the elect, but the truth of which they are signs belongs only to the latter.

The Gifts of God Are Offered to All, But Only Believers Appropriate Them:

It is indeed true that Christ together with His gifts is offered to all in common, and that the truth of God is not invalidated by the unbelief of men, but that the sacraments always retain their power; but not all are recipients of Christ and His gifts. Accordingly, on God's part nothing is changed, but where man is concerned each one receives according to the measure of his faith.

Believers Before and Apart from the Use of the Sacraments also Partake of Christ:

Moreover, as the use of the sacraments confers nothing more on unbelievers than if they were to abstain from them — indeed rather is fatal to them — so the truth of which they are figures is assured to believers even apart from their use. Thus in baptism Paul's sins were washed away which already had been washed away previously. Thus also baptism was the bath of regeneration for Cornelius, although this had already been given by the Holy Spirit [Acts 9:18; 22:16; 10:47f.]. Thus Christ communicates Himself to us in the supper, although He has previously imparted Him-

---

[54] Cf. Council of Trent, Session VII (3 March 1547), Canon 6, on the sacraments in general.

self to us and abides perpetually in us. For since all singly are enjoined to examine themselves, it follows that faith is required from them before they come to the sacrament. There is, however, no faith without Christ; but to the extent that faith is confirmed and increased by the sacraments, and the gifts of God are confirmed in us, to that extent Christ in a manner increases in us and we in Him.

Grace Is Not Bound to the Action of the Sacraments, But the Benefit of Them Is Sometimes Received After the Action:

The benefit which we derive from the sacraments ought by no means to be restricted to the time when they are administered to us, as though the visible sign conveyed with itself the grace of God only at that moment when it is being proffered. For those who are baptized in earliest infancy are regenerated by God in childhood or on reaching adolescence or even sometimes in old age. Thus the benefit of baptism lies open to the whole course of life, because the promise contained in it is perpetually in force. And it can sometimes happen that the use of the holy supper, which in the act itself benefits us too little because of our carelessness or sluggishness, may at a later time produce its own fruit.

The Idea of a Local Presence Must Be Put Away:

It is especially important that any idea of a local presence of Christ should be put away. For while the signs are here in the world, seen by our eyes and touched by our hands, Christ in so far as He is man must be sought nowhere else than in heaven and in no other way than with the mind and the understanding of faith. It is therefore a perverse and impious superstition to enclose Him under the elements of this world.

Explanation of the Words of the Lord's Supper, "This Is My Body":

Accordingly we reject as preposterous interpreters those who demand what they call a literal sense for the sacramental words of the Supper, "this is my body, this is my blood". For we maintain it to be beyond controversy that they are to be taken figuratively, so that the bread and wine are said to be what they signify. Nor should it be considered as something novel and unusual to transfer by metonymy the name of the reality signified to the sign, since similar modes of expression occur throughout

Scripture, and by speaking in this manner we are proposing nothing that is not found in the most ancient and approved writers of the Church.

Concerning the Eating of Christ's Body:

When we say that by the eating of His flesh and the drinking of His blood, which are here figured, Christ feeds our souls through faith by the power of His Spirit, it must not be taken to mean that there is any commixture or transfusion of substance, but that we draw life from the flesh once offered in sacrifice and from the blood poured out in expiation.

Against Transubstantiation and Other Follies:

In this way not only is the fiction of the papists concerning transubstantiation refuted but also all the gross figments and futile theorizings which either detract from Christ's heavenly glory or are incompatible with the truth of His human nature. For we consider it no less absurd to locate Christ under the form of bread, or to conjoin Him with the bread, than for the bread to be transubstantiated into His body.

The Body of Christ Is Locally in Heaven:

And lest there should be any ambiguity when we say that Christ is to be sought in heaven this manner of speaking signifies and expresses the distance between places. For although philosophically speaking there is no place above the heavens, yet because the body of Christ, in that it bears the nature and mode of a human body is finite and is contained in heaven as in a place, it is necessarily as far distant from us in terms of separation between places as heaven is from earth.

Christ Not To Be Worshipped in the Bread:

If, then, it is not right for us to conjoin Christ with the bread and the wine, much less may we worship Him in the bread. For although the bread is offered to us as a symbol and pledge of the communion which we have with Christ, yet because it is but a sign and not the reality itself, and does not have the reality included and fixed in itself, those who persuade themselves that Christ is to be worshipped in it make an idol of it.

[30 August 1549]

REPLY FROM ZURICH TO CALVIN'S LETTER OF 1 AUGUST 1549

The pastors, teachers, and ministers of the church of Zürich to their very dear brother John Calvin, faithful pastor of the church of Geneva, greetings.

Your immense zeal, Calvin, most respected brother in the Lord, and the unremitting labours by which you strive daily to throw light on the doctrine of the sacraments and to rid the Church of stumbling blocks which appear to have resulted from a somewhat imprecise explanation of these mysteries, are so far from being tiresome to us that we consider them to deserve not only praise and publicity, but also the best support and emulation that we can give. For since the sacred laws of our Prince, Jesus Christ, relate all actions to the cultivation of charity and to zeal in helping each other, they prohibit nothing more sternly than the placing of an obstacle in another's way that would prevent him from forming a right judgment concerning those things the knowledge of which is necessary or at least useful and salutary to men, or from discharging the duty which he owes both to God and to his neighbour; and with the same severity they enjoin the removal, as far as may be possible, of offences at which men are accustomed to stumble. For this reason we found the purpose of the visit which you and our esteemed brother William Farel paid us most creditable and especially worthy of churchmen; namely, that, in the first place, by friendly discussion we might expound mutually and in the simplest possible terms our opinion concerning the sacraments, particularly in respect of those articles over which there has hitherto been some degree of controversy among those who, in the case of other articles, have achieved remarkable unanimity in presenting a consistent doctrine of the Gospel; and, in the second place, that we should testify to our agreement by publishing a statement. Indeed, we see no way or plan more suitable for bringing religious controversies to an end or for dispelling empty suspicions where no discrepancy exists or, finally, for removing the offences which sometimes arise in the Church of God from the controversial opinions of teachers, than for the parties who seem to disagree or do in fact disagree to explain their mind, mutually and with the greatest openness, both by speech and by writing.

It would, however, be insufficient were they to keep the truth thus investigated and apprehended to themselves without its being made available to other men also, with a fuller explanation of those things which had been inadequately mentioned, a declaration in more familiar words of what had been too obscurely expressed, and the clarification in terms which are definite, appropriate, and meaningful of what had been ambiguously propounded. This method ever had the approval of the church fathers and was very often employed in resolving religious controversies; it was never without benefit to the Church; and, most important of all, it was approved by the supreme example of the apostles of Christ our Lord and God. For, as we read in Acts 15, it was precisely in this manner that the most serious dissension was settled, when the apostles and the genuine disciples of the apostles taught that hearts are purified by faith in the name of Christ and that men are saved by His grace alone; whereas others contended that it was obligatory to be circumcised and to keep the law of Moses.[55]

Accordingly we cannot but entirely approve your dedicated efforts, dear brother Calvin, and those of all godly men who study by every proper means to remove stumbling-blocks, to restore the tottering peace and tranquillity of the Church as they strive to present Christian doctrine in an ever clearer and fuller light by means of simple and precise explanation, and to dispel from men's minds empty occasions of discord or to lead back into true, substantial, and godly concord those who have had some disagreement in word and opinion. Moreover, we are induced to hope that the publication of a document in which we wish to give clear testimony of our agreement, both to the godly and to the enemies of the truth, will result in that fruit which you anticipate in your letter. For, by way of testing it, we have sent the draft of our mutual agreement to a number of the brethren, and here in Zürich also we have shown it to certain men who, having a love of Christ and the truth and being not unskilled in sacred things, have not only recognized that we are of one mind even in those articles over which, according to the supposition of many, there has hitherto been disagreement, but also have given thanks to Christ our Saviour since they perceive that we are united in God and in the truth, and entertain great hope of richer fruit in the Church.

Because of the cast of their mentality, however, some who, on hearing of our intention, have without difficulty expressed their approval, have desired a fuller treatment of this subject. But

---

[55] The reference is to the Council of Jerusalem, Acts 15:1ff. The particular allusion is to verses 9 and 11.

what would be the advantage of expounding at greater length that God is the author of the sacraments and instituted them for the legitimate sons of the Church, or how many sacraments were delivered by Christ to the Church, or which ones have been introduced by men, or what are the parts of the sacraments, or in what place, at what time, and by what sacred instrument these mysteries may suitably be enacted? That in these and a number of other articles of this kind there has been no semblance or suspicion of dissension between us is adequately proved by the published works which either our instructors of pious and sacred memory or we ourselves have written concerning the sacraments. But concerning the bodily presence of Christ our Lord, concerning the correct meaning of the words of institution, concerning the eating of Christ's body, and concerning the purpose, use, and effect of the sacraments (articles over which many think that hitherto our opinions, or at least our words have been in conflict) we have spoken so fully, so plainly and simply, that we trust that men eager both for brotherly concord and also for clearly expressed truth will not find that in our document either fulness or clarity of speech are lacking. We are confident, moreover, that the ministers of other churches in Switzerland will readily acknowledge that we have given expression to precisely the same doctrine of the sacraments as has for many years now been commonly accepted among Christian people, so that they will be the last to differ from us in the truth which we have confessed; and this we anticipate, not without strong reasons, from all the godly throughout the churches of other nations.

If, however, any person should produce a clearer explanation of the sacraments, we shall choose to join all the godly in using it rather than urge a single individual to subscribe to our agreement, in which we have employed the words of Holy Scripture and have concisely expressed in what sense we understand them, and also hold it as absolutely apparent that we do so in company with the Catholic Church. Even though this document should not remove the complaints of all whom any semblance of discord among us has hindered in the ways of the Lord, we shall none the less consider that it has admirably served its purpose in that we have given testimony to all, without any obscurity or camouflage, that we whom Christ has enabled to think and speak with unanimity concerning the doctrines of religion in no way disagree over the explanation also of the sacraments.

Farewell, most dear brother.

Zürich, 30 August 1549

All the ministers of the jurisdiction of Geneva subscribed to this agreement and sent a subscribed copy of it to Zürich on 20 December 1549. A copy of the same agreement was also brought to us subscribed by the dean[56] and officers of the church of Neuchâtel in the name of all the brethren, and on the same day, when we had assembled as usual, a copy was made.

[56] William Farel was the leading pastor of Neuchâtel, but his biographers give no indication that he ever bore the title of "dean."

1550

FURTHER VISITATIONS

On Friday 28 March 1550 the brethren, being assembled in general Congregation, elected as visitants of the country parishes Maîtres Calvin, Cop, and Raymond.[1] And then Messieurs, on being informed that these visitations were to be made, commissioned Seigneurs Pernet de Fosses,[2] and Jean Jessé[3] to accompany the ministers named.

On 8 June Maître Raymond visited Chancy and Cartigny with the delegates mentioned above.

On Sunday the 15th day of the same month Monsieur Calvin visited Coulogny and Vandoeuvres with the same delegates.

On the 22nd day of the same month Me Raymond visited Céligny and Genthod with the same delegates.

On the 29th day of the same month Me Raymond visited Russin.

Again, on Sunday 9 July[4]. . . .

[24 October 1550]

LETTERS TO DURAND AND NINAUX

On Friday 24 October 1550 the brethren, being assembled in Congregation, gave orders that letters should be written to Durand[5]

---

[1] Raymond Chauvet.

[2] Pernet de Fosses, a member of the Council, was one of the best-known citizens of Geneva during this period. His name appears frequently in the public documents.

[3] Pierre-Jean Jessé was another well-known member of the Council.

[4] The entry is uncompleted; and, moreover, the date is incorrect, as 9 July 1550 fell on a Wednesday. Probably Sunday 6 July was intended.

[5] Durand-Chârroux, from Onet-le-Château, Aveyron, in the canton of Rodez, had been pastor at Armoy since 30 May 1544.

and Ninaux,[6] the ministers of Armoy and Draillans,[7] instructing them to present themselves on the following Friday before the Congregation so that a decision could be taken concerning their transfer to other parishes, as Messieurs had demanded of us.[8]

The text of the letter[9] which was sent to each of them is as follows:

Since on Friday next[10] we shall be considering in Congregation the condition of the church entrusted to you, we have decided to invite you to be present at the consultation, if this is acceptable to you. For it is in your interests that you should be advised beforehand what we propose to do, and also it concerns the advantage of all. The fact that we have indicated a day to you should be a token that this business is to be conducted with moderate and with decent order. It will be your fault, therefore, if in the event of your being absent anything is transacted contrary to what you might desire. Farewell, most dear brother in the Lord. May the Lord govern you by His Spirit to the edification of the Church.

Geneva, 24 October 1550

John Calvin, *in the name of all*

Mes Durand and Ninaux failed to appear,[11] but Durand conveyed certain letters to Messieurs.

---

[6] Pierre Ninaux had been pastor at Draillans since 1544. He left his post in 1554 (see II, p. 63 below).

[7] The parishes of Armoy and Draillans, in Chablais, were at that time under the jurisdiction of Berne. As, however, ancient possessions of the chapter of Geneva were involved, the Seigneury retained the essential rights, and especially that of nominating the pastors of these parishes.

[8] The Council had its own particular reason for wishing to transfer these two ministers. Their parishes, as mentioned in the preceding note, were in a peculiar and somewhat equivocal position. Relations between Berne and Geneva were often turbulent, and it seems that Durant-Charroux and Ninaux had shown too much complacency in their attitude to Berne, without heeding the admonitions addressed to them from Geneva by the Consistory. The Council feared lest this affair, purely ecclesiastical though it was, might lead in the end to political complications; and it was for this reason that, after the councillor de Fosses had consulted with Calvin, the transference of these two pastors to other parishes was proposed.

[9] The letter is included in *Calvini Opera*, XIII, col. 647.

[10] 31 October.

[11] On Thursday 30 October, the eve of the proposed meeting of the Congregation, Calvin had told the Council that "he had heard that they were unlikely to come, although the pastor of Armoy was here" (in Geneva).

ABROGATION OF FESTIVALS

On Sunday 16 November 1550, after the election of the lieutenant[12] in the general Council, an edict was also announced respecting the abrogation of all the festivals, with the exception of Sundays, which God had ordained.

[12] Pernet de Fosses was elected *"Lieutenant de justice"*.

1551

Syndics: Chicand, Des Ars, Michel Blaise, Chamois[1]

ALLIANCE BETWEEN BERNE AND GENEVA RENEWED

On Sunday 8 March the alliance between the seigneuries of Berne and Geneva was renewed.

COMMOTION IN THE CITY

Because on the previous day, the 7th of the month, there had been a commotion in the city leading to bloodshed,[2] the ministers of the city, seeing the dangers which could ensue, and knowing that the trouble had not been settled and order had not been restored, presented themselves before Messieurs on the following Thursday, the 12th, in order to remonstrate concerning the danger into which they and the whole city could be plunged if order was not restored and condign justice administered.[3] The remonstrations were made by M. Calvin.

---

[1] The election of syndics took place on 8 February 1551. Concerning Antoine Chicand, see note 6 above. Jacques des Ars was, like Chicand, a prominent personage of the city, whose finances he supervised for a number of years and for which he carried out various diplomatic missions. Michel Morel (the name "Blaise" in the Register seems to be an inexplicable error) was a notary and a politician, less well known than his colleagues. François Chamois, another high-ranking figure on the Genevan scene, who was entrusted with various diplomatic missions, died in 1556.

[2] The allusion is to an incident symptomatic of the atmosphere then prevailing in Geneva when friction was beginning to show itself between the original inhabitants and strangers from elsewhere. 1549, in fact, saw the commencement of the era of refugees and the population of Geneva felt that it was being submerged by the new arrivals.

[3] The ministers hoped by this means to ensure good order and respect for the rights of the refugees and the laws of hospitality.

[15 May 1551]

INTRUSION OF TWO HERETICS

At the ordinary Congregation held on Friday 15 May, which was a day of censures, notification was given to the people that M. Calvin had warned several of the brethren (for there had not been time to communicate with all) that two heretics had come to the city with the sole intention of spreading their poison.[4] Everyone should be on their guard lest Satan should gain access to the flock and scatter it through their agency. Their errors were declared, namely, that no one is a Christian unless he is perfect, that there is no Church unless it is perfect and that the remission of sins is a deliverance which Christ has procured for us only in order that we may have this perfection.

This was amply refuted by Calvin, who showed by means of lively reasoning and testimonies from Scripture that we are indeed called to perfection and should strive after it, but that we have not yet achieved it and will not achieve it until we are stripped of this flesh: we journey and we run, but we have not yet arrived at the goal [see Phil. 3:12ff.]. Otherwise it would be futile for us to ask God to forgive us and to release us from our debts; for, being perfect, we would have no need of forgiveness or release.

JEROME BOLSEC REPRIMANDED

On the same day the Congregation of the brethren summoned to their presence Mᵉ Jerome Bolsec, a physician, who held certain mistaken opinions concerning free will and predestination,[5] and sternly reprimanded him, adducing passages of Scripture. Jerome, however, showed himself most obstinate until the passage from Ezekiel was read to him.[6]

---

[4] The registers of the Council provide some details concerning this affair. The two heretics in question — evidently Anabaptists — came from Paris. One of them, Michel Paulus, a goldsmith, was admonished by Calvin who apparently succeeded in convincing him of his error and leading him back to orthodox views. The other, Guillaume Guegnier, was imprisoned, and, persisting in his ideas, was subsequently, on 19 May, banished from the city.

[5] It is at this point that the affair of Jerome Bolsec, soon to take up a considerable portion of the Register (see pp. 137ff. below), has its beginning.

[6] The reference is not given, but it may perhaps be to Ezek. 18:25ff. or 36:26f.

[8 August 1551]

COMPLAINTS AGAINST M. PHILIPPE DE ECCLESIA

On Friday 7 August Nicolas, Pierre, and Claude Faloys, who were brothers, presented a petition to our Congregation containing a number of complaints against Maître Philippe de Ecclesia, their brother-in-law, in particular that Ecclesia was ill treating their sister and was unwilling to hand over her marriage contract, and also that he was saying slanderous things about her father and relatives.

When the brethren had read their petition and heard their complaint they deferred the matter to the following Friday, intending that de Ecclesia and his wife should then be present so that they could hear what answer they would have to offer to these complaints.

On Friday, the 14th day of the same month, de Ecclesia was present at the Congregation. As his wife had not arrived, the matter was postponed until after the dinner, and then, after having heard both parties, they were admonished by all to be reconciled to each other and were dismissed in a state of harmony.

The wife of de Ecclesia was reproved because of certain untruths in which she had been discovered and also because she had been rebellious against her husband.

De Ecclesia promised to hand over the contract as was required of him.

[28 November 1551]

LETTER FROM CALVIN IN THE NAME OF THE COMPANY
TO THE PRESBYTERY OF NEUCHATEL[7]

[7] This document, in the handwriting of Calvin, had formerly been pasted into the Register. In 1811 the Company of Pastors authorized its secretary, Charles Bourrit, to remove it so that it could be sent to M. Girod de l'Ain on behalf of the Minister of War, Clarke, Duke of Feltre, in Paris, who wished to possess a specimen of Calvin's handwriting. The subsequent fortunes of the letter are unknown, but it suddenly reappeared, about 1920, at an auction sale at which the Genevan Henri Fatio succeeded in purchasing it. His heirs restored it to the Company and on 13 February 1925 it was replaced in the Register. The document carries the information: "Taken from the Registers of the Venerable Company of the Pastors of the Church of Geneva, by a resolution of 1 February 1811. Charles Bourrit, Secretary." The text of the letter appears in *Calvini Opera*, XIV, coll. 211f.

Since there was discussion concerning our brother Heraldus[8] in our assembly today, and our brother Calvin explained that the pastors of the church of Neuchâtel were anxious to have a testimonial from us, it was unanimously agreed to write as follows: Heraldus has lived among us in a manner befitting a Christian man; he has been a frequent attender at our meetings and gatherings; and he has devoted himself sedulously to the other exercises of piety. However, when use has been made of him in any public office of the church there has been need to admonish him earnestly lest he should too easily fall into some fault, for in certain respects he has conducted himself with too little seriousness and thoughtfulness. But thereafter he has fulfilled the task entrusted to him with energy and becoming zeal. To many his disposition seemed colder than was necessary, particularly while he was an adherent of the papacy. With regard to his wife, we are able to say that she behaves herself in a manner worthy of the marriage bond and is a pious and godly helpmeet to him in the prosecution of his duty.

Geneva, 28 November 1551 [4 calend. decembris 1551]

John Calvin, *in the name of all*

[1551]

LETTER CONCERNING THE SCANDALOUS CONDUCT OF SIMON GOLAND, PASTOR OF THE PRESBYTERY OF TERNIER

Grace to you and peace from God our Father and the Lord Jesus Christ, most dear and honourable brethren.[9] Since there is between us such a harmony of doctrine and spirit that in feeding the flock of Christ we ought to labour in co-operation and to admonish each other concerning those things which affect the state of the Church, we have considered it our duty to complain to

---

[8] It seems likely that this Heraldus was Antoine Herault, a native of Saint-Julien in Dauphiné (Saint-Julien-en-Champsaur, Hautes Alpes, District of Gap, Canton of Saint-Bonnet) and thus a compatriot of Farel. He was admitted as an inhabitant on 12 July 1549. On 16 December of that same year he was recommended (assuming him to be the same person) to the pastors of Neuchâtel, Farel and Fabri, for employment in their territory. It is also known that he was installed as pastor of Valengin on 1 April 1552, where he seems to have remained for some ten years. At the beginning of 1562 he left for Vienne in Dauphiné and thereafter trace of him is lost.

[9] There is no indication in this minute of the persons to whom this letter was addressed, but they could hardly have been other than the pastors of Berne. The letter is also undated, but it must belong to the year 1551.

you about a pastor of the Bernese territory named Simon Goland,[10] whose custom it is frequently to resort to our city, of which he is a neighbour, not to teach or learn, but to indulge in dissipation and debauchery. This, indeed might seem of little account to some, were it not that with his dissipations he mingles impure language unworthy of a minister of the Word. For in order to please his companions in drinking and debauchery he boldly intervenes on their behalf against those by whom they are at times rebuked. Without any shame he declares that no private person may rebuke in public anyone who blasphemes or sins publicly in his presence, deriding and insulting good and faithful men who are unable to tolerate the blasphemies which are poured forth against Christ and religion and the sacred ordinances of God. Furthermore, he derides those who leave their homeland because of the tyranny which everywhere prevails in the papacy and betake themselves to a place where they may enjoy the pure preaching of the Word and administration of the sacraments, asserting that they would have taken care of their own salvation no less well if they had remained in their fatherland. Indeed, he is accustomed to pick out by name certain godly men who have left all for Christ's sake, declaring that they would have done better had they adhered to their former condition, since there is no reason why they should be so much afraid of participating in the mass, when they are compelled to do so. He maintains, moreover, that some parts of the mass are good, as is shown by the fact that Calvin has borrowed from it the thanksgiving which is ordinarily included when the supper is celebrated. Finally, he openly asserts that he does not agree with our doctrine.

Because we judged that this behaviour is most unworthy of a minister of the Word we sent two of our brethren to the classis of Ternier, which had assembled at Sacconex across the Arve,[11] so that they might make known the whole matter to their colleagues as they met together. But since we see that they have taken no steps to remedy so great a scandal, we have decided to write to you in this way; for we have the reliable testimony of godly men concerning these things. And we do not consider the matter to be of so little account that it should be entirely neglected or lightly passed over. We should be seriously to blame if we

[10] Pastor of Bernex in the presbytery of Ternier. The Latin form of his name in the text is "Golandus", of which the French equivalent may have been "Goulland".

[11] Sacconex au delà d'Arve, now Sacconex d'Arve, was actually a part of the Genevan territory, although situated in the bailiwick of Ternier which came under the jurisdiction of Berne.

closed our eyes to such impious utterances; and quite definitely we neither can nor ought to tolerate it when the true doctrine of Christ, which we hold in common with the other churches, is so foully dishonoured by one who ought to defend it to the utmost of his power. It was necessary, therefore, that we should be free from this blame and should perform our duty, lest, if these scandals were allowed to spread, you should accuse us, and rightly so, of silence or negligence. Accordingly, we commit these things to your piety and prudence, being hopeful that as you have the cause of religion at heart so you will withstand all who in any way injure it or bring it into disrepute. May the Lord ever govern you by His Spirit and protect and increase your church. Amen.

TESTIMONIAL FOR MATHIEU ISSOTIER

The pastors and ministers of the church of Geneva to all their godly brethren and colleagues.[12]

Since this our brother Mathieu Issotier[13] has for a long time lived not far distant from us — for he has been in charge of a parish in the Bernese countryside almost adjoining the walls of this city — the fact of our being neighbours has meant that he is well known to us. Moreover, all the time that he has held this position he has conducted himself honourably and without any suspicion of ill repute, he has maintained pure doctrine, and he has not been contentious. It is not because of any fault that he has been removed, but when the illustrious senate of Berne heard that he was regarded with hatred by certain wicked men and that he would be unable to lead a quiet life in the position which he held, orders were given that he should be transferred elsewhere before he suffered assault, which no one wished to happen. The outcome was that our innocent brother, thus unexpectedly removed from his post, chose to live privately among us, and from that time, although he has had to eke out a tenuous existence, has calmly borne his poverty and has made no attempt to break through it by resort to wrong practices, but has modestly

---

[12] The destination of this testimonial is not stated. It is possible that it was intended as a general testimonial which could be used wherever its bearer went.

[13] Mathieu Issotier was later a pastor in Provence, until 1562 (see p. 356 below). He was the brother-in-law of Sebastian Castellio, and on 31 August 1563 he was summoned before the Consistory for having distributed Castellion's *Conseils à la France Désolée*. Thereafter he ceased to be a minister.

restrained himself. As, therefore, he has led a life becoming to a Christian man, we believe that he will not prove our testimonial false.

[16 October 1551]

THE TRIAL OF JEROME BOLSEC[14]

Friday 16 October: After the exposition delivered on this day, according to custom, when Saint-André expounded the passage from the 8th chapter of St. John, "He that is of God heareth God's words"[Jn. 8:47], and after Maître Guillaume Farel had added what our Lord imparted to him, Maître Jerome Bolsec, of whom we have spoken above,[15] began once again to put forward his false propositions concerning election and reprobation, denying that they were *ab aeterno,* and saying with emphatic protestations and exhortations that no other election or reprobation should be recog-

---

[14] The Bolsec affair was the first of the great doctrinal controversies which disturbed the young church in Geneva. The importance which the Company attached to these laborious discussions is amply shown by the amount of space which they occupy in the present Register. The secretary has taken care to reproduce in their entirety all the documents of a theological nature which were contributed either by the pastors or by Bolsec, as well as the exchange of correspondence with the other churches on this subject. The texts which follow constitute the best source for this delicate affair, apart from the dossier of the criminal proceedings instituted against Bolsec by the Seigneury. There is, however, overlapping between these two sources. As was to be the case with the trial of Servetus two years later (see below, pp. 223ff.), the pastors were very closely involved in the judicial development of this affair, and it was they, naturally enough, who drew up the list of theological accusations against the erroneous opinions of Bolsec.

Jerome Bolsec, a Carmelite friar and doctor of theology of Paris, must have left his country about 1545 following the preaching of a somewhat too free sermon in the church of Saint-Barthélemy. He sought refuge with the Duchess Renée, in Ferrara, where he married and took up the study of medicine. But he soon left his protectress, for reasons which are not known, and found a position in Veigy in Chablais about 1547, in the service of Jacques de Bourgogne, Sire de Falais. It seems that he achieved an excellent reputation as a physician, which his later fortunes did not belie. As a theologian, however, who was at the same time a fervent adherent of the Reformation, he arrived at a position which, at one essential point, differed from the one Calvin had championed: it concerned the problem of predestination, the principle of which Bolsec was not prepared to admit. He had already been reprimanded by the pastors and the Council in March and again in May of this year (1551). Now the incident recorded here by the secretary of the Company took place; it led to Bolsec's imprisonment, trial, and finally his condemnation and banishment from Geneva.

[15] See pp. 132ff. above.

nized than that which is seen in the believer or the unbeliever. He affirmed, moreover, that those who posit an eternal decree in God by which He has ordained some to life and the rest to death make of Him a tyrant and, in fact, an idol, as the pagans made of Jupiter: *sic volo, sic jubeo, sit pro ratione voluntas*,[16] saying that this was heresy and that such teaching caused great offence. Then he declared that to attribute this opinion to St. Augustine was erroneous, as he would demonstrate; and, further, that various passages of Scripture had been corrupted in order to support this false and perverse doctrine, and that this was so even in the French translations. He cited Proverbs 16 where it is said that "God made everything for His glory, even the wicked for the day of his perdition" [Prov. 16:4], saying that "iniquity'" had been put in place of "the wicked", and that one should be very wary of such a translation. He alleged also that the passage in St. Paul's epistle to the Romans had been perverted and corrupted where it is said of Pharaoh that God raised him up that He might show His power in him [Rom. 9:17], saying that the word "eternally" had been added. He uttered several other calumnies and blasphemies by which he clearly showed the venom which lay hidden in his heart while he watched for the moment and opportunity for spewing it out in public, as he had already attempted to do in certain places.

An immediate reply was given by M. Calvin who defended this doctrine which had been faithfully taught in the Church for so long with the common consent of all instructors since the beginning of the Reformation; and point by point he replied to all his calumnies in such a way that the assembly was satisfied and much edified by the doctrine which he drew from the passages pertaining to election and reprobation.

At the conclusion of the Congregation one of the assistants of the Lieutenant who was present, Jean de la Maisonneuve[17] by name, in view of the scandal which Maître Jerome had occasioned in the Church and the blasphemies which he had uttered against God and His doctrine by saying that we were making an idol of Him, caused him to be imprisoned in the palace[18] and instituted an action against him, as is customary with such people.

---

[16] A quotation from Juvenal, *Satires*, VI, 223.

[17] Jean de la Maisonneuve, the son of Baudichon, must have been born some time between 1520 and 1526. His political career commenced in 1547 when he entered the Council of Two Hundred. In 1551 he was an official in the court of the Lieutenant. Subsequently he became a Councillor, and then a syndic; but he died in 1557.

[18] L'évêché, formerly the bishop's palace.

The brethren, both of the city and of the country, assembled after dinner to consider this case. It was decided that the principal points proposed by Me Jerome should be summarized and that then a petition in the name of the brethren should be presented to Messieurs, together with the articles, requesting the interrogation of Me Jerome regarding the subject of election and reprobation. This was done without delay; and then the articles were signed by all present and taken before Messieurs.

Petition From Bolsec to Messieurs

Most august Seigneurs: Your humble servant Jerome Bolsec, a subject of the magnificent and most august Seigneurs of Berne,[19] at present improperly and contrary to all law detained in your prisons, humbly entreats your Excellencies that the privileges and liberties of your magnificent city may be maintained and preserved for him and that he may be confronted with his accuser,[20] against whom he claims all expenses and damages and submits that he has said nothing which he does not hold to be true, and that he was wrongly reproved for what he said at the Congregation and unreasonably insulted before the whole assembly and church of the faithful. He demands also that his accuser shall be compelled to reply to the articles which the suppliant will present to him concerning the question which was disputed in the Congregation just as the suppliant has replied to those which were proposed to him by your Excellencies;[21] and, further, that if it is proved from the Word of God that the suppliant is in error (though he believes he is not), then those authors who hold the same doctrine shall be condemned and a prohibition placed on the printing, sale, and possession of their writings in your city and country, so that no one shall in the future be deceived by them and their false doctrine. Conversely he demands that if the contrary is found, namely, that your ministers hold and teach an

---

[19] Bolsec invokes, for his protection, the authority of Messieurs of Berne, of which state he was a "subject" by reason of his residence in Veigy, Chablais, in the home of the Sire de Falais, his patron.

[20] This is an allusion to the custom, prevalent in the administration of criminal law in Geneva, which required the accuser in a criminal action to submit to imprisonment until he had provided proofs that there was substance to his charge.

[21] See pp. 146ff. below. Bolsec's mention here of his having answered the list of questions which had been prepared by the pastors, but submitted to him by his judges, indicates that this petition was not written, as one would have expected, immediately following his arrest, but after the trial had been in process for some time.

opinion incompatible with the Word of God, then that doctrine shall be repudiated, prohibited, and condemned together with the books which teach it. In this way praise will be given to the truth and falsehood will be overthrown, without partiality or respect of any person, the honour of God will be maintained and exalted above all, and the Lord's Church will be fed and nourished on its own legitimate pasture of the truth gathered from the pure field of Holy Scripture, not from elsewhere, without adding to it or taking away from it. And in all this the suppliant humbly requests that justice may be administered to him rapidly and equitably, if it please your Excellencies, so that his means may not be unduly consumed in prison and litigation. May the Lord God be with you and keep you long in prosperity, judging just judgment.

[9 November 1551]

COPIES OF LETTERS WRITTEN TO THE COUNCIL ON BEHALF OF BOLSEC BY JACQUES DE BOURGOGNE, OF VEIGY[22]

(1) 9 November 1551

Most magnificent and honoured Seigneurs: It is now a long time since I was informed of the detention of Me Jerome Bolsec in your prisons. For my part, I have not wished to say anything, even though I have often been asked to do so by his wife, who is living here on the estate; for I have reckoned that being in the hands of your Excellencies he was so well placed that there was no need to intercede strongly that justice should be done to him — as indeed I am confident is at present the case, in no way doubting that you have the affair sufficiently at heart to prevent his suffering any wrong. In view, however, of the fact that the affair drags on for so long without making progress, and being constantly more and more importuned by his wife to write to you on his behalf since he has been of service to me, I have been

---

[22] Jacques de Bourgogne — so called as the natural great-grandson of Philippe le Bon — generally known as Sire de Falais, in Brabant, had left his high position in the court of Charles V to become an adherent of the Reformation and had formed a friendship with Calvin — a friendship which the Bolsec affair was to break. M. de Falais had settled in the immediate neighbourhood of Geneva, at Veigy in Chablais, which was in Bernese territory. He had welcomed Bolsec in his capacity as a physician, no doubt attracted by the originality of his character. He defended him, as we shall see, with much energy, appealing not only to the Genevan authorities, both civil and ecclesiastical, but also to Bullinger in Zürich and Haller in Berne.

unable to refuse her request. Thus, although I am aware that my authority can be of but little assistance to her, it is in good faith that I appeal to you to grant that justice may be well and rapidly administered to Me Jerome, especially as the cause of his detention is only that at the Congregation he expressed himself freely on a doctrinal issue, which all Christians ought to be permitted to do without being imprisoned for it. Since, moreover, I hear that Me Jerome has affirmed nothing so strongly that he is not prepared to retract it on a better way being shown to him from the Word of God, I pray you, Messieurs, to let him enjoy the accustomed liberties and immunities of your city, by releasing him from prison, so that he may practise his regular skill of which many people both here and elsewhere are in need.

Magnificent Seigneurs, if in anything I can be of service to you, you will always find me willing, with the help of God, whom, after my affectionate recommendations to your good favour, I entreat to keep you in His sanctity.

From Veigy, 9 November 1551

Entirely at your command and service,
Jacques de Bourgogne

(2) 11 November 1551

Most magnificent and honoured Seigneurs: The knowledge conveyed by your reply that my letter has been well received by your Excellencies[23] has encouraged me to address myself familiarly to you once again. I am not importunate by nature; but because I have always found you to be most humane and kindly I would consider it a misfortune if through failure to make known to you my need I should be deprived of your interest and good will. The fact is that your prisoner Me Jerome understands how to treat my physical ailments better than any other physician known to me, and I lean all the more heavily on his judgment because of his own choice he follows the treatment prescribed for me by doctor Andernar[24] of Strasbourg. It is to him, after

---

[23] M. de Falais' letter of 9 November had been read at the session of the Council on that same day (somewhat surprisingly, as the sessions were ordinarily held in the mornings; but the letter may possibly have been wrongly dated). The Council simply decided to press the trial on, while at the same time intensifying the security measures for the detention of Bolsec, who was requested to translate his answers into Latin.

[24] "Johannes Guinterius Andernacus", that is, Johannes Guenther (known in France by the name of Jean Gonthier), of Andernach in western Germany,

God, to whom I owe my life. For my first and humble request, therefore, I entreat that you will allow me the services of Me Jerome so that I may have his advice before the maladies of winter, to which I am subject, overtake me. It is necessary that the physician should be present to judge what is hidden in the internal parts. Otherwise I would not willingly inconvenience you if I could avoid it. Besides, he is paid for ministering to my needs; and it would, therefore, only be right if, with your approval, he were to fulfil his duty.

Magnificent Seigneurs, in approaching you like this it is not my wish to belittle or annoy you; for since I do not regard this as a criminal case (for the reasons which I have written to you) it is with all the more freedom that I put forward my request; and I am not acting in bad faith, but will be happy to return him to you whenever you please, on the understanding that you take an oath from him, binding also, if you so wish, his wife or his servant — for I respect him as a man of his word, when he has given it. If this is not acceptable, then, knowing how the matter stands, I shall make provision in the best way possible, praying you meanwhile to be so good as to let me have a word in reply so that I may make plans accordingly. And if there is any service which I can render to your republic I will employ myself in it to the best of my limited ability, with the help of God, whom, after having commended myself most affectionately to your good favour, I entreat to prosper your most magnificent Excellencies under His holy protection for ever.

From Veigy, 11 November 1551

Entirely at your command and service,
Jacques de Bourgogne

[16 October 1551]

ARTICLES WHICH WE HAVE EXTRACTED FROM THE OPINIONS HELD BY ONE CALLED MAITRE JEROME[25] THIS 16TH DAY OF OCTOBER 1551

1. After assenting to what had been said, or pretending to do so, in order to gain acceptance with the simple, he said that there

---

born in 1487, was a noted physician and hellenist. After living in Paris from 1526 to 1538, he settled, in 1540, in Strasbourg, and remained there until his death, in 1574. He was the master both of Vesalius and of Sturm.

[25] Here we return to the beginning of the trial and to the first document of accusation drawn up by the Company against Bolsec.

was a new and pernicious opinion contrary to Holy Scripture and most offensive to the Gospel, namely, that God determined before the creation of the world who should be saved and who should be damned, and that He did this before having foreseen who would and who would not believe.

2. He showed in his examination that he indeed admitted that God had from all time elected or reprobated those who should be saved or damned, but that this was in consideration of the obedience of the former to the Gospel and the rebellion of the latter.

3. As for the doctrine which we hold — namely, that before the foundation of the world God foresaw and foreordained those who should be His, without finding in them any reason for doing so, but choosing them of His own pure goodness, while on the contrary He reprobated those who should perish without our being able to assign any reason for His doing so — in the first place, Bolsec condemned this doctrine, as has just been said; and then he said that a certain Lorenzo Valla[26] invented it and that very few people competent in theology and possessing good sense accepted it; and, further, that it was rejected by all the ancient doctors, as all who have followed the teaching of the Gospel in our day hold and maintain in their writings.

4. Seeking to prove that none were reprobated except those who had first resisted God and His Word, he adduced the passages where God attributes the damnation of men to their own wickedness, saying: "It is not said that God will damn them because He has reprobated them, but because they have not believed". Thus he holds that in order of time unbelief must precede reprobation.

5. In confirming this opinion, he falsely cited what is not in the first chapter of St. John, namely, that Jesus Christ came to enlighten every man in this world [Jn. 1:9]; and his falsification of this passage was certainly malicious and impudent in view of the fact that his opinion had been refuted in the presence of the full Congregation.

---

[26] Lorenzo Valla (c. 1406-1457), the celebrated Italian humanist, several of whose writings were printed in Basle in 1540, was a pioneer of textual and historical criticism. He exposed the spuriousness of the so-called "Donation of Constantine," thus removing a chief prop of the temporal supremacy of the papacy. His book on the freedom of the will affirmed the impossibility of harmonizing divine omnipotence with human free will. His attacks on scholasticism were justified, and his critical comparison of the Vulgate with the Greek New Testament prepared the way for Erasmus and subsequent textual scholarship.

6. Moreover, although from the beginning he protested that the election of God was eternal and that we are saved by His grace, yet he then said and repeated: "Note well that Scripture does not say that we are saved because God has elected us, but because we have believed in Jesus Christ".

7. He went on to say that in order to render this false doctrine acceptable certain passages of Scripture had been corrupted, perverted, and falsely expounded. Among other passages, he cited the 16th chapter of Proverbs, saying that the French translation stated that God created the wicked for the day of iniquity, which is a wicked calumny; whereas the first translation of Neuchâtel has "for the evil day", and the edition of Geneva has "for the day of calamity" [Prov. 16:4].

8. He then said that we had falsely cited a passage of St. Paul, which in fact is not written as he quoted it, namely, that God raised up Pharaoh from all eternity [Rom. 9:17]. From this it is only too evident that he is a slanderer, accusing us of a deception which he has invented.

9. Citing the passage of St. Paul where he uses the analogy of the vessels which are made unto honour or dishonour, he said that we twisted it to mean entirely the contrary of what St. Paul intended [Rom. 9:21ff.]. He based his argument on St. Paul's statement that they were prepared for their destruction, but that God prepared the vessels of grace and salvation: as though by this Paul wished to say that the wicked prepares himself and not that he is predestined or foreordained by God.

10. Thereupon he condemned the doctrine of God which we follow, saying that it had the effect of making God a tyrant and an idol like Jupiter, such as the pagans had invented, and citing a verse[27] which speaks particularly of tyrants who by definition dictate their own pleasure.

11. He then added that in saying that God has predestined whom He will to life or to death we make Him the author of evil and iniquity.

12. He declared, further, that we give occasion to the wicked to blaspheme God by saying that there is nothing they can do about it if they are damned, and that it is not their fault.

13. Finally, he not only said that this was his opinion but also urged the people to beware of the false doctrine which he had condemned, which is the same as we preach every day, and in

---

[27] The reference is to Juvenal, *Satires*, VI, 223, already quoted above (note 16, p. 138).

which we are at one with all the churches which have broken away from the Pope. He did this, he said, in assurance of the truth of God.

[16 October 1551]

QUESTIONS FOR JEROME BOLSEC

In view of the trouble and offence which an individual named Me Jerome tried to cause today, the 16th of October, as he has already attempted to do previously, the ministers of the Word of God humbly pray that it may please Messieurs to have him interrogated on the following articles. They do this because it is the doctrine of the faith which is in question. The ministers put forward these articles here, however, only as a form of information, not because they are afraid of involvement should the need arise; but it is because they are fully confident that Messieurs, with all their authority will give the case adequate consideration that they regard it as sufficient to give information concerning the errors by which Me Jerome has tried to seduce and unsettle the people.

1. Whether he has not previously propounded the opinion which he maintained today, in presence of the full Congregation, and whether he was not answered immediately?

2. Whether he was not then admonished that he was at fault, and, although he did not assent to the reasons presented to him, whether he did not promise to pray that God would cause him to understand what was involved?

3. Whether he did not then falsely declare that we were unwilling to hear him?

4. Whether he does not believe that God has elected from among men those whom He pleases, without finding in them the cause, but simply because of His pure goodness and grace?

5. Whether faith does not proceed from the election of God and those who are illuminated receive such grace because God has elected them?

6. Whether those whom God has not elected do not remain in their blindness, as being reprobated by Him, that is to say, because He has not illuminated them by His Spirit?

7. Whether the whole race of Adam and the whole of mankind is not so corrupted that none is able to aspire to goodness unless God draw him?

8. Whether this grace of drawing is not special to certain persons, that is to say, to those whom God has adopted before the creation of the world?

9. Whether all would not remain in unbelief and obstinacy unless God changed the heart of those whom He pleases?

10. Whether, before having foreseen any difference between the one and the other, God did not elect the one and reject the other?

11. Whether the fact that some are illuminated and others not does not proceed from God's wonderful counsel, the first cause of which is unknown to us?

12. Whether it is not true that when the Gospel is preached, the reason why some believe and others do not is that God efficaciously calls those whom He has ordained to salvation?

13. Whether God does not work in His elect in such a way that, as well as the power to receive His grace, He gives them also the will?

14. Whether since the fall of Adam man is not so destitute of free will that he can do nothing but evil until God reforms him?

15. Whether such reformation is not a special gift which God bestows on those with hard and stony hearts, and not because of any good preparation which may be in them?

16. Whether in saying that we are saved by faith, he does not believe that this faith was given to us because God loved us from the time when we were His enemies and in ourselves were deserving only of His wrath?

17. Whether in saying that we are damned because of our rebellious nature, he does not believe that we have without our corrupt nature the root of unbelief and all evil, from which none can be delivered except those whom God delivers?

[20 October 1551]

Bolsec's Reply

The answers and confessions of Me Jerome Bolsec, native of Paris, inhabitant of Veigy, made by order of the syndics, their excellencies Antoine Chicand, Jacques des Ars, Michel Morel, and François Chamois, on 20 October 1551 in the presence of their excellencies Amblard Corne, Michel de Larche, Domaine d'Arlod, Amyed Gervaix, Guillaume Beney, Pierre Jean Jessé, Claude de

Lestral, Jean de la Maisonneuve, Jean Pernet, Pierre Dorsière,[28] the *sautier*[29]

After he had solemnly taken the oath, the prisoner Me Jerome was enjoined according to the customary form to speak the truth, on pain of forfeiting the case and a fine of sixty sous. When interrogated about the cause of his detention he replied that he did not know. He requested, however, to be permitted to write his replies and admissions or denials, and this was granted. He prepared and wrote them out in the terms which follow.

To the first question I answer:

I contradicted the statement that those who obey the Word of God are the elect whom God has determined to save, and those who do not obey it are those whom He has reprobated from the beginning, since these words imply that the will of God is the cause both of the acceptance of the faith and of the rejection of the faith, which is false.

To the third, I answer:

I praised what was well said, not what was ill said, namely, what at the beginning I said was false.

To the fourth, I answer:

After some discussion, having praised what was truly said, I said that there were some statements which merited a fuller explanation.

To the fifth, I answer:

I mentioned various erroneous opinions which I repudiated by the Word of God, and others by reason, such as that of the Manicheans.

To the sixth, I answer:

I said that at the present day there was an opinion opposed in a certain respect to the Manicheans and that those who affirmed it

---

[28] This impressive court of justice includes nearly all the political personalities of mid-sixteenth century Geneva.

[29] The *sautier* (the term appears for the first time only in 1528, applied to a Genevan functionary) was in particular the guardian of the city hall, charged with the execution of the orders of the Council.

were guilty of three evils: firstly, because they corrupt the text of the Word of God; secondly, because they expound Holy Scripture wrongly; and, thirdly, because they attribute to the ancient doctors things which they did not say.

To the seventh, I answer:

In the writings and in the speech of the ministers of this city I have heard or read this same error or opinion which I repudiate, and again I have seen it in the writings of other modern authors.

To the eighth:

In sermons and Congregations I have heard things which are holy and conformed to the Word of God, but the view or opinion which I oppose and reject is not in accordance with the Word of God, but contrary to it.

To the ninth:

I have read a little in their writings, and I adore and reverence as truth what is in conformity with the Word of God; but what I have said is false I cannot accept.

To the tenth:

The opinion concerning the reprobation and perdition of the damned, namely, that it is the will of God, is untrue and involves absurdities which are much to be feared and are the cause of stumbling.

To the eleventh:

Among the other authors, Zwingli, in his book on Providence,[30] has been even more absurd than Monsieur Calvin; none the less, Monsieur Calvin differs little from him, when the matter is properly understood.

To the twelfth:

I have not seen them all; if I had the time I would be the better able to answer whether there could be some such.

---

[30] Zwingli preached a sermon on Providence (*De Providentia*) at the Colloquy of Marburg, which he revised and expanded for publication, in 1530.

To the thirteenth:

Yes.

To the fourteenth:

I have never heard Monsieur Calvin preach anything which is not holy and good, excepting what he said in the Congregation concerning the cause of the perdition of the damned.

To the fifteenth:

At a meeting of the Congregation I spoke urging the church, ministers as well as assistants, always to hold fast to the simplicity of the Word of God, and I put forward nothing scandalous at the Congregation but only propositions taken from Holy Scripture; then one day when I was in Geneva I was summoned to Monsieur Calvin's house where all the ministers of this presbytery were assembled; and there I complained to Monsieur Calvin and his colleagues that they were wronging me in speaking ill of me and rebuking me as they were doing, and that to the extent that I was shown by the Word of God to be in error I was ready to retract my opinion. Thereupon Monsieur Calvin attempted to prove both by text and by reason that I was in error. But so far was he from convincing me that I reckoned I had satisfactorily met all his arguments, excepting for one authority which I promised to consider more carefully. As, however, they were unwilling to give me a hearing, several more of them spoke; for they regarded me as convicted of heresy.

To the sixteenth:

The other opinions which I maintained on the first occasion when I spoke in opposition to Monsieur Calvin were much the same in content. It is true that we did not speak in this way before, for on that other occasion we spoke only of universal views and propositions concerning God, which I wished to be held in their universality. But on this later occasion the disagreement was caused over the question of the perdition of the damned, which he said was the will of God — a doctrine which I judge to be false.

The inquiry extended no further, but awaited his answers and the formulation of his case.

[21 October 1551]

The answers of Me Jerome, detained by order of Messieurs the Syndics, their excellencies Antoine Chicand, Jacques des Ars, Michel Morel, and François Chamois, on 21 October 1551 in the presence of their excellencies Amblard Corne, Pierre Bonne, Henri Aubert, Claude Dupan, Pierre Jean Jessé, councillors, and their excellencies Jean Pernet, Jean François Philibert Donzel, Jean Cousin, Jean Du Mollard, Julien Bocard, Lestral, Rigotti, the sautier, the souldan.[31]
His excellency Jean de la Maisonneuve acted for the Lord Lieutenant.

To the first I answer that I did not advance my own propositions but those which I mentioned yesterday, namely, that the universal propositions of Scripture be left in their entirety, and I received an immediate, but not an adequate, answer; and so after the Congregation I spoke to Monsieur Abel[32] and then to Monsieur Calvin, showing them that their answer was not adequate.

To the second I answer as I did yesterday, and once again I say that, as we agreed, I prayed God incessantly that He would give me grace to understand the truth, indeed I pray for this continually, and I desire that they should do the same so that the Church may not be divided over opinions.

To the third I answer No, but that I offered to write down what I thought, for in speaking and disputing one gets heated and drawn into contentions which are uncharitable and unchristian; Monsieur Calvin, however, said that he did not wish this and that it was enough for me to be present there. He then held me to be stubborn and intractable, as was reported to me and as the two ministers from Vevey,[33] who were most surprised at this, know to be the case; and once again the minister from Veigy said to Me Pierre Viret that I ought to be given a hearing; but Me Pierre Viret replied that this had been done both at Geneva and at Lausanne, and that there was no need to discuss the matter further.

To the fourth I answer that God has elected from among men

---

[31] That is, the gaoler. Bolsec now appears before an enlarged court and finds himself compelled to answer the same questions as on the previous day. For *sautier*, see note 29 above.

[32] That is, Abel Poupin.

[33] The two ministers from Vevey were François de Saint-Paul and Augustin Marlorat. Following Bolsec's trial Saint-Paul, who was a compatriot of Calvin's, openly opposed the strict Calvinistic doctrine of predestination and withstood his colleagues in Lausanne, Beza and Viret.

those whom He has pleased, that is to say in Jesus Christ, apart from whom none is acceptable to God, as the apostle says, and that He has elected them not because of any good which was first in them, but simply because of His goodness and grace.

To the fifth I answer that faith does not depend on election, but that we ought to consider faith and election together; for before man can be considered elected of God he must be loved, and before we consider him loved of God we must take into account in virtue of whom it is that we are loved of God, that is, Jesus Christ whom God has given, with whom there is neither before nor after and to whom therefore the following three things are present: the union of man with His Son through faith, the love which comes through this faith, and the election of the believer which is through faith in Jesus Christ. Over this the holy doctors of old are in agreement, as are also three learned and highly esteemed persons of our day, Melanchthon, Bullinger, and Brenz, together with others.

To the sixth I answer that the rest do not remain in the blindness of their corrupt nature, but are duly illuminated by God's grace, which, as St. Paul says, is ever given abundantly beyond the measure to which sin abounds [Rom. 5:20f.]; and I maintain that those who say that they are abandoned by God in their blindness because He so wills it dishonour God and misunderstand Holy Scripture and speak contrary to it, to whose number Sr Calvin belongs.

To the seventh I answer Yes.

To the eighth I answer that there is an ambiguity in the word "drawing", for there is a violent drawing, which I do not accept, and there is a sweet and fatherly drawing, which God employs with His rational creatures, and that in general He communicates this to all, without abandoning any except those who despise it and rebel against it; for it is after such persons have rebelled frequently against God's grace and sweet admonitions that they are then abandoned, but not from the beginning and by the purpose and decree of God.

To the ninth I answer that in order to receive faith it is necessary for God to change the heart of stone, that is to say, the heart that is obstinate and hardened in evil doing, and to give a heart of flesh, that is to say, a heart capable of understanding; and God makes His grace available to all, as He has promised by the prophets.

To the tenth I answer that it is unnecessary to say that God has foreknowledge of one thing more than of another, for with Him there is neither past nor future, but all things are present; and accordingly I say that at one and the same time He sees the difference between believers and unbelievers and the election of the former and the reprobation of the latter.

To the eleventh I answer that I do not desire to enter into this wonderful and secret counsel of God and I am content to stop at the simple Word of God which says that those who believe in His Son will be saved and that unbelievers will be damned, and that He sent His Son into this world to the end that all might believe in Him. In brief, I say that Scripture does not lead us higher than this and it should be enough to stop at this, without wishing to go further and confuse the minds of the simple.

To the twelfth I answer that it is not my understanding that God has ordained to save some rather than others, but that those who believe do so through efficacious grace, whereas in the case of the others who do not receive faith the grace of God which causes one to believe is not efficacious because they do not take it and esteem it as it deserves, so that their failure to believe comes from their contempt and rebellion, not from the decree of God.

To the thirteenth I answer that it is God who gives the heart of flesh and an understanding capable of understanding the word of salvation, who, having illuminated a man's understanding, causes him to believe, and who constantly increases His gifts and graces in His elect, that is to say, in those who believe perfectly.

To the fourteenth I answer that after the fall man was not entirely deprived of free will, for then he would have been a brute beast without reason, but that his will remained damaged and corrupted in such a way that he has frequently and virtually always judged good to be evil and evil good. Consequently, he has always needed to hear the law of God and to follow it with the help of God's grace, and in order to believe in Jesus Christ he has needed special grace and drawing.

To the fifteenth I answer that those whom God has reformed through Jesus Christ have been reformed by special grace, and that the heart of flesh has been placed in them, and the heart of stone removed, through the free gift of God, without any deserving on their part [Ezek. 11:19; II Cor. 3:3].

To the sixteenth I answer that God gave us faith because of the love which He bore toward us before we loved Him, for in us He found nothing worthy to cause Him to love us, and that this love was solely on account of His fatherly mercy.

To the seventeenth I answer that it is in our corruption and wicked nature that we have our damnation and are children of wrath, and that it is not possible that any should be saved from such corruption and damnation unless God should deliver him through His Son Jesus Christ.

After the Lieutenant had received his answers and confessions he requested that justice should be done to him and that the case should be proceeded with. Thereupon the prisoner demanded his discharge and the termination of his detention. And after having heard the parties we referred to the good pleasure of Messieurs the consideration of his answers and the further formulation of his case.

[22 October 1551]

Further repetitions made before Messieurs the Syndics, their excellencies Antoine Chicand, Jacques des Ars, Michel Morel, François Chamois, etc.[34]
His excellency Jean de la Maisonneuve acted for the Lord Lieutenant.

After having sworn to speak the truth, and having been asked whether it was not preferable to speak the truth and whether everything which he had affirmed was true, and whether he wished to add or retract anything, Bolsec replied that he had spoken nothing but the truth and that what he had spoken had been spoken in good faith, and that he believed it to be the truth, but that if he were shown by the Word of God to be in any error he was ready to be corrected; while, on the contrary, if he was not shown to be in error he did not think that he ought to abandon an opinion which accorded with Holy Scripture. He wished, however, to be subject to the correction of Messieurs and of Scripture.

THE REPLIES GIVEN BY THE MINISTERS OF THE WORD OF GOD TO THE ANSWERS WRITTEN BY MAITRE JEROME BOLSEC

In the first place, with reference to the answers he has given to the articles proposed by order of Monsieur the Lieutenant: concerning the first and second they say that Me Jerome has shown himself presumptuous in condemning without any distinction a statement, which, as he says, could only be false in one sense; and so he cannot deny that he has resorted to calumny in condemning it altogether, which is inexcusable.

[34] This took place on the following day, 22 October 1551.

Concerning the fifteenth they say that he particularly exhorted the people and not the ministers, saying: "Christians, beware lest you be deceived", etc., maintaining also that he was certain that he had the Spirit of God in what he said.

And when he was summoned so that his error could be reproved, he rejoined that he had made a complaint. Then he was reproved because he had falsely and wrongly complained in a letter that he had been slandered, and for this he asked forgiveness. It was protested, also, that he had been treated with nothing but kindness. Thereupon the falsity and error of his opinion was reproved; and at this he was so distraught that he changed his position and contradicted himself more than twenty times, as may be verified by persons of good character.

With reference to the remaining articles proposed in the presence of Monsieur the Lieutenant: because the answers are not of great importance, or because they resemble those which follow later, in order to avoid undue length they leave it at that.

As regards the answers given to the articles presented to Messieurs by the ministers:

1. Concerning the first, they say that what he had previously stated in the Congregation tended in sum to the same conclusion, namely, that God did not elect those whom He pleased from among men by His free goodness, but rather in consideration of the fact that they would accept His grace and put it to good use, and that He reprobated none from the beginning, but that those who remain rebellious to the end reprobate themselves. They say, moreover, that he was adequately answered at the time. As for the universal propositions which he alleges — in particular the passage where St. Paul says that God wishes all to be saved [I Tim. 2:4] — it was explained to him that St. Paul did not intend this of every single man, but of all estates of men. As for the passages in Ezekiel where God says that He does not desire the death of the sinner, but rather that he should be converted and live [Ezek. 18:32], it was explained to him that the prophet only intends that God exhorts all in general to repentance, but that His arm and His power are not revealed to all who hear the preaching, as is declared in the 53rd chapter of Isaiah [Is. 53:1], and, indeed, that conversion is a special gift of grace. Further, concerning faith, he was told that all who believe in Jesus Christ will indeed be saved, but that not all are given the light to believe, as Moses says: "The Lord hath not given you an heart to perceive" [Deut. 29:4]; again, as Jesus says in Matthew 16: "Flesh and blood hath not revealed it unto thee, but my Father

which is in heaven" [Mt. 16:17]; again, in the first chapter of St. John which states that those who are born of God believe in Jesus Christ [Jn. 1:12]; and again in the sixteenth chapter: "No man can come to me except the Father draw him" [Jn. 6:44, 65]. The doctrine was so amply derived from Scripture that he should have been quite satisfied.

2. Concerning the second answer, they say that, seeing him to be stubborn after he had been convicted of error, they exhorted him to pray God to bring him into line with the truth, and that the doctrines which he claims to hold are false.

3. They say that there was never any question of getting heated in dispute, nor indeed was there any hostility toward him, but he was treated with every kindness. As for his being held to be stubborn and intractable, they say that there was good reason for this; but that his claiming of the two ministers from Vevey as witnesses is false.

4. They say that the answer is neither straightforward nor unequivocal, but that he beats about the bush, as will be more apparent in the following answers.

5. They say that it is a most manifest heresy to deny that faith depends on election, for, as St. Paul says, those whom God foreknew He predestinated, and those whom He predestinated He also called, Rom. 8 [vv. 29ff.]. Again, the first chapter of Ephesians says that God has blessed us with every spiritual blessing according as He has elected us in Jesus Christ before the creation of the world to be holy and without blame [Eph. 1:4]. Thus Paul shows that the reason why we are led to Jesus Christ is because God has elected us, adding that He has predestinated us according to the good pleasure of His will [Eph. 1:5], and, further, that His grace has abounded in us in all wisdom in order that He might make known the mystery of His will, according to His good pleasure which He has purposed, etc. [Eph. 1:8f.]. Again, Jesus Christ says that those whom the Father has given Him will come to Him [Jn. 6:37], from which it follows that this giving is prior. Again, St. Paul says that he obtained mercy, not because God foresaw that he would believe, but in order that he might do so; for he says that in doing this, God wished to make known His mercy for the instruction of those who should believe, I Tim. 1 [v. 16]. And this accords with his statement in the first chapter of the second epistle, that it is according to the purpose of God and not according to our works [II Tim. 1:9]. Again, St. Peter greets the elect of God who have been sanctified according to His foreknowledge [I Pet. 1:2].

With regard to Maître Jerome's assertion that before a man can be considered elect of God he must be loved by Him, and before he is loved we must take into account in virtue of whom it is that he is loved; and, further, that three things must go together, namely, the union of man with Christ through faith, the love which proceeds from faith, and election which is through faith: the ministers say that these opinions are the result of gross ignorance and that he subverts the very foundations of Christianity. For it is specifically stated, in the fourth chapter of the first epistle of John, that God loved us before we loved Him [I Jn. 4:10, 19], and we know that those whom God has elected often remain in error for a great part of their lives, and that God draws them when it pleases Him. They do indeed admit that it is only through faith in Jesus Christ that we can apprehend our election and know that we are loved of God; but they add also that we must first be apprehended of God, as is said in Philippians 3 [v. 12]. Similarly St. Paul says in the fourth chapter of Romans that God calls things which are not as though they were [Rom. 4:17]. That is why in the fifth chapter of the same epistle he says that God reconciled us to Himself even when we were His enemies [Rom. 5:10]. But it was because He loved us that He was moved to do this, as we read in the third chapter of St. John [v. 16]. It follows, therefore, that for His part God loves us even from the time when, for our part, we are His enemies.

With regard to his assertion that his views are in harmony with those of the ancient theologians, it is the greatest impudence to make such a claim, seeing that St. Augustine openly affirms the contrary in hundreds of passages, especially in the two books which he entitled *De Praedestinatione Sanctorum;* also in his book *De Dono Perseverantiae;*[35] also in his book *De Praedestinatione et Gratia;* also in his book *De Correptione et Gratia;* also in letter 59 to Paulinus, in letter 105 to Sixtus, in letter 106 to Boniface; also in his first book to Boniface, chapters 19 and 20, and in the second book, chapters 5 and 7, and in the fourth book, chapters 6 and 9; also in his fourth book against Julian, chapter 8, and in the fifth book, chapter 3; also in the first book *De Peccatorum Meritis et Remissione,* chapter 21, and in the second, chapter 18; also in his book entitled *Enchiridion ad Laurentium,* chapters 96 to 105; also in the sermon on the words of the Apostle, 7, 11, and 20. He also cites passages from St. Ambrose to the same effect, such as that written by him in his commentary on Luke 9: "Had Christ

---

[35] Actually, the book *De Dono Perseverantiae* was the second part of the treatise *De Praedestinatione Sanctorum.*

so wished He would have made holy those who were not, but He calls those whom He pleases and gives His fear to whom He wills." And another ancient doctor, Prosper,³⁶ condemns those who say that we obtain grace from God by the merit of faith. What is more, in chapter 24 of his first book of Retractations St. Augustine corrects himself and acknowledges that he was at fault in not having taken into account the grace of God which precedes faith in the election of those whom He pleases without regard to their faith. Accordingly the ministers say that Me Jerome has done them a grave injustice in saying that they falsely claim St. Augustine for their side.

With regard to his assertion that of the theologians now living there are three who are on his side, namely, Melanchthon, Brenz, and Bullinger,³⁷ the ministers reply that he has misunderstood Melanchthon; for all that Melanchthon counsels is that we should not investigate the election of God with a curiosity and audacity that probe into His secret counsel, but should be content that He has adopted us by Jesus Christ, of whom we are made members through faith. This is something which is daily and diligently taught in this city — a fact of which Me Jerome cannot be ignorant seeing that it is also plainly declared and expounded by Calvin, to mention none other, both in his *Institutes* and in more than thirty passages in his commentaries. Moreover, that this is what Melanchthon intended is apparent from the letters written to Calvin in his own hand, which can be produced.

As for Brenz, Me Jerome is most impudent in claiming that he concurs with his heresy, especially since, when commenting on the fifth chapter of St. John, Brenz says that before the creation of the world God elected some and rejected the rest; again, on the sixth chapter, that God gives His faith to those whom He pleases, because He has mercy on whom He will and hardens whom He will, explaining that the reason for this is that God elected some before the creation of the world, and that those whom He has elected He calls; again, on the fifteenth chapter he writes: "So far as God and His immutable purpose are concerned, those whom He has elected before the creation of the world cannot perish and those

---

³⁶ Prosper of Aquitaine (c. 390-c. 463) was a great supporter of Augustine's doctrine of predestination. Augustine wrote his two treatises *De Praedestinatione Sanctorum* and *De Dono Perseverantiae* after receiving information from Prosper and Hilary of the opposition to his doctrine of grace in Southern Gaul. In later life Prosper adopted less strict views.

³⁷ Melanchthon, Brenz, and Bullinger were, in fact, less rigorous than was Calvin in their definitions of the doctrines of election and grace, though all three held firmly to the truth of election.

whom He has rejected cannot be saved", adding a very strong clause, "even if they should perform all the works of the saints"; again, in homily 72 on the Acts, he says: "Since we are all damned, if God elects some in order to give them salvation it is of His mercy, and if He leaves the rest to perish this is not a cruel injustice but a condign judgment".

As for Bullinger, Me Jerome does him a serious wrong, seeing especially that in commenting on the ninth chapter of Romans he says that God wished to show that it was within His power to kill and to make alive, to elect and to reject, according to His counsel and free choice; again, on chapter 2 of the first epistle to Timothy he agrees, as in the preceding passage, with St. Augustine. The ministers, however, do not claim just one or two for their side but as many as God has used for the restoration of His Gospel in our time.

6. They say that it is a damnable heresy to deny that those who remain in their blindness remain in it because of the corruption of their nature; for Scripture is full of testimonies to the fact that we are all ignorant and blind, that in us there is only darkness, and that we cannot understand the things of God, but that they are foolishness to us. That it is not the case that the Spirit of God is given to all for their illumination, but is a special gift, is seen from I Cor. 1 [vv. 27ff.] and 2 [vv. 10ff.] and John 1 [vv. 9ff.] and 6 [vv. 37, 63ff.], Is. 53 [v. 1], and other similar passages. With regard to the assertion that all are duly illuminated by God's grace, if he means in so far as God binds Himself to them, the ministers agree with him; but if he is saying that they are illuminated in order to come to salvation, the contrary is apparent in the whole of Scripture, as has already been shown. As for his assumption that grace abounds according to the degree that sin abounds [see Rom. 5:20], they say that this is either a stupid or a malicious perversion of St. Paul's meaning, for he is not speaking of the number of persons, but of the manner in which God works in His children. Thus St. Paul says that grace surpasses condemnation. But condemnation extends to all, as he says. It follows, therefore, that he is not dealing there with the question as to how many people participate in the grace of Jesus Christ, but as to how this grace prevails in those to whom it is given. As for his assertion that to say that some are abandoned by God because He so wills it is to dishonour God, they reply that Me Jerome utters a wicked blasphemy against the Holy Spirit, who has expressly declared by the mouth of St. Paul that God hardens whom He will, even particularly saying that this was shown in the case of children who were still in their mother's womb and

had done neither good nor evil, and relating all to the secret counsel of God and to His will as He has ordained it, which to us is incomprehensible, Rom. 9 [vv. 11ff.].

7. They agree.

8. While they are in agreement over the seventh article, concerning the answer which he offers to the eighth they say that it is a superfluous cavil to speak of a violent drawing of God, seeing that they teach daily that God gives us the will to follow Him and not that He drags us by force. Of this Me Jerome cannot be ignorant, since it receives adequate expression in the writings of Calvin which refute and condemn him, and thus he is self-evidently a calumniator. As for his assertion that God draws all rational creatures, this has already been adequately refuted, and it is clearly in opposition to this that St. Paul says that God calls those whom He has predestinated, Rom. 8 [v. 30], and also that He has mercy on whom He will, Rom. 9 [v. 15]. Likewise, St. Luke says that those believed who were ordained to eternal life [Acts 13:48]. At this point, indeed, Jerome shows himself to be a true Pelagian, since he denies that God grants believers both to will and to do His good pleasure, as St. Paul declares, Phil. 2 [v. 13]; for from this it follows that all unbelievers have not been drawn, since they have not had the will.

9. They say that by a false interpretation Me Jerome corrupts the passage from Ezekiel, chapters 11 [v. 19] and 36 [v. 26] where God promises to give a heart of flesh, explaining this as a heart capable of obeying Him; for the prophet expresses much more when he adds that God will cause us to obey His commandments. He does not say that God will give only the ability and the capacity, but also that He will give the fulfilment. And this is what St. Paul means when he says that God gives "both to will and to do". There is yet another error and falsification in Me Jerome's claim that this was promised to all by the prophets; for on the contrary, it was spoken only to those who truly belong to the Church of God and to His people: as is apparent in Jeremiah 31 [v. 34] and Isaiah 54 [v. 13]. And this is how our Lord Jesus interprets it in John 6 [v. 45]. But, apart from this, the words of the prophet are quite explicit, for he is addressing only the children of the Church.

10. Concerning the tenth, they are astonished that, in maintaining that there is neither first nor second with God, Maître Jerome did not recollect the distinction which is taught to schoolchildren, namely, that what is neither before nor after in time is none the less in a certain order. Now, this is how God foresaw

in their order the fall and damnation of men before the remedy which He gave in Jesus Christ. It cannot be regarded as absurd, then, that He chooses to save those whom He pleases without regard to any difference. St. Paul, in fact, shows clearly that there is nothing distinctive in us which causes us to be preferred to others, apart from the action of God, I Cor. 4 [vv. 6f.]. It follows, therefore, that the grace of God precedes every difference, since it is this which creates the distinction.

11. Concerning the eleventh, they say that to speak as Me Jerome does is indeed to becloud the understanding of the simple with empty and frivolous sophistry. There is none so simple, however, as not to be able to perceive his stupidity. He says that the Word of God leads us no further than this statement: "He who believes on the Son has eternal life" [Jn. 3:36]. On the contrary, the ministers declare that faith comes by hearing, as St. Paul says in Romans 10 [v. 17], and that we cannot believe if the Gospel is not preached to us. But since it is evident that God ordains that the Gospel is preached to some and not others, it is the greatest impudence to wish to hide from sight something which is so obvious. When St. Luke says in Acts 16 that Paul was forbidden by the Holy Spirit to proclaim the Word of God in Asia, and, again, that the Holy Spirit prevented him from going into Bithynia [Acts 16:6f.], it is apparent that God causes the rain to fall where He wills in order to give the means of believing in His Son. It is also a malicious device of Satan to wish to obscure the grace of God which He declares in particular to those to whom He sends the preaching of His Gospel. St. Luke speaks of this in Acts 14 [v. 16] where he says that in time past God allowed the nations to wander in their own ways. If Me Jerome replies that this was because God foresaw that preaching would not have been to their profit, Jesus Christ says the contrary: "Woe unto thee, Chorazin! woe unto thee, Bethsaida! for if the mighty works which were done in you had been done in Tyre and Sidon, they would have repented long ago in sackcloth and ashes," Matt. 11 [v. 21]. In brief, we are in no way departing from Holy Scripture in saying with Moses and David that God elected the nation of the Jews from among all the peoples of the world in order to reveal His will to that nation, because He loved it, Deut. 4 [v. 37], 7 [vv. 6ff.], Ps. 147 [v. 11], and not because of their worthiness or righteousness, Deut. 9 [vv. 5ff.].

12. Concerning the twelfth, they say that his assertion that God has not ordained to salvation some rather than others is entirely contrary to St. Paul's affirmation that God has mercy on

whom He will and hardens whom He will, Rom. 9 [v. 18]; which corresponds with what God said to Moses: "I will be gracious to whom I will be gracious and will show mercy on whom I will show mercy", Exod. 33 [v. 19]. Again, St. Paul says that those who love God are called according to His purpose [Rom. 8:28]. But when Me Jerome adds that those who believe, believe through grace, it is full of sophistry; for all are equally perverse and are unbelieving by nature. None, therefore, can believe unless his heart is touched by God, just as we are told that God opened the heart of the woman who believed Paul's teaching, Acts 16 [v. 14]; also, that He opened the understanding of His disciples so that they might understand the Scriptures, Luke 24 [v. 45]; and, again, in John 6 [v. 37]: "All that the Father has given Me shall come to Me". Now, it is evident that all do not come, and so it follows that all are not led of God. The fact is that Me Jerome holds that by their own free will men render the grace of God efficacious. As for his assertion that the failure of some to believe comes from their contempt and rebellion and not from the decree of God, the ministers affirm that they teach the same thing daily. The word failure, in fact, cannot be associated with God. But it is mistaken to conclude from this that all those who are destitute of the Spirit of God do not remain in their unbelief.

13. Concerning the thirteenth, they say that Maître Jerome evades the issue and does not answer the question; for he was asked whether God does not give to His elect the will to come to Him as well as the power, to which he answers that He gives them a heart which is capable, wishing to indicate that the grace of God can do nothing of itself, unless men render it effective by their free will, just as though God hung an apple in the air for any to take who will. From this it would follow that the grace of God does not profit us at all excepting through our merit. St. Paul says, on the contrary, that it is not of him who wills, nor of him who runs, but of God who shows mercy, Rom. 9 [v. 16].

14. Concerning the fourteenth, they say that Me Jerome speaks just like a papist when admitting that man has need of the grace of God as though of himself he could in part aspire to what is good; for this is to make free will the companion of the Holy Spirit. To the contrary, however, it is affirmed that every imagination of man's heart is only evil, Gen. 8;[38] again, that all are perverse and corrupt and none seek God, Rom. 3 [vv. 10ff., 23]; again, that their heart is blinded and in darkness and that they are spiritually dead, Eph. 2 [vv. 1, 5]; so much so that they

---

[38] *Sic.* The reference is to Gen. 6:5.

cannot have a single good thought, II Cor. 3 [v. 5]; and, again, that every affection of the flesh, that is to say, of our nature, is enmity against God, Rom. 8 [vv. 7f.]. And as for his assertion that man would be a brute beast if he no longer possessed free will, he will have to argue against St. Paul who says that the natural man is enslaved, sold under sin, Rom. 7 [vv. 14, 25], and against Jesus Christ who proclaims that all who are not set free by Him are slaves, John 8 [vv. 31ff.].

15. Concerning the fifteenth, the ministers reply that Me Jerome has not adequately answered their question, and does nothing but cavil in his customary manner, thinking up subterfuges to cover up the error which he holds concerning free will; for he does not answer whether God bestows grace particularly on some rather than others when all have hearts as hard as stone.

16. Concerning the sixteenth, they say that Me Jerome's answer is not to the point; for the question put to him implies that the free love by which God has adopted us is the cause why He gives us faith. Jerome, however, contradicts what he has already said in answer to article 5, namely, that God does not love us when we are without faith. But now he declares that God loves us even when we are His enemies. And from this it follows that with God there is both before and after, which was precisely what he denied where the order of election was concerned. For before calling us He loves us as His creatures lost and damned in Adam; and after having called us He loves us as members of Jesus Christ who are formed again in His image.

17. The seventeenth and last article has no need of a reply.

* * * * *

These replies were presented to Messieurs, and Bolsec was called before the ministers who spoke with him personally pointing out to him clear passages from Scripture and from St. Augustine; for the books had been brought to the city hall. This was done on two separate days, with the result that Maître Jerome, not knowing what to say — apart from beating about the bush — said that the judgment of the neighbouring churches should be sought, and that he would submit himself to them. To this the ministers agreed.

Meanwhile he was forbidden by Messieurs to teach and order was given for him to leave prison on providing adequate security, but confining him to the city with a ban on his leaving it, on pain of being held as a defrauder and a wicked man.

As, however, Jerome did not produce the security he remained a prisoner in the palace.[39]

Messieurs gave orders that the preceding articles together with the answers and replies should be translated into Latin and sent to Basle, Zürich, and Berne; and this was done.

Articles Proposed by Jerome Bolsec to Maitre Jean Calvin Requiring Him to Answer Categorically and Without Human Reasoning or Empty Similitudes, but Simply by the Word of God

Firstly, whether he does not admit that every article of faith and every doctrine which is taught in the Church of our Lord ought to be proved by numerous authoritative passages from the whole of Scripture which are plain and evident and cannot be turned to a different meaning?

Whether he does not admit that one ought not to speak of God otherwise than Holy Scripture teaches, and that one should not add to or take from the Word, but accept it in simplicity?

Why it is that he adds to the words of St. Paul in Romans 9 [v. 17], where he speaks of Pharaoh, "I have raised thee up that My name might be declared", etc., putting more at the beginning than the text contains?

By what precise and manifest passage of Holy Scripture he is able to prove that the eternal will and decree of God are the cause of the sins which the wicked commit and of their perdition?

Which of the following two opinions is the better: that God compels men to sin or that he makes it inevitable without compulsion, and what is the difference that he finds between these two opinions; and let him prove which is the better by the Word of God?

Whether he does not admit that the wicked Jews held this opinion from the time of the prophet Ezekiel, as it is written in the 33rd chapter where they said that they were weighed down and overwhelmed with their sins and that it was impossible for them to do better and that they were bound to do evil?

Whether he wishes to deny that God refutes this wicked opinion in this same 33rd chapter [vv. 10f.] when He says to Ezekiel: "Therefore, O thou son of man, speak unto the house of Israel: Thus ye speak, saying, If our transgressions and our sins be upon us, etc.; say unto them, As I live, saith the Lord God, I have no pleasure in the death of the wicked, but that the wicked should turn from his way and live"?

Whether he does not admit that in ancient times the heretics

---

[39] *L'évêché;* see note 18, p. 138 above.

known as Cainites held such opinions, namely, that men are necessitated by the decree of God to sin and that all things are done by necessity, and whether he does not admit that they were condemned and refuted by the Greek doctor Epiphanius in his book against heresies?[40]

By what express and manifest authority of Holy Scripture does he prove what he has written in his *Institutes*, namely, that God has not created all men for the same end but some for salvation and others for perdition; and how does he harmonize such views with what is taught in the catechism preached in Geneva, namely, that the principal end and supreme good of man is to know God?

Since the creation is an act which proceeds from the goodness and love of God, as all theologians christianly hold, how is it credible that the goodness and love of God could have created some in order to kill and destroy them, seeing that killing and destroying are acts of hostility and hatred? — and let him base his answer on a plain text of the Word.

If the wicked were created by God to the end that they should not know God, but rather in order that they should be hardened, rebellious against God, and damned, how it is that they are rebellious, seeing that they do only what God wills and that for which they were created?

Whether there is an explicit text in Holy Scripture which teaches what he has written in his *Institutes*, namely, that not only did God foresee the fall of Adam, and in it the ruin of all his posterity, but also that He willed it thus and ordered and determined it thus by His own counsel?[41] — and let him quote the explicit and plain text.

What was it in Adam that caused him not only to be abandoned by God but also to be necessitated to sin, seeing that in him there was no original sin; and what is the cause of God's being able justly to forsake and damn the children of Adam?

While God counteracted the sin of Adam so gloriously by the blood of His Son Jesus Christ, and His name thereby became all the more glorious, how it is possible to say that God willed and determined that sin should be committed so that He might be glorified by this means, seeing that St. Paul says [Rom. 6:1f.]

---

[40] Epiphanius (c. 315-403) was Bishop of Salamis. His *Panarion* or *Refutation of All Heresies* was designed to describe and expose every heresy by which the Christian Church had been threatened. The Cainites are mentioned in chapter xxxviii. Earlier references to the heresy of the Cainites are found in Irenaeus, *Adversus Haereses*, I, xxxi; Hippolytus, *Refutation of All Heresies*, VIII, 20; and Pseudo-Tertullian, *Adversus Omnes Haereses*.

[41] Cf. *Institutes*, III, xxiii, 4ff.

that it is not right to do evil in order that good may come of it?

Let him quote the explicit text where what he says in his *Institutes* is written in the Word, namely that God wills and determines that all which He foresees should be done, and that He foresees only those things coming to pass which He has determined shall come to pass.

Whether it is honourably said of God and in harmony with the Word to say that God willed and ordained that the men of Sodom and Gomorrah should commit their vile and detestable sin against nature, that the Israelites should worship the golden calf, and likewise all other sins, of which God had foreknowledge? — and let his answer be based on Holy Scripture.

If the Sodomites and Israelites, together with all wicked men, did only what God willed and ordained, and that because they were created and necessitated to do so, how it is comprehensible that God should be angered, exasperated, and provoked to wrath, as Holy Scripture testifies? — and let his answer be based on explicit passages of Holy Scripture.

If there is in God a will other than that which is revealed to us in Holy Scripture, what is it called and how is it that he has knowledge of it, since it has not been revealed? — and let his answer be based on an explicit text of Scripture.

Let him prove from Scripture and explain how it is that God wills iniquity to be done, since it is written in Psalm 5 [v. 5], Ezekiel 18 [v. 32] and 33 [v. 11], and Wisdom 1 that God does not will iniquity.

Let him state whether there is any accident in God, and whether God's understanding, will, and memory are not the substance of God and God Himself.

Let him state how it is that there is simplicity in God, seeing that he says that there are two wills in God and how it is that there is unity, since in Him there are two contraries, to will and not to will, to please and not to please, to ordain and to forbid the same thing; and let his answer be based on Scripture and proved by explicit texts.

Since the will of God is the substance of God Himself, and is the cause of the sins which men commit, does it not follow that God is the cause and author of sins? Let his answer be based on the explicit text of the Word of God.

Since the written law is the declaration of the one and perpetual will of God, by which He forbids iniquity as displeasing to Him and commands righteousness as acceptable to Him, how can it be understood that God wills iniquity, seeing that God is immutable? Let his answer be based on the explicit text of Scripture.

Calvin's Reply

With reference to Me Jerome's assertion that he insists on the article that God is not the author of sin, there was no need at all for him to raise this question, since it is a doctrine which we have always preached and maintained in our writings — indeed, I have written a book on this very subject.

With reference to his assertion that Zwingli wrote a book entitled *De Providentia Dei* in which he teaches that God not only induces and urges men to sin but compels them, I have not the least doubt that this is an impudent calumny; for in so far as I have had leisure to read the book I have found all along that he says the exact contrary — indeed, in eight or ten of the book's pages he protests more than twenty times that God is neither the cause nor the author of sin and iniquity, and also opposes those who state that evil deeds are performed by the providence of God. When Me Jerome is compelled to point to the exact passage I hope that he will perceive his stupidity and malice in this as in other things. All, however, that he might be able to adduce from Zwingli would in no way help his defence, for he has come here to attack our doctrine of set purpose, and we are not obliged to maintain all that has been written by others. It is, therefore, a frivolous subterfuge to wish to accuse us in the person of another: let him go to Zürich to argue about Zwingli, if he so wishes.

As for myself, he falsely slanders me when he says that I have written that God necessitates men to sin. To begin with, this terminology that God necessitates is not my language but a jargon of monks which I never use. But it is also malicious impudence to say that I have ever applied the term sin to God or to His will. What I have said is that the will of God, in that it is the supreme cause, is the necessity of all things; but time and again I have stated that God for His part disposes and controls all that He does with such equity and justice that even the most wicked are compelled to glorify Him, and that His will is neither a tyranny nor an irrational whim but is in fact the true rule of all good. Moreover, I have particularly stated and affirmed that men are compelled to do neither good nor evil, but that those who do good do so of a free will which God gives them by His Holy Spirit, and that those who do evil do so of their own natural will which is corrupted and rebellious. Me Jerome is thus shown at every point to be a slanderer who perverts good doctrine and the pure truth of God.

He covers over, however, the errors and blasphemies which he has propounded, such as, for example, his assertion that we are not saved because we have been elected by God; again, that election does not precede faith; and again, that no one is reprobated solely because of the corruption of his nature. These are notorious heresies, and he has been sufficiently convicted of them.

He also passes over and hides the fact that he has called our doctrine the heresy of the Cainites, as though we were to say that Judas redeemed the human race when he betrayed Jesus Christ, and all the other wicked charges with which he has defamed the doctrine of God which we faithfully hold. He thinks, indeed, that the false accusations which he has made against us, especially that we have falsified passages from the Bible, will be forgotten.

He says nothing about his having exhorted the people to beware lest they be seduced and much else besides, even while he has been in prison; or about his having said, only a week ago, "Shame, shame, you and Calvin are all heretics!"; and that I had besought Messieurs even with tears that the matter might not be taken any further.

He attempts, finally, to hide the wicked and disgraceful errors which are involved in his doctrine, such as his assertion that God gives to all a heart capable of obeying Him by faith, which implies that He does not give the will, but that man of his own free will accepts, if he so chooses, the grace of the Holy Spirit, so that our election and salvation are founded upon our merits. He asserts, in fact, that man has not lost his free will and that if he did not have free will, he would be a beast.

Again, the error of his assertion that the grace of God is equal for all and that men decide for themselves whether they are saved or damned, as though God does not elect by His free goodness those whom it is His will to have for His children, and having elected them does not reform their hearts and affections in order to bring them to Jesus Christ, and as though, having brought them to Christ, He does not establish them right to the end.

COPY OF THE ARTICLES PRESENTED TO MESSIEURS BY THE MINISTERS FOR BOLSEC'S INTERROGATION[42]

1. Whether he did not condemn the doctrine of those who say that God has by His counsel determined whom it is His will to save or to damn, and what arguments he used in condemning this doctrine? Whether he did not say that this is a false and per-

---

[42] This new series of questions proposed to the judges by the ministers is not dated, but it was probably drafted by Calvin during the last days of October.

nicious opinion, most offensive to the Gospel, and whether he did not in fact call it a heresy?

2. Whether he did not say that this opinion originated with a certain Lorenzo Valla, and that very few men of good sense who are versed in theology accept it; indeed, that it is rejected by all the ancient theologians, and that those who hold it do St. Augustine great injustice by maintaining that he agrees with them?

3. Whether he did not show in his explanation that he directly opposed free election, denying that it is the cause of our salvation; and whether he did not make the assertion: "It is not said that men will be saved because God has elected them, but because they have believed"?

4. Whether he did not say that for the purpose of approving this false doctrine several passages from the Bible had been perverted and falsely expounded, indeed, that the passages themselves had been corrupted and falsified; and in particular whether he did not cite the 16th chapter of Proverbs [v. 4], saying that there was a French translation that ought to be corrected which states that God created the wicked for the day of iniquity?

5. Whether he did not say that a passage from St. Paul — the 9th chapter of Romans [v. 17] — had also been falsified to state that God raised up Pharaoh from eternity?

6. Whether he did not say that those who attribute the election of some and the reprobation of others to the will of God make Him an idol like Jupiter as the pagans used to do; and whether he did not cite in this connection a Latin verse, with the effect of attributing tyranny to God, namely: *Sic volo, sic jubeo, sit pro ratione voluntas*?[43]

7. Whether he did not say that by affirming that God has predestined to life or to death those whom He has willed He is made the author of evil and iniquity, and that occasion is given to blaspheme Him?

8. Whether he did not say that we open the way for the wicked to accuse God by saying that it is not their fault that they are damned?

9. Whether he did not urge the people to beware of this false doctrine (as he called it) which was so offensive, adding that he was speaking in assurance of the truth of God?

10. Whether he did not state quite openly that he wished to attack and condemn the doctrine which is preached here and which has hitherto been proclaimed in the Congregation?

---

[43] Juvenal, *Satires*, VI, 223.

11. Whether he did not repeatedly urge the people as mentioned, inciting them to rebel, if possible, and to cause trouble and division in the Church?

12. Whether he was not also responsible for other outrageous and harmful actions?[44]

[14 November 1551]

CORRESPONDENCE CONCERNING THE BOLSEC AFFAIR

I. *Copy of a Circular Letter Addressed by the Company of Pastors to the Swiss Churches*[45]

There is a certain Jerome here who, having abandoned the monk's cowl, became one of those wandering physicians who by deception and trickery accumulate so much impudence that they are ready and eager for any audacity. It is now eight months since this man endeavoured, in the public assembly of our church, to overthrow the doctrine of the free election of God which we, together with you, teach as it is received from the Word of God. At first, indeed his rashness was curbed with all possible moderation. But he did not cease to make a nuisance of himself everywhere with the purpose of shaking the simple from this article of the faith, until, more recently he belched forth his poison without restraint. For when, according to our custom, one of the brethren was expounding the passage in John where Christ declares that those who do not hear the Word of God are not of God, and had said that as many as are not born again of the Spirit of God obstinately resist God to the end, because obedience is a special gift which God bestows on His elect, this worthless

[44] There follows at this point a Latin translation of the questions put to Jerome Bolsec, his answers to them, and the subsequent rejoinders of the ministers, each question, answer, and rejoinder being taken in turn. Of these, numbers 1 to 3 are omitted, doubtless because they did not concern matters of doctrine, and also 7 and 17, because there was agreement on them — though the question introducing the 8th answer and rejoinder is in fact a conflation of questions 7 and 8. This Latin version was prepared for submission to the churches of Basle, Berne, and Zürich so that they might advise their colleagues in Geneva how they might bring this Bolsec case to a suitable conclusion. The inclusion of an English translation would be superfluous here, especially as any variations of the Latin from the French are of no particular significance.

[45] The copy of this letter in the Register is not dated, but the date is easily ascertainable from the original which is preserved in Zürich and reproduced in *Calvini Opera*, VIII, coll. 205ff. (For the date see next note). The address on the document in Zürich is in Calvin's hand.

fellow stood up and protested that it was a false and wicked opinion, invented by Lorenzo Valla, which had sprung up again in our day, that the will of God is the cause of all things. It was in this way, he said, that sin and the blame for all evils were ascribed to God, so that He became saddled with a tyrannical will such as the ancient poets had invented for their god Jupiter. Jerome then turned to the other article, affirming that men did not obtain salvation because they were elect, but that they were elect because they believe, and that no man was reprobated merely because God so willed it, but only those who turned away from the election which is common to all.

In raising this question he assailed us with many atrocious insults. On hearing of the matter the prefect of the city put him in prison, chiefly because he had incited the people in a tumultuous manner not to let themselves be deceived by us. Next, a report of the affair was made to the Council, where he proceeded to defend himself with no less obstinacy than temerity. Meanwhile, when he kept on claiming that there were many ministers in the other churches who agreed with him, we requested our Council not to pronounce a final judgment before the answer of your church had been received showing that this worthless fellow was dishonestly laying claim to your support. At first, being overcome with shame, he did not oppose this appeal to the churches, but he complained that because of your friendship with our brother Calvin you would naturally be prejudiced. The Council, however, resolved to consult you as we had requested. It is an additional fact that he has implicated your church, for, while condemning Zwingli above all others, he pretends that Bullinger is of one mind with him. He has even snatched cunningly at an opportunity for causing discord among the ministers of the territory of Berne.

Now, we desire that our church should be rid of this pestilential person, but in such a way that he does not become injurious to our neighbours. While, however, it is of great importance to us and to the public peace that the doctrine which we profess should be confirmed by your approval, yet there is no need for us to use many words in seeking your cooperation. Our brother Calvin's *Institutes,* which in particular Bolsec has presumed to attack, are not unknown to you. There is no point in our explaining with what reverence and moderation he discourses on the secret counsels of God, because his book is by itself an adequately clear witness. Nor, indeed, do we teach anything here except what is set forth in God's holy Word and has been held in your church ever since the restoration of the light of the Gospel.

It is generally agreed that we are justified by faith; but the substance of God's mercy is seen when we understand that faith is the fruit of free adoption, and that adoption is the consequence of the eternal election of God. This impostor, however, not only pretends that election depends on faith but also that faith itself springs no less from man's own impulse than from heavenly inspiration.

Again, it is not disputed that the fact that men perish is to be attributed to their own wickedness. But in the reprobate whom God by His secret counsel passes over and abandons as unworthy we are given a notable admonition of the need for humility. Jerome, however, will not grant that anything has been justly done by God unless the reason for it is plainly to be seen. But with us it is a settled and acknowledged doctrine that it is wrong to describe God as sharing in the blame for the sins of men or in any way to apply the notion of sin to Him. Yet this is not to deny that by some secret and incomprehensible counsel He manifests His power through Satan and the reprobate as instruments of His wrath, at one time instructing the faithful in patience, at another inflicting on His enemies such punishment as they deserve. But this profane trifler exclaims that when we make God's providence the explanation of all things we involve Him in guilt. In short, he removes all distinction between ultimate and hidden causes and proximate causes, so that, for example, he will not let us speak of the calamities with which holy Job was afflicted as the work of God without making God equally guilty with the devil and the Chaldean and Sabean robbers.

We trust, then, that, as the mutual fellowship between us demands, you will not scruple to uplift and affirm by your subscription the doctrine of Christ on which the impieties of this rash and irresponsible man have been heaped. Because we are confident that you will do this spontaneously and gladly it would be superfluous to bother you with tiresome and detailed petitions. You may count on us in turn to be always ready to fulfil our brotherly obligations whenever we can be of any service to you.

Farewell, most dear and estimable brethren. May the Lord govern you by His Spirit, bless your labours, and guard your church.[46]

---

[46] In the original there follow the date — 14 November 1551, in Calvin's hand — and the signatures:

Your brethren and colleagues,

Joannes Calvinus	Abelus Poupinus
Jacobus Bernardus	Ludovicus Trepperellus
Ludovicus Cogneus	Nicolaus Gallasius

Franciscus Bourgoinus
Raymondus Chauvetus
Michael Copus
A Sancto Andrea
M. Malisianus

Joannes Pyrerius
Nicolaus Parens
Joannes Faber
Joannes Baldinus
Philippus de Ecclesia

[21 November 1551]

II. Reply from the Ministers of Basle[47]

To the most excellent and learned servants of Christ, the pastors of the church of Geneva, their respected brethren and colleagues in the Lord — Greetings.

Respected brothers in the Lord, we have received your letter and have read and considered it as fully as possible in the short time available. It grieves us that Satan so tirelessly sows tares in godly churches, attempting to disturb our concord to the great peril of God's glory, and to damage other churches also by branding his mark on them. This affair points plainly to the extreme depravity of persons who act in this way. The nature of the trouble persuades us to send you a brief reply, for a longer reply would seem to be unnecessary and also the use of too many words might lay us open to suspicion in the eyes of some.

This Jerome is unknown to us, and no doubt we are unknown to him. We are sure, therefore, that he has no better knowledge of our doctrine: it is impertinent and mendacious of him, then, to claim us as companions of his error. We have long since made public the confession of our faith, and up till now it has been without blame. As, moreover, we handle everything in it in the simplest manner, so also in the place where we treat of election we do so in an orthodox manner. Perhaps we may say a word about our opinion on this subject. God has elected us in Christ Jesus before the foundation of the world, Eph. 1 [v. 4]. He sent the Word of the Gospel, which concerns Christ the Son of the living God: he who receives Him by faith is saved; he who does not receive Him is condemned, Mk. 16 [vv. 15f.]. This Word is sent throughout the whole world, for God wishes all men to be

---

[47] The Register contains the original of this letter, written in the hand of Myconius. It is reproduced in *Calvini Opera*, VIII, coll. 234ff. Oswald Geisshäuser who was known as Myconius (1488-1552) was a native of Lucerne. He studied in Basle where he associated himself with Erasmus, and subsequently he collaborated with Zwingli in Zürich. After Zwingli's death he returned to Basle and succeeded Oecolampadius as head of the church there.

saved and to come to a knowledge of the truth, I Tim. 2 [v. 4]. He is the common God of all; Christ is the common Saviour of all.

But not all believe who hear. The Father does not draw all. For Christ says in Jn. 6 [v. 44]: "No man can come unto me, except the Father which hath sent me draw him. . . . It is written in the prophets, And they shall be all taught of God". Those, therefore, whom He draws believe; those whom He does not draw do not believe; and among the latter are those who are drawn, as we say, and yet do not believe because they refuse God's drawing. They do as Christ says in Jn. 3 [v. 19]: "This is the condemnation, that light is come into the world, and men loved darkness rather than light". Carnal desire takes pleasure in sin and openly despises the life which is of God. Such persons, then, while they are condemned, are the cause of their own condemnation, just as those who are saved have reason for thanksgiving, since it was not in their power to be drawn. While, therefore, the latter give thanks because they have been effectively drawn, the rest might seem to have cause for complaint against God, because they have not been drawn with good effect. This only we say: what takes place is plain enough; but why it takes place is due to a hidden cause which God alone knows. Nor it is for us to inquire into this cause. But this much is certain: that they rejected the Word which was preached to them because it was contrary to their inclinations.

The remaining questions which are seen to be in doubt we leave to God. While they may be reverently investigated by us, yet, if we genuinely wish to know something for our own peace, it is better that we should start from faith rather than from the foreknowledge of God or from predestination and election, except as necessity requires, as we have briefly shown: and this is especially desirable when we are instructing the simple, for in this way our teaching is not bound up with doubtful questions by which it could be side-tracked, but is given with prayers for the acquisition of faith which is fruitful in good works. You see then our simplicity with regard to this question, which is the most difficult and intricate in religion. And so we ask the Lord to keep us in this simplicity right to the end. We do not wish, however, to be accused of obstinacy: if anyone can give us better instruction from the Word, our acquiescence will be unhesitating and prompt.

It is in this way that we wish to reply to your very clear letter. We contribute nothing to the dispute which you have described except what we offer in this letter — which seems to us much more straightforward than the conflicting views of a disputation. This fellow Jerome, indeed, not only acts the sophist but also seems in some respects to smack of heresy. We have noted the examples you give. We know of no way in which what he twists as a saying of Valla applies to us; for we attribute to God nothing but mercy and goodness and similar qualities. We simply state therefore that we are elected in Christ, that faith follows the Word heard and received, and that those who have faith and keep it to the end are saved, while those who do not have it are condemned. If election took place before the foundation of the world, it must necessarily be so. Let this man seek others, then, to support his errors: we are otherwise instructed by the Word of God. We affirm also that we are justified by faith, by means of which we make Christ ours together with every merit of His passion, as befits the elect of God, for He elects them in Christ. Those who lack this faith are not justified, because they also lack election and the adoption of sons and whatever belongs to the inheritance of the kingdom.

Here, then, you have the response which we felt we should give to your letter. We think that there is nothing which can be offensive to you or which is not catholic. Take our brevity and simplicity in good part, therefore. Greetings in the Lord to you and your church, and please for your part pray God for us.

Basle, 21 November 1551

Vuolfgangus Vuissenburgus Thomas Gyrfalconius
Marcus Persius Valentius Boltz
M. Simon Sultzerus Osvaldus Myconius[48]
Jacobus Truckenbrot

[48] These names are all written in the hand of Myconius; thus they are not properly signatures.

[21 November 1551]

III. Letter from Simon Sulzer to Calvin[49]

To his most distinguished and respected brother and colleague in the Lord, John Calvin: Greetings.

It grieves us greatly that your church is being troubled by this irresponsible man whose nature is, it would seem, to stir up strife. Myconius, however, has already written in our name about this. But we are much more grieved and distressed because of the persecution which you tell us has broken out afresh as a result of the King's public edict and which is being carried out with the shedding of the blood of many martyrs;[50] for just at this very time numerous persons had caused us to hope that shortly a door for the Gospel would be opened in France. But Schärtlin's son,[51] who recently arrived here, intimated that a royal decree had been proclaimed forbidding for the present that anybody should be put to torture in the name of religion, which has caused some to think that the report that has reached you is either false or at least exaggerated. Nevertheless we resolved unanimously that our magistracy should be approached and requested to take up the cause of Christ and our afflicted brethren, together with the three other evangelical orders. When I acted accordingly yesterday I brought back a most favourable reply, namely, that they would consult with the Bernese first of all, to whom a delegation will be sent in the near future. An agreement with them should

---

[49] The Register contains the original of this letter. The pastor and theologian Simon Sulzer, a native of Berne, was associated with Calvin and especially Viret, in spite of his Lutheran sympathies which became more marked each year. In 1548 he was banished from Berne following the colloquy of Lausanne on the holy supper, in which he sided with Viret. He settled in Basle, where he served as a minister and ultimately succeeded Myconius as *antistes*. This letter, less official than the preceding one, is the reply to a personal letter written from Lausanne a few days previously by Calvin and addressed to Myconius and Sulzer.

[50] The edict of Chateaubriand, issued on 27 June and registered by the Parliament of Paris on 2 September, was a considerable intensification of the rigorous measures already taken against the Evangelicals of France.

[51] Sebastian Schärtlin, knight of Burtenbach, was a noted adventurer of war in the service at first of Charles V and the city of Augsburg, but afterwards he passed over to the service of the Reformation and the city of Basle. He was proscribed by the Emperor and judged an undesirable person by the Diet in 1550, despite his friendship with Bullinger. Thereafter, together with his elder son Hans Sebastian, who was also a military leader — and undoubtedly the one to whom reference is made here — he entered the service of the king of France, though remaining a Protestant.

make it possible to undertake fruitful intercession with the king for the mitigation of this cruel edict. They will also communicate with Zürich and Schaffhausen. For, since they have brought back an unsympathetic reply to the letter which was given to this man's father, Francis, they feel that careful consideration should be given to the method by which the king may be most easily and effectively influenced, and it is probable that they will arrange the sending of a delegation for this purpose. Moreover, so that I may promote this by every possible means, I shall assiduously commend this course to our trusted friends in Berne, and I think that you and our brother Viret ought to take the first opportunity to do the same. I hope, however, that you will let us have even fuller information concerning such things as have been definitely and reliably reported to you from France; for we have more confidence in you than in rumours brought from elsewhere.

We have no news except that a letter tells us that Magdeburg has at last been liberated from its blockade, on tolerable terms, thanks to the zeal of certain good and distinguished men.[52] It has not yet been possible to ascertain the nature of these terms; I entertain the hope, however, that this church, which hitherto has been so obedient to Christ, has been mercifully treated by the Lord, and that in the future it will be zealous for the glory of His name.

Farewell now, my most dear and respected brother in the Lord. Salute your colleagues for me.

Basle, 21[53] November 1551

Entirely yours,

Simon Sultzerus

[52] Magdeburg had capitulated on 3 November after a famous siege and a heroic defence; but liberty of religion was accorded to the inhabitants of the conquered city.

[53] The paper has been torn so that the second figure in this date is missing. But the date of the letter from Myconius, which arrived in Geneva at the same time, makes it reasonable to conclude that this letter from Sulzer was written on the same date, namely, 21 November 1551.

[27 November 1551]

IV. Reply from the Ministers of Zürich[54]

To the most distinguished men and faithful pastors of the Church of Christ at Geneva, most respected doctors and ministerial colleagues and our most dear brothers:

We have been greatly grieved to hear, dear brethren, that the church which the good Lord has appointed you to serve has been troubled; for we recognize and acclaim the outstanding gifts which the Lord has generously bestowed on you and your church. Not only is it a refuge for faithful men who have been driven from their fatherland by savage tyranny, but also the preaching of the truth, which is the proclamation of Christ, has gone forth from it into the neighbouring territories and throughout the whole of France. This gives Satan no pleasure, for he is the enemy of the pure truth and of Christ's glory. He rages, therefore, and strives to trouble and scatter your church. At no time since the restoration of evangelical doctrine have we been more savagely assailed by antichrist and his master the devil, the prince of darkness, than at present, when we find him not only arraying against us the most powerful rulers through the instigation of false bishops and prophets, but also raising up false brethren in our very midst, stirring up quarrels and altercations, and inciting innumerable libertines and the fury of the populace. And all these things conspire to bring it about that our ministry may be disparaged and dismissed, the churches of Christ troubled and scattered, and once again falsehood, imposture, and antichristianity may gain the ascendance. If ever there was a time for vigilance, it is now most of all plain that we should watch and pray, for should we be deprived of grace from above and the protection of the eternal God we could easily be scattered by some trifling incident.

With regard to this present affair of Jerome, we suggest that every avenue should be explored to see whether you cannot come together in mutual understanding and be reconciled in the Lord. In your judgment Jerome has conducted his case in an intemperate manner; but, our brothers, we look for moderation in you also,

---

[54] This document in the Register is beyond doubt the original letter, since its two pages carry the customary marks of folding; moreover, the writing does not correspond to the hand of any of the Genevan pastors who, acting as secretaries of the Company, might have had the task of copying the text of this letter. At the same time, however, it bears no signature, nor exterior address, nor evidence of sealing. It could have been joined to another fold. The letter is reproduced in *Calvini Opera*, VIII, coll. 229ff.

for you seem in your letter which has been given to us to be extremely severe. It is important ever to remember that prophetic and evangelical utterance descriptive of Christ our Lord: "He will not strive, nor cry out, nor will anyone hear his voice in the streets; a bruised reed He will not break, and smoking flax He will not quench, until He brings forth judgment unto victory" [Is. 42:2f.]. While we do not deny that we have to deal more strictly with those who are incorrigible and stubborn, yet we do not wish to tighten the chains of a captive man, unknown to us, as we have not been appointed his judges.

As for the doctrinal issue over which you have been disputing, there was no need for you to ask our opinion concerning election and reprobation, and concerning faith and human ability, since you cannot be ignorant of what it is, especially from our last consensus, in which we consider this question has been fully covered. But since others interpret differently what we have said, and good men among you desire to hear once again our view, concisely set forth, so that they may be able, though not present with you and us, to form a judgment concerning the agreement or disagreement in our doctrine, we propose to set forth the following few points for the consideration of the godly.

In the first place, we maintain that election, by which God from eternity elects undeserving sinners and embraces them in Christ, and through which we have all things that pertain to life and salvation, is entirely gratuitous and that the whole salvation of man (which is the foundation of faith) is to be attributed to the free mercy of God, as the apostle says: "It is not of him that willeth, nor of him that runneth, but of God that showeth mercy" [Rom. 9:16]; and again: "He hath chosen us in him before the foundation of the world, that we should be holy and without blame before Him in love, having predestinated us unto the adoption of children by Jesus Christ to himself, according to the good pleasure of His will, to the praise of the glory of His grace, wherein He hath made us accepted in the beloved" [Eph. 1:4ff.].

Secondly, we teach that the faith by which we embrace Christ is not obtained because of any merits of our own, but that it is given by the mere grace of God through the Spirit and the Word, and that the same grace of God increases and preserves the same faith in us, as the apostle says: "Unto you it is given in the behalf of Christ not only to believe in Him but also to suffer for His sake" [Phil. 1:29]; and elsewhere the apostles say: "Lord, increase our faith" [Lk. 17:5]. Accordingly Augustine writes, in chapter 3 of his work on the Predestination of the Saints, that we know that faith is preceded by grace. Hence we attribute nothing to the unregenerate powers of men except corruption, willful sin, blame, and punishment, and to those who are regenerate by the Spirit of God we attribute the willing performance of good on account of the Spirit of God, as the apostle says: "The natural man receiveth not the things of the Spirit of God" [I Cor. 2:14]; and again: "We are not sufficient of ourselves to think anything as of ourselves, but our sufficiency is of God" [II Cor. 3:5]. Elsewhere he speaks to the same effect: "It is God who worketh in you both to will and to do of His good pleasure" [Phil. 2:13]. Again, in the Gospel we read: "If the Son shall make you free, ye shall be free indeed" [Jn. 8:36]. "For where the Spirit of the Lord is, there is liberty" [II Cor. 3:17]. None the less we know that the remnants of the flesh remain, for, as the apostle teaches, what we do not wish we do, and so with the mind we serve the law of God, but with the flesh the law of sin [Rom. 7:15, 25], so that throughout the whole of life the regenerate man finds that what he does is done by grace. This was the experience of David when he said: "Enter not into judgment with thy servant, for in thy sight shall no man living be justified" [Ps. 143:2].

Thirdly, the fact that the reprobate do not believe the Word of God, but wickedly live in opposition to God, ought to be attributed to them, not to God, who justly and condignly condemns those whom He condemns, since it is in man, not in God, that sin inheres. "As for God, His way is perfect" [Ps. 18:30], and God does not will iniquity. "The Lord is righteous in all His ways, and holy in all His works" [Ps. 145:17].

Finally, we do not remove the proper order from the process of salvation. We neither reject nor confuse proximate and remote causes. We acknowledge that God laid His hand on Job in excess of his guilt. We acknowledge that He made use of Satan and his hosts, who, however, are least of all to be absolved from guilt, because their eye was evil. But Job himself bears witness: "The Lord gave and the Lord hath taken away" [Job 1:21]; he says not: "The Lord gave and the devil hath taken away."

This is our view, concisely set forth in this letter, and more fully explained in our writings and from it those who wish to do so may, without being present, and without fear or favour, easily form a judgment concerning our agreement or disagreement. We love you as brothers, we love your church, and with all our heart we pray the Lord graciously and kindly to bring all your troubles to a happy conclusion. Pray the Lord for us. Long may you live and flourish, respected and beloved masters and brothers in Christ.

Zürich, 27 November 1551

[22 December 1551]

V. *Reply from M. Farel and the Ministers of Neuchâtel*[55]

To our most respected brethren and colleagues the pastors of the most holy assembly in Geneva, servants of our Lord Jesus distinguished for the excellence both of their piety and of their doctrine: Greetings.

May Christ Jesus, who conquered and triumphed on the cross, preserve your church, which in the past has been assailed and molested in so many ways and all but destroyed, and is now attacked by Satan with all his force. Christ was betrayed by one man, Judas, deserted by the eleven, arraigned before one man, Annas, and subsequently before his son-in-law Caiaphas, and was condemned to death by conspiring enemies. Then he was taken before Pilate, by whom He was sent to Herod, and at last was condemned by a judge who pronounced Him innocent, because he knew that it was on account of envy that He had been handed over. Good God! how many Judases has the Church had as traitors; how many times has she been sold at home and abroad; how long and how many times she has been deserted by almost all the churches! They know who have laboured to establish and preserve her. How many high priests have condemned to death how many leaders, to say nothing of private individuals! Not only have the scribes and Pharisees conspired with the priests, racked with envy, to bring about the ruin of the Church, but even those who wished to be regarded as foremost among the heralds of the Gospel. Neither the Pilates nor the Herods nor any other powers that the world admires can tell how the Church was able to survive even for a single hour so many and such great assaults. Nobody came to you who did not hear terrible things openly uttered of your church and especially of its pastor, whom the ravagers of the flock hate beyond measure. Inside the city nothing was heard but the most offensive language of the envious; between cups in all the drinking-houses nothing was left unsaid against the church, even what should have been to her commendation. And these things were also done at home by

---

[55] The Register contains the original of this letter, which bears, at the foot of the second page, four signatures. The first could be that of Fabri; but Farel has added, undoubtedly in his own hand, a brief postscript. The letter is reproduced in *Calvini Opera*, XIV, coll. 221ff.

pastors of whom the church and its members deserved well, and whom formerly godly pastors had acknowledged as brothers and colleagues in the work of the Lord. What do we think was done by wicked men far distant, *Cortesios, Carolos et id genus impios*?[56] But although all these things caused many to fall, yet they could not prevent your church from daily rising, growing, and becoming more illustrious, numerous, and saintly. Now at length Satan and all who are his have taken the step of selecting an instrument most fitted to the perdition of himself and others, namely, this altogether profane fellow Jerome, who is no better versed in holy things than the filthiest pig, without the least fear or reverence profanely overturning everything with his unclean snout; and who with his fellow-conspirators has taken it upon himself to attack the ark in which the godly trust and, moreover, to stir up that question which enrages the wicked and, as he is busy doing, to remove the godly from the most firm rock of election on which they know that they are established in Christ, to whom they have been drawn by the Father because they are elect from eternity, for which no cause can be given or assigned except the sole will of God as He elects whom He wills.

Again, he tries to construct a cause of reprobation other than the will of God and shamelessly proceeds to deny that there is such a thing as reprobation and predestination to death from eternity. And when that outstanding elected instrument says that it is not of him who wills nor of him who runs, but of God who shows mercy, having mercy on whom He will and hardening whom He will [Rom. 9:16, 18]; and when he refers explicitly to the hidden and incomprehensible counsel of God, he most fittingly, but at the same time most simply, answers every query that can be raised: "O man, who art thou that repliest against God? Shall the thing formed say to him that formed it, Why hast thou made me thus? Hath not the potter power over the clay, of the same lump to make one vessel unto honour and another unto dishonour?" [Rom. 9:20f.]. This simple and absolute answer ought to be sufficient for all men, and for us especially it should be sufficient that God so wills and decrees things. And since His will is most holy and blessed, it ought to be accepted and reverenced by us, not accused and blamed as the cause of evil, seeing that God is the author and cause of such great good. Since, indeed, we rightly acknowledge that God is the author and creator of all

---

[56] These words, underlined in the original, are presumably, an allusion to the persecutions sanctioned by the French court.

things that exist (and only a wicked or insane man would say that He is the creator of things which have never been formed) in such a way that it is well with His creatures and they enjoy a life of blessedness, it is from God alone that they have this, not from themselves, but it is of grace and mercy which through the kindness of God the elect experience in accordance with His eternal decree. And, contrariwise, the failure of the reprobate to achieve this and to live is due to themselves alone, because they are not participants of grace and mercy and have not been endowed with eternal life, but are left to themselves so that they deservedly perish, as from eternity they have been ordained as vessels of wrath.

But, without wishing to be invidious, who has explained all these things in a purer, truer, and more godly manner than our brother Calvin in his superb *Institutes,* where he treats of predestination? Let Jerome and any other mortal man bite and gnaw; they will not be able to overthrow any point of a truth so sure and settled, but they will only bring upon themselves what is foretold of those who dash themselves against a rock, that is, they will be broken to pieces. We are greatly encouraged, most dear brethren, because in what is holy, good, and right you all feel and approve the same things. You have also received godly instruction from that great servant of God whom you share with us — may Christ preserve him for you and you with him! As for that ungodly trouble-maker and all his associates, if they do not repent God will punish them severely. We had heard earlier from Farel that he was behaving wickedly and entertained ungodly opinions; and now your letter informs us more fully of the obstinacy of this villainous wretch who tries to overthrow and confuse everything which our brother Calvin has written and proved concerning God's hidden counsel of election and reprobation and which you religiously hold and teach together with him. We also, indeed, have held and taught the same from the time when the Gospel began to be preached again, as now we still hold and teach it. We believe that the good will of God, which approves the godly and teaches them to be patient and also punishes the wicked, is as far from the bad will of the devil and the ungodly as God is removed from Satan and the ungodly who are impelled by Satan. Moreover, when God allows evil things to happen to us we must realize that the purpose is that as suppliants we should reverence and call upon Him, that in His holiness and benevolence He may turn things to the advantage and benefit of His own whom He has elected; and again when we see Satan and those whom he impels labouring only for our ruin and performing all kinds of mischief, we should pray to be delivered from him.

This sacrilegious insolence is the greatest affront to the supreme majesty of God when it involves Him in the crime of the devil and the Chaldeans and others who ill-treated Job. He is a treacherous subverter of Scripture if he denies that Job truly said that the Lord gave and the Lord took away, and that it came to pass according to the Lord's good pleasure. Such great impiety can in no way be tolerated. God has ordered that those who are in positions of leadership have a duty to discharge in removing stumbling-blocks from the Church and in preventing disturbers of the peace from troubling the Church and the godly.

This is the reply, respected brothers, which in the short time available we would offer to your letter. We must not be content with human reason and we must not pretend to a false kind of simplicity. We must not, on the plea of having something else to do, desert the godly and their cause; nor must we favour the ungodly man who, despite many warnings, always goes from bad to worse, and for whom it is as natural to be false as it is foreign to good men. We have been content to remain in apostolic simplicity respecting the clay and the potter and the vessels made unto honour and unto dishonour; and we have been content to accept and admire God's wisdom, will, and eternal counsel, rather than invent untruths and objections with shameless Jerome [see Rom. 9:20f., 11:33ff.]. You have dealt with this matter wisely and we believe that all good men will approve what you have done. May the Lord Jesus preserve you and His holy people together with the government, removing all who are reprobate.

Farewell, and please assist us with your prayers, as we also pray for you. Be mindful of Toussain.[57]

Neuchâtel, 22 December 1551

Your [58] true brethren in the Lord, who desire not only to approve by letter your holy and pure doctrine concerning God's foreordination and to condemn the impious and sacrilegious Jerome, but also to bear witness to it by word of mouth and, if possible, to

---

[57] Pierre Toussain. Concerning his circumstances, see pp. 87ff., 93ff. above. During the last months of 1551 the situation in Montbéliard seemed critical for Toussain and his colleagues; and the citizens of Neuchâtel, their near neighbour, were disturbed by it.

[58] This paragraph is in a different hand, beyond doubt Farel's.

do so openly and more fully. I Farel have signed in the name of all together with several of the officers and delegates.

Fabri[59]
P. Clementi[60]
Johannes Drogy[61]
Grury[62]

[59] The four signatures that follow are autographs. Christophe Fabri had been a colleague of Farel since 1546, and later became his successor.
[60] Pierre Clément was professor and pastor in Neuchâtel.
[61] This was probably Jean Droz, pastor at Bevaix.
[62] This person has not been identified.

[9 January 1552]

VI. Letter from Oswald Myconius of Basle[1]

To the learned and pious John Calvin, Christ's minister in the church of Geneva, his respected brother and colleague in the Lord: Greetings.

We have received a letter written on the 4th of January this year by Bolsec from prison,[2] in which he says that he is surprised that we dissent from him and also that we call him a heretic since he entirely approves our opinion. He requests that we should write again on these matters. Accordingly on 8 January we consulted as to what should be done here; for it was felt that no action should be taken without your knowledge, especially in the case of one who is being held in captivity. A courier is leaving shortly for Geneva. Therefore I seized my pen, since the Lord seemed to have provided this man at an opportune moment. I shall briefly set down what we wish to tell you. We would like to know what your judgment is of our opinion now that Bolsec has said that it is the same as his; for if this is the case, we have misunderstood the brethren's letter, since it contains things from which we dissent as well. For example: where they write that he holds that "men do not obtain salvation because they are elect but are elect because they believe". This is directly opposed to what Paul writes about our being elect in Christ before the

[1] The letter in the Register is the original in the hand of Myconius. It is reproduced in *Calvini Opera*, coll. 239f.
[2] This letter from Bolsec has not been found.

foundation of the world [Eph. 1:4]. Here we do not agree with him at all. We ask, therefore, whether you would say that we agree with him, for we do not wish to send him any reply before hearing from you. And if what you say does not accord with our thought, we will give a clearer declaration of our belief. For we value you and your whole church so highly that we have no desire to dissent lightly from you on account of a single individual whose doctrine and whose person are both unfamiliar to us. We hear from some that he is not a bad man; nevertheless, we prefer to believe those whose trustworthiness we have known and experienced hitherto, so long as nothing different is established — an eventuality which we do not anticipate.

Beyond this we have not said, nor do we wish it said, that he is a heretic, since we are not convinced that he is such. But we wrote as follows: "This fellow Jerome, indeed, not only acts the sophist but also seems in some respects to smack of heresy". We added an example which explained what we had in mind. You will see from these few lines what we wish to know from you in this protracted business. We do not wish our churches to be divided just when the Papists are striving to destroy them utterly, and that too with human ravings. We have enough enemies, and we do not want more, if it can be avoided. Men whom we would least wish are rising from our midst, among whom is Osiander[3] who has invented something previously unknown to us on the subject of justification. We shall write about this on another occasion, if you are unaware of it.

Greetings to you with the brothers in the Lord. Basle, 9 January 1552

Yours,

Os. Myconius

in the name of the brethren.

We have sent a note to Bolsec so that he may know why we have not written.

---

[3] Andreas Hosemann, known as Osiander, (1498-1552) the German Reformer and theologian who had participated in the Marburg Colloquy (1529) and the Augsburg Diet (1530), had published his work on justification in 1550. This work constituted a departure from the Reformed position in that he maintained that justification was far more than the imputation to the believer of Christ's righteousness in that it was the actual impartation of that righteousness. Thomas Cranmer married Osiander's niece in 1552, the same year that he was appointed Archbishop of Canterbury.

[11 December 1551]

Decision on the Trouble Caused by Bolsec

On Friday 11 December[4] the ministers decided that as the communion was getting near, it would be well to remedy this trouble which had been caused by Maître Jerome, so that steps could be taken to ensure that the sacrament was not polluted by any who might have been infected with his error. In order to do this it was resolved that on the following Friday the matter should be placed before the Congregation, with M. Calvin explaining the situation and then each of the ministers in order adding briefly what our Lord had given him for the confirmation of doctrine.

This was done on the following Friday, which was the 18th; and all the ministers, both from the city and from the country, announced one after the other their judgment concerning this matter.

On Thursday the 23rd[5] of the month Maître Jerome was banished to the sound of the trumpet from the territory of Geneva.

[4] That is, in the year 1551.

[5] Thursday was the 24th. On the preceding day, Wednesday the 23rd, the sentence was registered by the Council and thereby rendered effective; but it is very likely that the sentence was not in fact executed until the next day.

1552

Syndics: On Sunday 7 February 1552 Messieurs Bouteiller,[6] Philippin,[7] Hudroid du Molard,[8] and Vandel[9] were elected as syndics.

[March 1552]

BANISHMENT OF M. JEAN DE SAINT-ANDRE
FROM BERNESE TERRITORY

On Sunday[10] M. Jean de Saint-André, minister of Jussy, was arrested when on his way to preach at Foncenex and imprisoned at Gaillard by the officers of that place for having said and preached that those who had received communion on Christmas Day had received the communion of Christmas and not of Jesus

---

[6] Jean-Ami Curtet, known as Bouteiller, was one of the most considerable and influential statesmen of the young Seigneury. He was entrusted with numerous diplomatic missions, and between 1530 and 1565 was syndic on nine occasions. He died in 1567.

[7] Jean Philippin was perhaps less remarkable as a personality than Bouteiller, but this was the sixth term as syndic. He managed to keep himself above the quarrels of his fellow-citizens and thus was able to render great services to his troubled city. He died in 1556.

[8] Hudriod du Molard, another distinguished Genevan statesman, personified and on more than one occasion was the mouthpiece of the old-style Genevans against the policy which favoured the admission of foreigners. In 1555, a year in which he was Lieutenant (cf. p. 306), he became involved in the affair of the Libertines, and, although he could not be identified with them, he voluntarily chose exile, quitting Geneva in 1556.

[9] Pierre Vandel, unlike du Molard, was closely associated with Ami Perrin as one of the leading Libertines, and was opposed to Calvin from the beginning, while at the same time being one of the most determined shapers of Genevan independence. Following the events of 1555, he fled and was condemned to death for contumacy.

[10] The date is left blank in the Register.

Christ, making more of that day than of any other, as though the sanctity of the supper depended on days. For this he was cruelly treated in prison and banished from the territory of Messieurs of Berne.[11]

DIFFICULTIES OVER APPOINTMENT TO JUSSY

After Saint-André had returned to this city Messieurs ordered the election of a minister who should be sent to Jussy and that Saint-André should serve in the city. Accordingly, the brethren of both country and city assembled on 18 March and proceeded to an election. After calling on the name of God they gave order that Maître Philippe de Ecclesia should go to Jussy and Maître Jean Fabri to Vandoeuvres in place of de Ecclesia. De Ecclesia, however, was unwilling to acquiesce in this arrangement and advanced a number of objections which the brethren were unable to accept. De Ecclesia then said that he would bring his objections before Messieurs and that if Messieurs ordered him to go to Jussy he would go, but not otherwise. Fabri agreed to go to Vandoeuvres.

On the following Monday M. Calvin, M. Abel,[12] Jacques Bernard, and Mathieu[13] appeared before Messieurs and announced what the ministers had resolved. De Ecclesia replied to this, excusing himself from going to Jussy. Fabri also spoke to the same effect. Thereupon Messieurs ordered that de Ecclesia should remain at Vandoeuvres and Fabri in the city, and that the ministers should proceed to a new election.

When the ministers objected that they could not have acted better and more conscientiously than they had done, and could not choose others than those they had already chosen, Messieurs said that if they did not hold a new election then they would do so themselves. Moreover, when the brethren held fast to their decision, Messieurs sent word by the *sautier*[14] to M. François Bourgoin that it was their wish that he should go to Jussy in order to preach and reside there. M. Bourgoin reported this to the breth-

---

[11] Foncenex, which was a short distance from Jussy, belonged at that time to the Bernese mandate of Gaillard. Calvin travelled to Berne to defend Saint-André, but in vain. Saint-André was banished from Bernese territory and in consequence was unable to continue his ministry in the Bernese village of Foncenex, which was attached to the Genevan parish of Jussy. This necessitated certain changes in the allocation of the Genevan pastors.

[12] That is, Abel Poupin.

[13] That is, Mathieu Malesier. In the Register a blank space is left for the surname.

[14] See note 29 (p. 147) above.

ren, who, after calling on the name of God, resolved to appear before Messieurs to object that they ought not and could not proceed in this way when appointing or moving ministers, and that it meant the breaking of ecclesiastical order and policy. This was duly done. Messieurs, however, held fast to their first decision.

Bourgoin now informed the brethren that, as he had no testimony to this call other than the wish of Messieurs, he could not vacate his present post to go to the country, and that the assurance which he had had hitherto in the exercise of his office was entirely the result of his legitimate calling in accordance with ecclesiastical order; if this was lacking, he could not continue to exercise his ministerial office with a good conscience. He therefore requested the brethren to consider this and give him their counsel, protesting that if he was not sent with their approval and consent he would resign from the ministry.

Thereupon, on Friday 22 April, the brethren both of country and city decided that Bourgoin had no just reason for resigning and that for the time being it would be better for him to accept this constraint, with which, however, none of the brethren were in agreement. The following Monday two ministers from the city and two from the country appeared before Messieurs to protest that we could not give our consent to so violent an infraction of ecclesiastical order, since such an example could only be prejudicial to the future.

When Me Jean Fabri's turn came to speak, he announced that he was prepared to go to Jussy and that he would announce this before Messieurs. This was approved by the brethren both because it resolved the situation and also because it deprived Messieurs of any pretext that at the beginning he had not consented to go to Jussy.

On the 25th day of the same month Calvin and Fabri appeared before Messieurs together with two brethren of the country in order to present their objections, as above. Messieurs, none the less, declared that they held fast to what they had ordered[15]

Meanwhile, however, de Ecclesia was accused by someone

---

[15] The reason for the opposition of the Council to the Company's decisions is not clear, nor do the Council's Registers throw any light on the situation; but no doubt this disagreement was a reflection of the state of tension existing between the partisans of Calvin with their favourable attitude to foreigners and the defenders of traditional Genevan exclusivism. In the number of the latter there were, as we have seen, at least two syndics, namely, du Molart and Vandel (notes 8 and 9, p. 187 above).

called Osias[16] of having committed certain acts of usury and was admonished by the brethren to clear himself. Messieurs were advised of this and undertook an investigation.[17]

The brethren were also informed that de Ecclesia was on familiar terms with Maître Jerome Bolsec and that Bolsec had urged him to conceal these acts of usury.

They were informed, further, that on Easter Day de Ecclesia had preached that the body of Jesus Christ is not in one particular place, but is everywhere.

[3 June 1552]

VISITATION OF PARISHES

In the general Congregation on 3 June, which was the day of censures before Whitsun, the brethren ordered that the visitations of the country parishes should be carried out in the customary manner. They deputed Calvin, Abel,[18] and des Gallars to do this and decided that in the meantime Messieurs should be informed. Accordingly, on the following Monday, the 6th day of the month, Calvin appeared before them, and at his request they ordered that the visitation should take place and deputed as their representatives Messieurs Jean Chautemps and Claude de Lestral.

The visitation was commenced on Sunday 24 July by des Gallars with M. Claude de Lestral, accompanied by one of Messieurs' officers. On that day they went to Jussy and Foncenex, where Me François Bourgoin was officiating for the time being.

On Sunday 31 July Me Abel went with the delegates named above to Russin and Dardagny.

On Sunday 7 August Monsieur Calvin went to Satigny.

On Sunday 14 August Me Abel went to Chancy and Cartigny.

On 21 August des Gallars visited Nédan and Bossey.

On the 28th Me Abel visited Céligny and Genthod.

On 18 September des Gallars went to Moëns.

---

[16] Osias, or Ozias Martin, was an inhabitant of Thonon.

[17] De Ecclesia had already been the cause of much trouble to the Company (see pp. 92f., 105ff., 133 above). The present case is resumed on pp. 201ff. below.

[18] That is, Abel Poupin.

[July 1552]

LETTER FROM FIVE STUDENTS IN PRISON IN LYON[19]

To our brothers of the church of Geneva: Grace and peace from our good God and Father through Jesus Christ our Saviour be multiplied to you. Amen!

Very dear brothers in our Lord Jesus Christ, since you have been informed of our captivity and of the fury which drives our enemies to persecute and afflict us, we felt it would be good to let you know of the liberty of our spirit and of the wonderful assistance and consolation which our good Father and Saviour gives us in these dark prison cells, so that you may participate not only in our affliction of which you have heard but also in our consolation, as members of the same body who all participate in common both in the good and in the evil which comes to pass. For this reason we want you to know that although our body is confined here between four walls, yet our spirit has never been so free and so comforted, and has never previously contemplated so fully and so vividly as now the great heavenly riches and treasures and the truth of the promises which God has made to His children; so much so that we seem not only to believe and hope in them but even to see them with our eyes and touch them with our hands, so great and remarkable is the assistance of our God in our bonds and imprisonment. So far, indeed, are we from wishing to regard our affliction as a curse of God, as the world and the flesh wish to regard it, that we regard it rather as the greatest blessing that has ever come upon us, for in it we are made true children of God, brothers and companions of Jesus Christ, the Son of God, and are conformed to His image; and by it the possession of our eternal inheritance is confirmed to us. Further, we are bold to say and affirm that we shall derive more profit in this school for our salvation than has ever been the case in any place where we have studied, and we testify that this is the true school of the children of God in which they learn more than the disciples of the philosophers ever did in their universities — indeed, that it must not be imagined that one can have a true understanding of many

[19] The martyrdom of the five young men who were arrested in Lyon on returning from their studies in Lausanne is well known. It aroused strong emotion in the Reformed world and occupies considerable space in the correspondence of Calvin (see *Calvini Opera*, XIV, *passim*). Yet the present letter seems to have escaped the notice of the editors. Though without signatures and without any indication of place and date, its attribution to the students imprisoned in Lyon is scarcely a matter of doubt.

of the passages of Scripture without having been instructed by the Teacher of all truth in this college. It is true enough that one can have some knowledge of Scripture and can talk about it and discuss it a great deal; but this is like playing at charades. We therefore praise God with all our heart and give Him undying thanks that He has been pleased to give us by His grace not only the theory of His Word but also the practice of it, and that He has granted us this honour — which is no small thing for vessels so poor and fragile and mere worms creeping on the earth — by bringing us out before men to be His witnesses and giving us constancy to confess His name and maintain the truth of His holy Word before those who are unwilling to hear it, indeed, who persecute it with all their force — to us, we say, who previously were afraid to confess it even to a poor ignorant labourer who would have heard it eagerly.

We pray you most affectionately to thank our good God with us for granting us so great a blessing, so that many may return thanks to Him, beseeching Him that, as He has commenced this work in us, so He will complete it, to the end that all glory may be given to Him, and that, whether we live or die, all may be to His honour and glory, to the edification of His poor Church, and to the advancement of our salvation. Amen!

Those whom you know
Received on Friday 15 July and read at the Congregation of the brethren.[20]

[5 August 1552]

ANTONIO BARGIO AND HIS WIFE ELIZABETH

On Friday 5 August Antonio Bargio, a Piedmontese, and his wife Elizabeth, a native of Crete, appeared before the brethren both of city and of country. They declared that a marriage had been contracted between them in Venice and that they had lived together as man and wife, although their marriage had not been solemnized in church. They requested that, now that they had come into the Christian Church and wished to live in accordance with the Reformation of the Gospel, the affirmation and declaration which they had made in our presence should be admitted as confirmation of their marriage, since they had no one available who could give additional testimony.

---

[20] This note is in the hand of the Company's secretary.

The Count of Martinengo,[21] an Italian preacher, was then heard. He stated that he knew Bargio to be a man with knowledge of God and His truth.

The parties were then interrogated to ascertain whether they had been living together affectionately as man and wife. They replied that this was so and that they had two children.

Thereupon, by the decision of the brethren, they were admonished and reproved because they had not contracted their marriage in the presence of Christian brethren to avoid scandal; and they were told to serve God from now on and to live in a manner edifying to their neighbours.[22]

[24 June 1552]

LETTER FROM AN UNKNOWN LADY PERSECUTED BY HER HUSBAND BECAUSE OF HER FAITH[23]

Sirs, in the name of God and our Lord Jesus Christ may it please you to listen to the affliction of an unfortunate Christian woman who is subject to a husband that is an idolater and persecutor of Christians, not just at this moment, but for more than ten years now. Will you please excuse her if for the present she does not disclose her name, for with the help of the Lord it will shortly be revealed to you if you approve her leaving him with whom she has been placed through the power of her father and brothers, whom she did not dare to disobey. It is true that at that time she had no knowledge of the Gospel, but some time after the marriage it pleased the Lord to open her eyes to know her God, so that her husband and nearest relatives noticed it. Thereupon, torn by conflicting loyalties, she came to the point of speaking out openly for her God, who gave her a little more liberty in confessing her faith, which was taken well enough by her husband. He, however, held her all the time to the papal idolatry, forcing her

---

[21] Celse Martinengo, of Brescia, was a friend of Zanchius and a disciple of Peter Martyr (Vermigli). For his preaching of the Gospel he was obliged to leave Italy in 1551. Responding to a call to Geneva, he arrived there in March 1552 and was at once established as pastor of the Italian church, where he remained until his death in 1557.

[22] The conclusion of this affair is missing.

[23] The Register contains the original autograph of this letter. It is reproduced in *Calvini Opera*, XIV, coll. 337ff. The identification of this lady — certainly of high rank and near to the Court — is difficult. The name of Madame de Cany, to whom Calvin wrote on several occasions, has been suggested.

to go to mass and to undertake journeys and pilgrimages and make vows to the saints. After six years of this he became so enraged that he sought other means for persecuting Christians because of the Gospel. Some he threw into prison; others he charged before the judges and nobility, of the kingdom, for he is a powerful nobleman with an income of ten thousand francs, and his word is well received among our robed and mitred bishops. He also forbids his wife to speak to any whom he suspects of listening to the Gospel. Knowing his fury, she keeps silent when she sees him blaspheming against Jesus Christ and His members in this way. This has the effect of making him still more frenzied, for he complains to all his household that she speaks no evil of those whom he calls Lutherans, that she belongs to their sect, and that he needs no further evidence. She admits this, knowing how displeasing it is to God to keep silence before men. He also threatens to throw her into the water or to commit her to perpetual imprisonment or to some other secret death, with the result that she has had to continue in this papal idolatry.

She requests you in the name of the Lord Jesus to inform her whether the law of marriage compels her to live with her husband, or whether the Gospel permits her to leave him and to seek liberty to live to the glory of God in a place where she can publicly call upon His name. Knowing, moreover, the family to which she belongs and the nobles of the realm with whom she is connected and who enjoy great favour with the king, she requests you most affectionately to let her know whether, if she were to withdraw herself to you and her return were demanded by the king or by her husband, you would give her up; for it is certain that he would not come to look for her, unless it were for the purpose of amusing himself by having her burnt or doing her slowly to death in a permanent dungeon.

She sends this gentleman to you, Sirs (hoping that you will show that charity which has the approval of the Lord Jesus Christ). He will describe to you the rest of her sad life; and, in order that you may give all the more credence to what she says, she has asked one of her closest friends to write to several persons of her acquaintance assuring them that this letter is not a fabrication, but truthful, as she herself knows it to be. If, further, it is permitted to speak and complain of grievous and severe assaults, be assured, Sirs, that no creature could have endured more than she, for she suffers every kind of affliction of both spirit and body: apart from the strict servitude in which she is held, so that she does not dare to confess her God, so many unpleasantnesses are heaped upon her that the enumeration of them would take too long; but the carrier of this letter can tell you of them, if you wish to take the trouble to ask him, Sirs.

There are, besides, close relatives of her husband who have made confession of faith with her and have frequently spoken of the things of the Lord together, but who have banded against her, giving themselves over to sensual living and deserting Jesus Christ. In their revolt they perpetrate numberless persecutions, even against those who in time past have declared their faith to them, bringing accusations against them, causing them to be thrown into prison, and forcing them to offer themselves in military combat. In addition to all this, Sirs, her husband is their accomplice, ordering and attempting to compel her with all his power to incite others against one of our brothers in Jesus Christ, whom he is holding prisoner, because she has more friends than her husband, and he wishes her to engage them immediately for the execution of what he calls justice. She would rather die, Sirs, than do this. Even when he notices her pretences to conform to papal idolatry he resorts to extreme cruelty. Once, Sirs, when she was very seriously ill he required her to confess herself, which she was unwilling to do except to one whom she knew to be a believer. He then became so enraged with her that he refused to let her speak to the person whom she had requested, saying that they were both of them heretics. After she had recovered, one Easter Day, when she was still very weak from her illness, she was compelled to receive her Easter communion from the hand of a priest, and in order to escape further idolatry she remained in the chapel of her home, keeping with her a small number of faithful servants. Her husband was so greatly enraged against her, and against her servants even more than her, that he was unwilling to see them, saying that they were all heretics and that he would have them burnt, cursing and blaspheming the name of Jesus Christ, so much so that his poor wife was compelled to keep away from him. If she wished to perform any charitable acts, such as visiting the sick or giving to the poor, he would never permit it; nor would he allow her to sing psalms or hymns or anything in praise of the Lord, since he hated this more than anything else in the world, with the result that neither she nor her servants dared to possess the psalms in French nor any books speaking of Jesus Christ; indeed, persons were appointed to keep a watch on her. He himself needed only to catch her at this to use it as an occasion for causing her further vexation. If any of his or her relatives die, he compels her to pay for masses to be sung for them and to be present at them, and if he suspects the beliefs of any he tries to compel her to slander and speak evil of them and to praise idolaters with him.

For the concluding part of her long and sad life, she entreats you humbly, Sirs, both you Messieurs of the Church and you Messieurs of the City, to meet together to formulate a reply to her sad request so that she may have a resolution of her case, for she has no desire to live any longer in this idolatry being deprived of all means of serving Jesus Christ, of obeying His commandments, and of confessing her faith. She would prefer the condition of a servant with you, Sirs, rather than to continue in an exalted position in this idolatry. Will you, then, be so kind as to give a ruling under your seal as to whether a woman is permitted to leave her husband for the reasons described above, and for others also which you may learn from the carrier of this letter; and also whether, if she were with you and the king or other great noblemen demanded it, you would deliver her up? These things she commends most humbly to your goodness.[24]

From France, 24 June 1552
Received 22 July 1552

[22 July 1552]

REPLY TO THE PRECEDING LETTER[25]

With reference to the appeal made to us by a noble lady who because she wishes to follow the true and pure religion is ill treated by her husband and held in most severe and cruel servitude, and with reference to the inquiry contained in her letter, namely, whether it would be lawful for her to leave her husband and withdraw herself here, or to some other church, where she could live with peace of conscience, we have unanimously agreed to give the following reply.

In the first place, we bear in mind the perplexity and anguish in which she must be, and we are affected with such pity and compassion that our heart goes out to her, praying God that it may please Him to grant her such relief that she may have cause to rejoice in Him.

---

[24] Ordinary precaution required that this letter should bear no signature.

[25] The original of this letter is lost, but a copy has been preserved in the Register. Its composition may with reasonable certainty be attributed to Calvin, and it has been published in all the editions of the Reformer's letters. It is reproduced in *Calvini Opera*, X, coll. 239ff.

Since, however, she requests advice as to what she may be permitted to do, it is our duty to state in reply purely and simply what God shows us by His Word, closing our eyes to all else. We pray her, therefore, not to be exasperated if our counsel does not conform entirely with her desire; for it is imperative that both she and we should follow the Master's orders without mingling our feelings with them.

It must be remembered that the situation in marriage is such that a believing spouse cannot voluntarily leave an unbelieving partner, as St. Paul shows in the 7th chapter of the First Epistle to the Corinthians [v. 13]; and there is no doubt that St. Paul intends this even when the believing husband or wife has to suffer a great deal, for in his day the pagans and the Jews were no less inflamed against the Christian religion than are the papists today. But St. Paul enjoins that the believing partner should endure bravely and persevere with constancy in the truth of God, and should not desert the partner who is hostile.

In brief, we ought to prefer God and Jesus Christ to all the world in such a way that fathers, children, husbands, and wives are of no account to us, with the result that if we can be loyal to Him only by renouncing all, then this is what we must do. But this is not to say that Christianity should abolish the order of nature when the two are able' to exist together. It is fitting rather that a Christian wife should redouble her efforts to fulfil her duty to her husband who is an enemy of the truth, so that if possible she may win him, as St. Peter says in the 3rd chapter of his first canonical epistle [v. 1].

Moreover, as things are today in the papacy, a believing wife is not fulfilling her duty if she does not use every endeavour to lead her partner into the way of salvation. Even when she is met with extreme obstinacy, there should be no semblance of her turning from the faith, but she should rather affirm her resolution and constancy, whatever the danger it may involve.

On the other hand when persecution arises it is permissible for a partner to flee, after she has fulfilled what is her duty. For when husband or wife have made confession of faith and have shown, if necessity demands, that they ought to and can in no way consent to the abominations of the papacy, then, if persecution arises against them for this reason and they find themselves in extreme danger, they may justifiably avail themselves of a means of escape, should God provide one. For flight from persecution when one is compelled to it is not the same thing as a voluntary divorce.

Now, the noble lady who requests our advice is very far from having reached this point in the performance of her duty. For according to what she herself says in her letter she is only silent and dissimulates. When pressed to defile herself with idolatry she yields and complies. This being so, she has no excuse for leaving her husband, without having made a more adequate declaration of her faith and without having endured and resisted greater compulsion.

She must pray God, therefore, that He will strengthen her, and then she must battle with more constancy than hitherto, in the power of the Holy Spirit, both with all sweetness and humility to show her husband what faith she holds, and also to make it clear to him that for her to comply with his demands would be to sin against God. We do not overlook her husband's roughness and cruelty of which she has told us; but all this does not prevent her from being courageous, while commending the outcome to God. For we may be assured that when, because governed by fear, we do not dare to put our vocation to the test, this proceeds from lack of faith; and this is not a foundation on which to build.

If, after having put to the proof the things we have said, she finds herself in grave peril, and her husband is persecuting her to the death, then she may avail herself of the liberty which our Saviour grants to His followers for escaping from the fury of the wolves.

As for the question of personal security, the gentleman who carries this letter will inform her what we have said by word of mouth, giving the reason why we have not gone further.

22 July 1552[26]

[29 July 1552]

THE QUESTION OF PUBLIC PENITENCE

The question was put to us, whether the rule of discipline is consonant with the Word of God whereby a man who has gravely sinned, causing public offence to the Church, is compelled by the authority of pastor and elders to give formal evidence of his penitence.

The answer, in our judgment, is that if any man who offends the Church by his evil example truly and earnestly repents, he should confess his sin before the Church so that he may be reconciled. For if any individual is injured by us, we know what Christ

---

[26] The Register carries no record of the signatories to this letter.

commands. Surely an offence by which the consciences of the godly are wounded ought not to be treated more lightly than an injury which involves only the loss of prestige or money. The Church ought to be of much greater importance than any individual. It follows, therefore, that there is no true and sincere penitence when the one who has fallen into sin refuses to make satisfaction for his offence. Moreover, that the Church may legitimately demand this is apparent from the spiritual guidance which the apostles give. Paul commands the elders who ought to be obeyed before all others to rebuke sinners in the presence of all so that others also may fear [I Tim. 5:20]. Paul wishes this to be carried out for the common example of all, and so presbyters should rebuke in the presence of all. If, therefore, any individual is an offence to the Church, he is rightly by this rule restored to grace and admitted to the sacred supper of the Lord, after he has first acknowledged his fault. And the course which Paul followed with the Corinthians should be accepted as a general rule [I Cor. 5:1ff.]. For although he dealt very mildly with him who committed incest with his step-mother, yet he commanded him to be restored to grace only after he had publicly confessed his sin, as is plain from the context of the second epistle. There he warns them to take care lest the unhappy man should be overwhelmed with grief [II Cor. 2:6ff.], from which it appears that he had previously given evidence of penitence with mourning. He speaks, again, of his fear lest God should humble him and he should be compelled to mourn over those who had sinned and had not evinced penitence for their fornication and uncleanness and lasciviousness [II Cor. 12:21]. By the term penitence he indicates that profession by which the churches ought to bear witness to their newness of life. Indeed, Paul's assertion that the Corinthians had humbly confessed their faults has no little relevance to this matter. How can we fail to see that what the whole body of the Church did not hesitate to do is important for the private individual? Moreover, the writings of the ancient authors testify that this form of confession was in constant use in all the centuries. Remove it, and there remains no further vestige of discipline in the Church. Christ ordered the unworthy to be excluded from the supper [Mt. 22:8, 11ff.]: how, then, is it allowable to admit those who have caused offence until they seek pardon by confessing their sin? Then again, how can one who has shown no desire to remove an offence he has caused conscientiously approach the holy table?

We, therefore, approve this custom of giving testimony to penitence in the presence of the people, and we deny that it is a rash or merely human invention. It has, rather, been enjoined by our heavenly Master, and in our judgment it should be carefully retained and religiously encouraged wherever it is found. Further, the Consistory may decide to require of sinners what they used formerly to do by admonition of the pastor and elders. In advocating the exercise of this discipline, however, we think that the brethren should discuss it among themselves and that the Consistory should announce, having regard to their opinion, what would seem to be useful for the edification of the Church.

> *The ministers of the Genevan church, both those who preach Christ in the city and also the brethren who had come from the country, unanimously gave this reply to the ministers and brethren of the church of Neuchâtel.*[27]

[7 November 1552]

CRITICISM OF CALVIN'S INSTITUTES

On Monday 7 November Maîtres Guillaume Farel and Pierre Viret,[28] who had come to this city because of the troubles here,[29] appeared before Messieurs to object against the defamation of doctrine which was taking place in taverns and restaurants and also against the accompanying debauchery. They complained, too, against Troillet,[30] who had propounded teaching similar to

---

[27] The date given at the head of this communication — 22 July 1552 — and also this statement concerning the senders and the destination are in a hand different from that of the text.

[28] Farel and Viret had arrived in Geneva a few days earlier to support Calvin in this affair, which promised to be difficult.

[29] The allusion is to the agitation which had prevailed in Geneva for several weeks — at least since August — in connection with the dispute between the notary Troillet, belonging to the Libertine party, and Calvin. Troillet had publicly and severely reproached Calvin both because of his doctrine and because of his behaviour in the city. This is, in fact, a fresh episode in the senseless warfare between the two main streams of Genevan politics.

[30] Jean Troillet belonged to an old established Genevan family and had at one time been a hermit in Bourgogne. On coming over to the Reformation, he returned to Geneva and had hoped to be appointed to the post of pastor. Calvin, however, opposed the appointment, judging him to be ill fitted for such a post. The disappointed Troillet became a notary and from then on fostered a relentless enmity against Calvin, seizing every opportunity to attack him. What the Register records here is the climax of this animosity. But there seems to have been a happy ending, as the account that follows indicates; for Troillet was simply censured, acknowledged his faults, and was reconciled with Calvin.

that of Maître Jerome,[31] finding fault with the doctrine of predestination as it is set forth in M. Calvin's *Institutes*.

On the following day Calvin and Troillet were summoned and the matter was debated. The conclusion was adjourned to the next day, the 9th day of the month, when an extraordinary session of the Council was held and prayers were advanced by one hour. The judgment which follows was then given.

[*9 November 1552*]

Having given a hearing to the honourable and learned ministers of the Word of God, Maître Guillaume Farel and Maître Pierre Viret, and after them the honourable Monsieur Jean Calvin, minister of this city of Geneva, and the nobleman Jean Troillet, also of Geneva, in their statements and responses, debated at length, concerning the *Christian Institutes* of Monsieur Calvin, and having carefully considered the whole matter, the Council announced its judgment that, all things having been heard and understood, Calvin's book of the *Institutes* was a good and godly composition, that its doctrine was godly doctrine, that he was esteemed as a good and true minister of this city, and that thenceforward no one should dare to speak against this book and its doctrine. They ordered both parties and all others to abide by this ruling.

Signed: C. Roset, *by order of the Syndics and Council, and sealed with the seal of the Seigneurie*

This judgment was announced in the presence of the parties mentioned above. Troillet, who acknowledged his fault, declared his agreement with it. He confessed that there had been a misunderstanding and went and shook hands with Calvin.

[*14 November 1552*]

PHILIPPE DE ECCLESIA ARRAIGNED

On Monday 14 November 1552 the ministers both of city and country were summoned before Messieurs. Also present were Maître Philippe de Ecclesia and Messieurs Farel and Viret. The case of de Ecclesia, which has been mentioned above, was briefly reviewed with respect to his acts of usury and disloyalty, also the familiar terms on which he had been with Mᵉ Jerome[32] and

---

[31] That is, Jerome Bolsec.
[32] That is, Jerome Bolsec.

the favourable opinions he had held of Jerome's doctrine, which he had repudiated by his signature in common with the other ministers. To this de Ecclesia had no answer to offer by way of defence or excuse. Messieurs therefore censured and condemned him. Yet they asked us to pardon him once again and to keep him in our Company in the position which he had been occupying, on condition that he requested forgiveness and acknowledged his fault. We protested that we could not take him to be other than he had shown himself to be on so many occasions and that there was no hope of amendment.

On the following Friday, which was the 18th of the month, de Ecclesia presented himself at our Congregation, but he was informed, by decision of the brethren, that as there was an insufficient number present his case would be postponed for two weeks, when all the brethren from the country would be summoned.

On Friday 2 December de Ecclesia presented himself and he was reproved in accordance with the decision announced by Messieurs. Since, however, it was impossible to draw from him any confession or sign of repentance, the case was adjourned to the day of censures.

On Friday 16 December 1552 the brethren from both city and country assembled in general Congregation for the hearing of censures.

Me Philippe de Ecclesia, whose case had been adjourned to this date, appeared before the brethren, and it was pointed out to him that he had not complied with the conditions laid down by Messieurs nor shown any true sign of repentance for rectifying his fault — something required of a minister of the Word more than of any other person; and, further, that he had openly kept himself separate from our Company and had been found in places where God and His doctrine were blasphemed.

He in turn replied that he had confessed to having been found with Me Jerome and in the company of others with whom he had conducted himself in an unseemly manner. If his doctrine had been at fault, he was willing for us to impose such correction as we might think fit; but he insisted that he had not approved of Me Bolsec.

He was asked whether he had not associated himself with Troillet when he was opposing our doctrine. He replied that for this reason he was no longer keeping company with Troillet.

Again, whether from the time when Troillet started to say that we made God the author of sin he had not connived with him in this matter. He replied that he had never spoken with him on this subject.

Again, whether Troillet had not maintained in his presence that our doctrine was false. He replied that he had never spoken ill of our doctrine. When pressed to reply more precisely, he said that he did not remember that Troillet had spoken ill of it.

Again, whether, when he was in a gathering where the doctrine of God was being blasphemed, he had not remained silent, and when some man had rebuked him, asking him how he could endure this, he had replied: "I won't say anything". De Ecclesia replied that he had heard nothing of this. The person concerned was named as Jean-Louis Favre,[33] a citizen. He said that he did not remember this.

Again, whether he had not told a man that he had a book on the subject of predestination, because he had not wished to reply to this person in the presence of others. He said that this was not so.

Again, whether he had not said that the sole reason why the brethren were unwilling to accept him in the Congregation was because he had been unwilling to go to Jussy. He replied that this was not so.

Again, whether he had not told Bodin[34] that when he had explained his opinion on the subject of predestination before the Congregation he had not revealed everything — No.

Again, whether he had not held Osias[35] and Bardel[36] to be bad characters, and yet had been on familiar terms with them. He said that this was not so.

Again whether he had not been the accomplice of those who reviled our doctrine, as had been stated in the sentence delivered by Messieurs. He denied this.

Because the brethren did not find in de Ecclesia what they had hoped for, and because he had shown no repentance since the judgment delivered by Messieurs, he was informed that they could no longer accept him in their Company, and he was admonished to consider whether he could conscientiously retain the office of a minister in the church.

De Ecclesia then presented himself before Messieurs, accusing

---

[33] Perhaps this was Jean-Louis, the son of Antoine Favre, who that year was auditor of accounts. As the name Favre was common in Geneva it could well have been someone else.

[34] Jean Bodin was the author of a work entitled *The Republic*.

[35] See note 16, p. 190 above. Osias was about forty years old.

[36] Jean Bardel, an inhabitant of Hermance, was a draper, aged about thirty-two. He seems to have been associated with de Ecclesia, especially as a debtor.

the brethren of unwillingness to accept him and of having tried to open new proceedings against him, by cross-questioning him and setting up a tribunal and writing down his replies. He charged that by doing this we were usurping Messieurs' authority, and he blamed and calumniated the brethren in several other ways. Thereupon Monsieur Calvin was summoned, and he made plain the nature of his calumnies, pointing out that we had instituted no form of legal procedure and had required no oath, but that we had acted as before God, in whose presence it was necessary to proceed in truth. He declared, moreover, that, in accordance with Messieurs' own injunction, there was need for de Ecclesia to show some sign of repentance. There was nothing better he could do than to confess and acknowledge his faults without resorting to dissimulation. As for the writing down of what he said, he himself knew that it was our custom to make a written record of what was transacted in our Congregation; indeed, he himself had been party to this, as could be proved by his signature, which we would produce if necessary. There was no question of this being something novel or unusual, for the ministers of the territory of Berne did the same, and in fact it had always been the practice. What is more, the ministers of Berne administer the oath to their dean, which is something we do not do, as we follow the simplest possible procedure.

On 23 December the ministers were summoned before Messieurs in connection with this affair. We were informed that it was the wish of Messieurs that we should be reconciled with Me Philippe, and they ordered this to be done. Then all the ministers of the city and also Mes Jacques Bernard and Mathieu Malesier replied that we could not acknowledge de Ecclesia as a brother and could not consent to be ministers with him without wounding our conscience. Thereupon Messieurs deputed certain delegates, namely, Monsieur the Syndic Philippin, Sr de Lestra,[37] and Sr Guillaume Benoît,[38] who were also members of the Consistory, and ordered us to meet with them after dinner in order to resolve this affair. Accordingly we assembled after dinner that day, but since not all the delegates were present the matter was deferred. Meanwhile we requested the syndic to make it plain to Messieurs that the supper could not be administered by de Ecclesia without scandal, and that one of the preachers of the city should be sent for this purpose.

[37] Probably Claude de Lestra, a councillor since 1537.
[38] Guillaume Benoît, a councillor since 1544, was an apothecary. In 1556 he was deposed for having forbidden compounds in his shop.

On the same day and at the same hour Messieurs proposed to us that some reconciliation should be made in the case of those who had been banned from the supper by the Consistory. Monsieur Calvin replied at once in the name of all the brethren, making two requests on our behalf: firstly, that they should not give the ministers the authority which belonged to the whole Consistory, of which each of us was a member, since it was not for us as individuals to deprive anyone of the supper, nor did we have authority, apart from the decision of the Consistory, to re-admit those who had been deprived; and, secondly, that they should exhibit the same impartiality to all.

Philibert Berthelier[39] was then sent into our presence. He showed the same or even greater rebelliousness than before, saying that it was not his understanding that the Consistory possessed such authority nor that the people were bound by its decisions. Messieurs therefore confirmed the sentence of the Consistory and pronounced him unworthy of the supper.

Philibert Bonne[40] was also heard, but he gave no more evidence of repentance.

As for the others, their hearings were deferred to the next day so that they could present themselves at the Consistory, an extraordinary meeting of which was being held in connection with the question of the supper.

With regard to the case of Me Philippe de Ecclesia, this could not be proceeded with until 6 January because the brethren from the country could not assemble before that date, owing to the celebration of the supper and also the severe wintry conditions. Accordingly they were instructed to attend without fail on 6 January.

On that day all were present. Assembled with us were those whom Messieurs had delegated to hear de Ecclesia. He came in and offered the same excuses as on previous occasions, speaking of reconciliation and protesting that he wished us no harm and that all should be forgiven, without in any way acknowledging

---

[39] Philibert Berthelier, son of the hero and martyr for Genevan freedom, was one of Calvin's most intransigent adversaries in Geneva. Communion was forbidden him in 1551 because he had publicly declared that he was "just as good a man as Calvin," and despite his repeated protestations, this ban was regularly renewed. In defiance of the authority of the Consistory, Berthelier appealed to the Council, and the latter attempted to set aside this ban, to the great offence of Calvin's followers.

[40] Philibert (or frequently Jean-Philibert) Bonnaz (or, phonetically, Bonne: the final -az was not pronounced), was the son of a great Genevan merchant and younger brother of the syndic Pierre Bonnaz, but, unlike the latter, an adherent of the Libertine party. He left the city in 1555.

his faults or showing signs of repentance. He was asked to withdraw and, after discussion, it was unanimously resolved both by Messieurs' delegates and by the ministers that, as he had neither satisfied the requirements imposed by Messieurs nor had fulfilled his duty to God and his church, the matter should be reported to Messieurs. The ministers, moreover, stood firmly by their declaration that they could not accept him as a pastor.

On Monday 20 January 1553 Messieurs informed M[e] Philippe that the ministers were justified in bringing the action against him and that everything had been substantiated.

On Monday 27 January Messieurs resolved that de Ecclesia should be deposed, setting Easter as the termination of his engagement.

* * * *

The Syndics for the year 1553 were Ami Perrin, Etienne Chapeaurouge, Domaine d'Arlod, and Pernet de Fosses.

[2 December 1552]

TESTIMONIAL GIVEN TO M. BERNARD ARNAIL

The ministers of the Word of God in the church of Geneva to all good, faithful, and godfearing persons:

Since M[e] Bernard Arnail,[41] doctor of medicine, has decided to retire to some place where it is possible that he will not be so well known as he is here, and to the end that he may not be held in suspicion or in ill repute by all God-fearing persons, he has requested us to give him a testimonial in accordance with what we know to be the truth, with the help of which he will be able to show how he has lived in France and why he has withdrawn to these parts. We have made inquiries concerning his life and have learnt from trustworthy persons that when he was in France he conducted himself honourably and without reproach, showing commendable zeal in his attachment to the pure doctrine of the Gospel. Here, moreover, he has continued to be well thought of,

---

[41] Nothing further is known of the activities in Geneva of this physician. He went to Moudon, in the canton of Vaud, where he received an allowance from the local authorities. In 1557 he departed bearing a certificate attesting his good character, his professional ability, and his zeal for the Reformation. Subsequently, he settled in Berne.

and in his way of life has set the good example of a Christian man. Having, then, such commendation of him, we pray that God will give him grace to continue well. As for his knowledge of the art of medicine, since we are not competent judges of this we leave the judgment to those who have more understanding and skill than we.

2 December 1552

[16 December 1552]

DEATH OF LOUIS COUGNIER
AND APPOINTMENT OF JEAN MACAR TO RUSSIN

On Friday 16 December 1552 the death occurred of Maître Louis Cougnier,[42] minister of the Word of God at Russin. On this day all the brethren from both city and country were assembled to hear censures. When these had been made, it was immediately resolved to make provision for the church at Russin which through the prolonged illness of Maître Louis had for a long time been deprived of regular ministrations. After invoking the name of God, several worthy persons were nominated who were in good standing in this church. Since, however, it was not then possible to form a decision concerning the willingness and intention of these persons, the matter was postponed to nine o'clock the next day.

On this day the brethren reassembled and, after invoking the name of God, began their deliberations. After taking various considerations into account, Me Macar[43] was elected minister of Russin. He was at once sent for and the situation was explained to him, together with the decision of the brethren; and he was admonished concerning the nature and obligation of the ministry, and also its difficulties.

Macar accepted the charge with modesty. He was required to expound Psalm 110 on the following Monday, the 19th, before proceeding to his examination. On the Monday he expounded this psalm, and after they had heard him the brethren pointed out what they found to criticize. On the same day his examination commenced and continued on the next and on various other days. In

[42] Louis Cougnier (see note 12, p. 63 above).
[43] Jean Macar was moved from Russin to the city of Geneva in 1556 (see p. 316 below). He served as minister in Paris for a short and critical period in 1558.

the course of the examination he was given the opening part of the 4th chapter of the epistle to the Hebrews as the text for his sermon. On the 28th day of the month Macar preached his sermon before the Consistory after the lesson, in the presence of the ministers of the city and the syndics Philippin and Amblard Corne.[44] On Wednesday 4 January 1553 the examination was completed, the criticisms offered, and the articles and customary admonition read, and on the following day, the 5th, Macar was presented to Messieurs, before whom he took the oath. On Friday the 6th, order was given by the brethren that he should officiate at Russin and that he should be presented there. On the Sunday following, the 8th, des Gallars went to present Macar at Russin and Dardagny, and with him, delegated by Messieurs, were Sr Pernet de Fosses, châtelain of St. Victor, and Sr Jean-Louis Ramel, châtelain of Peney.[45]

[44] Amblard Corne was a business man and a Genevan magistrate, and a personal friend of Calvin, who thought highly of him.
[45] Jean-Louis Ramel (born 1501), châtelain of Peney, is less well known than his father, of the same name, who was one of the most notable magistrates of Geneva at the beginning of the sixteenth century.

1553

[6 January 1553]

CERTAIN ARRANGEMENTS FOR PREACHING

On Friday 6 January the brethren gave order that from then on Maître Jean Fabri and des Gallars should take over Maitre Abel's[1] week at the Madeleine and should share between them the two weeks at St. Gervais and the Madeleine. The reason for this was that Messieurs had requested that someone should take the place of Me Abel, since he could not be heard.[2] Monsieur Calvin was asked to give the sermon on the day of prayers in this week, in accordance, however, with his convenience and without his being under any compulsion. Instead of this Wednesday sermon Me Jean Fabri was to preach on the Saturday for Calvin at the Madeleine. This arrangement was to continue until more suitable provision could be made.

[20 January 1553]

ARTICLES PRESENTED TO MESSIEURS AGAINST PHILIPPE DE ECCLESIA

In order that Messieurs may see that everything we put before them concerning Maître Philippe is true, we pray them to be pleased to hear in the first place the testimonies of those who

---

[1] That is, Abel Poupin.

[2] The arrangements for preaching during the week in the different churches of the city are set out in the Ecclesiastical Ordinances of 1541 (see p. 40 above). The duties were portioned out, each pastor being responsible in turn for a week's preaching in one of the churches. Abel Poupin was probably advanced in years and already a sick man. He died a little over three years later, on 5 March 1556, "after a long and painful illness and numerous relapses" (see p. 314 below).

were examined in connection with the charge of usury, from which they will find that we were compelled to bring to their attention the scandal involved.

Articles on which we pray Messieurs to examine the brothers-in-law of Maître Philippe:

Whether they had not heard that he had taunted his wife, their sister, and them too, that their father had been burnt, and whether they did not complain about this insult.

Again, whether they had not heard that he behaved himself badly at home as well as elsewhere in a manner that was unbecoming to a minister of the Word of God, and whether they did not complain about this.

Again, whether they had not heard that there was discontent because of his acts of usury and also because of his conduct with Osias.

In particular, they ask that Maître Nicolas Fabri, one of the three, should be interrogated:

Whether he had not warned Maître Philippe that his reputation was at stake, pointing out that Osias was a man of evil fame and that it was not seemly for him to be associated with him in such things; and whether Maître Philippe did not reply that arguing was no crime.

Again, whether he did not know the kind of life Maître Philippe had led previously, and that he should reveal what he knows.

Again, he should reveal what he knows concerning the opinions he had heard expressed by Maître Philippe to the effect that there were many errors in the catechism of Geneva.

May it please Messieurs also to interrogate Maître Jean Bodin[3]:

Whether he has not known Maître Philippe intimately for a long time as a man who says one thing while he thinks another.

Whether Maître Philippe did not tell him that in his house he had a book on predestination which he would show him when they were alone and not otherwise.

Again, when he was summoned before the Company of ministers, whether this was not simply to know the truth concerning certain opinions which he was reported to hold.

Again, whether he was examined by means of interrogation.

Again, whether Maître Philippe did not speak to him as follows: "Were you not asked in the Council chamber whether the ministers had required you to take the oath when they summoned you before them?" And, when Bodin had replied that no such thing

---

[3] Concerning Jean Bodin see note 34, p. 203 above.

had happened, whether Maître Philippe did not rejoin: "Those Messieurs have lost their memory".

Again, whether he had not been far from understanding that Maître Philippe wished only to accuse us of having usurped a measure of jurisdiction.

Again, whether it was not a fact that this had never been Maître Philippe's intention. Bodin should reveal all that he knows about this.

Drawn up on Friday 20 January 1553 and presented to Messieurs the same day.

On Friday 20 January it was announced . . . .[4]

[26 April 1553]

LETTER FROM LAUSANNE CONCERNING FABRI AND VITALIS[5]

To their most faithful fellow-servants of Jesus Christ, the most watchful ministers and pastors of the church of Geneva, their most respected brethren and masters: grace to you and peace from God our Father and our Lord Jesus Christ. Amen!

In October of last year we indicated to you, most reverend brethren and masters, the accusations preferred by your colleague Fabri[6] against François Vitalis,[7] and we requested that you would undertake the conduct of this case which is common to both our churches. Accordingly, that you might the more easily do this, we ordered Vitalis to go to you. Just at that time, however, the plague struck at his home and he was in great distress because of many sorrows, to which we can bear testimony. Now he has told us plainly that he wishes to proceed to Geneva for the purpose of hearing your judgment in this case. He has requested us to remind you of our earlier letter in which it was stated that he was ready to defend himself against and refute Fabri's accusations. Once

[4] This minute has been left unfinished.

[5] The letter in the Register is the original in the hand of Jean Ribit. This letter has been published in *Calvini Opera*, XIV, coll. 523. For the reply from Geneva see pp. 218ff. below.

[6] That is, the pastor Jean Fabri.

[7] Jean Fabri was the Genevan pastor. François Vitalis, an obscure pastor of the territory of Vaud, had been accused of immorality and wished to exculpate himself before the Genevan pastors. The *Manuals* of Lausanne mention him as having subsequently ministered to the victims of the plague in Lausanne about 1556, and thereafter as being pastor at Savigny and deacon of Lutry at the end of 1559.

again, therefore, we turn to you, desiring you of your kindness to undertake this case, and, if it is not a trouble to you, to inform us by letter of its outcome.

Farewell. May Christ long keep you in safety to the glory of His name!

Lausanne, 26 April 1553

In the name of the Colloquium of Lausanne,

Joannes Ribittus,[8]

Cordially yours.

[10 February 1553]

LETTER FROM TREPPEREAU EXCUSING HIMSELF FOR LEAVING HIS PARISH[9]

To the most learned and no less godly pastors of the Church of Geneva, ever honoured masters in Christ: Salvation to you and peace from God our Father through Christ in the Holy Spirit.

My respected brethren and fathers in Christ, I imagine that you are not unaware of what happened to me in Berne, for from the letter sent to the magnificent Senate of Geneva you will have learnt, I suppose, the nature and magnitude of the burden which I have undertaken. The fact is that I was neither able nor obliged to concern myself with the care and administration of the church at Céligny, and so I commended that church to Christ, the true and supreme Pastor of all churches, who will rule you by His Spirit and guide you in the choice of a suitable minister for that church. I regret very much that I was unable to meet you before my departure. I would have explained openly and simply the reasons for changing my sphere of work, which I do not doubt are appar-

---

[8] Jean Ribit, of Faucigny, had studied in Paris and Zürich and was an excellent Hellenist. In 1540 he succeeded Conrad Gessner at the Academy of Lausanne. At the time of writing this letter he was dean of the presbytery of Lausanne. Subsequently, in 1559, he resigned and spent some time teaching at the College of Geneva. He completed his career as professor of biblical exegesis in Orleans, where he died in 1564. In the canton of Vaud the term *colloquium* designated a sub-division of the presbytery.

[9] The letter in the Register is the original in the hand of Treppereau. Concerning Louis Treppereau and the circumstances of his departure from Céligny (see note 6, p. 63 above).

ent to some of you, and on account of which, I trust, I would be excused by those among you who wished some action to be taken against me. I hope, however, to come shortly to Geneva and to speak with you about all the things which may seem to you to be to the advantage of the church. Meanwhile, if I have offended you in any way, either privately or publicly, I ask that through Christ the Conciliator of all and through the common ministry of the Word you will pardon me.

Farewell, ever honoured fathers and masters in Christ.

10 February. Nyon

From him who is entirely yours,
Ludovicus Trepperellus

This letter was received on Saturday 11 February 1553 by the hand of Maître Pierre, brother-in-law of Treppereau, to whom the brethren gave the unanimous reply that, for our part, we did not intend to reply in writing to Maître Louis, but that he could tell him, if he wished, that none of us knew the reasons for his change, that we had all protested against it, and that it was impossible to excuse him as he requested in his letter. He had wronged the brethren by pretending that someone had been in communication with him, when in fact no one knew or approved of his action, as even now we are unable to approve it. As for his excuse that he was unable to speak with us, this is sheer mockery of the kind that he is accustomed to use; for when, on the Thursday, he was in this city and appeared before Messieurs, he could quite easily have presented himself at our Congregation on the following day.

[30 March 1553]

LETTER FROM LAUSANNE REQUESTING A TEACHER FOR THEIR COLLEGE[10]

To the most faithful ministers and pastors of the church of Geneva, men distinguished for both piety and learning, our most dear and respected brethren and colleagues: Grace to you and peace from God our Father and our Lord Jesus Christ. Amen!

Although we have long and carefully been seeking a man whom we could put in charge of the first class of our college, yet we

---

[10] The letter in the Register is the original in the hand of Jean Ribit.

have not succeeded in finding anyone really suitable here. Accordingly, most honoured brethren and colleagues, we beg you to help us in this matter, urging you not to fail us at this juncture. You are not ignorant of what is owed by the members of the one body to their fellow-members. You will remember that some years ago, when your college was deprived of a teacher, at your request we sent you our beloved brother Enoch,[11] whom you deemed worthy to be placed in charge of your college. Now, therefore, if you have a man who could take charge of the class mentioned — that is, who is competent to teach Greek and Latin and is a lover of pure religion — we earnestly request you to send him to us with your commendation. If there is anything further you wish to know, our brother Theodore Beza, who has undertaken this commission in our name, will easily enlighten you.

Farewell. May Christ prosper you more and more by His Spirit to the praise of His own name and the benefit of the Church! *Lausanne, 30 March 1553*

In the name of the ministers and professors of Lausanne,

Yours cordially,

Joannes Ribittus, *Dean*

This letter was delivered on 3 April and the following reply was sent.

REPLY TO THE PRECEDING LETTER

Greetings. No doubt our brother Theodore Beza has reported to you how, on the receipt of your letter, we immediately set to work with due earnestness and diligence to find a suitable teacher for the first class of your college; and, just when it seemed that no one was particularly willing to take on the post, we had the timely offer of this brother who, although at first he showed himself difficult (for he had just cause for excusing himself), yet, whether submitting to entreaties, or yielding to advice, or overcome by reasoning, at length gave his consent. In our judgment he is an upright and modest man who will perform his duties faithfully and without offence to the Church.

---

[11] Louis Enoch occupied several posts in the churches and schools of Geneva. It was in 1550 that he was appointed principal of the collège de Rive, the chief educational establishment in Geneva before the founding of the Academy and the College in 1559.

[10 April 1553]

LETTER FROM THE FRENCH CHURCH IN STRASBOURG CONCERNING TROUBLE-MAKERS NAMED TAPETIER AND NICAISE

To the most distinguished master John Calvin and his colleagues in the church of Geneva: Grace to you and peace from God our Father through Jesus Christ our Lord and Saviour.

Some months ago a certain man named Nicolas Tapétier arrived here from Geneva, sent (in my judgment) not by God, nor by you the servants of God, but by the father of all division and discord, Satan himself. He has been troubling and upsetting us and our little church, and infecting it with his poison. What is still worse, another individual, a companion of this fellow, called Nicaise is daily expected, and his arrival is likely to be in accordance with the working not of God but of Satan. I would that God might prove me to be a false prophet! In the meantime I am unable to keep silence when I consider what is being done at the instigation of these men, or rather of Satan acting through them. Both of them are better known to you than to me, for they lived with you in Geneva for some time.

Since, therefore, it is in the interest of you all (and, of course, of us) to watch over not only your own church but also ours, and indeed the whole Church of God, we ask you all and beseech you through Jesus Christ our Saviour to be so good as to inform us by means of a letter signed by you (if this proposal of ours meets with your approval) how these two individuals we have mentioned behaved themselves when in your city — what sort of persons they were, what fruit the Gospel of Jesus Christ produced in them, etc. With this help from you we shall be able, if need be, to resist them to the face before the whole church, so that this field of the Lord may be purged of weeds and tares and the good seed of God may grow and bear fruit.

In short, we suggest that, in the event of some of your citizens coming here from Geneva, it will be desirable for you to notify us by letter what sort of persons these two men were in your midst, and we in turn will do the same for you. For in this way the ungodly goats and also the godly sheep will be known and recognized wherever they go and wherever they are; and the goats will be driven out, while the sheep will be kept in safety. Worthy fathers, make provision for what is good; for the love of God urges us and duty compels us to be importunate with you.

You may learn about the state of our church from the bearer of this letter, our and your brother Antoine de Chéry, to whom we have confidently entrusted this whole business. Pray for us. May the Lord God long keep you all well and safe in the service of His holy Church, to the glory of His name and the edification of us all. Amen!

Strasbourg, 10 April 1553

>Your brother and fellow-servant,
>
>Joannes Garnerius,
>
>in his own name and in the name of the elders of the church

This letter was delivered to us on 21 April 1553.

[22 April 1553]

REPLY TO THE PRECEDING LETTER

Grace to you and peace from God our Father through Jesus Christ.

It grieves us, most honourable brethren, that your church, which has been assailed more than enough by enemies from without, should now be disturbed by worthless fellows from within. If only we had authority to act more effectively for the relief of your situation the will would certainly not be lacking, especially as those who are now molesting you went forth from here.

Realizing that both men are dishonest and tiresome persons, bent on sowing discord, it was our constant fear that they would do damage, whether here or elsewhere, either by troubling the godly or by deceiving the simple, as is their custom; but it is fitting that we should be ready to endure these conflicts by which the Lord in His wisdom from time to time exercises His Church. Since, moreover, it is our duty to curb such men according to our ability, we have willingly and unanimously agreed to send you the evidence for which you have asked.

With respect to Nicolas Tapétier: he lived for a while in a godly and Christian manner among us, excepting that he was a sharp-tongued man, stormy in temperament, and constantly quarreling at home. Before long he was also found to be bibulous and addicted to gluttony to such an extent that his moderate means were insufficient to support his extravagances. This resulted in his going to Italy in the hope of finding greater fortune there. But before this, when he had not succeeded in obtaining from charity as much as he wished for the satisfaction of his greed, he had shown himself to be as arrogant as he was greedy.

As for Nicaise, from the first he had given many plain evidences that he was a headstrong and factious man. It was customary for him to inflame his naturally immoderate temper by drinking with others and this led to his being the cause of numerous disturbances.

At length they both gave more ample proof of their true nature. When a certain ungodly minister of Satan attempted to upset our church by denouncing the free election of God, these two mercenary opportunists began, at first secretly, but afterwards, when they had gathered boldness, more openly, to make themselves a nuisance. Our brother Calvin called Nicaise to him and calmly admonished him that he would do better to devote his energy to learning rather than to gabble rashly about things of which he was ignorant. Although he had petulantly attacked our doctrine, he was assured of pardon for what was past. He expressed gratitude and clearly stated his satisfaction.

A few days later they both left together. During their travels they attempted to denigrate us and our church and also spued forth wicked blasphemies against the sacred providence of God. On the return of Nicaise to our city, our brother Calvin reported him to the magistrate because he did not cease from his evil speaking and our patience had been taxed to the limit. His case was heard and he was banished from our society. It was, we think, a bad conscience that stopped Nicolas from returning. Meanwhile his wife and children were compelled to beg. This shows what an example of piety he is, for he abandoned his own children, evincing less concern for them than a savage beast. The impostures and deceits of Nicaise are better known in Lausanne.

The Lord grant that your church may be purged of such counterfeits or rather plagues and may glorify God in a state of tranquillity and decent order. There are two reasons why we have not before now given you a word of warning concerning these two men: firstly, it was not by our decision that they betook themselves to your city, and, secondly, we wished to avoid the mistake of too much severity. We are sure that you, who have experienced to your own hurt how harmful and poisonous these vagabonds are, will take such steps as lie open to you to ensure that others are warned against them, especially the brethren at Metz and Vézelay: for if they flee from you, we suspect that they will make their way thither.

Farewell, most dear and cordially respected brethren. May the Lord guard you by His power, govern you by His Spirit, and enrich you with every blessing right to the end.
Geneva, 22 April

        Your brethren and fellow-workers,

Joannes Calvinus	Michael Copus
Abelus Poupinus	Joannes a Sancto Andrea
Nicolaus Galasius	Joannes Faber
Raymondus Calvetus	Joannes Macarius

[28 April 1553]

REPLY CONCERNING THE DIFFICULTIES BETWEEN FABRI AND VITALIS, SENT TO MESSIEURS OF LAUSANNE[12]

When your letter was delivered to us by François Vitalis it was the day of our Congregation, and, since he had come to clear himself, we fixed an hour for him to be heard. After listening to his complaints and to Fabri's reply, we decided that the situation should be briefly summed up. We were hampered, however, by the fact that Fabri had no letter which would have helped us to form a more definite judgment. But, so far as we can trust our memory, the main issues were raised in the midst of the accusations. When Vitalis blamed Fabri for whatever misfortunes he had suffered, Fabri excused himself by saying that he had written only at your request and that it ought not to be held against him that, impelled by concern for the public safety of the Church, he had freely warned you; and it should at least be seen whether the things he reported to you are true or false.

On coming to the actual charges, Vitalis confessed that when he was a prior he had kept a concubine in the monastery, but that she had been shared with some others, although he did not deny that his conduct had been especially shameful. When it was objected that in excusing himself before you he had not spared Fabri, as though he had been a companion in his vice, he replied that he had never spoken in this way, but on the contrary had testified that Fabri had been neither associated with nor privy to his offence. When Fabri said that he had sent a letter warning him that the concubine should be expelled and threatening to take action, he denied that the letter had been delivered to him. Fabri rejoined that its receipt had once been admitted. Our brother

---

[12] This is the reply to the letter of 26 April from the pastors of Lausanne (see p. 211 above).

Raymond[13] also declared, before Vitalis acknowledged these things, that the whole matter had been narrated to him by Fabri in such a way that there could be no suspicion that anything had been made up on the spur of the moment. This Vitalis confirmed, except that he sought pardon on the ground of his blindness, since at the time he was a stranger to Christ. But a little later, in the course of discussion, he began to boast that he had taken pains to promote the Gospel. Fabri, however, insisted, while Vitalis kept silent, that the concubine would never have been removed from the monastery except through fear of legal action.

The second charge concerned Vitalis' complaint that Fabri had said that he had persecuted innocent and godly men because of their faith, in support of which he had produced nothing more substantial than suspicions. It was indeed established, from the statements made by both, that certain kinsmen of Vitalis had come armed to take Fabri off to prison, and that shortly afterwards Vitalis had left the place where he had begun to preach and had followed them. From this Fabri concluded that he had not been ignorant of the plot nor uninvolved in the conspiracy. But Vitalis declared that he had fled, overcome by fear because he was in danger of suffering the same fate. When both had been heard, we reproved Fabri for unjustly accusing a Christian brother on the basis of so obscure and unsubstantial a suspicion — adding that if anything was hidden from us today, the time would come when God would be the judge.

The third charge concerned the woman whom Vitalis had brought with him. Fabri denied that he had written anything other than that Vitalis had behaved dishonestly and set a very bad example by keeping a concubine while still involved in monastic superstitions and by continuing this sordid relationship for more than a whole year. Plainly, we were unable to absolve Vitalis of all blame in this matter. We leave it to God to judge whether he conducts himself with as much modesty and forbearance as he now promises to do. It is, frankly, difficult to expect that a young and lusty monk, who was scarcely sprinkled with the merest drop of godliness, should refrain from the girl whom he had previously kept as his wife.

The final charge was that his departure had been less than honourable. To this Vitalis replied that when a prior was to be appointed he had accepted this office so that he might be more free. . .;[14] meanwhile a rumour had arisen which had compelled

---

[13] That is, Raymond Chauvet.
[14] The text is defective here because this page of the Register has been damaged.

him to take flight. He denied the charge. We were compelled to suspend judgment.

We will not presume to pronounce a verdict on this whole case. It seems that there were long-standing quarrels between the two men arising from mutual jealousy and the antipathy of one of them. We fear that a measure of animosity still remains in their minds, and yet we cannot suggest the origin of the new and sudden offence which has caused Fabri maliciously and hostilely to damage with his testimony him whom at first he had commended, perhaps too generously, and tried to help.

Farewell, most honourable and respected brethren. May the Lord ever be present with you, govern you with His Spirit, and protect your church.

Geneva, 28 April 1553

Johannes Calvinus
Abelus Pouppin
Nicolaus Gallasius
Michael Copus

Raimondus Calvetus
Johannes a Sancto Andrea
Franciscus Borgoignus
Johannes Macardus

[12 May 1553]

NICOLAS COLLADON APPOINTED TO VANDOEUVRES IN PLACE OF DE ECCLESIA

On 12 May 1553 Maître Nicolas Colladon[15] was elected in place of Maître Philippe de Ecclesia; and, after having expounded and preached in accordance with our custom, and having been examined, was presented to Messieurs on Thursday, the 18th. They then assigned him to Vandoeuvres and Cologny.

FRANÇOIS BOURGOIN REQUESTS A CHANGE OF PARISH

After receiving a request presented by M. François Bourgoin that he should be moved from Jussy to another parish or be per-

---

[15] Nicolas Colladon was the son of an advocate from the province of Berri in France who had sought refuge in Geneva in 1550. He had been studying in Lausanne since 1549, and from now on was to play an important role in the Genevan church and in the Company, of which he was to be secretary from 1562 to 1571. He was a faithful friend and devoted colleague of Calvin. From 1566 on he taught theology in the Academy, but in 1571 he was dismissed for having dared to criticize the government. Thereafter he was a professor first in Heidelberg and then in Lausanne, where he died in 1586.

mitted to return to the city, Messieurs gave order that he should return to the city and that des Gallars should go to Jussy.

Messieurs did this, however, without giving any notification to the ministers, who had no knowledge of it apart from what Bourgoin reported to them. The brethren told him that they could not approve what he had done, that it was not by their decision that he had done it, and that they could not consent to des Gallars going to Jussy. They therefore counselled him to present himself before Messieurs and, if he was agreeable, to tell them that he could not conscientiously support the decision that des Gallars should leave the city.

[27 May 1553]

LETTER TO THE COMPANY FROM MACAR, WHO WAS IN BERNE[16]

To my very dear and respected brethren, the ministers of Geneva: Greetings.

Since, contrary to hope, the Lord has given me some hope of a tolerable solution, the brethren consider it necessary for me to remain here with our brother du Moulin[17] until Friday next[18] lest they should omit any part of their duty. I realized how inconvenient this would be, both because of the impending communion day and also because of our day of censures, but I decided that I ought to obey the brethren, who are pleased with nothing that is displeasing to you. Accordingly there is, I think, no need for me to make excuses for being prevented from administering the Lord's supper in my parish or for my inability to be present on the day of censures; but it is fitting rather that you should intercede with the Lord with all earnestness, as you have done hitherto,

---

[16] The letter in the Register is the original in the hand of Macar (see note 43, p. 207 above). Macar had gone on a mission to Brne where, it seems, he had joined Calvin who at the same time was negotiating with the authorities of Berne the delicate question of ecclesiastical ceremonies — a dispute which was holding up the interchange of territories between Geneva and Berne. Although Macar makes no mention in this letter of Calvin's presence in Berne, it is probable that he had written in Calvin's name as well as his own.

[17] Claude du Moulin was pastor in the bailiwick of Thonon. Subsequently he became an instructor in the College of Lausanne. In 1559 he resigned and went to Geneva, and then to France, where he suffered martyrdom in 1574.

[18] That is, 2 June.

that, since He has begun to give some token of His good will towards us in this matter, He may continue to watch over His Church which, through the unjust calumny of a single man, has had to pass through a crisis of no small magnitude. Meanwhile, as the consideration of my duty is always a matter of concern to me, I shall with increasing importunity ask those men who at first arrogantly excluded us, but now show themselves ready to hear and take notice of our doctrine, not to afford any further occasion for the utterances of slanderers. Moreover, if those impudent and worthless fellows, concerning whose calumnies we await witnesses so that they may be convicted and pay the just penalty of their crimes (if indeed we may hope for this much) — if these men, I say, continue their fabrications against us (for they are consummate architects of lies and slanders), we shall oppose their false accusations. In brief, we shall unceasingly urge here that the rumours spread everywhere concerning sound doctrine, thanks to the obscurity of the most recent rescript or to the silence of Messieurs of Berne, may be extinguished; and if the testimony given to the piety of one man is less than just, at least it will be apparent that the reputation of our church is damaged neither openly nor indirectly. If we succeed in obtaining this from them whom God has wished us to supplicate, we shall have occasion for praising Him from whom all good things come; but if not, we shall rejoice to have fulfilled our duty as far as we were able to do so; nor shall we collapse in tearful self-pity, as those think who in their envy prefer to slander us rather than do good to anyone.

May the Lord govern you by His Spirit, honoured brethren ever esteemed by me. My companion du Moulin sends you many greetings.

Berne, 27 May

Your ever obedient servant,
Jo. Marcarius

* * * *

SYNDICS FOR THIS YEAR: AMI PERRIN, ETIENNE DE CHAPEAUROUGE, DOMAINE D'ARLOD, PERNET DE FOSSES

July 1553

FONCENEX

On the [blank] day of July Maître François Bourgoin requested the advice and assistance of the brethren, since he had heard a report that inquiries had been made about a sermon preached by him at Foncenex in which he had criticized the witnesses who had given evidence against Jean de Saint-André.[19] It was resolved to make all possible investigations to establish the truth, and even to go to the place itself the better to ascertain the facts. Despite the circumstance, however, that Messieurs had been repeatedly requested to sanction this procedure, it was ordered in the Council, without our being present and without in any way having communicated with us, that Maître Nicolas des Gallars should go to Jussy and Foncenex and that Bourgoin should return to the city. The brethren, feeling that they had been wronged because the order of the church had not been duly observed, protested to Messieurs, who, however, refused to budge from their decision. Accordingly, seeing that there was nothing further they could do, they sent Maître Abel Poupin and Maître Jacques Bernard to protest again before the Council that, although we would acquiesce in this change for the sake of peace, yet we could not accord it our approval.

[August 1553]

THE TRIAL OF MICHAEL SERVETUS
THE THEOLOGICAL DISPUTE

Servetus — Lieutenant, P. Tissot. — (The Venerable Company had been called before the Council when Servetus was examined. The Council had ordered a summary of his errors to be made.)

On 13 August of this year Michael Servetus was recognized by certain brethren[20] and it was decided that he should be imprisoned lest he should further infect the world with his blasphemies and heresies, seeing that he was known to be altogether beyond hope of correction. Thereupon, a certain person had filed a criminal action against him, setting down a number of articles which contained a collection of the most notorious errors of Servetus.[21] Several days later the Council ordered that we should be present

---

[19] Jean de Saint-André was secretary of the Company of Pastors from 1552 until his death in 1557. This part of the Register is written in his hand. He left his parish to placate the Bernese, who had imprisoned him for attacking from his pulpit in Foncenex their custom of celebrating Holy Communion on Christmas Day (see p. 187 above).

[20] In the Madeleine church at the Sunday sermon, *"post prandium"*. See *Calvini Opera*, VIII, col. 725, n.l.

[21] This accuser of Servetus was Nicolas de la Fontaine, Calvin's secretary. It was the practice in Geneva for such an accuser to be imprisoned until evidence in support of his charge was forthcoming (see note 20, p. 139 above).

when he was examined.[22] When this was done the impudence and obstinacy of Servetus became all the more obvious; for, to begin with, he maintained that the name of the Trinity had been in use only since the Council of Nicea and that all the theologians and martyrs prior to that had not known what it was. And when the plainest evidences were produced from Justin Martyr, Irenaeus, Tertullian, Origen, and others, so far was he from showing any shame that he poured out all sorts of absurdities in a most insulting and offensive manner.

At length Messieurs, realizing that the trial would go on interminably unless some means was found of curtailing it, ordered that a selection of the erroneous and heretical propositions contained in his books should be made, and that when he had replied in writing we should demonstrate briefly the falsity of his opinions, so that the whole might be sent to the neighbouring churches for their advice.[23]

OPINIONS OR PROPOSITIONS TAKEN FROM THE BOOKS OF MICHAEL SERVETUS WHICH THE MINISTERS OF THE GENEVAN CHURCH DECLARE TO BE IN PART IMPIOUS AND BLASPHEMOUS AGAINST GOD AND IN PART FILLED WITH PROFANE ERRORS AND INVENTIONS, AND ALL ENTIRELY FOREIGN TO THE WORD OF GOD AND THE ORTHODOX CONSENSUS OF THE CHURCH.

The Reply of Michael Servetus to the Articles of John Calvin

Calvin arrogates to himself the authority to write articles after the manner of the Sorbonne masters[24] and capriciously condemns whatever he wishes without adducing any reason from Holy Scripture. Either he altogether fails to understand my mind, or he cunningly misrepresents it. I am therefore compelled briefly

---

[22] The date was 17 August. Calvin presented himself before the Council and accepted responsibility for the accusation which he had entrusted to Nicolas de la Fontaine. The Council resolved that "Monsieur Calvin and any one whom he wished to associate with himself should be enabled to assist Nicolas with his replies and to point out the errors and the passages in proof of them."

[23] On 21 August the Council had made provision for consulting the governments of the Protestant cantons.

[24] The theological school of the Sorbonne in Paris was famous for its method of disputation known as the *actus Sorbonicus* in which a scholar propounded and defended a particular thesis against all comers. It is said to have been introduced by Francis of Mayrone (d. 1325), a pupil of Duns Scotus.

to set out my whole position here and to adduce reasons in my favour, before I reply to his articles one by one.

A BRIEF REFUTATION OF THE ERRORS AND IMPIETIES OF MICHAEL SERVETUS OFFERED, "AS COMMANDED",[a] BY THE MINISTERS OF THE GENEVAN CHURCH TO THE MAGNIFICENT SENATE[25]

[a] *You offer yourself as the prime accuser: then you take care to be commanded, you dissimulator!*

When the dogma or rather bluster of Servetus that all trinitarians are atheists first began to cause a disturbance he defended himself by maintaining that the name of the Trinity *had been invented* by Athanasius and the fathers of *the Council of Nicea.*[b][26]

[b] *The real Trinity was then made public; for formerly there was a disposition of the Trinity, as I have taught from Irenaeus and Tertullian, nor does Justin teach otherwise, to say nothing of Origen.*

But even after he had been convicted of falsehood and impudence by the testimony of Justin Martyr,[27] Origen[28] and others of the fathers, he did not cease to wander away from the point. Accordingly, our Magnificent Council, intending that a limit should be

[25] In the following exchanges the words in italics were underlined by Servetus and he added comments on them either between the lines or in the margin. These comments are here placed in smaller italics immediately following material to which they pertain. They are identified by corresponding lower case letters of the alphabet. It was evidently between 15 and 18 September that Servetus studied and annotated these passages; for on Friday 15 September the Council agreed to the request of the prisoner that Calvin's rejoinders should be communicated to him, and that if he in turn should write anything it should be shown to Calvin. On 19 September the Council considered the remarks made by Servetus and decided to consult with the churches of Switzerland without delay.

[26] The thought of Servetus and his criticism of the Trinity — which is the subject of this present theological dispute — were strongly influenced by his reading of the church fathers of the ante-Nicene and Nicene periods who were involved in the first great christological controversy. Beyond doubt, it was when he was staying in Basle that Servetus became acquainted with their writings. Tertullian and Irenaeus, his principal sources, had just been printed for the first time, and in the circle of Ecolampadius and his colleagues Servetus would have been able to consult other more or less recent editions of patristic writings.

[27] Justin Martyr was one of the Christian Apologists of the second century. Servetus would not have had first-hand knowledge of his works since they were first printed in Paris in 1551 by Robert Estienne. His one quotation of Justin comes from a passage in Irenaeus where Justin is cited (*Adv. Haer.*, IV, vi).

[28] The works of Origen (c. A.D. 185-253), the great Alexandrian scholar and most prolific of the Christian authors of the early Church, were printed in Paris by Josse Bade from 1512 on.

set to the disputation, desired us to write down the *bare*ᶜ proposi-

ᶜ *This is the way you invent things.*

tions which in our judgment were impious and incompatible with the true faith, so that if Servetus had any kind of explanation he might produce it openly and prove his assertions with whatever reasons he could muster. We in turn were to show from the Word of God that we had condemned nothing rashly. This was resolved in the presence of Servetus, who offered no objection. We have done as desired. Because to enumerate all his errors would take too long, we have *in good faith*ᵈ presented certain verbatim extracts

ᵈ *Cain-like faith, homicidal.*

so that from them a judgment concerning the whole book[29] might be formed. It will now be apparent whether Calvin has arrogated to himself the tyranny of the Sorbonne, by condemning rashly and without reason, or whether in fact Servetus has with his customary petulance and without any shame calumniously twisted what we, as the case required and as ordered by the Council, have set out under the main heads which have been called in question.

SERVETUS My whole point was that this name "Son" is properly and always attributed in Holy Scripture to the Son of man, just as the name "Jesus" and the name "Christ" are properly and always attributed to the same. In proof of this I adduced all the places of Scripture where this term "Son" occurs, which always designates the Son as man. I affirm that it is impossible to find any place in the gospels where this term "Son" occurs in which it does not stand for the Son as man. If, then, this is how Scripture always understands it, we also ought always to understand it in this way.

I said that the reason why the second person in the Godhead was formerly called a person was because he was a personal representation of the man Jesus Christ, already subsistent hypostatically in God, and visibly resplendent in the same Godhead. It is because this explanation of "person" is unknown to Calvin, and because almost the whole argument hangs upon it, that I here adduce references from the ancient doctors of the Church.

[29] The reference is to Servetus' *Christianismi Restitutio* which was published in this same year, 1553, at Vienne in Dauphiné, and which was the principal cause of his conviction. It is cited throughout the course of the disputation. The *Christianismi Restitutio* was condemned first in France and then in Geneva, and burnt at Champel with its author. Only three copies of the original edition are still in existence. It was reprinted in exact reproduction (with the same pagination) by Mürr in Nüremberg in 1790.

MINISTERS With regard to his assertion that his purpose was to prove that the name "Son" is everywhere attributed to Christ as man, it is easy to show even from the pages of his own book *how frivolous this cavil is.*ᵃ His real purpose was *to deny*ᵇ that

> ᵃ *See what I say at the beginning of my book, page 5, and in book 3, page 92, and in my first letter to you, page 577, and at the very beginning of my work addressed to Melanchthon, page 689.*[30]
> ᵇ *That is a falsehood.*

the Word of God, who clothed Himself with our flesh, was anything; *to deny*ᶜ that He was begotten of the Father before all ages;

> ᶜ *That is a falsehood.*

and with more than appalling abuse to rend asunder all the faithful who confess that the *Son of God*ᵈ was *eternal.*ᵉ We affirm

> ᵈ *As personal.*
> ᵉ *I also confess it on pp. 582 and 733.*

also that *the Word of God*ᶠ clothed with flesh, and God manifested

> ᶠ *Not the man himself.*

in the flesh, was properly *and truly*ᵍ the Son of God. And Calvin's

> ᵍ *I always call the man himself Son, just as Scripture does.*

words are found in the fifth chapter of his Institutes[31] to the effect that *even as man*ʰ Christ is *truly*ⁱ the Son of God, although not by

> ʰ *And also as God He is the Son, therefore there are two sons.*
> ⁱ *Various trifles are complex.*

reason of His human nature. Thus Servetus wickedly lies when he says that *we have imposed our own meaning on "Son".*ʲ He

> ʲ *Thus he plainly says that the Son is called man by virtue of the union, not naturally so.*

fancifully maintains, further, that Christ is the Son of God *for the reason that*ᵏ *His flesh is heavenly*ˡ and divine, compounded *of*

> ᵏ *Not for that reason alone.*
> ˡ *Like the heavenly manna, John 6, so the second man from heaven is heavenly, I Cor. 15* [Jn. 6:32f. and I Cor. 15:47].

*three uncreated elements.*ᵐ As for his contention that the name

> ᵐ *I said, on pages 120, 164, and 193, that their original was in the archetype of the Word. But you shamelessly turn everything to a bad meaning.*

"Son" is nowhere found in the gospels except with reference to

---

[30] Servetus is referring to his *Epistolae triginta ad Joannem Calvinum Gebennensium concionatorem* and to his *De Mysterio Trinitatis et veterum disciplina, ad Philippum Melanchthonem et ejus collegas, Apologia*, which were appended to his *Christianismi Restitutio*.

[31] Actually, in chapter VII of the editions of the *Institutes* current in 1553, and in book II, chapter XIV, 4 of the subsequent and final edition of 1559.

Christ as man, this is a matter over which *there is no dispute.*ⁿ

> ⁿ *On the contrary, for you perfidiously refuse to acknowledge that the Son is properly and always man.*

Consequently he has no excuse for causing a disturbance; yet he has *perniciously troubled*º the Church by fabricating the enormi-

> º *It is you who perniciously trouble the Church with your teaching of Simon Magus.*[32]

ties for which he contends. Clearly, there is nothing remarkable if the apostles call *the Word of God*ᵖ manifested in the flesh "Son".

> ᵖ *No, the man precisely, who as man is the Word and Jesus Christ.*

But it must also be seen whether that Word was not *begotten*ᑫ of

> ᑫ *In a personal manner.*

the Father before all ages. Concerning this deep mystery nothing can be said more plainly than what is found in the first chapter of John [v. 1], namely, that *the Word was with God.*ʳ For the eternal

> ʳ *You are ignorant of what the Word properly is.*

majesty and the unity of essence and *the distinction of person*ˢ are

> ˢ *That is true.*

plainly expressed there. Servetus plays with *the term "person",*ᵗ

> ᵗ *I take the word "person" in its most proper sense, while you misuse it.*

pretending that it is *an idea or a resplendence.*ᵘ The words of

> ᵘ *Substantial.*

John, however, *do not support*ᵛ such a cavil. And when *Christ*ʷ

> ᵛ *You fail to understand them.*
> ʷ *Man.*

speaks, in the 17th chapter [v. 5] of the glory which He had with the Father from the beginning, He means by these words not that He was merely glory or *an idea,*ˣ as Servetus imagines, but rather

> ˣ *I speak of a true hypostasis.*

that He was *wisdom,*ʸ which was *begotten*ᶻ of the Father and

> ʸ *The very person of Christ.*
> ᶻ *In a personal manner.*

*resides*ᵃ in Him, and that He participated in His glory. A real

> ᵃ *Truly.*

distinction is also apparent in the first chapter of the Epistle to the Hebrews [v. 3], where the Apostle calls *the Son*ᵇ the express

> ᵇ *The man Christ.*

*image*ᶜ of the substance of God the Father. For unless His own

---

[32] The allusion is to the incident recounted in Acts 8:9ff.

     ᶜ *As I have explained in bk. 3. p. 116, and likewise Tertullian, pp. 41, 336, 353, and 354.*

substance was from the Father, this statement of the Apostle that the Son is His express image would not stand. He, then, who acknowledges that the Father is eternal God, as Scripture declares Him to be, will not deny that *the Son*ᵈ also is eternal. He who

    ᵈ *Truly.*

confesses that the world was created by God the Father through His Word will concede that a *real*ᵉ distinction is necessary. More-

    ᵉ *Irenaeus teaches to the contrary, in the seventh place which I have quoted from him, and Tertullian also.*

over, if we like to wrangle over a word, the name Son of God refers to something *beyond human*ᶠ nature in the 30th chapter of

    ᶠ *That is a falsehood. On the contrary, it is a prophecy of Christ, and on p. 31 of his letter to the Philippians Ignatius applies it to Christ as man, and likewise Tertullian, p. 251. Who will not see how destitute of the truth you are when you have no other place to produce concerning the Son?*

Proverbs [vv. 3f.]. For the rest, since certain things will have to be said about this matter *in the appropriate places*,ᵍ we shall for the moment *pass over*ʰ many things.

    ᵍ ᵃⁿᵈ ʰ *He will produce nothing else from Holy Scripture. The case is already judged, and you are intent on awarding the victory to him.*

Because he *misapplies*ⁱ numerous testimonies of the ancient

    ⁱ *You are a worthless and shameless twister.*

writers it is *opportune*ʲ to point out how unworthily and futilely

    ʲ *Evidently.*

he distorts their words and how improperly he claims their support.

Passages From Tertullian

SERVETUS 1. The first place in Tertullian is found on pp. 200 and 201 of bk. 2 *Against Marcion*[33] where he says that God formerly assumed human senses and feelings, that God moved about in the form and with the other attributes of the human con-

---

[33] *Adv. Marc.*, bk. II, ch. 27. Tertullian's *Adversus Marcionem* belongs to his Montanist period and is the most extensive of his writings. His works were printed in Basle in 1521 by Beatus Rhenanus at the press of Frobenius, and there were several new impressions during the course of the next thirty years. No doubt Servetus became acquainted with Tertullian's writings during his stay in the territory of the Rhine. His quotations are not taken from the first edition of 1521 but from the impression of 1528. Tertullian was born in Carthage c. A.D. 160 and died some time after 220.

dition, that God conformed Himself to humanity, and that Christ Himself was visible in the Godhead. "We profess", he says, "that Christ always acted in the name of God the Father, that from the beginning He had converse with men, and that He communed with the patriarchs and prophets". And a little further on: "Christ was appointed by the Father for this very purpose, learning even from the very beginning that state of a man which he was in the end to become". And on p. 201, when teaching that God has never been seen, he says that Scripture means "that the Father is invisible, in whose authority and name He who appeared as the Son of God was God; but with us Christ is received in the person of Christ". He points out that He is called a person because the person of Christ was formerly seen, and He is thus a personal Son.

MINISTERS The first place that he adduces contains nothing other than that the Son of God formerly appeared to the fathers *in the form of a man*,[a] which was a prelude to the still future

[a] *Subsisting in the same Godhead, which he for that reason calls the person of Christ in God: but you are deaf when it comes to hearing the name "person" where you don't wish to hear it.*

incarnation. This is the unanimous tradition of *all*[b] the ancient

[b] *You are talking nonsense.*

doctors of the Church, and also of the theologians of the *Sorbonne*.[c]

[c] *You are talking nonsense.*

But it is irrelevant to the argument of Servetus.

SERVETUS 2. The second place is on p. 138 of the book *Against the Jews*,[34] where he says: "He who spoke to Moses was the Son of God Himself, who also used always to appear visibly. For no man has ever seen God the Father. Therefore it follows that it was the Son of God who spoke to Moses and was seen by him". At that time, then, it was the Son, the man Jesus Christ, who was visible.

MINISTERS In this second place Tertullian teaches that it was always the *Son of God*[a] who was seen. From this fact Servetus concludes that there always existed some visible substance from

[a] *He does not differ from the Father except by the distinction of visible and invisible, as on pp. 429, 430, and 431.*

which the body of Christ was compounded. But Tertullian means that Christ was seen by a dispensation, not in accordance with His

---

[34] *Adversus Judaeos*, ch. IX.

nature,[b] under a sort of type. We now cast back these same words

   [b] *The nature of a word is to represent: it is for this reason that Tertullian assigns a body to the Word.*

against Servetus; for if it was always the Son who was seen, it *necessarily*[c] follows that *the Son*[d] has always existed.

   [c] *That is true.*
   [d] *As personal.*

SERVETUS 3. The third place is on p. 41 of the book on the Resurrection of the Flesh,[35] where he says that the flesh of Adam was formed from the earth and shaped to the likeness and image of God, which is Christ, who already at that time had such a likeness in God. "That which God formed", he says, "He made according to the image of God, namely Christ. He who was constituted in the likeness of God did not think it robbery to be equal with God". Tertullian cites this saying of Paul to the Philippians [2:6] saying that Christ was already formerly constituted in the form and likeness of God, and he declares that it was the same form and likeness of God to the image and similitude of which the flesh of Adam was conformed. There was, therefore, a visible likeness and person of Christ, then already resplendent in God.

MINISTERS This third place, since it affirms nothing except that *the image*[a] of God in which man was created was the Son,

   [a] *Did you confess the form and likeness of flesh subsistent in the Word? O shameless twister!*

requires no refutation: for we have always *professed*[b] this very

   [b] *You lie openly against the mind of Tertullian.*

thing.

SERVETUS 4. The fourth place is on pp. 335 and 336 of the fifth book *Against Marcion*[36]: "Who was it that said in the person of Christ, 'Let there be light'? [Gen. 1:3]. Who was it that said to Christ concerning the enlightenment of the world, 'I have set thee to be a light of the Gentiles'? [Is. 49:6; quoted in Acts 13:47]. 'O Lord, he says, 'the light of thy person, or of thy countenance, has been set upon us' [Ps. 4:6].[37] Now the person of God is Christ the Lord; and this person is called by the Apostle the image of God [II Cor. 4:4]. Therefore Christ was the person of the Creator who said, 'Let there be light'". This is what Tertullian writes. Notice how many times he repeats the noun "person": and what

[35] *De Resurrectione Carnis*, ch. VI.
[36] *Adversus Marcionem*, bk. V, ch. 11.
[37] Here Servetus indicates the two meanings of πρόσωπον (used in the Septuagint). His argument revolves around the term "person".

he understands by "person" is precisely the appearance of Christ already hypostatically resplendent and truly speaking in the creation itself. Moreover, he expounds the expression "the image of God" used by the Apostle in Colossians 1 [v. 15],[38] calling it the divine appearance of Christ which was resplendent in God.

MINISTERS He proves nothing from this fourth place save that Christ is *the person of God*[a]: but in turn he could have

[a] *He says that the very appearance of man is the true person and image in God: but Satan has blinded your eyes.*

elicited from the context that *the person of Christ was in the Father*.[b] For the rest, the *sense*[c] of the writer is simple, that the

[b] *Would that you believed this!*
[c] *Of which, plainly, you are ignorant.*

hypostasis of the Father shone forth *in the Son*,[d] since the essence

[d] *By what phantasms?*

was the same.

SERVETUS 5. The fifth place is on p. 351 of the same bk. 5,[39] in the following words: "The Apostle says that Christ is the image of the invisible God [Col. 1:15]. But we affirm that the Father of Christ is invisible, knowing that it was the Son who always appeared in ancient times in the name of God, as His image. He does not proceed, however, to make any distinction between a visible and an invisible God." There is a very beautiful passage, next to the preceding, which teaches that in the essence of God there is no real distinction between the Father and the Son, as between two invisible things, as the tritheists fondly imagine, but that there is only a personal distinction between the invisible Father and the visible Son, which he also calls a formal disposition in God in his book *Against Praxeas* — on pages 418, 419, 420, 429, and more clearly still on pages 430 and 431.[40]

MINISTERS The sum of the fifth place is that God the Father, who in Himself is invisible, was always visible in the Son. This we *gladly embrace*:[a] not because *there was a visible essence of the*

[a] *By propounding absurdities.*

Son,[b] but because God shone upon men through *the light*[c] of His

[b] *On the contrary, Tertullian particularly contends there that the substance of the Son is visible and corporeal.*
[c] *Concealed from you.*

---

[38] See also Servetus' next section.
[39] *Adversus Marcionem*, bk. V, ch. 19.
[40] *Adversus Praxean*, ch. IIff.

wisdom, and because the Word of God was the bond of communication between God and men. *How wickedly Servetus*ᵈ attempts

ᵈ *O blindest wretch!*

to overthrow the real distinction is obvious to all, without our having to say anything. In what sense the disposition is called *formal*ᵉ we shall explain *elsewhere.*ᶠ

ᵉ *This is our whole inquiry, not to be glossed over here.*
ᶠ *Where? Defeated, he deceitfully turns tail.*

SERVETUS 6. The sixth place is on pp. 353 and 354 of the same book,[41] where he says that Christ was formed in the likeness of God, and that elsewhere the Apostle calls Christ the image of the invisible God [Col. 1:15] precisely because he places Him in the likeness of God. Therefore, He was truly the image of God and of man, resplendent in God and restoring man. These are golden words which ought to be perpetually remembered.

MINISTERS In this sixth place he is exposed as *a falsifier,*ᵃ

ᵃ *It is only you who falsely attempt to corrupt the sense of Tertullian, who speaks always of the visible image, form, and likeness.*

for Marcion, wishing to prove that the body of Christ was imaginary, seized on the saying of Paul that Christ was found in fashion as a man [Phil. 2:8]. Tertullian retorts that He is said at the same time to have been in the form of God [Phil. 2:6]. And hence he concludes that form is not something *contrary*ᵇ to true substance.

ᵇ *But there was a form and likeness in the very substance of God, just as in the substance of the flesh; so that in either case the fashion and likeness belong to the substance. This is what he says.*

His words are: "Will it not equally follow from the passage where the Apostle places him in the likeness of God that Christ is not truly God, if He was not truly man because He was constituted in the likeness of man? For in both cases the true substance will have to be excluded if likeness or similitude or form is attributed to a phantom. But if in likeness and image, as the Son of the Father, He is judged to be truly God, then also as the Son of man, in the likeness and image of man, He is found to be truly man." Servetus, however, cunningly, or rather *wickedly,*ᶜ supposes of his

ᶜ *You are a Simon Magus, always wicked and perverse.*

own imagining that He was therefore *truly*ᵈ the image of God and

ᵈ *In either case the idea of a phantom being excluded.*

of man, resplendent in God, and restoring man. Then, applauding

---

[41] *Adversus Marcionem*, bk. V, ch. 20.

his own fallacy, he exclaims: "These are golden words which ought to be perpetually remembered".

SERVETUS 7. The seventh place is on pp. 422 and 423 of the book *Against Praxeas*,[42] where he affirms that the Word is something substantial, so constructed in the Spirit that a certain reality and person can be seen. He says that the Word signifies or represents something, but not in such a way that it is an empty thing. Our word, he points out, is a kind of structure projected into the air, and it vanishes away. But the Word of God, constructed in the Godhead itself, ever remains, as he says, in its own representation. He says, moreover,[43] that there is here no προβολή or emanation of one thing from another: therefore there is no real distinction as between two separate entities; but in the very Godhead of the Father there is an emanation, the construction of the Word, and a formal disposition. Hence there arises, he says, the economy, dispensation, or disposition of the Trinity, constituted in as many names as God has wished. See likewise p. 419.[44]

MINISTERS This seventh place is so far from lending him any support that, rather, it pointedly opposes his *raving*.[a] For

> [a] *Tell me, you wretch, why on p. 422, line 4, and on p. 423, line 1, Tertullian says that the Word was formed and constructed by the Spirit and Wisdom? What kind of construction was that? Visible? Corporeal? as he says it was.*

although he quotes *words*[b] neither accurately nor honestly, yet he

> [b] *See lines 4, 5, and 6.*

says that the reality can be seen. But what follows in this same passage of Tertullian is *much clearer*[c]; for he *denies*[d] that the Son,

> [c] *He is digressing, to avoid answering.*
> [d] *That is true.*

or Word, who proceeded from such great substances and made such great substances, Himself lacks substance. He then inquires whether the Word of God, who is called the Son and Himself shares the name of God, is something void and empty. "In what form of God was he?" Tertullian asks. "Certainly in some form, not in none." Again: "Whatever was the substance of the Word, I call it a *person*[e] and assign it the name of Son; and while I ac-

> [e] *Visible.*

knowledge the Son I affirm Him to be *second*[f] to the Father". The

> [f] *By disposition.*

---
[42] *Adversus Praxean*, ch. VII.
[43] Ch. VIII.
[44] Chs. II-IV.

sum-total of this is that he *asserts*ᵍ a *real*ʰ distinction. How much

ᵍ *That is a falsehood.*

ʰ *Nothing such is ever heard in Tertullian, but only in disposition.*

greater, and less tolerable, is the *shamelessness*ⁱ of Servetus when

ⁱ *On the contrary, the shamelessness is yours.*

in the midst of such clear light he does not hesitate to spread clouds of smoke. By the device of denying that he has introduced πεοβολή he thinks to drive from himself the ill-will which heretics have maliciously and slanderously engendered. Meanwhile Tertullian makes it plain that he is speaking of "two, God *and His Word*ʲ,

ʲ *As something invisible from which something visible appears, according to his explanation.*

the Father and His Son; just as the root and the fruit are two things, but conjoined; a fount and a river are two distinctions, but indivisible; the sun and its ray are two forms, but in combination. For everything which proceeds from something else is necessarily second to that from which it proceeds, yet not for that reason separate. Where, however, there is a second, *there must be two* ;

ᵏ *By disposition, as he says.*

and where there is a third, *there must be three.*ˡ Now the Spirit

ˡ *By disposition.*

is a third, proceeding from the Father and the Son." At length he concludes: "Thus the Trinity, flowing down from the Father by interfused and connected steps, in no way disturbs the monarchy and at the same time guards the state of the economy". If there were a single drop of modesty in Servetus, would he have dared to wrest this passage for the purpose of denying the *real*ᵐ distinc-

ᵐ *Had Simon Magus not blinded you, you would have seen that a real distinction is never spoken of there, but a formal disposition. On p. 442 he removes any distinction between the Word and the Spirit, and indeed quite openly denies it.*

tion?

SERVETUS 8. The eighth place is on p. 15 of the book on *The Flesh of Christ*[45], where for the purpose of demonstrating the human person of the Word he uses three arguments: from angels, from the Holy Spirit, and from the soul. The first is stated as follows: "You have read and believed, Marcion, that the angels of the Creator have assumed human form, and have even assumed a body so real that Abraham washed their feet (Gen. 18), Lot was rescued from the Sodomites by their hands (Gen. 19), and an

[45] *De Carne Christi*, ch. III.

angel also wrestled with a man (Gen. 32). If, therefore, this has been permitted to angels, which are inferior, much more is it permitted to the Word of God". He repeats this on p. 89.

MINISTERS This eighth place, since it teaches nothing except that the Son of God was *truly able to be clothed with* human flesh^a,

^a *No: He truly had a human form beforehand.*

and that angels were truly enveloped in human bodies, is plainly in our favour and *refutes*^b Servetus.

^b *Simon Magus is refuted.*

SERVETUS 9. The ninth place is on p. 16 of the same book[46] where, citing from the gospel [cf. Mt. 3:16, Jn. 1:32], he says that the Holy Spirit descended on Christ in corporeal form, in corporeal appearance, in corporeal shape, and he affirms that there was the solidity of a body in the very substance of the Holy Spirit. The same is therefore also the case with the Word. But, as is customary in Tertullian, the body must be understood as a truly visible substance.

MINISTERS This ninth place has no other purpose than *that we may know that the Son of God has appeared in the true*^a sub-

^a *No: that we may know that beforehand there was a true visible form in the Godhead.*

stance of flesh. Servetus madly *accommodates this to his raving*^b,

^b *Are you not ashamed to close your eyes to so obvious a truth?*

that there has always been a visible substance of man in God.

SERVETUS 10. The tenth place is on p. 19 of the same book[47] where, repeating the argument from angels already mentioned, he says that the Lord Jesus Christ Himself appeared to Abraham at the same time in the company of the angels (in Gen. 18, as above), and that then already Christ Himself was learning to converse with, to liberate, and to judge men, in the true, not feigned, substantial form of a man.

MINISTERS From this tenth place nothing more can be legitimately elicited than from the others, namely, that Christ *appeared*^a to the patriarchs in the company of angels, which no

^a *In the true substance of the Godhead.*

one has ever denied. And here too the criminal falsity of the man is apparent. Tertullian's words are: "Already at that same time

---

[46] *Loc. cit.*
[47] *Op. cit.*, ch. VI.

the Word of God was learning to converse with and to liberate and to judge the human race in the garb of a flesh which was not as yet born, since it was not yet the time for it to die before both its nativity and its mortality were announced". Servetus, however, gives these words an unnatural meaning when he says that then already Christ was learning to converse with and to liberate and to judge men in the true, not feigned, *substantial form*[b]

[b] *Was not that true corporeal garb a true substantial form?*

of a man.

SERVETUS 11. The eleventh place is on p. 24 of the same book[48] where he argues concerning the soul that, while it is an existent spiritual substance, yet it has the form of a body, and preserves its human shape after separation from the body. Therefore such a form is not inconsistent with the Word of God too.

MINISTERS In citing this eleventh place he raves in a manner of which he ought to be ashamed. Tertullian is disputing there against heretics who *feign that the flesh of Christ*[a][49] was changed

[a] *That is a falsehood, for on the contrary they deny the flesh of Christ.*

into a body, and he maintains that the substances and natures are different. But Servetus takes it in an opposite sense, fondly imagining that there is a corporeal form in the spiritual substance of Christ. This is nothing *other than*[b] to side with the heretics against

[b] *It is you who are raving.*

whom Tertullian is fighting.

SERVETUS 12. The twelfth place is found at line 15 of p. 29 of the same book[50] where he says that Christ Himself emanated as man from God Himself, and, at line 33,[51] that the Son of God is from the seed of the Father. Calvin objects to these two statements as though I were guilty of great crimes. He shouts, but proves nothing. He displays his ignorance and manifestly shows that he has never read Tertullian. Irenaeus also speaks of the seed of the Father in book 4, ch. 51, p. 262.

MINISTERS He corrupts this twelfth place no less shamelessly than perfidiously — as though Tertullian taught that Christ

---

[48] *Op. cit.*, ch. XI.
[49] This would seem to be a *lapsus calami*, and for "flesh" we should read "soul", or "divinity", as in the Latin and French editions of Calvin's *Defence of the Orthodox Faith Concerning the Holy Trinity*.
[50] *Op. cit.*, ch. XVII.
[51] *Ibid.*, ch. XVIII.

as man, as Servetus imagines, *emanated from God*[a] and is the Son

[a] *It is the truth.*

of God *from the seed of the Father.*[b] We admit, indeed, that

[b] *It is the truth.*

something similar is found there, but with a very different meaning. "God", he says, "sent down His Word into the womb of a virgin. And, to reply more simply, it was not fitting that the Son of God should be born of human seed, lest, if He were wholly the son of man, He should fail to be also the Son of God. Therefore, in order that He who was already *the Son of God from the seed of God the Father, which is the Spirit,*[c] might be the Son of

[c] *Remember that for Tertullian the Word and the Spirit are the same, as he himself testifies on p. 442. For him also Wisdom and the Holy Spirit are the same (see pp. 369 and 422) because he never acknowledges a real distinction.*

man, that flesh alone had to be assumed which was from the flesh of man, without the seed of a male. For the seed of a male was unnecessary for one who had the seed of God. Thus, just as before He was born of the virgin He was able to have God as His Father without a human mother, so likewise when He was born of the virgin He was able to have a mother without a human father." He concludes at length that the flesh of Christ was made from that flesh in which He was born, indeed that its substance was received from His mother alone without male seed. So great, however, is the depravity of Servetus that he hopes to camouflage his execrable error with the pretence that *the flesh of Christ*[d] was produced from

[d] *The flesh of Christ truly partook of divinity, even when it was in the sepulchre.*

the heavenly substance of God.

SERVETUS 13. The thirteenth place is on pp. 32 and 34 of the same book[52] where he says that that man who is the fruit of the womb, the flower and stem from the root of Jesse, a male opening the womb, is Himself properly the Son of God, who is also the son of Mary. And he says the same on pp. 109, 245, and 246.

MINISTERS We embrace this thirteenth place without controversy; but at the same time this must remain fixed, that the Word of God, who, as clothed with our flesh, is *properly called*

[52] *Op. cit.,* chs. XXIf.

the Son of God and Christ,ᵃ is worthily accounted to be the eternal

   ᵃ *You say that "Christ" is properly a name of man and "Son" a name of Deity. But now by some kind of sophistry you confuse the two.*

Son of God because He is *the Word begotten of the Father before the ages.*ᵇ

   ᵇ *As begotten, Christ Jesus was begotten in a personal manner as man.*

SERVETUS   14. The fourteenth place is on p. 43 of the book *The Resurrection of the Flesh*[53] where he says that the soul performs its vital operations through the body in such a way that for it to be separated from the body would be as though it should die. This is the language I have used. Calvin then deceitfully charges me with having said that souls are mortal, whereas both there and in hundreds of other places I have always taught the opposite.

MINISTERS   He tries in vain to cover over his impious and profane error by citing this fourteenth place. What Tertullian says there is that through the flesh the soul is supported by every instrument of the senses. From this it in no way follows that *the soul was made mortal like the flesh.*ᵃ

   ᵃ *It is most shamelessly that you charge me with this.*

SERVETUS   15. The fifteenth place is on p. 71 of the same book[54] where he quotes Paul to the effect that the glory of God and the true light of God are known by us in the face of Jesus Christ [II Cor. 4:6]. I have written extensively concerning this vision of the true divine light in the face of Jesus Christ in my third book on the Trinity. But Calvin, blind as ever, is unwilling to see God in this way. Tertullian confirms this same divine vision in the face of Jesus Christ from the saying of Christ Himself, on p. 436 of his book against Praxeas.

MINISTERS   He mischievously twists this fifteenth place, *as though the spiritual substance of Christ were visible from the beginning, whereas Tertullian intends no such thing;*ᵃ indeed, his

   ᵃ *You are so shameless that you would deny that snow is white.*

words convey a quite different sense, namely, that the Father was visible in the Son because He manifested Himself through His

---

[53] *De Resurrectione Carnis*, ch. VII.
[54] *Op. cit.*, ch. XLIV.

Word as He pleased. This interpretation has the consent of all ages.

SERVETUS There are innumerable other places in Tertullian concerning the visible person and form of the man Christ, who is ever resplendent in God, as, for example, on pages 212, 213, 219, 228, 229, 327, 331, 430, 432, 438. The same man Christ walked in paradise, talking with Adam face to face. He closed the ark after Noah had entered into it. He descended in the form of a man to judge the tower of Babel, to speak with Abraham, to destroy the Sodomites. He appeared to Jacob, and to Moses in the bush. He was seen in the fiery furnace of Babylon, when His appearance, as we read in Daniel 3, was said to be like to the Son of God. Tertullian cites these and other passages on pp. 431 and 432.

16. I shall add one further place where the identity of the face of Christ, both formerly and now, is beautifully shown. On pp. 428 and 429 of his book *Against Praxeas*[55] and on p. 272 of his book *Against Marcion*[56] Tertullian cites Exodus 33, where Moses asked to see the face of God which was then hidden. Moses did not see it then, but after the coming of Christ he saw it in the transfiguration on the mount, as we read in Mt. 17, and thus it was then that Christ granted his request, as Irenaeus beautifully teaches in bk. 4, ch. 37, p. 243, and also Tertullian on p. 272. The face of Christ is always to be understood therefore as the same as is now resplendent in heaven, as was seen in the transfiguration of Mt. 17, as was seen by Paul, Acts 9, and by John, Rev. 1, shining with uncreated light above the brilliance of the sun. If it were possible for the humanity to be separated now from that light, the light of God would still remain in the form of a man which was already conformed to man: and thus from eternity it was resplendent in God. For the divine form is never changed. But now to turn to Irenaeus.

MINISTERS It remains for us to cite, instead of the innumerable other testimonies which *this windbag*[a] pretends to have, a

[a] *O you Simon Magus, a man bewitched!*

few, but *perfectly clear*[b] and definite, places from which the true

[b] *You ridiculous mouse!*

meaning of the writer may be understood.

On p. 421 of his book against Praxeas[57] Tertullian maintains that the nativity of the Word was perfect *in the creation of the*

---

[55] *Adversus Praxean*, ch. XIV.
[56] *Adversus Marcionem*, bk. IV, ch. 22.
[57] *Adversus Praxean*, ch. VII.

world,ᶜ and on the following page he says that *He was begotten*ᵈ

   ᶜ *Contrary to what you teach.*
   ᵈ *In the creation. But this is a begetting of which you are completely ignorant.*

when He proceeded from the Father.

In the same book he reasons that the Son *has always existed*ᵉ

   ᵉ *In His own person and substance.*

because the Father has always existed; and that they are *distinct*ᶠ

   ᶠ *By personal disposition.*

because of the relationship between them.

On p. 425 of the same book[58] he writes: "We prove from the Scriptures that God the Father made His Word a Son *to Himself.*ᵍ

   ᵍ *As personal.*

For if He calls Him Son, and if the Son is none other than He who has *proceeded from the Father Himself*,ʰ then He will be the Son,

   ʰ *The visible from the invisible.*

and not the same as the One from whom He proceeded. For He did not proceed from Himself. You, however, who say that the Father is the same as the Son make the same person both to have produced from Himself (and Himself to have proceeded from) that which is God." What more obvious *proof*ⁱ of a real distinction

   ⁱ *Some proof!*

could be asked?

On p. 426 of the same book[59] he distinguishes between the persons in this real sense. "For", he says, citing Psalm 110, "it is the Spirit who speaks, the Father to whom He speaks, and *the Son*ʲ

   ʲ *The Son is there compared with the Father, that is, Christ with God, as he explains there, on line 9. For these are prophecies of the man Christ.*

of whom He speaks. In the same manner also other passages, which are spoken now to the Father concerning the Son, now to the Son concerning the Father, now to the Spirit, establish each person in His own proper character." The argument continues to p. 428.

On p. 429 of the same book[60] he explains how Christ may be both visible and invisible. "*The Visible and the Invisible are one and the same*", he says; "*and since both are the same it follows*

---

[58] Ch. XI.
[59] *Ibid.*
[60] Ch. XIV.

*that He is invisible as the Father and visible as the Son."*ᵏ By these

> ᵏ *It is Praxeas who said this, and Tertullian cites it with disapproval. But you understand nothing. I have taught, on pp. 96 and 731, that formerly the Word also was invisible.*

words he indicates that the Word was invisible in His essence, but that by dispensation he was the image of God.

On p. 435 of the same book[61] a *real*ˡ distinction is asserted with-

> ˡ *No: in line 2 it is called a disposition.*

out any obscurity in the following words: "Undoubtedly He who was from the beginning is shown to be other than He with whom He was. The Word of God is other than the Lord God, although the Word is also God: God, however, in that He is the Son of God, not the Father. He through whom all things were made is *other*ᵐ than He by whom all things were made."

> ᵐ *Other by disposition is what he says, line 28.*

On the same page he thunders against the whole teaching of Servetus when he says that it would be more tolerable *to proclaim that the two are divided than that the one God*ⁿ *assumes different*

> ⁿ *This is an incongruous deduction since both are denied.*

guises.

That an *interior*º hypostasis is meant is apparent on p. 441[62] where

> º *I have stated both an external and an internal hypostasis on p. 705 of my book.*

he says that the Father became visible in the Son by *the*ᵖ mighty

> ᵖ *His.*

works, not by *representation of His person.*ᑫ And a little further on

> ᑫ *Which means separate representation, of the kind that Philip requested* [the allusion is to Jn. 14:8ff.] *as he says in line 13.*

he adds that in this way *the property*ʳ of each person is apparent.

> ʳ *But I have clearly taught, on p. 273 of my book, that the persons are distinguished by the property of action.*

He explains, moreover, *that*ˢ the Father was seen in the Son, not

> ˢ *By works and miracles, is what he says there.*

by sight, but by intelligence.

Nor otherwise will what is found on p. 443[63] make sense (". . . it is not into a unipersonal God that He commands them to baptize: for we are immersed not once, but three times, into the

---

[61] Ch. XXI.
[62] Ch. XXIV.
[63] Ch. XXVI.

separate persons at the mention of each name separately") unless *a real distinction*[t] is affirmed.

> [t] *Who denies that the man who is the Son is really distinct from God the Father?*

On the same page[64] he shows how far he recoils from the raving of Servetus, that the flesh of Christ is of *the substance of God*,[u]

> [u] *It truly participates in God's substance.*

when he says: "The flesh is not God so that it could have been said of it, 'That *holy*[v] thing shall be called the Son of God', but

> [v] *Holiness is related, not to the flesh, but to the Spirit: for this reason he says, in the last line, that it was the Holy Spirit that was born.*

He who was born in it *is* God". Again, a little further on, at the beginning of the following page, he writes: "Did the word become incarnate by being as it were transfigured into flesh, or by being clothed with flesh? Certainly by being *clothed*.[w] For it is neces-

> [w] *I teach all these things everywhere, and they are not at all to the point.*

sary to believe that God is immutable and incapable of form, as He is also eternal. But transfiguration is the destruction of what previously existed. For everything which is transfigured into something else ceases to be what it had been, and begins to be what it has not been. It follows, therefore, that He must be understood to have become flesh at the time when He came to be in the flesh, and was manifested and seen and handled by means of the flesh. For if the Word became flesh by transfiguration and a change of substance, there would now be one substance, a kind of mixture of flesh and spirit, like *electrum* compounded of gold and silver which ceases to be either gold or silver since a *tertium quid* produced from both is neither one nor the other. But we find everywhere that He is both the Son of God and the Son of man, both God and man, without doubt distinct according to each substance in its own special property, inasmuch as the Word is nothing other than God nor the flesh anything other than man." At length he concludes: "We see that there is a twofold state, not confused, but conjoined in one person — Jesus, God and Man. But if this were a *tertium quid* compounded from both like *electrum*, no distinct proofs of either substance would be apparent: either the Word would be mortal or the flesh would be immortal, if the Word had been converted into flesh."

[64] Ch. XXVII.

We think that there is *no need to accumulate more*ˣ evidence,

    ˣ *There is no need for you to wander away from the point any further.*

since the emptiness of this man is demonstrated plainly and soundly enough by these places.ʸ

    ʸ *You have omitted the sixteenth place from Tertullian concerning the vision, both formerly and now, of the divine face of Christ, and the manner in which the desire of Moses to see that face was fulfilled. You will find a comparison of Irenaeus, p. 243, with Tertullian, pp. 272 and 429, very beautiful.*

Passages from Irenaeus Concerning the Human Person of the Word

SERVETUS 1. The first place from Irenaeus is in bk. 4, ch. 17, pp. 216 and 217, where he says that the Jews departed not knowing that He who in human shape spoke to Abraham and Aaron and Moses was the Son of God, the Word of God, Jesus Himself, who already had formed man to His own image, and who also Himself was already the likeness of God. Irenaeus teaches very plainly that in the Word there is a human person, the likeness of man, to the image and similitude of which the flesh of Adam was moulded, as he openly teaches on p. 298. He teaches, further, that the same Word was the divine likeness, which at one and the same time was the Word and the Spirit, without real distinction. For in the spiritual substance of the Father itself the likeness and representation of the Word was stamped, as the seventh place from Tertullian has already taught us, with which the teaching of Irenaeus is in complete harmony.

MINISTERS Since this first place only teaches that it was Jesus who spoke to the patriarchs in the form of a man, it is illegitimate for Servetus to derive from it that there is *an eternal apparition of man*.ᵃ What he cites from p. 298 is *just a fabrication*.ᵇ

    ᵃ *O you shameless fellow! Do you think that when He was seen it was only an apparition? Unless God was changing, His divine form remained constant.*

    ᵇ *These are Irenaeus' words there, at line 23: "There was a mixture of breath and divine Spirit in Adam's flesh, which was moulded according to the image of God". This image, therefore, was in the flesh. He says, moreover, that the Spirit of God was implanted in man, which this sorcerer denies.*

SERVETUS 2. The second place from Irenaeus is in the same book 4, ch. 15, p. 215, where he says that Abraham, taught by the representation of the Word, knew that the Son of God would become man. Do you hear, Calvin, that in the Word there is the representation of man? You have never heard it said that the Word is in any place unless He represents. Again, it is characteristic of a word to be expressed or uttered. When, therefore, John says, "In the beginning was the Word", it should be understood that there was an utterance in the Godhead representing Jesus Christ.

MINISTERS This second place, that Abraham was taught by a representation that the Son of God would become a man among men, is irrelevant to the present issue; for Servetus absurdly gathers from this that *there is no word unless it represents.*[a]

[a] *If only you had some knowledge of grammar and language, you would realize that the proper function of a word is to represent. It is appropriately called* Parole *in French because of this very signification. But Satan so overturns you in everything that you always abuse everything.*

SERVETUS 3. The third place is in the same book 4, ch. 8, p. 211, where he cites a certain senior disciple of the apostles to the effect that the Father who Himself is measureless was formerly measured in the Son; just as he says afterwards that the invisible Father was seen in the Son. For in this immeasurability and invisibility of the Father's light the visible form of the Son appeared, stood forth, and was produced, consisting in a certain kind of measure. And thus the Father, in Himself immeasurable, was measured in the Son; just as the Father, invisible in Himself, was rendered visible in the Word.

MINISTERS He shows similar shamelessness in this third place. Irenaeus quotes the opinion of an unknown man to the effect that the measureless Father was measured in the Son. Servetus thereupon *divines*[a] that he was one of the disciples of the

[a] *Irenaeus quotes him in this way throughout, and everywhere praises him.*

apostles. But this is of little consequence. What is indefensible is for him to take this word "measure", which *is there applied to the creation of the world,*[b] and to transfer it to the substance of

[b] *That is a falsehood:* Irenaeus *is there passing from one thing to another.*

Christ. For Irenaeus explains his own meaning when he says: "God does all things by measure and in order, and with Him there is nothing unmeasured, because nothing is disorganized". Afterwards he adds: "The Son is the measure of the Father, since He also comprehends Him". The things Servetus has tacked on are *his own*^c inventions.

 ^c *No, they are the statements of Irenaeus and Tertullian.*

SERVETUS 4. The fourth place is in the same book 4, ch. 37, pp. 242 and 243, where, quoting the words of Isaiah 6: "I have seen with my eyes the King, the Lord of hosts", he states: "They saw the Son of God conversing as man with men". And a little further on: "The Word spoke with Moses, appearing before his eyes, just as one might speak to his friend" [see Is. 6:51, Ex. 33:11, Num. 12:8]. He then teaches how Moses desired to see His face, which he afterwards saw transfigured on the mount; and points out that it was always the same face of Christ through which God was seen, and is now seen.

MINISTERS This fourth place is ineptly adduced, for in it *Irenaeus plainly teaches that by the Spirit of prophecy*^a the patri-

 ^a *You, most shameless of men, fail to see that what is being described there is the appearance of a reality then present, and standing before their eyes.*

archs saw that the Son of God would suffer, who was then impassible. But all this is no less consonant with our faith than it is contrary to the figments of Servetus.

SERVETUS 5. The fifth place is on p. 298 of bk. 5, where he says that the body of Adam in its entirety, the very flesh of Adam, was moulded from the clay of the earth in the image and similitude of God; precisely because Christ was already in the likeness and form of God, as the third place from Tertullian has already taught us.

MINISTERS The explanation of this fifth place was given earlier when we expounded *the third place from Tertullian.*^a For

 ^a *Let the judicious reader judge for himself, and let him take careful note of the mind of the author.*

none of us is so foolish as to deny that Christ is the eternal *image*^b

 ^b *An invisible phantom.*

of God. We assert, indeed, that the *image*^c which was hidden in

 ^c *Which image?*

God has shone forth in man. For Servetus, however, there is no *image*^d unless it is visible.

 ^d *Very properly so.*

SERVETUS 6. The sixth place is in bk. 1, ch. 2, p. 20, where he says that the Church received from the apostles the proclamation that God the Father Almighty is one, and that Jesus Christ His Son, who was born of a virgin, is one. Therefore if the birth truly took place from a virgin, He truly became the Son from the virgin. He adds afterwards that He is the Son of the invisible Father, for he always teaches that the Son is visible.

MINISTERS As is his custom, he shamelessly distorts this sixth place. Irenaeus says there that the right faith is in God the Father,[65] in one Son of God, incarnate for our salvation, and in the Holy Spirit, who foretold through the prophets the birth of Christ from a virgin, and His death and resurrection. We leave it to the readers to judge *how wickedly this corrupter alters the words.*[a] So frivolous, in fact, is his interpretation that we might

[a] *That is a falsehood. It is the very thing that both you and I say: why then do you so wickedly attack it?*

with better reason argue that Irenaeus *indicates a double birth;*[b]

[b] *Who would deny this?*

whereas what he clearly declares is that this birth from a virgin was foretold by the Spirit.

SERVETUS 7. The seventh place is in bk. 2, ch. 18, p. 84, and ch. 47, p. 117, where he says that God is the whole Logos and the whole Spirit, and that there is no real distinction. He teaches the same thing more obviously in ch. 48, p. 118, where he states that the Logos is the Father. And in ch. 56, p. 126, he says that the Father made everything through the Word, that is, through Himself. Similarly, in bk. 1, ch. 19, p. 41; bk. 2, ch. 2, p. 66; and bk. 4, ch. 52, p. 263, he says that the Father did not create through the Word as though through some other entity, but because He said, "Let there be", and it was so. Irenaeus says, moreover, that he learnt this from the disciples of the apostles.

MINISTERS He is false when he says that in this seventh place *a real distinction is denied;*[a] for Irenaeus teaches nothing

[a] *If the λόγος is Himself the Father, He cannot be really distinct, p. 118.*

there except that the complete fulness of the Godhead is in the Son and in the Spirit, as the unity of essence requires. What is found in ch. 48 of bk. 2 accords with this. In ch. 19 of bk. 1 nothing other is found than that the Father created all things

---

[65] Still more accurately, ".... in one God: the Father, ... the Son, ... and the Holy Spirit ...".

through the Word.[b] But this falsifier substitutes that He did not

[b] *That is, through Himself, as is said on p. 126.*

create through the Word as though through some other entity. The other places are in agreement; nor is our own confession other than what is there handed down.

SERVETUS 8. The eighth place is in bk. 2, ch. 10, p. 76, where he says that the Scriptures concerning the Word and the Spirit do not refer to distinct entities, but to dispositions of God. And in the same book, ch. 47, p. 115, he says that the Word and the Spirit are a mystery and disposition of God who exists, subsists, is communicated, and discloses Himself in this way. The emission is not made like rays from the sun, for that would rend and divide God, as he says in bk. 2, ch. 17, p. 82.

MINISTERS There is a similar distortion in this eighth place. Irenaeus denies that where Scripture speaks of God in the plural number a diversity of gods is indicated, but rather *dispositions which are in God.*[a] Instead of a variety of gods Servetus substi-

[a] *Which there are the Word and the Spirit.*

tutes distinct entities. No one of a sound mind, however, would not repudiate the emanations such as Valentinus and other fanatical men have invented.

SERVETUS 9. The ninth place is in bk. 2, ch. 6, pp. 143 and 144, where he says that in former times the Son of God was manifested to Abraham and to numerous others. In bk. 4, ch. 3, pp. 208 and 259 he says that the law was given to Moses by Christ Himself. "How", he asks on p. 224, "was Christ the end of the law if He was not also the beginning of it?" Abraham wandered on his pilgrimage with the Word, and in Him he saw Christ, as he says in bk. 4, ch. 12, p. 212. Jacob saw the same Word, bk. 4, ch. 23, p. 221. In former times the Word used to ascend and descend in the form of a man, bk. 4, ch. 26, p. 224, and ch. 27, p. 227. The same Word, the man Jesus, was seen in the furnace in Babylon; and He was also seen by Daniel in the clouds of heaven, bk. 4, ch. 37, p. 244. He is the same who used to speak with Adam in paradise, bk. 5, p. 314. In the Word, therefore, there was a visible person, and a true hypostasis, never changed, but as such ever permanent.

MINISTERS There is nothing to cause *difficulty*[a] in this ninth

[a] *He speaks of a true visible image, you of an invisible phantom. This presents no difficulty to Calvin!*

place. Servetus, however, is plainly pulling wool over our eyes when he insists so strongly on proving the eternity of Christ. We are, indeed, familiar with his sophistry that the flesh of Christ was eternal in a resplendent appearance; but to refute this presents no problem. For Irenaeus intends nothing else than that Christ who at length was manifested in the flesh, was the eternal Word[b] of God, and God.

[b] *Subsisting in a visible hypostasis.*

SERVETUS 10. The tenth place is in bk. 4, ch. 33, p. 235, where he says that the name of Jesus Christ belongs to the Father Himself, and that His image is the image of the Father. "Just as, were a king to paint the likeness of his son", he says, "he would rightly say that it was his own likeness and the likeness of his son, both because it is of his son and because he himself produced it". He vividly expresses what we have already taught from Tertullian concerning the image of Christ and of God; so that it is established that in this matter Irenaeus is in complete agreement with Tertullian: and also Clement, and indeed Peter himself, whom we shall now hear.

MINISTERS This tenth place *exposes the crass ignorance of Servetus.*[a] Irenaeus is concerned only to show that the glory of

[a] *No, it exposes your most shameless subterfuge. The place is absolutely plain.*

Father and Son is common and therefore one. This remarkable interpreter uses this as a pretext for *mixing the persons*[b] so that

[b] *That is a falsehood.*

no distinction remains.

For the rest, it is worth taking the trouble to draw attention to a few places, so that the great injury that Servetus does to Irenaeus in pretending that he is party to his errors may be obvious to all.

Bk. 3, p. 192: "If He did not receive *the substance of flesh*[c]

[c] *This is beside the point: he is speaking against the sorcerers who denied the flesh of Christ.*

from man, He was made neither man nor the Son of man; and if He was not made what we were, He did no great thing in that He suffered and rose again. But since ours is a body taken from the earth and *a soul receiving breath from God,*[d] everybody admits

[d] *You, together with Simon Magus, deny this death of the soul.*

that the Word of God was made this too, recapitulating in Himself His own handiwork." *Because, however, this place is mutilated,*[e]

[e] *Look elsewhere; you'll find no help here.*

we shall take what he says on p. 214 of bk. 4, namely, that *the only begotten Son came to us*ᶠ *recapitulating in Himself His own*

ᶠ *Who will deny this? It was thus that Christ Himself came to us from God Himself.*

handiwork. On p. 216 of the same book that stupid fiction of the eternity of the visible substance is *refuted*,ᵍ and the *eternal*ʰ hypo-

ᵍ *That is a falsehood.*

ʰ *Truly.*

stasis of the Son is affirmed. His words are: "All who from the beginning have prophesied have had the revelation from the Son Himself, who in most recent times *was made* visible and able to suffer".ⁱ What he says in the same fourth book near the end of

ⁱ *Because formerly He was hidden and at last appeared openly.*

p. 239 is also to the point: "For the Word and Wisdom, the Son and the Spirit, *are always present with God*,ʲ by whom and in

ʲ *Who has denied this? But listen to what he says there, namely, that the substance of the creatures was in God Himself. You, however, blinded as you are, always deny with Simon Magus this deity of ours.*

whom He freely made all things".

Passages from the Apostle Peter and his Disciple Clement

SERVETUS 1. The first place is from pp. 14 and 15 of the first book of Clement,⁶⁶ where the apostle Peter says: "When therefore Abraham wished to know the causes of things the true prophet, Jesus Christ, appeared to him and disclosed all that he desired. And when everything had been duly and adequately taught, the true prophet Jesus withdrew again to His invisible abode". Who would desire further testimony than this? Was not He who appeared to Abraham the Word of God? the personal Son? the Son Jesus Christ?

2. The second place is on the same page 15: "When the Israelites were afflicted," he says, "the true prophet Jesus appeared to Moses and struck the Egyptians with plagues from heaven, and led the people of God out of Egypt".

---

⁶⁶ The references are to the *Clementine Recognitions,* a pseudonymous work belonging to a later age than that of Clement of Rome, whose name it bears. Internal evidence suggests that it comes from the early part of the third century. Addressed to James the Lord's brother, it professes to reproduce the instruction given to Clement by the apostle Peter. The original text, in Greek, is lost, but a Latin version was preserved in the writings of Rufinus (d. 410). A printed edition was published in Basle in 1526.

3. The third place is on p. 21 of the same book 1, where Peter says: "Christ, who was from the beginning and eternally, was present, though secretly, yet constantly, with the godly through each successive generation, and especially with those by whom He was awaited, to whom also He frequently appeared".

4. The fourth place is on p. 37 of bk. 2, where Peter says of Christ, the true prophet: "The true prophet from the beginning of the world, through the course of the ages, hastens towards the rest,[67] everywhere appearing and correcting".

5. The fifth place is on p. 78 of bk. 4, where Peter says that when God made man in His own image and likeness, He implanted in His work a certain breath and odour of His divinity. He teaches that the image of the body is in God. In opposition to Simon Magus and his disciples Peter teaches that divinity has been implanted in us, by reason of which we possess a measure of free will. Tertullian, on p. 181 of his second book against Marcion, says that God communicates His substance to us through the perception of the soul; and, on p. 182, that man has freedom of will because he is the *afflatus* of God, who Himself is free and self-controlling. He teaches the same thing repeatedly on pp. 185 and 420. Nor does Irenaeus teach otherwise, ever defending free will against the sorcerers. No one in the history of Christianity has ever taught differently, except that sorcerer Calvin.

Passages from the Fictitious Peter and the Imaginary Clement

MINISTERS Though it is hidden to no one that this book which pretends to the name of Clement is a patchwork of fantasies badly put together by some ignorant monk, yet Servetus adduces nothing from it which we would not willingly grant him. But for him to obtain all is still to profit nothing. We confess that the Son of God was always first among the angels, performed the office of the highest prophet, and through all the ages was *secretly present with the holy patriarchs*.[a] None the less, the argument of

[a] *In true visible form.*

Servetus is without substance, so that he is plainly seen to be a man destitute of common sense while he trifles in this feeble manner. But since he takes such great pleasure in these fantasies, by what effrontery does he *conceal*[b] the letter of Sixtus,[68] which is

[b] *My concern there is with the sayings of Peter, not of others; although I could also accept the sayings of others.*

---

[67] The rest, that is, of His kingdom which He will establish at last.
[68] A letter attributed to Pope Sixtus III (432-440).

inserted there, p. 76, concerning the eternal unity of Father, Son and Spirit? Also, the letter of Hyginius[69] follows a little further on, p. 60, in which the eternal generation of the Son is asserted, which Servetus assails with such slanders as he can *muster*.[c] In

[c] *That is a falsehood.*

addition, there is the letter of Soterus,[70] on p. 63, which states that the Son was made Christ according to the flesh, but was begotten of the Father according to His divinity. Thus the wicked error of Servetus concerning the *mixed*[d] generation of Christ is overthrown.

[d] *That is a falsehood.*

In the letter of Eutychianus[71], pp. 78 and 79, the *communicatio idiomatum*[72] is asserted, to which Servetus is so hostile that, exhaling the *afflatus* of an evil demon, he says, in his ninth letter to Calvin, on p. 602, that this doctrine *partakes*[e] of the mark of the

[e] *On p. 703 of my Apologia*[73] *I affirm a* communicatio idiomatum *between the Word and the man, free, however, from your illusions.*

beast.

We wonder also for what reason he now buries Ignatius[74] whom hitherto he has so haughtily *appropriated as a patron*.[f] On p. 22,

[f] *I have quoted many things from him in my Apologia and also elsewhere.*

in his letter to the Magnesians he, whoever he may be, declares that Christ[g] *was begotten of the Father*[h] before the ages. Again,

[g] *The man.*
[h] *I declare the same.*

on p. 31, in his letter to the Philippians, he teaches that the saying of Solomon [Prov. 30:4]: "What is His name, *or the name of His Son?*"[i] ought to be referred to Christ, inasmuch as He is God the

[i] *That is, the man Christ, as he says. If you were not blind, you would see that this is contrary to you.*

Word. Again, on p. 51, in his letter to the Smyrneans, he testifies

---

[69] Pope Hyginius lived in the second century and is mentioned only by Irenaeus. All the letters attributed to him are without doubt spurious.

[70] Soterus, another second-century pope, wrote a letter to the Corinthians.

[71] The letter of Eutychianus, who was pope from 275 to 283, was addressed to the bishops of Boeotia.

[72] The doctrine of the *communicatio idiomatum* asserts that in the person of Christ there is a communion of the divine and human attributes.

[73] That is, his *Apologia* addressed to Melanchthon.

[74] Ignatius, one of the Apostolic Fathers, was Bishop of Antioch and suffered martyrdom in Rome c. A.D. 110. On the journey to his martyrdom he wrote seven letters, four from Smyrna and three from Troas, to churches in Asia Minor and Rome and to Polycarp, Bishop of Smyrna. The letters were printed by Lefèvre d'Etaples in 1498.

that the only-begotten Son^j is God the Word, but that according

  ^j *He says Christ.*

to the flesh He is the son of the virgin from the stock of David. Again, on p. 74, in his letter to the Ephesians, he writes: "We have as physician Jesus Christ who, before the ages was the only-begotten Son,^k and in the beginning was the Word; but afterwards

  ^k *Man in the form of God.*

He also became man of the virgin Mary, the incorporeal in a body, the impassible in a body that could suffer, the immortal in a mortal body". Indeed, a clearer distinction between the two natures of Christ could not be expressed. Servetus, however, *mixes these natures with such confusion*^l that he makes *God*^m flesh

  ^l *That is a falsehood. I teach quite openly, on p. 201 and on p. 590, in my sixth letter to you, that the divine form in Christ is neither confused nor made other nor changed.*
  ^m *A participant in God.*

and *denies*^n that the Word has a distinct hypostasis from the

  ^n *That is a falsehood.*

Father.

SERVETUS It now remains for me to reply to Calvin's articles in turn.

With reference, first of all, to the title, one cannot help being amazed at the shamelessness of this man, who declares himself to be orthodox when he is a disciple of Simon Magus, as I have already plainly shown in my *Apologia*. Who would call a criminal accuser and a murderer an orthodox minister of the Church?

A BRIEF REFUTATION OF THE SOPHISTRIES WITH WHICH SERVETUS HAS ATTEMPTED TO JUSTIFY HIS ERRORS AGAINST WHICH WE HAVE OBJECTED[75]

MINISTERS Perhaps he was afraid the judges would be unaware of his eloquence as a wanton slanderer if he did not call Calvin a *murderer*^a and spew out a string of insults against him.

  ^a *Truly so, and a follower of Simon Magus. Deny that you are a murderer and I will prove it by deeds. You dare not deny that you are a Simon Magus. Who, then, may trust you and believe that you are a good tree? In so just a case I stand firm and do not fear death.*

We, however, shall apply ourselves simply to the issues before us.

---

[75] The second part of the theological dispute with Servetus commences here. The thirty-eight propositions discussed were extracted by Calvin and the Company of Pastors, in proof of his heresy, from Servetus' work *De Trinitatis Erroribus Libri Septem*.

THE FIRST OPINION or proposition taken from the books of Michael Servetus: That all who maintain that there is a Trinity in the essence of God are tri-theists, and really atheists, and that the God they postulate is tripartite and multiple. Again, that theirs is a speculative not an absolute God; that their gods are imaginary, the illusions of demons (Bk. 1 on the Trinity, p. 30). To this corresponds what he adds on the following page: "Since you like dreaming, fix your eyes on phantoms, and then you will see that without three phantoms your Trinity is incomprehensible". At length he concludes that all trinitarians are atheists.

SERVETUS I have already replied often enough to this first article, and it is established from the authors I have cited that there is no real distinction of three invisible entities in the essence and unity of God. But there is a personal distinction between the invisible Father and the visible Son. In the second manner the Trinity is most piously believed, but not in the first.

MINISTERS It is proved from all his books[a] that the name
  [a] *That is a falsehood.*
"trinity" has always been specifically *rejected*[b] by Servetus as sacri-
  [b] *That is a falsehood. I use the name "Trinity," and teach it, on p. 22, and "the most true Trinity" on p. 24 and pp. 273 and 704, 705f.*
legious and detestable. Now, however, he makes a pretence of a personal distinction. For, as we shall see later, a "person" is for him nothing *else than a transfiguration of God.*[c] Further, he openly
  [c] *No, a hypostatic form.*
abandons all *distinction between Word and*[d] Spirit, affirming that
  [d] *I remove a real, not a personal, distinction.*
the Spirit is one and the same with the Word. This prodigious farrago of blasphemies, which readers will find in the places we have cited, admits, therefore, of no excuse and *deserves no pardon.*[e]
  [e] *Let pardon be granted, then, to Simon Magus.*

OPINION 2. That the Jews have the support of so many authorities that they would rightly be amazed at the tripartite God introduced by us (Bk. 1 on the Trinity, p. 34).

OPINION 3. That the postulation of a real distinction in the incorporeal Godhead gave Muhammed a reason for denying Christ (Bk. 1 on the Trinity, p. 36).

OPINION 4. That these three incorporeal distinctions in God cannot be sustained and are an imaginary triad (Bk. 1 on the Trinity, p. 29).

SERVETUS The reply to the second, third, and fourth articles is the same. What I say about Muhammed is in a measure confirmed to be true by the Turks today.

MINISTERS Since he passes over in silence what we consider to be deserving of grave censure, let him be judged by reading what we have quoted. Nor is it any kind of excuse that today the Turks say that the Trinity is a stumbling-block to them, since it does not follow from this that it was a *just*[a] reason for the apos-

[a] *You impostor, you invent, all alone, what is just.*

tasy of Muhammed. But we have already briefly *shown*[b] that his

[b] *That is a falsehood.*

haughty *repudiation*[c] of invisible and secret hypostases in the one

[c] *I repudiate a real distinction in God.*

essence of God is opposed to the whole teaching of Christianity. For unless there had been a real distinction between God the Father and God the Word, *the Word would not have been able*[d]

[d] *Unhappy man, you are ignorant of the dispensation of so great a mystery.*

to descend and assume flesh without the Father becoming man at the same time.[e] Everyone, therefore, who *confuses*[f] the real

[e] *The person of the Word is man.*

[f] *It is only you who are confused. You rely on sophistical reasons alone, unrelated to the Scriptures, and founded on false premises.*

distinction between the Father and the Son drags the Father from His heavenly throne and nails Him to the cross. Moreover, Paul does not say that Christ was the form of God, which would suit the fabrication of Servetus, but that He was in the form[g] of God.

[g] *It is the same thing.*

If before He assumed flesh He was *in the form of God*,[h] it was not

[h] *If He was in the form of God, the distinction was formal: you are speaking against yourself.*

lawful for Him to grasp at the real hypostasis, which would sustain this form in itself: otherwise the form *would have vanished*[i] apart

[i] *Fairy tales: as though there were such things as accidents and subjects in God!*

from a subject. And the triple invocation of the divine name in baptism would be absurd unless *Father*,[j] *Son*,[k] and Spirit really

[j] *God.*

[k] *Man.*

differed from each other. A proper and separate name is assigned to each. Unless we acknowledge reality in the Son[1] and the

[1] *He is gripped by frenzy.*

Spirit, it must follow that baptism is illusorily celebrated in an empty name of a non-reality as far as Father and Son are concerned. We shall not waste time over *the shift of Servetus*[m] that

[m] *I maintain that, as Christ and as Jesus, the Son is properly said to be from man.*

it is in the flesh that the person of the Son is really distinct from the Father; for from this postulate *he derives*[n] the distinction that

[n] *That is a falsehood.*

the flesh of Christ is God. But the Godhead is understood by us as something very *different*,[o] indeed as eternal. Finally, with re-

[o] *To your people this is blasphemy.*

gard to *the person of the Spirit*[p] it is always firmly held that, while

[p] *The person of the Spirit subsists perceptibly, just as the person of the Word subsists visibly. I have taught this on pp. 163, 164, 704, 705, etc.*

His substance is invisible, yet He has a distinct name by reason of His own proper power.

OPINION 5. With the purpose of concealing his impious doctrines, he confesses that there was indeed a personal distinction in God, but in doing so he understands only an external person which does not truly subsist in the presence of God — as in bk. 3 on the Trinity, p. 92, where he says that from the beginning the Word was ideal reason, which already represented man: that in the Word with God there was a pattern of the future man Jesus Christ. Again, on p. 229 of Dialogue I[76] he says that there is no real difference between the Word and the Spirit. Again, on p. 189 of bk. 5 on the Trinity he says that there was no real generation or spiration in God.

SERVETUS Whenever there was occasion, I have always professed that both internally and externally there is a subsistence of the Son in God Himself. Moreover, you contradict yourself. For if He was ideal reason, then He was internal. It is evident that you do not know what you are talking about. What you posit concerning the real difference has already been conceded and demonstrated by me. Read carefully the places which I have designated, I beseech you, and put on the heart of a Christian man, praying that the truth may be revealed to you.

[76] This refers to *Dialogorum de Trinitate libri duo, de justitia regni Christi, capitula quattuor*, which was published in 1532.

MINISTERS If he had always professed that there is a subsistence of the Son *internally*ᵃ in God, he would not have troubled

ᵃ *I propound an internal hypostasis on pp. 705 and 734 and elsewhere throughout.*

the Church over the subject of the real distinction. For *subsistence*ᵇ is either an empty phantom or something real. If he admits

ᵇ *True subsistence is formed internally in God Himself.*

that the Son subsisted internally in the Father, then He is *really*ᶜ

ᶜ *This does not follow.*

distinct from Him. There is nothing *contradictory*ᵈ in our words;

ᵈ *Horrible monstrosity.*

but he will mingle earth and heaven sooner than he will be able to reconcile the fictions which he heaps together — namely, that there is no person that is not visible, and that *the person of the Son was internally in God;*ᵉ that the hypostasis of the Son was

ᵉ *The same person that was internal was externally displayed as visible.*

from the beginning, and that it was the Son only in figure; that the substance of the future Christ was in the cloud and the pillar of fire, and that He was compounded from uncreated elements in the womb of His mother. Thus we have every reason for complaining that he deceitfully covers over the impiety of his teachings while he opposes the term "person", *not understanding*ᶠ any

ᶠ *You don't understand your own self, and you shout out like a blind man in the desert: as the spirit of vindictiveness burns so fiercely in your breast, wisdom cannot enter your malevolent mind.*

hypostasis which dwells inwardly with God, but only a likeness, an appearance, and a representation.

OPINION 6. To make it quite plain that the persons are confused by him, the following is found on p. 86 of bk. 2 on the Trinity: "The same wisdom was formerly Word and Spirit because there was no real distinction: wisdom itself was the Spirit". And on p. 164 of bk. 5 on the Trinity he explains that the whole mystery of the Word and the Spirit was the resplendent glory of Christ.

SERVETUS To this sixth point I reply that things which were not separate cannot have been confused. In chapters 17 and 37 of his fourth book Irenaeus interprets the same wisdom as the Holy Spirit, and so also does Tertullian in his books on the flesh of Christ, against Hermogenes, and against Praxeas, where see p. 442. Solomon, too, when he testifies that wisdom was given to him understands it of the Holy Spirit [Cf. I Kings 3:5ff., II Chron. 1:7ff.]. Ecclesiasticus, Baruch, and the Book of Wisdom show the same thing [Ecclus. 2:26, 7:12; Bar. 3:9ff.; Wis. 1:1ff.], as already quoted in my eighth letter to you. I say that the whole mystery of the Word and the Spirit was to the glory of Christ because in Him is the whole fulness of the Word and the Spirit. You unhappy man, to persist in condemning things that you don't understand!

MINISTERS In his reply he openly overthrows every *distinction*[a] between the Son and the Spirit and fills his cheeks with the

a *Every real distinction.*

breath of Sabellius.[b][77] From this it is clear that whatever he con-

b *That is a falsehood.*

fessed previously concerning the Trinity and the persons was full of unadulterated deceit. For had he conceded *ex animo* that there are three persons in God, *the Word should have been distinguished from the Spirit at least in form and dispensation.*[c] But he contends

c *This I have said a thousand times.*

that *the selfsame wisdom is the* Spirit,[d] as much as to say that *the*

d *This does not contradict what has preceded, and it is what Tertullian teaches on pp. 369, 422, and 442.*

selfsame Spirit[e] was crucified and rose from the dead. Paul,

e *You are raving: it is the man who was truly crucified.*

however, speaks very differently when he proclaims that Christ was raised[f] from the dead by the Spirit of God, in Romans 8 [v. 11].

f *In no way contrary to me.*

Elsewhere, also he teaches that *Christ was declared*[g] to be the

g *As man.*

Son of God with power according to the Spirit of holiness, in Romans 1 [v. 4]. The testimonies which Servetus ignorantly cites or wickedly misapplies[h] in support of this error must be guarded

h *It is you who misapply, being devoid of understanding.*

against. Irenaeus and Tertullian sometimes *improperly mingle*[i] the

i *Only Calvin properly concocts, like Simon Magus.*

Spirit and the Word, because the Spirit descended into the womb of the virgin and supplied the place of the male semen. We admit that the term "wisdom" is not always to be understood hypostatical-

---

77 Sabellius, third century, gave his name to the heresy of Sabellianism, a form of modalistic monarchianism, which denied the independent subsistence of the Son in the Godhead and taught that the Father suffered as the Son (patripassianism).

ly, but as a special gift of the Spirit. So also when there is mention of "the word" it is more often intended of the word preached than of that inner Word who was always with God. But Servetus, *who forces the same sense*[j] on a word with a variety of meanings

[j] *That is a falsehood.*

wherever it occurs, does not hesitate to impose the penalty of his hallucination on God.

OPINION 7. Although he denies any real distinction between the three persons before the incarnation of Jesus Christ, yet he says that Christ was honoured with such great glory that He is not only very God of God, but also that He is God from whom another God proceeds (Bk. 5 on the Trinity, p. 185).

SERVETUS I said "a God other than Christ", another mode of the Deity. Moreover, I added the following: "If this manner of speaking offends you, I will say another person of the Deity". Why must you turn into a calumny what I have set right in the same place? Your hostility is everywhere apparent!

MINISTERS The arrogance of this man is certainly amazing when he allows himself to state that *another*[a] God is the same as

[a] *Other than Christ. And you, wretched man, do not blush to speak of another deity. But you may do everything with impunity. Add the correction which I have supplied in that place.*

another mode of the Deity, and thus savagely assails all godly men who have dared to say that there are three real persons in the one God. But what is the point of this new mode of the Deity? In the same place he interprets it as another person of the Deity. It is then concluded that *there was no person of the Spirit*[b] until

[b] *That is a falsehood.*

He emerged all of a sudden at the resurrection of Christ. There is thus *a double error*[c] in that he assigns *the beginning of the per-*

[c] *That is a falsehood.*

son[d] of the Holy Spirit from that time, and also in respect of that

[d] *That is a falsehood.*

person *postulates*[e] another God.

[e] *No such thing.*

OPINION 8. That Jesus Christ is the Son of God in so far as He was begotten of God in the womb of the virgin Mary, and that this was not only by the operation of the Holy Spirit, but because God begot Him from His own substance (Bk. 1 on the Trinity, pp. 11 and 12, and also the letter to Calvin, 1 and 2).

SERVETUS Is not one called the son of him by whom he has been begotten? Accordingly I say that God produced this Son from His own substance from eternity. Hence He is said to be naturally from God.

MINISTERS Although he tries to avoid censure by in part *withdrawing his errors here*,[a] yet his explanation is by no means

    a *That is a falsehood: I have said the same thing in the very same words on pp. 56 and 207 and in my first letter.*

acceptable. For if the man Christ is *naturally*[b] from God, and

    b *By natural generation.*

was begotten from the substance of God in so far as He is man, *it follows*[c] that He does not share with us in human nature. And

    c *A fairy tale: as though participation in Deity means that it is impossible to share in human nature. These things are unworthy to be propounded in the presence of learned men.*

this blasphemy, in which Servetus so blandly indulges, completely overthrows the whole hope of redemption.[d] The falsity of this

    d *That is a falsehood.*

teaching is clearly exposed by the testimony of the apostle when he affirms that, apart from sin, Christ was *like*[e] us in all things

    e *He was like us in all that He received.*

[Phil. 2:7; Heb. 2:17, 4:15]. But I say that the whole of our redemption is torn up by the roots if it is not *a fact*[f] that the Son of

    f *Of course it is a fact.*

God participates with us in the true likeness of human nature. How can Paul's assertion that through the obedience of one man many are made righteous [Rom. 5:19] be sustained unless our sin was expiated in *the same nature*?[g] Where is that fellow-feeling

    g *What? without participating in Deity?*

which the apostle teaches to be necessary in a mediator [Heb. 4:15], if the likeness of nature is *taken away*?[h] Where is the relationship

    h *You are trifling.*

of brothers[i] [Heb. 2:11, 12, 17] if the origin of Christ's flesh is

    i *The state of Deity takes away none of these things. I beseech you not to torment yourself with such frivolities.*

taken from heaven while ours is derived from earth? Where is the hope of resurrection, if Christ had not once clothed Himself with a mortal and transitory body similar to our own? We see, then, *how lethal*[j] this fabrication is which, by sundering and shat-

    With lethal rage you, in company with Simon Magus, fume against the flesh of Christ, as though it did not possess its divinity when it was in the tomb.

tering the bond of our unity with Christ in respect to the community of human nature, separates us from His life. Moreover, that he wrote in a manner very different from what he now *pretends*[k] is

[k] *That is a falsehood.*

apparent from the places that have been cited, and *will soon be apparent*[l] from other places. For everywhere he rages against

[l] *Of course!*

those who believe that the Word was begotten from eternity,[m]

[m] *That is a falsehood.*

maintaining as he does that generation *originates*[n] only from the

[n] *That is a falsehood: on the contrary, I maintain that it is from eternity.*

flesh. Let us look at some examples.

OPINION 9. That the Word of God descending from heaven is now the flesh of Christ, in such a way that it is the flesh of Christ from heaven (Bk. 1 on the Trinity, pp. 17 and 18). Again, on p. 73 of bk. 2 on the Trinity: that the body of Christ is itself a body of deity, and that His flesh is divine, flesh of God, heavenly, begotten from the substance of God. Again, on p. 231 of Dialogue 1: that the soul of Christ is God, that the flesh of Christ is God, and that both the soul and the flesh of Christ were from eternity in the very substance of the Godhead.

SERVETUS The Word is now the flesh of Christ in hypostatic union. Thus I plainly say that the flesh of Christ is from heaven according to the essence of Deity, and that the same flesh is spoken of as manna given from heaven. The remaining points I concede, in the sense explained by me there: which is what you beg for here, unhappy man. But you leave out the primary truth, being ignorant of the faith in which you must be justified.

MINISTERS It is well known with what artifices *heretics*[a]

[a] *This heretical Simon Magus constantly breathes out hateful things against the flesh of Christ.*

used formerly to wrap up their utterances, partly in order that they might avoid an open confession of the truth, partly that they might camouflage the perversions they had uttered. The error of Servetus is inexcusable, that *the soul of Christ is God*[b] and the

[b] *Was not the hypostatic union of the Word in the separate soul of Christ, deifying it? Read what I have written on p. 270.*

flesh of Christ is God, just as Christ Himself is God, and that the flesh of Christ is from heaven and from the substance of God. For *he confuses*[c] the two natures. Indeed, he reduces the true humanity

[c] *That is a falsehood.*

to nothing.[d] What is more, *he pretends*[e] that Deity is in some

[d] *That is a falsehood.*
[e] *That is a falsehood.*

sense passible. Then *he mixes all together.*[f] He excuses all these

[f] *That is a falsehood.*

enormities with a single word, namely, that the Word is flesh by hypostatic union. But there is no hypostatic union when *the humanity itself*[g] is said to have come from heaven. And the ex-

[g] *The divine flesh itself. If the blood is called the blood of God in Acts 20, then the flesh is called the flesh of God. In Jn. 6 it is called the bread of God which is from heaven.*

planation to which he directs us precludes these subterfuges; for on p. 232 he says: "The soul of Christ breathes from eternity the total animation of the world in the very essence of Divinity; but His flesh, begotten from the substance of God, has the essence of Deity". Meanwhile he calls us unhappy and beggarly on the ground that we take occasion to censure him through our ignorance of the primary truth. *For him, however, the primary truth*[h] is

[h] *The primary truth and justifying faith is to know assuredly that this man is by nature the Son of God. But you think that you are justified by acquaintance with Simon Magus.*

that there is *no distinction*[i] between the two natures of Christ.

[i] *That is a falsehood.*

OPINION 10. On p. 77 of bk. 2 on the Trinity he says: "The essence of the body and soul of Christ is the Deity of the Word and Spirit"; and, "From the beginning Christ's relationship is one of body as well as of soul". Again, on p. 87 of bk. 2 he writes: "The substantial Deity is not only in the soul but also in the flesh of Christ". Again, on p. 164 of bk. 5: "God was Word and Spirit, variously dispensing Word and Spirit into body and soul".

SERVETUS That is called essence by which anyone is sustained. Are you not ashamed to allege such great things here and yet to produce no justification for censure? Do you imagine that the ears of the judges will be deafened merely by your doglike barking?

MINISTERS With his customary arrogance he accuses us of barking like dogs, when in fact we have put forward not a single syllable of our own. He inquires whether we are not ashamed to allege such great things, and to censure nothing justly. But we have only discharged the duty laid upon us by the Council.[a] Nor,

[a] *How you fabricate! As you were so anxious to accuse, the Council permitted you to oppose me in writing.*

indeed, if he had any measure of modesty, should the liberty of defending himself which has been granted him prove tiresome to him. When he said that the essence of the body and soul of Christ was the Deity of the Word and Spirit, and that from the beginning Christ's *relationship was one of body as well as of soul*,[b] was cen-

[b] *A relationship of Deity which is in body and soul simultaneously.*

sure of so abominable an error difficult? For unless true humanity, similar *to our own*,[c] corruption apart, is found in the flesh and soul

[c] *And it is similar, while also possessing Deity.*

of Christ, He ceases to be a mediator, *because He will not be man*.[d] It will be no more troublesome to refute the raving that

[d] *Do you say that an invisible entity is man, and that man himself is not man?*

God was Word and Spirit, variously dispensing Word and Spirit into body and soul. For it is not obscurely that *he asserts*[e] the

[e] *That is a falsehood.*

transmutation of Deity[f] into the human nature of Christ. This

[f] *Do you call communication transmutation?*

is to tear Christ right away from us. For where is the bond of brotherhood if we do not partake *of the same nature*,[g] but instead

[g] *It is disgraceful to revert so often to the bestiality of man.*

He *who was to be the redeemer*[h] was made man from the beginning

[h] *Of both natures.*

by a secret infusion from the Word and the Spirit? Moreover, *what body was crucified*,[i] and what soul endured the pains of

[i] *The very body in which God dwelt, as Ignatius says, on p. 12.*

extreme grief and death, when according to Servetus, the essence of both was nothing other than a dispensation of Word and Spirit or an infusion into a new form? But as Paul says that *a man who is a heretic*[j] and refuses to be admonished stands self-condemned

[j] *Such as is Simon Magus.*

[Tit. 3:10f.], so these errors refute themselves without any need for long disputation.

OPINION 11. In order that he may show that for him the divinity of Christ is a mockery, he explains that He is spoken of as the wisdom and the power of God and the brightness of His glory, just as if He were called some kind of excelling wisdom and power (Bk. 2 on the Trinity, p. 87).

SERVETUS You act unjustly in everything and quote this place inaccurately. I have not said what you impose upon me.

MINISTERS He protests that he is treated unjustly since he has not spoken in this way. But after proposing the question whether the man Christ is called the wisdom and the power of God, he adds that the Scotists have great difficulty with abstract names, but not the Hebrews, because with the latter it is commonplace for what *excels*[a] to be designated of God. Let the readers

[a] *In this manner I was preparing a way from the minor to the major.*

now judge whether this common manner of speech accords with the saying about Christ [I Cor. 1:24]. For what sort of deity of Christ is this if it is regarded as only an excellence?[b]

[b] *Do not more sublime concepts concerning the deity of Christ follow there also?*

OPINION 12. That from the beginning Jesus Christ was man with God in His own person and substance (Bk. 2 on the Trinity, p. 90). Elsewhere, however, he attributes two persons to Christ (Bk. 4 on the Trinity, p. 129).

SERVETUS The first part is perfectly true: would that you understood it aright! In Himself Christ is one person, but in Him there is truly the Holy Spirit, who is also a person.

MINISTERS Regarding the first[a] part, we have touched some-

[a] *John says that he had seen that which was from the beginning* [I Jn. 1:1]. *What is that?*

what on this above in connection with the opinion that the person of the man Christ should be understood as a figuration in God,[b]

[b] *Irenaeus calls it a figuration on p.* 217.

and His substance as *a conflation*[c] which Servetus calls a dispen-

[c] *You mendaciously impute new terms to me: the deceptions, therefore, are yours.*

sation of God into flesh. When he wishes us to approve such deceptions with a single nod, why is he angry if we prefer to believe God?[d] The second part is absurd in every respect. He explains

[d] *You derive nothing from God.*

that Christ has two persons because *in Him there is truly the Spirit*,[e] who is also a person. But it will be possible to extend this

[e] *Do you deny that Christ was truly anointed with the Holy Spirit?*

further: because in Him there is truly the Father, as He Himself declares [Jn. 14:10f.], *therefore He has three persons*.[f] It is im-

[f] *I say that in Christ there is God, who is three persons.*

possible for him to excuse himself in this way without perverting all *the principles of piety.*g

g *What you call principles of piety are sophistries invented by men.*

OPINION 13. After confessing that the Word of God had been made man, he says that this Word was the seed of Christ (Bk. 4 on the Trinity, p. 145). Again, that this is something different from the Son (Bk. 1 on the Trinity, p. 23). Again, that the Word by whom the world was created had been produced by His grace: whence it follows that He and the Word are not the same (Bk. 2 on the Trinity, p. 85). Again, that the Word of God was the dew of the natural begetting of Christ in the womb of the virgin, just as semen is of the begetting of animals (Dial. 2 on the Trinity, p. 260). Also that the Son of God was naturally begotten of the Holy Spirit through the Word (Bk. 1 on Regeneration, p. 355).

SERVETUS I mean "seed" in the sense of the twelfth place of Tertullian, and of Irenaeus as there quoted, and of Philo[78] on p. 201 of my first Dialogue, where the whole of your calumny is dispelled in the plainest manner. In the place which you cite from p. 23 "word" is used for the voice from heaven saying that this is the Son of God [cf. Mt. 3:17, 17:5]. You have neither read nor understood that place, and accordingly, what you quote is beside the point. Who does not see that the deity of the Word is in reality something different from the man who is the Son? I concede that the other things which you add are true.

MINISTERS Since he brings forward nothing to the point in his reply, let the readers only open their eyes to consider what he has said. For if *the Word was the seed*a of Christ, and some-

a *In chapters 45 and 55 of Isaiah and Psalm 71 the Word is called dew, cloud, and rain* [cf. Is. 45:8; 55:10; Ps. 72 (71):6] *causing Christ to germinate. On p. 201 I explained "seed" as Deity acting in the place of seed.*

thing different from the Son, the doctrine that the Word was made flesh *falls to the ground.*b Now *he pleads*c that in one place he

b *How so?*

c *That is a falsehood.*

usedd "word" for the voice of the Father. But this is a futile cavil;

d *Not I, but John himself, as there quoted: I Jn. 5.*

for in the whole context he is seeking to prove that the Word is

---

[78] Philo of Alexandria, the Jewish-Hellenistic philosopher of the apostolic period.

something different from[e] the Son. And this he asserts openly

[e] *Man.*

enough when he says that in the creation of the world the Word was produced by Christ's grace; and elsewhere that He was *the dew*[f] of the natural begetting; and, again, that Christ was begotten

[f] *As David and Isaiah say.*

through the Word. When he obstinately defends all these things as true it is obvious that the mystery of our redemption is *overthrown*[g] by him, since John's declaration that *the Word*[h] was made

[g] *That is a falsehood; it is your inventions that I am overthrowing.*
[h] *See p. 266.*

flesh [Jn. 1:14] *vanishes into thin air.*[i]

[i] *That is a falsehood.*

OPINION 14. That the Word of God was the seed of Christ's begetting. And just as all things that beget first conceive seed in themselves, which they transmit to the foetus outside of themselves, so the seed of the Word was in God before the Son was conceived in Mary (Bk. 4 on the Trinity, p. 146). Again, that the paternal seed of Christ's begetting effected precisely the same thing in Him as the created seed of a father does in each of us (Dial. 2 on the Trinity, p. 254).

SERVETUS I concede all this because deity has acted in place of seed, as I have explained on p. 201 of my first Dialogue.

MINISTERS We indeed confess that in forming the flesh of Christ *the power of the Spirit*[a] took the place of the seed. But

[a] *Irenaeus says that this same thing is the power of the Word, and that the seed was the Word mingled with its own plasma, on p. 263, line 1. Tertullian likewise calls the seed the Word, and at the same time the Spirit, on pp. 29 and 442.*

this is in no way comparable to the fantasy of Servetus that the Word was the seed of begetting.

OPINION 15. That through the action of God's Spirit the body of Christ came into being, since by the divine Word, as though by the dew of Christ's begetting, He mingled Himself at the same time with these created elements of earth; and that inasmuch as the divine and the human breath of His soul were implanted and coalesced, there came into being one hypostasis of His spirit, which is the hypostasis of the Holy Spirit (Bk. 5 on the Trinity, p. 165). And previously he had said that in Christ there are three elements from the substance of the Father (Bk. 4 on the Trinity, p. 159).

SERVETUS This again I concede, if you understand the last of paternal elements, mentioned because of their ideal relationship in God.

MINISTERS From this it is apparent how blind is his obstinacy. The whole of Scripture proclaims that Christ is *the seed of Abraham*[a] and the son of David. Servetus compounds His flesh

[a] *And the seed of God, in Malachi* 2 [v. 15] *and the branch of God, in Isaiah* 4 [v. 2].

from four elements, *three of which he pretends are uncreated*,[b]

[b] *I say that there are four created elements in Him, just as there are in us: but to Him I add the substance of the Word, which I say was the exemplar, expressing in Him the force of three superior elements as of the heavenly dew; see pp.* 120 *and* 256. *These are great mysteries, unknown to Simon Magus.*

as we shall see shortly. Thus the Christ of Servetus will be quite other[c] than He who was *promised*[d] of old in the law and the

[c] *Nothing of the sort.*

[d] *Such a one was promised as would spring from the heavenly dew of the Word, as on pp.* 120 *and* 256.

prophets. A horrible *confusion*[e] of the two natures is implicit in

[e] *That is a falsehood.*

his words; for he wishes there to be one hypostasis in which God and man are commingled, on the ground that they have *coalesced*[f] into one essence.

[f] *As soul and flesh without confusion. If there was a substantial union, a single substance results from it.*

OPINION 16. So that he may pervert the apostle's assertion in Hebrews 2 [v. 16], that Christ did not assume the nature of angels but the seed of Abraham, he explains it as meaning that He liberated us from death (Bk. 2 on the Trinity, p. 90).

SERVETUS I pervert nothing, but I accept both interpretations; while you quote and teach everything falsely there.

MINISTERS *We have quoted nothing falsely*[a] as he with his

[a] *The number was corrected afterwards.*

customary dishonesty charges. For he maintains that this passage of the apostle should be interpreted to mean that Christ was about to liberate the human race from death, as though *He would take*[b]

[b] *He does so every day: for the verb is in the present tense.*

it into His bosom. And he then *deceitfully distorts*[c] eight or nine

[c] *That is a falsehood.*

testimonies of Scripture lest he should be *compelled to confess*^d

^d *Most worthless wretch, have I ever denied it?*

that Christ is of the seed of Abraham.

OPINION 17. That God is the Father of the Holy Spirit: which is nothing else than to confuse the persons, such even as he fashions them (Bk. 5 on the Trinity, p. 187).

SERVETUS It is your mind that is confused, so that you are unable to understand the truth: I am speaking by way of metaphor.

MINISTERS If *a metaphor*[a] excuses Servetus here, there will

> As Christ says that spirit is born of spirit, John 3 [v. 6] so Athanasius teaches that the Holy Spirit is born of God, as I have quoted on p. 41. Tertullian teaches the same, on the last line of p. 443.

be nothing in religion which may not be eluded. He admits that the person of the Son, after He became man, was really distinct from the Father. Scripture proclaims that He is uniquely one; but to Him Servetus *adds*[b] the Spirit, as though there were a second

^b *That is a falsehood, because the relationship is different.*

begetting. What else will remain secure for us in Scripture? For mutual relationship demands that if Christ is the only-begotten Son of God, God should not be the natural[c] Father of anyone else.

^c *Truly.*

In addition, he specifically compares the Word and wisdom with the Spirit in this place. By the same figure, he says, He is called *the Father of the Word.*[d]

^d *If you understand the Word without the person of man. That wretch truncates my sentences so that by hook or by crook he may trap me.*

OPINION 18. To show how he makes play with the term "persons" he says that there was one sole personal image or appearance, which was the person of Christ in God, and which was also communicated to the angels (Bk. 3 on the Trinity, p. 102).

SERVETUS I have already cited the authors who agree with what I say of the term "person", not making play at all, but using the words properly which you deceitfully misuse.

MINISTERS Since we have already *clearly shown*[a] either that

^a *That is a falsehood.*

he has never understood the opinions of the ancient authors, or that he *deceitfully perverts*[b] their testimony, it remains for our

^b *It is you alone who have deceitfully perverted their writings.*

readers to take notice of his deception. Previously, in the first article, he confessed that the Trinity is piously believed, provided that it is not a matter of belief in *invisible*[c] persons. Now, when

[c] *Three really distinct entities or persons.*

he leaves only one person,[d] let him deny, if he can, that he is a

[d] *You wretch, that is a falsehood! What I said was that in the creation of man there was one personal image and visible appearance, and that the flesh of Adam was conformed to this image. This does not prevent the Holy Spirit from being called a person, and even the Father, in His own mode.*

dissimulator.

OPINION 19. That there are three elements from each parent in Christ as well as in us; but that earthly matter is derived from the mother alone in Christ, as also in all things that are generated. From this it follows that He did not have a body similar to ours, which is the same as to destroy our redemption (Dial. 2 on the Trinity, p. 250). He expresses this still more fully on p. 194 of bk. 5 on the Trinity, where he says that in us there are only created elements, but that in Christ there are both created and uncreated elements together with the substance of the Spirit of God communicated substantially to the flesh itself.

SERVETUS Christ's body is similar to ours, except for sin, and with the further exception that it participates in deity.

MINISTERS When Servetus replies that the body of Christ is similar to ours with this exception, that it participates in deity, the apostle must be condemned for carelessness, since it occurred to him only to except sin; for he declares that *Christ was in all things similar to us*[a] in His human nature, except for sin [Heb.

[a] *This refers to the properties of man. The objection is so stupid that if Calvin had a grain of intelligence he would be ashamed to repeat it so often. Tell me, wretched man, whither Christ was similar to us in deity? If the humanity of Christ were granted as you wish, then He would be a mere creature. But it is dissimilar to ours in that it is made glorious by the presence of the true deity in Him.*

4:15]. Servetus opposes this and obtrudes the much greater distinction that Christ's body was compounded of three uncreated elements, and *had no more than a fourth portion from His mother,*[b]

[b] *That is a falsehood, you clumsy slanderer: for I attribute all four created elements to His mother. Read the comments which I have now written on article 15. This article 19 which you have written shows that you are a falsifier.*

which itself also was *converted*[c] into Deity. Paul, however,

[c] *That is a falsehood.*

teaches very differently when he affirms that according to the flesh Christ is the son of David and descended from the fathers, in Romans 1 [v. 13] and 9 [v. 5]. He does not designate a part only of the flesh there, but *the flesh in its entirety*,[d] in respect of which

[d] *The whole flesh — that, namely, which is distinct from deity — is from the seed of David. This sorcerer is shocked because I make the flesh of Christ, which was begotten of the Holy Spirit, a participant of deity.*

Christ is the son of David. There also he plainly distinguishes the deity *from the flesh*[e] and teaches that Christ is the Son of God

[e] *From a creature of flesh.*

because He has something *greater than flesh.*[f]

[f] *Truly.*

OPINION 20. That the heavenly dew by overshadowing the virgin and intermingling itself with her seed and blood transformed the human matter into God (Dial. 2 on the Trinity, p. 263).

SERVETUS Transformation there is glorification and illumination.

MINISTERS In the fables of the poets there is no metamorphosis so *ridiculous*[a] as this propounded by Servetus, that the Holy

[a] *It is the sorcerer who treats the flesh of Christ ridiculously.*

Spirit transformed the human into God, *because the humanity of Christ was glorified.*[b] But *quality*[c] is very different from matter.

[b] *Glorification is called transformation in Mt. 17 [v. 2] and Phil. 3 [v. 21]; see also Dial. 2, pp. 270 and 271.*

[c] *Wretched man, do you say that the glory of Christ is a quality? On the contrary, the divine light is substantial.*

OPINION 21. He confuses the two natures by saying that the created and the uncreated light were one light in Christ, and that a single substantial soul was formed in Christ from the divine Spirit and the human soul (Dial. 2 on the Trinity, p. 268). Indeed, on the next page he says that the substance of the flesh and the substance of the Word are one substance. At length he concludes that the flesh of Christ possesses the substance of the Word corporeally, the substantial life-giving divine Spirit, and thus that it is truly heavenly and of the substance of God, the flesh of the Word, the flesh of God, which has eternal existence (Dial. 2 on the Trinity, p. 271).

SERVETUS He who coheres with God is one Spirit with Him. Is it confusion when two are united into one? Are soul and flesh confused when they make one man? Unhappy man, you are ignorant of the very principles of things.

MINISTERS Let our readers judge whether the opinions which *we have condemned*[a] admit of any excuse. Servetus, however,

[a] *Just as you have condemned astrology, though you have never had even a nodding acquaintance with it. It is thus that you pass judgment on things of which you have no knowledge.*

clamours that *we have no knowledge*[b] of the elements of things

[b] *Truly, but only of grammar.*

because we do not concede that the soul of Christ was formed from the Holy Spirit and the human soul. We admit that the soul is united to the body in such a way as together to produce man, but each retains its own property. *Union, however, is something very different*[c] from substantial unity.

[c] *Wherever there is substantial union there is unity. Just as the rational soul and the flesh is one man, so God and man is one Christ.*

OPINION 22. That since Jesus Christ participates in God and man He cannot be called a creature, but one who participates in creatures (Dial. 2 on the Trinity, p. 272).

SERVETUS What follows immediately after?

MINISTERS He smiles arrogantly because it seems absurd to us that Christ ought not to be considered a creature *in so far as He is man.*[a] But his insouciance comes from the fact that *he does*

[a] *It is you who have added this, you impostor.*

not attribute human nature to Christ,[b] but fabricates an empty[c]

[b] *That is a falsehood.*
[c] *That is a falsehood.*

phantom for himself, in order that he may tear Him away from us, lest He should be bone of our bones and flesh of our flesh, and lest we in turn should be *His flesh.*[d]

[d] *We do indeed participate in His flesh and bones, Eph. 5 [v. 30].*

OPINION 23. That the selfsame deity which is in the Father was communicated to the Son Jesus Christ immediately and corporeally; that afterwards it was communicated spiritually to the apostles by His mediation through the ministry of an angelic spirit; indeed, that deity was implanted corporeally and spiritually in Christ alone by nature, but that holy and substantial breath is given by Him to others (Bk. 1 on the Trinity, p. 22).

SERVETUS This is true.

MINISTERS When without any embarrassment Servetus passes over what is plainly repugnant to the first *elements*[a] of Scrip-

[a] *Of which you are completely ignorant.*

ture, he displays his stupidity all the more shamefully. If the deity of the Father was communicated immediately and corporeally to Christ, *it follows*[b] that He was not God before He appeared as

[b] *From the corner to the wall, O crafty logician!*

man. For the adverb "immediately" was so placed as to *take away*[c] the eternal hypostasis of the Word. Let our readers consider

[c] *That is a falsehood.*

what sort of deity is Christ's if He has it *in common*[d] with us.

[d] *By the same nature God freely communicates His glory to us, Jn.* 17 [v. 22].

OPINION 24. That just as the Word descended into the flesh of Christ so the Holy Spirit descended into the souls of the apostles (Dial. 2 on the Trinity, p. 264).

SERVETUS This is just a kind of similitude, as I show there.

MINISTERS Whatever excuse Servetus may make, *the comparison*[a] is absurd and quite unacceptable. For what connection

[a] *There are various analogies there even of plants and worms.*

is there between the descent of the Word into flesh and the descent of the Holy Spirit into souls, unless Servetus attributes a merely *interchangeable*[b] deity to Christ so that he may make us gods

[b] *No, a natural deity.*

equal with Him. Moreover, he explains his meaning there, namely, that *there is an elementary and divine substance of the Spirit*[c]

[c] *Communicated to the elementary spirit of Christ.*

which is diffused into us, just as there was an elementary and divine substance of the body of Christ. Let our readers *carefully consider*[d] and clearly recognize that under the name of Christ

[d] *Let them consider you a Magus, a phantom without any truth.*

Servetus dreams up a phantom.

OPINION 25. He confuses the persons when he says: "By nature and voluntarily the λόγος was an ideal relation and emanation, the resplendence of Christ with God, the Spirit of Christ with God, His light with God"; from which it follows that there was no substance, since there was only a figure of that reality which was not yet, and meanwhile He was no different from the Spirit (Dial. 1 on the Trinity, p. 208).

SERVETUS It is yourself you confuse, not understanding what you are talking about, as though that which subsists hypostatically in God were not true substance.

MINISTERS Would that Servetus understood[a] what hypo-

[a] *Would that you did!*

stasis is! When, however, he babbles ignorantly of unknown things he deprives whoever does not subscribe to his ravings of reason and judgment. In the first place, *he substitutes an idea for the Word of God,*[b] *who was God with God.* Secondly, he makes the Word a

[b] *Augustine and Clement of Alexandria and others speak in the same way, as quoted by me on pp. 140 and 141.*

resplendence, so that it is a visible appearance, *not an inwardly subsisting reality.*[c] Thirdly, *he says that the Logos is the Spirit*[d]

[c] *That is a falsehood.*

[d] *I speak of the Logos there, and I speak of the Spirit there, but not as being altogether the same, since there were always two hypostases.*

of Christ, whence it follows that the Spirit was made flesh. Thus Christ will not be the Word of God manifested in the flesh, but the Holy Spirit made man. Fourthly, he says that the Word was *the light of the Word*[e] — a definition by which the substance is

[e] *I said the light of Christ, and now you falsely say the Word.*

taken away.[f]

[f] *Is not the light of God substance?*

OPINION 26. That before the advent of Christ no hypostasis of the Spirit was seen (Bk. 5 on the Trinity, p. 197). From this it follows that there was no hypostasis or person, since, according to what he affirms in his books and states in his answers, there is no person that is not visible. Corresponding to this is his assertion on p. 217 of Dial. 1 that the Spirit of God was a shadow in the creation of the world.

SERVETUS In the Word the person is called a visible hypostasis, in the Spirit a perceptible hypostasis.

MINISTERS He makes the hypostasis of the Spirit perceptible, although it is not visible. *Let him say*[a] by what sense He was

[a] *I have already explained this on p. 198: read it if you wish.*

perceived. He ought, however, to remember how violently *he belabours all pious persons*[b] *who separate person from visibility and*

[b] *To point out error is piety, not criminally to accuse.*

form.[c] Thus he is plainly *at variance*[d] with himself, as has already

[c] *Contrary to the force of the term.*

ᵈ *In what respect?*

been seen earlier. Moreover, the second place convicts him even more clearly of shamelessness, where he says that *the Spirit was a shadow*ᵉ in the creation of the world: unless he wishes *to main-*

> ᵉ *For the reason that He did not then shine forth clearly. Read pp. 191, 192, 196, and 265. You know very well that I have explained everything, and so you are acting against your conscience.*

*tain*ᶠ that hypostasis is nothing other than shadow.

> ᶠ *You are trifling.*

OPINION 27. So that it may be known what kind of eternity he attributes to Christ, we quote the following: "Just as all things are now in God, so they were in Him before the creation in the same order, and Christ first of them all". Again: "God, eternally decreeing by His eternal reason the corporeal and visible Son, showed Himself visible through the Word in the substance of such an appearance" (Dial. on the Trinity, p. 205).

SERVETUS   All is well, except that you have a perverted mind.

MINISTERS   Servetus will certainly get first prize for insults! When he is asked how he understands Christ to be eternal God, the explanation he offers is that Christ was eternal just like all other things, though he says that *in order Christ was first.*ᵃ When

> ᵃ *Who alone was the form of God's substance, and the visible splendour of His glory: these words are added there, but you have perfidiously omitted them so that my opinion may seem to be more objectionable.*

all pious minds are scandalized at so sacrilegious an utterance, Servetus simply says that all is well. Let our readers notice what person, idea, and hypostasis mean to him here, namely, *some kind of imaginary eternity*ᵇ which *Christ and stones*ᶜ have in common.

> ᵇ *No, a truly formal substance.*
>
> ᶜ *No such thing.*

Nor is an explanation lacking, for he adds that God, decreeing by His eternal reason a visible Son for Himself, showed Himself visible in this way.ᵈ The deity of Christ, then, will reside in this,

> ᵈ *A Son such as He previously preformed hypostatically.*

that by an eternal decree of God He was *ordained*ᵉ Son.

> ᵉ *Substantially formed and displayed.*

OPINION 28. That as long as Christ moved about in mortal flesh He had not yet received the new Spirit whom He was to receive after His resurrection (Bk. 5 on the Trinity, p. 185). Again, on p. 195 of Bk. 5 on the Trinity, that Christ before His resurrection had not yet obtained the full glory of God, but afterwards received the new Spirit. That therefore now Christ alone contains hypostatically within Himself the full glory of Word and Spirit. What he writes on p. 231 of Dialogue 1 on the Trinity also corresponds to this, namely, that God breathed the supervenient Holy Spirit into Christ, just as into us, and by another dispensation breathed the total deity anew in the same way as He renewed His prior Spirit in the resurrection, a new Spirit having been given whom the Spirit given in the Jordan adumbrated.

SERVETUS All this is true, if you understand it properly.

MINISTERS Before Christ died John the Baptist proclaimed: "We have all received of *His fulness*,[a] and grace for grace". Again:

[a] *Christ always had the fulness of the Spirit, but before the resurrection He was not glorified, Jn. 7 [v. 39]. He is called the new Spirit, therefore, on account of the new glory. The whole Christ, indeed, became a new man, and all things became new.*

"The Father does not give the Spirit by measure" [Jn. 1:16, 3:34]. Servetus *propounds a Christ denuded*[b] of His Spirit. Nor is it

[b] *That is a falsehood.*

merely a question here of the measure of gifts, but he in fact deprives Christ of the new Spirit.[c] If what he maintains is true,

[c] *You are raving.*

when Christ died He did not contain hypostatically within Himself the whole glory of the Word and the Spirit. That being so, *He had lost*[d] the glory which He Himself testified had been His with

[d] *All things were preserved in the body and the soul.*

the Father in the beginning before the creation of the world [Jn. 17:5]. But what does he think to gain by contending that God breathed the supervenient Spirit into Christ, just as into us, and that by some kind of *dispensation*[e] He breathed the total deity

[e] *The new glory.*

anew? What sort of deity had Christ when He died if afterwards the Father breathed *the total deity*[f] into Him? If he had said

[f] *The same deity by the new dispensation.*

that *a new grace*[g] was infused into Christ's human nature there

[g] *What do you call grace? a created quality? There is no such quality in Christ, but only the very deity itself. These infused qualities of yours belong to Simon Magus and his imitators. We are truly partakers of the divine nature, 2 Pet. 1, and the temple of the living God who truly dwells in us, 1 Cor. 3 [v. 16], 2 Cor. 6 [v. 16], Jn. 14 [v. 17], Acts 2 [v. 4].*

would at least have been rather more colour for his statement. By no pretext, however, can the assertion be excused that Christ received the new Spirit[h] only at the resurrection. Now the hinge

[h] *The Spirit of glory.*

on which the question turns is: In what does the deity of Christ consist? By saying that *the total deity*[i] was breathed into Him

[i] *The same deity.*

after He rose from the dead, Servetus teaches that He was *a half-God*[j] during the time that He was here on earth. But John affirms

[j] *That is a falsehood.*

that it was then that His glory was seen — glory which was appropriate to the only-begotten Son of God [Jn. 1:14].

OPINION 29. That in the substance of God there are parts and partitions, not in the same way as in creatures, but in accordance with the distribution of dispensation, in such a way that in the partition of the Spirit each portion is God (Bk. 3 on the Trinity, p. 121). Moreover, where he affirms that our spirits have existed substantially from eternity he adds that they are consubstantial and coeternal with God (Dial. 1 on the Trinity, p. 226). In another place, however, he declares that the Spirit by which we are illuminated can be extinguished (Bk. 4 on Regeneration, p. 555).

SERVETUS Nearly all this is true, except that the Spirit of God is not said to be extinguished in Himself; but in a certain manner He is extinguished in us, because when we are extinguished He withdraws.

MINISTERS If these things are true, what falsehood will it not be permissible to utter? If in God's substance there are *parts and partitions,*[a] and if each portion is God, what nonsense will it

[a] *By a particular dispensation of Deity.*

not be possible to invent concerning the majesty of God?[b] In fact,

[b] *With Simon Magus you confine God in a corner: I say that He is all in all.*

he fabricates a God for us who is as craftily versatile as any Proteus. But there is nothing new in this license of his, since *he permits*[c]

[c] *I say that all entities are sustained in God.*

himself to suppose that there are accidents in God, in Epistle 7 to Calvin. What follows is even more execrable, namely, *that the spirits of the regenerate are coeternal and consubstantial with God.*[d]

[d] *The regenerate are truly partakers of the divine nature, which, in its own separate modes and separate dispensations, is ever eternal. In them is the substance of the eternal Spirit, eternal light; their abode has been prepared from eternity in God Himself; a kingdom has been prepared*

for them from eternity; and their names have been written in heaven from eternity. Eye has not seen, nor has ear heard, these eternal things which have thus been prepared for us in God [cf. I Cor. 2:9]. *If Calvin gave attention to these things he would not fling such detestable accusations at others.*

And yet he says elsewhere *that these same spirits are extinguished,*[e]

[e] *Wretched man, see my first answer. See in what sense Paul warns against extinguishing the Spirit, in* 1 *Thess.* 5 [v. 20].

not only when we die, but when we fall from the grace of God. As an inventor, he will be *more ingenious still*[f] if he can reconcile

[f] *You are lower than the lowest.*

the doctrines *that a substance coeternal with God is extinguished*[g]

[g] *That is a falsehood.*

and that God is immutable and without shadow of turning [Jas. 1:17].

OPINION 30. That by the breadth of God the Spirit of deity was from the beginning implanted in all things (Dial. 1, p. 138).

SERVETUS This is absolutely true: but you, unhappy man deluded by Simon Magus, are ignorant of it, with the result that, by maintaining that the will is enslaved, you make us stocks and stones. See the last place cited from Clement and Peter.

MINISTERS Behold the moderation of this captive man who *maniacally*[a] clamours that they who do not affirm substantial

[a] *Yours is the mania, which causes you to persecute to the death.*

deity in the soul of man are disciples of Simon Magus! But none *of the prophets*[b] and none of the apostles or martyrs ever *makes*

[b] *You now keep quiet about the theologians, who all have always taught thus in Christianity.*

mention[c] of this Spirit of deity. We know, indeed, that the soul

[c] *On the contrary: Genesis 2 and 6, Job 33 and 34, Psalm 103, Eccles. 12, Isaiah 42 and 57, John 1, Acts 17, and many other places. Similarly, I have already given quotations from Peter, Clement, Irenaeus, Tertullian, and all the others.*

of man was adorned *with heavenly gifts*[d] which were related to

[d] *With magical qualities.*

the glory and image of God, and indeed we willingly admit that these gifts are divine; but *that fictitious deity*[e] which Servetus calls

[e] *O horrible blasphemy!*

an afflation from the breath of God has nothing in common with the infused graces of God.

OPINION 31. That whenever in the law the Spirit of God is said to be in anyone it is not to be understood of the Holy Spirit of regeneration (Bk. 5 on the Trinity, p. 192).

SERVETUS He is usually received in this way, in those who were not prophets.

MINISTERS Both specifically and *in general he has denied that the Holy Spirit was given under the law to the fathers.*[a] But

[a] *That is a falsehood. See p. 192. The Spirit is received in one way in the prophets and in another way among the populace. I said that by the name of the Jews the populace should be understood, but that in the prophets there was another relationship, as you will find on pp. 557 and 650.*

since the whole of Scripture proclaims that believers now are endowed with none other Spirit than was formerly granted to the fathers, and David's petition is well known: "Take not thy Holy Spirit from me" [Ps. 51:11], and since there can be no faith or godliness except from the Holy Spirit, he brazenly excuses himself with a single little word.

OPINION 32. That angels were formerly worshipped as gods by the Jews (Bk. 5 on the Trinity, p. 184) in such a way that they call them their gods (the following page). What he says on p. 218 of the first Dialogue corresponds with this, namely, that under the law God was never truly worshipped, but angels who foreshadowed Christ were worshipped; and again, on the following page, that Abraham believed in him who foreshadowed Christ.

SERVETUS It was in this way that nearly all things happened to them in figures.

MINISTERS We also confess that things which have been openly revealed to us in Christ were shown to the fathers in figures. But from this Servetus falsely infers his sacrilegious invention *that angels were worshipped*[a] as gods by the saints. For Abraham was

[a] *God was worshipped in an angel, and an angel himself was worshipped — see Joshua 5 and Judges 6, etc.*

no less correctly instructed than any of us concerning the pure worship of the one God. The calumny, therefore, that angels were their gods[b] and that God was never *truly*[c] worshipped under the

[b] *They are called gods, in Genesis 20 and 35, etc.*

[c] *In accordance with the comparison we have made, there was a shadow then, since the light of truth had not then been manifested as it has been now.*

law, is excessively shameful. He speaks as though none of the saints of that time *understood*ᵈ the meaning of the command:

ᵈ *You are trifling.*

"Thou shalt love thy God". If it was not properly Christ, but an angel who foreshadowed Him, in whom Abraham believed, where is that *hypostasis*ᵉ and vision which Servetus earlier described in

ᵉ *It was concealed beneath a veil, because of Adam's sin. This I have explained in hundreds of places.*

such splendid terms? See how consistent he is with himself.

OPINION 33. Although he asserts that Christ or the Word had no real hypostasis from the beginning, none the less he affirms that the angels and the elect were really in God from the beginning (Bk. 4 on the Trinity, p. 135).

SERVETUS What you have concocted is a falsehood. No creature existed really except from the moment of its creation.

MINISTERS Let the passage be examined where he says that the spirits not only of the just but also of all men and all things were luminous *forms in God from eternity.*ᵃ Then he adds: "The

ᵃ *The angels existed really after they were created; we existed exemplarily from eternity.*

angels also were in God from the beginning".ᵇ Now he accuses us

ᵇ *If you were not a deceiver there would be no ambiguity here.*

of falsehood, when in fact we have quoted his false ravings word for word. He imagines that his impiety will be covered over if he now says that no creature existed really except from the moment of its creation. But there he argues about the manner in which all created things existed always in God. Moreover, the adverb "really" is explicitly used there.ᶜ

ᶜ *Of the angels created from the beginning: differently from us, as you by a shameless falsehood impute to me.*

OPINION 34. He maintains that the substantial deity is in all creatures (Dial. 1, p. 213).

SERVETUS God is in all things by reason of essence, presence, and power, and He sustains all things.

MINISTERS There is no controversy as to whether God is in all things by reason of essence, presence, and power, and as to whether He sustains all things. But *from this*ᵃ it does not follow

ᵃ *It is the same thing.*

that *the substantial Deity*ᵇ is in all creatures; and very much less

ᵇ *You have already heard this from Irenaeus and others. Substance is that by which we are sustained.*

what he declared before the judges, namely, that the pavement on *which we walk with our feet*[c] participates in deity, and that even

[c] *You said that when moving your foot you were not moving in God. Therefore it is in Satan that you move. We are in God, in whom we live and move and have our being* [Acts 17:28].

in devils[d] all things are full of gods.

[d] *Even if you were an evil demon, it is by God that you would have been sustained hitherto.*

OPINION 35. After patching together many perverse and pernicious ravings concerning the substance of the soul in pp. 220 to 225 of the first Dialogue, he concludes at length that the soul is of God and of His substance; again, that the created inspiration was implanted in it together with deity; and again, that through the Holy Spirit by a new spiration it combines substantially into the one light with God.

SERVETUS Take away the word "substance" from it and you will find the rest to be true, and that it is only you who are raving in company with Simon Magus.

MINISTERS The fierceness of the man is astonishing, that he should accuse those who do not agree with his Manichean views of raving in company with Simon Magus. *He wrote*[a] that the soul

[a] *That is a falsehood.*

is of the substance of God.[b] We pointed out his error. Let the

[b] *I openly teach that the soul was created, on pp. 178, 225, 260, and in other places. I said that angels and souls have a likeness to the substance of the Spirit from which they have emanated.*

word "substance" be taken away, he says, and everything will be true. Why has he not himself taken it away? Why in fact did he take the trouble to express himself in a manner which he knew was *hateful to all godly men*,[c] namely, that souls are produced by

[c] *Deity is hateful to you, you Magus.*

God's propagation? He openly *glories that he is a Manichean*[d] and

[d] *That is a falsehood.*

does not accept reproof.

OPINION 36. Although the soul is not God, he makes it God through the Spirit, who indeed is Himself God: so much so that He holds it is wrong to doubt that both our soul and the Holy Spirit of Christ have an elementary substance essentially joined to themselves in the same way as the Word has flesh joined to Himself. Furthermore, he holds that things both created and uncreated combine into one substance of soul and Spirit (Bk. 5 on the Trinity, pp. 181 and 182).

SERVETUS It is true that many things combine like this into a unity, just as bones, flesh, nerves, soul, form, and spirit combine into one substance of man.

MINISTERS When he has propounded a horrible blasphemy he avoids the issue with foolery. Everybody agrees that many things combine into one. But it is too absurd to conclude from this *that the soul is made God*,[a] as things created and uncreated

[a] *Are we not made gods on account of the gifts of the soul?*

combine into one substance of the soul, so that the soul has the elementary Spirit conjoined to itself just as the flesh of Christ is united to the Word. It is obvious that by such ravings *all the mysteries of redemption*[b] are profaned.

[b] *Tell me, wretch, how this follows.*

OPINION 37. He has written and also spread abroad terrible blasphemies against pedobaptism, as is sufficiently plain throughout the four books on Regeneration, and especially from the conclusion on p. 576. Again, he states that mortal sin is not committed before the age of twenty.

SERVETUS I admit that I wrote this. When you teach me otherwise I will not only accept it, but I will also kiss your footprints.

MINISTERS Were he a man *of mild and docile spirit*[a] nothing

[a] *As it would become you to behave towards me, even if I were deluded by an evil spirit, as the apostle teaches you,* 2 Tim. 2[vv. 25f.].

would become him less than his fierce and unrestrained raging when *he says*[b] that pedobaptism is a detestable abomination, the extinc-

[b] *I have already admitted that I wrote this; I have not seen your reasons for teaching the opposite.*

tion of the Holy Spirit, the desolation of the Church of God, the confusion of the whole Christian profession, the abnegation of the renewal made through Christ, and the trampling underfoot of His whole kingdom. Nor is it only in one passage that he blusters out these offensive utterances; but with every possible malediction he assails and belabours the sacred administration of pedobaptism, of which God is the author, as we have shown with solid arguments. And what diabolical arrogance to absolve adolescents from mortal sin until they have passed their twentieth year!

OPINION 38. That the soul is rendered mortal through sin,

just as the flesh is mortal; not that the soul returns to nothing any more than does the flesh, but that it dies when it is painfully deprived of vital actions, and is kept languishing in hell, as though with no further prospect of life (Bk. 4 on Regeneration, p. 531). He forms the conclusion, on the following page, that the regenerate have a soul different from what it previously was because of the renewed substance and because of the new deity which is added.

SERVETUS The very place that you quote against me proves that you are acting dishonestly; for there I say that the soul as it were dies and is kept languishing in hell. Therefore if it is languishing, it is still living. See what I write concerning the survival of the soul on pp. 76, 229, and 718. In a certain sense it is called another soul in the regenerate, just as on account of new accidents it is called a new thing.

MINISTERS Let our readers pay attention to the charge of dishonesty, the false infamy of which is laid upon us. We have quoted his words *in good faith*,[a] not omitting even a syllable that

[a] *In a previous accusation you told a different falsehood.*

might have the effect of extenuating his offence. He now pleads that he said that the soul "as it were" dies. This, indeed, is true; but it increases his impiety all the more. For when it might seem that the death of the soul is alleviated by that note of similitude, he adds: "By *another more significant*[b] relationship the soul is

[b] *Spiritual death, or the death resulting from sin, is called more significant. Why this raving from Calvin?*

rendered mortal through sin, just as the flesh is", etc. He certainly ought not to have *published*[c] the book if he did not wish to be

[c] *Would that all your sorcery were still in your mother's womb!*

caught in such manifest calumnies. Elsewhere, it is true, he does not deny that souls survive after death, but maintains that they are driven about like frail shadows, having scarcely any power of themselves (p. 229). To this the following is added on p. 233: "We have said that the elements of the soul itself are corruptible and that for that reason it is blown about hither and thither, as though denuded of its substance, and at length, in some manner subjected to an evil demon because of Adam's sin, it is dragged down to hell, as though never to be restored to the body again". What, then, does he expect us to think of his statements, according to which now the elements of the soul are blown about in the air, now souls are as though denuded of their own substance, now are said as it were to die, now by a more significant relationship are delivered up to death together with the flesh?

Since, were we to follow through every single one from the immense labyrinth of his errors,ᵈ there would scarcely be any

ᵈ *I wish I were free to make a catalogue of your errors!*

prospect of ever emerging, we considered it would be more satisfactory to set down only a selection; and because of the difficulties of the present time the brevity of our replies should be pardoned. Indeed, we have had only two days for our work. This, however, needs no apology, since it has been abundantly sufficient for the exposure of his enormities. Our readers should be warned that this unhappy man has left not one main point of doctrine untouched by his corruption. In the freedom of the will *he is a Pelagian.*ᵉ⁷⁹ He holds a doctrine of perfectionism like the Cathari,

ᵉ *Any one who is not Simon Magus is a Pelagian to Calvin. Thus absolutely all who have belonged to Christianity are condemned by Calvin, including the apostles, and the disciples of the apostles, and the theologians of the ancient Church, and all the rest. For no one excepting that Simon Magus ever completely took away the freedom of the will.*

Novatus, and similar groups.ᶠ⁸⁰ He destroys the law of God to

ᶠ *That is a falsehood.*

such an extent that *each man's own ideas*ᵍ are the rule of living.

ᵍ *That is a falsehood.*

He plucks faith away from the promises. He overthrows *free justification by faith.*ʰ He deprives the fathers who died under the law

ʰ *That is a falsehood.*

of all spiritual grace,ⁱ as though they were fed like earth-bound

ⁱ *That is a falsehood, you worthless wretch.*

pigs. By his fantastic scheme of regeneration he plunges the simple into the snares of the devil, and in this respect he is clearly a libertine. But he has scattered the poison of his impiety still more widely. For twelve years ago when the Lyon Bibles were printed he sullied their margins with many pernicious fabrications.⁸¹ The faithful know that nowhere is the virtue of Christ's death better attested in the Old Testament than in Isaiah 53; yet what the

---

⁷⁹ Pelagius, who flourished in the early part of the fifth century and from whom the heresy of Pelagianism was derived, denied original sin and affirmed the freedom and ability of man to choose good or evil.

⁸⁰ The Novationists of the third century, who were also known as the Cathari, were members of a rigorist sect.

⁸¹ The reference is to the first edition of the Bible prepared by Servetus, which was printed in Lyon in 1542.

prophet affirms concerning the provision of our reconciliation, the expiation of sins, and the removal of the curse, this corrupter diverts to Cyrus, because in his death the Jews paid the just penalties of their sins. Whoever therefore sincerely and prudently considers these things will acknowledge that his object was, by extinguishing the light of sound doctrine, to overthrow the whole of religion.

Joannes Calvinus

Abelus Poupinus
Jacobus Bernhardus
Nicolaus Gallasius
Franciscus Bourgoinus
M. Malisianus
Reimondus Calvetus
Joannes Pyrerius

Michael Copus
Joannes Baldinus
J. a Sancto Andrea
Joannes Faber
Joannes Macarius
Nicolaus Colladonius

SERVETUS[82] There has now been enough clamour, and this is a great crowd of signatories. But what passages do they adduce to establish that the Son is invisible and really distinct as they assert? They adduce none at all, nor will they ever adduce any. To have done so would have been fitting for so many ministers of the divine Word who everywhere boast that they wish to teach nothing that is not proved by solid passages of Scripture. But no such passages are now found. My doctrine, therefore, is condemned only by shouting, but without any reason and without any authority.

Michael Servetus signs, on his own indeed here, but he has Christ for his most sure protector.

To John Calvin: Greetings.

What I said about your being ignorant of the principles of things was done for your good, if you are now willing to understand. The main principle of which you are ignorant is that every action comes about through contact. Neither Christ, nor God Himself, acts on anything which He does not touch. Indeed, He would not be God if there were anything that escaped His contact. You dream up imaginary qualities, like the servitudes of lands. Neither the power of God, nor the grace of God, nor any such thing is in God which

---

[82] This brief paragraph and the letter to Calvin which follows were written by Servetus as a conclusion to the marginal comments he had inserted in the refutation presented by the Ministers. The date of their composition must be placed between the 15th and the 18th of September.

is not God Himself; nor does God send a quality into any part in which He Himself is not present. God, therefore, is truly in everything, He acts in everything, and He touches everything. Everything is from Him, through Him, and in Him. When, therefore, the Holy Spirit acts in us, His deity is in us and He touches us. I have also found you to be in error in another matter during the disputation. For the purpose of preserving the force of the law you quoted Christ's words, "What is written in the law?" and "Keep the commandments" [Lk. 10:26, Mt. 19:17]. Consider, that the law was then not yet fulfilled, nor taken away. Consider again, that Christ, while He was among men, wished the law to be kept. The man also to whom He was speaking was subject to the law. Accordingly, Christ then referred him to the law as to a superior authority. But afterwards, when everything was fulfilled, all became new: the old had been taken away. Similarly, He commanded another man to show himself to the priest and to offer a gift. Ought we therefore to do the same? He commanded a lamb and unleavened bread to be prepared for Him at the passover. Are we to make the same preparations? Why do you act the judaizer today by using unleavened bread? Consider these things, I beseech you, and read carefully my twenty-third letter. Farewell.

This whole business of Servetus, as it is written above, has been sent by Messieurs to the churches of Berne, Basle, Zürich, and Schaffhausen in order to obtain their judgment.[83]

[September 1553]

PHILBERT BERTHELIER[84]

At the beginning of September 1553 this church was greatly troubled since Philibert Berthelier, who had been excommunicated and forbidden the sacraments because of his rebellion against the Consistory, had been granted absolution by Messieurs, without the Consistory being given a hearing. This action was opposed by the ministers, who unanimously declared that they could not admit this man, or others like him, to the supper until the Consistory had evidence of his repentance, and had absolved him. It was ob-

---

[83] The dossier was sent on 21 September by the hand of an official messenger. Cf. the correspondence of the Council on this subject, in *Calvini Opera*, VIII, coll. 802-804.

[84] The dispute between Berthelier and the Consistory, which was to raise important problems in connection with the relationship between church and state in Geneva, had had its beginning in the preceding year (1552). (See p. 205 above, note 39.)

jected, moreover, that the order of the Church laid down that authority to forbid or admit to the Lord's supper belonged to the Consistory, and not to Messieurs.

Maître Jean Calvin protested publicly from the pulpit, in the same sermon when the supper was administered, that under no circumstances would he receive such a rebel at the supper, and that it was not for men to compel him to do what was scandalous, but that Messieurs rather should be urged to prevent Berthelier from presenting himself at the sacrament.

On 7 September the ministers of the city, with the exception of M. Jean Calvin, appeared before Messieurs to voice the same protest as Calvin had made. They declared that it was not lawful for them to break the oath they had sworn to maintain the order constituted in this church in accordance with the Word of God, and as laid down also in Messieurs' own ordinances.

Messieurs replied that it was not their intention to introduce any innovation into their ordinances, but that on the contrary they wished what was contained in them to remain fixed and inviolable; and they gave the ministers the book of their ordinances so that they could examine the relevant articles.[85]

On the following day, the 8th, the ministers presented themselves again before Messieurs to show them that the articles in the book of their ordinances concerning the order of the Consistory were contrary to the ruling they were trying to enforce on them, and that by proceeding in this way the very authority which these same articles conferred would be removed from the Consistory. Thereupon the ministers returned to Messieurs their book of ordinances and presented them with the following plea in writing:

CONCERNING THE ORDER OF THE CONSISTORY

The ministers of the Word of God in this city of Geneva unitedly remonstrate with their right honourable Seigneurs, Messieurs the Syndics and Council of Geneva, over the dispute which has recently arisen as to whether those persons should be banned from the supper who have been banned by the Consistory, until such time as evidence has been given of their repentance.

Illustrious Seigneurs, we shall not protest at length the desire which we have to obey you, as we are bound to do, because we prefer to give proof of this by our deeds, as you have always been aware; so much so, that we can truly say that we endeavour, as far as we possibly can, to conform to your will. But if there are times

---

[85] These ordinances are given above, at the beginning of this volume, pp. 35ff.

when our conscience forbids us to comply with your injunctions, we pray you, in the name of God, to receive our excuses indulgently and to give heed to pleas that are backed by good and just reasons, so that we may be able to fulfil the duties of our office faithfully, both towards God and towards you. For we shall never serve you with a loyal and free spirit if we do not uprightly and openly follow God's commands without turning to the right hand or the left.

It is a question of knowing to whom it belongs to ban from the supper those who are unworthy and unfit to receive it. Since, however, you have declared that it is your intention to observe your ordinances which were passed in the General Council, it would be superfluous for us to assemble here a variety of reasons for proving to you that we are requesting nothing except what is of God and His Word. Accordingly, without entering into a protracted debate, we state that the matter is defined clearly enough in your ordinances, where it is precisely specified to what persons the supper is forbidden. Furthermore, this authority is given to the Consistory: something which is clearly expressed four times.

This in no way contravenes the added requirement that the offender is to be reported to you, for these words do not imply that the Consistory is not to proceed with the correction and discipline which have been entrusted to it, and in short to carry out all that is there laid down, but their purpose is that you should take action against contemptuous persons who refuse to respond to spiritual punishment. In actual fact it is not said that such persons are to be reported to you so that you may decide whether the supper should be forbidden them or not, but, as is plainly stated in another place, that in all which concerns civil justice, and particularly where there is need for imposing some punishment or restraint, the report shall be made to you with the decision of the Consistory, and that the judgment shall be reserved to you. But here it is simply said that the Consistory, after having ordered what is in accordance with its office, namely, the banning from the supper of those who show themselves unworthy, shall report the matter to you, so that, if there are any who behave contemptuously, they may be reprimanded by you who have the power of the sword.

What is more, this does not refer to all to whom the supper is forbidden, but only to those who obstinately persist in teaching and disseminating false opinions and errors or who are rebellious and despise the order of the church, since in such cases the danger is much greater and there is need for justice to be administered. As for those who fail to submit to admonitions, whether they deny their faults after being convicted of them, or continue to behave badly, and also those guilty of some offence which merits the forbidding of the supper to them for a period of time, so that they may have an opportunity to humble themselves and others may not fall so easily into similar faults, nothing is said of having to report them to you, since this is not required in the first instance, but only if they persistently despise spiritual discipline.

Thus, illustrious Seigneurs, you see that in your ordinances there is neither doubt nor obscurity, but that it is plainly left to the Consistory to determine to whom the supper should be forbidden. And, finally, it is stated that it is the office of the minister to turn away those who contumaceously and rebelliously present themselves at the Lord's table in defiance of such a ban.

There is, especially, no requirement that a man who is manifestly contemptuous of the Consistory should be admitted to the supper; for it is tantamount to his wishing to triumph by despising those who have been delegated by you to represent the body of your church and to have charge over the spiritual realm which God wishes to be zealously guarded and maintained. It would, indeed, be better for there to be no political administration than for it to suffer disruption by such disorder, and for the Consistory to be altogether abolished than to suffer such indignity. You know, however, right honourable Seigneurs, that if ever anyone has complained of too great severity, we have always been ready to account for our action and to silence all voices to the contrary; for we are well aware that we have no right, even though men should permit us, tyrannously to do what seems best to us without saying why we do it.

What is more, if we do not refuse to account for our action even to the humblest, we are far from disdaining to observe a similar modesty towards you, to whom we owe honour and reverence, as to our superiors.

But just as you see that we are prepared to do whatever is right and just, so when you see that we have been falsely complained against we pray you to stand by us and to repel with vigour those who only seek to cause trouble so that they may cover up their sins. For, as we have always insisted, if those who are the most rebellious and unwilling to behave with humility succeed in being accorded more privileges than those who are good and peaceable, this can only lead in the end to a dreadful confusion.

Accordingly, illustrious and honoured Seigneurs, we trust that you will be pleased, in the name of God, to attend to this matter and to put right all future scandals in such a way that God may be honoured without contradiction, the order of the church may continue uninterrupted, you may enjoy an undisturbed tranquillity, and we may serve you in peace. For so far are we from presuming to diminish your authority that we pray God earnestly to increase it and to cause it to flourish to the glory of His name. And to this end we wish to use our own small power, without sparing even our lives, if need be. Therefore, if your prerogatives are to be preserved safe and secure, it is not against us that you should contend.

The matter was deferred by Messieurs and for the time being no reply was given.[86]

[12 October 1553]

LETTER FROM THE COMPANY OF PASTORS OF GENEVA TO THE BELIEVERS OF CERTAIN ISLANDS IN FRANCE[87]

Most dear brethren, we praise God that He has given you, in your captivity, the desire to serve Him faithfully, so that you are more afraid of being deprived of His grace than of exposing yourselves to the dangers into which the malice of men may bring you. For the brother who bears this letter has told us that you have requested him to return to you as soon as possible, and that you wish by every means to advance in blessing and to be confirmed in the faith of the Gospel. Today, in fact, there is more need of this than ever. Moreover, this admirable zeal of yours must be steadfast, so that you make constant progress along the road of salvation.

With regard to the man,[88] he is known to you, and, as far as we are concerned, since he has shown himself to be a God-fearing man here and has conversed with us in a manner that is holy and beyond reproach, and has always adhered to good and sound doctrine, we do not doubt that he will behave himself faithfully elsewhere and supply you with bread for your edification.

With regard to the advice which he has requested in your name, we propose that you should keep to the following order. In the first place, you should be diligent in assembling together for the purpose both of joining in prayer and of being instructed and admonished by him and by others whom God shall give you, and whom He has graciously enabled to minister to you. Further, you should courageously separate yourselves from idolatrous practices and from all superstitions which are contrary to the service

---

[86] The dispute was resumed on 7 November (see pp. 291ff. below).

[87] This letter is a response to a request from a number of Reformed Christians living on the islands off the coast of Saintonge in Western France (Oléron, Marennes, etc.). Philibert Hamelin, the bearer of this letter, was to become the first pastor of the small Reformed community that had been formed there. After a very active ministry in this part of France, Hamelin suffered martyrdom in 1557.

[88] Philibert Hamelin. Mention of his name would have endangered him.

of God and to the confession which all Christians make to Him, for to this we are called. When in time God has made you so to advance that you will be like a body of the church that maintains the order just described, and when there are some who are resolved to keep themselves from the pollutions which prevail in your place, then you will be able to enjoy the use of the sacraments. But we consider that it would be ill-advised for you to start with them, or even to be in a hurry to celebrate the holy supper before a proper order has been established among you. In fact, you will do much better to abstain from them, in order that you may in this way be induced to search by what means you may be rendered fit to receive them: namely, as we have already said, by regularly meeting together in the name of God, being united as a single body, and separating yourselves from idolatrous practices, which it is unlawful to mix with holy things. Likewise it is not lawful for a man to administer the sacraments to you unless you are recognizably a flock of Jesus Christ and a churchly form is found among you.

Meanwhile take courage and dedicate yourselves wholeheartedly to God who has purchased you through His own Son at such cost, and surrender both body and soul to Him, showing that you hold His glory more precious than all that this world has to offer. May you value the eternal salvation which is prepared for you in heaven more than this fleeting life. Therefore, and in conclusion, most dear brethren, we shall pray the good Lord to complete what He has begun in you, to advance you in all spiritual blessings, and to keep you under His holy protection.

12 October 1553

Signed Charles d'Espeville *in the name both of himself and of his brethren.*[89]

[*27 October 1553*]

DEATH OF SERVETUS

On Friday 27 October, having received the decisions of the churches of Berne, Basle, Zürich, and Schaffhausen concerning the affair of Servetus,[90] Messieurs condemned him to be taken to Champey and to be burnt alive there. This was done without any

---

[89] Charles d'Espeville was a cover-name which Calvin felt it discreet to use on occasions.

[90] The texts of these letters are given in *Calvini Opera*, VIII, coll. 808ff.

sign of repentance for his errors being given by Servetus at the time of his death.[91]

[7 November 1553]

AUTHORITY OF THE CONSISTORY

On Tuesday 7 November the Council of Two Hundred was convened in connection with the question of the authority of the Consistory and to consider the problem respecting to whom it belongs to excommunicate and to absolve. Before the Two Hundred had entered, however, Messieurs declared that it was their intention to reserve to themselves the power of absolving those who had been banned from the supper.

Thereupon the Consistory asked to be allowed to consult among themselves and, having withdrawn, resolved that they could not possibly consent to the pretensions of Messieurs, which were contrary to the order of the church, and they requested to be heard before the Council of Two Hundred.

In the presence of the Council Maître Jean Calvin, speaking for the Consistory, stated the case most adequately and explained why it was impossible to acquiesce in the pretensions of Messieurs; and then the declaration which had previously been presented in writing to Messieurs by the ministers was read before all.

On the following Thursday, after hearing the decision of the Council of Two Hundred that the whole right of forbidding from and readmitting to the supper should be taken away from the Consistory, the ministers presented themselves before Messieurs and unanimously declared that they were unable to consent to this ruling, and that to compel obedience would be to drive them from their charge, for they would choose this or death rather than consent to the abandonment of so holy and sacred an order, which had for so long been observed in this church. The ministers – and especially M. Jean Calvin, in accordance with the written promises he had received from Messieurs[92] – requested to be heard before the Council of Two Hundred and the General Council. This was not granted, but they were told that the request would receive attention.[93]

---

[91] For the text of the sentence pronounced against Servetus and further details of his execution see *Opera Calvini*, VIII, coll. 827ff.

[92] This is, beyond doubt, an allusion to the promises made to Calvin when he returned to Geneva in 1541.

[93] The dispute was resumed on 21 December (see p. 293 below).

On Friday 10 November the Council of Two Hundred was authorized to proceed to the election of the Lieutenant, and Messieurs wrote concerning this to the Seigneurs of Berne, Basle, Zürich, and Schaffhausen.[94]

[1 November 1553]

OBJECTIONS TO FAREL'S PREACHING

On Wednesday 1 November, prior to the matters mentioned above, Maître Guillaume Farel, who had come to this city, preached a sermon in which he exhorted and strongly criticized the youth, some of whom were offended, and even some who were not present at the sermon complained about it, although he had already departed to Neuchâtel. They alleged that he had called them all atheists. Thereupon an inquiry was instituted.

On Saturday 11 November M. Guillaume Farel, who had been informed of the trouble stirred up against him,[95] returned to this city and was commanded by Messieurs not to preach until the matter had been resolved.

On the following Monday Maître Jean Calvin, M. Abel Poupin, M. Jacques Bernard, and M. Mathieu Malesier appeared on behalf of all the ministers before Messieurs to protest against the injustice done to M. Guillaume. M. Pierre Viret was also with them.

On the same day also a considerable number of citizens of Geneva appeared before Messieurs to oppose the complaints which had been laid against M. Guillaume Farel, objecting that the complainants had misrepresented the position by making their complaint in the name of all the citizens, whereas they, who were citizens, had not consented and would never consent to it, since they esteemed Farel as a true servant of God and his preaching as good and godly, and had received profit and edification from his exhortations.

It was then ordered by Messieurs that M. Guillaume Farel should be recognized as a true pastor, as he had always been, and it was declared that he had preached and fulfilled his office faithfully. There were indeed many who called him father because he had begotten them in our Lord and because he had been the first to raise up the church here. After this Messieurs wrote a letter to Messieurs of Neuchâtel informing them that Maître Guillaume,

---

[94] A contemporary German translation of this letter is given in *Calvini Opera*, coll. 685f., and the replies from Berne, *ibid.*, coll. 690f., and from Zürich, coll. 699ff.

[95] By a letter from Calvin; see *Calvini Opera*, XIV, coll., 662f.

after having preached as he was accustomed to do, would return when he wished, accompanied by a herald, and that his expenses would be paid by this city. All this was a great consolation to the children of God and a cause of confusion to the wicked.

[21 December 1553]

PHILIBERT BERTHELIER

On Thursday 21 December the Consistory was summoned before Messieurs in connection with the case of Philibert Berthelier, who insisted on being admitted to the supper. The Consistory opposed this until such time as Berthelier should give evidence of repentance and humble himself before the Consistory, against whom he had been rebellious. Immediately François Berthelier, who had accompanied his brother, burst out, in the presence of Messieurs, with outrageous accusations against the ministers, asserting that they wished to tyrannize and dominate and were disobedient to the Seigneurie. Because of these harmful and monstrous accusations Messieurs commanded him to leave. As for Philibert, no further ruling was given, except that he should continue to abstain from the supper.

On the same day François Berthelier was summoned before the Consistory and asked how he could conscientiously partake of the Lord's supper in view of the outrageous things he had uttered that morning in the presence of Messieurs. He, however, continued his calumnies, declaring that so far as the Consistory was concerned he was addressing himself only to the ministers, whose treatment of his brother had been satanical, in holding him to be excommunicated and reprobate, without being able to produce any reason for doing so. He claimed, further, that he had power to give absolution just as much as they had to excommunicate, with a number of other outrageous utterances. Thereupon he too was banned from the supper, and it was resolved that on the following Tuesday all the members of the Consistory should present themselves before Messieurs to complain of the outrageous charges which had been made by François.

1554

Syndics: Amblard Corne, Pierre Tissot, Claude Dupan, Michel de l'Arche.

Lieutenant: François Chamois.

[8 March 1554]

FRANCOIS BERTHELIER

On Thursday 8 March, by order of Messieurs, François Berthelier attended the Consistory where he declared that he had been carried away by affection for his brother, with the result that he had said things against the ministers which should not have been said, and that he was sorry for having said them. He requested that he should be readmitted to the supper, which had been forbidden him. After various exhortations this was granted.

[22 March 1554]

PHILIBERT BERTHELIER

On Thursday 22 March Philibert Berthelier also attended the Consistory by order of Messieurs. He was sent out and recalled three or four times, but refused to acknowledge his fault and his rebelliousness, despite the fact that a number of good and godly admonitions were addressed to him. Accordingly, the ban against his partaking of the supper of our Lord remained in force.[1]

---

[1] For the conclusion of this matter, see p. 305 below (24 January 1555).

[3 June 1554]

RAYMOND CHAUVET ARRESTED AT DRAILLANS

On Sunday 3 June Maître Raymond Chauvet, minister of the Word of God in Geneva, went by order of Messieurs to preach at Draillans, where he had already been the previous Sunday, in the absence of M. Pierre Ninaux, the minister of that place, who had gone to France to attend to personal business without permission of Messieurs, although it was by them that he had been instituted as minister of Draillans. After the service an officer of Thonon detained M. Raymond, requiring him to appear immediately before the bailiff of Thonon, on pain of a fine of 25 écus. M. Raymond complied and presented himself before the bailiff, who inquired why he had preached in Draillans. When he replied that he had done so by order of Messieurs he was placed under arrest in the château of Thonon. The matter was taken in hand by Messieurs of Geneva since they were directly concerned, and they sent notification to Berne of a day for meeting to discuss the action of the bailiff.[2] The day designated was 15 July. Meanwhile M. Raymond remained under arrest, which the bailiff was eager to prolong, since Chauvet was paying the expenses, though unwillingly, in view of the fact that he was in no way to blame.

[July 1554]

A LIBELLOUS BOOK HANDED TO MESSIEURS

While these things were going on, in the month of July, a book, anonymously written by hand, was handed to Messieurs by Seigneur Pierre Vandel.[3] Vandel said that some unknown person had sent it to him. The book was full of calumnies and insults against the Seigneurie, against whom it was directed. There were also accusations against the churches and Seigneurs of Zürich and Neuchâtel, and especially a number of false and wicked charges against M. Jean Calvin. Finally, the last part of the book was a commen-

---

[2] Geneva retained certain ecclesiastical rights, including the appointment of the pastor, over the village of Draillans, although it was situated in the Bernese territory of Chablais, to the south of Thonon.

[3] Pierre Vandel was closely associated with Ami Perrin in the agitations against Calvin of 1555. In all probability the presentation of this pamphlet was part and parcel of the Perrinist campaign designed to undermine Calvin's authority.

dation of Servetus, Jerome [Bolsec] and other heretics, condemning the power which administered physical punishment to them.[4]

On Monday 2 July the ministers of the city and some from the country presented themselves before Messieurs to petition that, in view of the fact that in this book God and the order which He had raised up were dishonoured, the churches and godly republics defamed, their Seigneurie held in every kind of contempt, and all of us described as cowardly and pitiable because we submitted to the dictatorship of one man who was more immoderate than any pope or bishop ever was in Geneva, they would be pleased to give attention to such false and infamous charges and to suppress such wicked calumnies.

On the same day M. Guillaume Farel, who had been sent by the ministers of Neuchâtel because they were wickedly attacked in this same book, also lodged a complaint with Messieurs in the name of all his brethren.

[7 July 1554]

ANDRE VULLIOD BANISHED

On Saturday 7 July Vulliod, a notary, was banished by Messieurs because of execrable blasphemies which he had uttered. Their sentence contained the following words: "Although the supper was legitimately forbidden him by our Consistory, he rebelliously presented himself to receive it. For this reason", etc.[5]

[25 July 1554]

RAYMOND CHAUVET RELEASED

On Wednesday 25 July Seigneur Jean Lambert[6] was sent to Thonon on behalf of Messieurs to bring back M. Raymond, the minister mentioned above, following the decision made by the *commis* at the meeting in Lausanne.

---

[4] Viret and Farel attributed this pamphlet to Bolsec, M. de Falais, and perhaps Vandel himself. Calvin suspected Castellio.

[5] The banishment was temporary, for a similar case, lasting from 1 July 1558 to 29 August 1559 ended in the perpetual banishment of Vulliod, once again for blasphemy. *Calvini Opera*, XI, col. 583 gives a summary, but telescopes the two cases.

[6] Jean Lambert was a member of the Small Council and was to become First Syndic in 1555.

[12 August 1554]

JEAN DE MONTLIARD APPOINTED TO DRAILLANS

On Sunday 12 August M. Raymond went to Draillans by order of Messieurs and the decision of the ministers for the purpose of presenting as pastor Maître Jean de Montliard, called de Molrey,[7] who previously, namely, on 18 May of the present year 1554, had been elected as minister and had been appointed to Céligny.

[August 1554]

M. ANDRE LE COUR APPOINTED TO CELIGNY

In the same month of August Maître Jean de Montliard, before going to Draillans, presented M. André Le Cour[8] as minister in Céligny, who previously, namely, on Thursday 2 August, had been presented to Messieurs by the brethren for the taking of the oath.

[14 September 1554]

TESTIMONIAL FOR JEAN DE PIOTAY, SURGEON

On Friday 14 September letters testimonial were granted to Jean de Piotay, a surgeon of Carpentras,[9] on the authority of certain reputable persons of this city who testified to the excellence of his life and conduct, together with his wife.

[21 September 1554]

A SCOTSMAN

On the following Friday, the 21st, a certain Scotsman[10] requested the brethren to give a hearing to the arguments by which he claimed to be able to demonstrate that he had received a revelation and had been called by the Lord to go to the churches, and

---

[7] Jean de Montliard, the son of Nicolas de Mellevaux, was a pastor in the Genevan territory from 1554 to 1563.

[8] André le Cour was later sent as pastor to his native town of Issoire (Puy-de-Dôme).

[9] Jean de Piotay, from Carpentras (Vaucluse), had been living in Geneva since 1550. He was "barber" in the plague hospital from 1556 to 1565.

[10] The identity of this unnamed Scotsman is not known.

also to the princes who had supported the Reformation, in order that he might intervene for the bringing about of peace and unity and the settlement of all disputes. In proof of his calling he adduced certain quite inappropriate passages of Scripture. He requested also that two or three members of the Congregation should be nominated to hear his reasons under more leisurely conditions. His object was to obtain authorization from this church to proceed with his enterprise. The ministers, however, replied that, while they did not wish to hinder him from employing himself in accordance with the gifts which he had received from the Lord, they were unable to give recognition to his revelations, and that he had misused Scripture in the attempt to authenticate his calling, which in their judgment proceeded from his imagination rather than from God. As for the request that certain of the brethren should be designated to hear him further, they could not consent to this since he had already explained his proposals amply and at length to some in particular and to the majority of those assembled for that purpose. Nor were they able to grant him letters testimonial, since he was unknown to them; though if he should employ himself to the benefit and advancement of the Church they would glorify God.

[4 October 1554]

JOURNEY OF JEAN FABRI TO BERNE

On Thursday 4 October Maître Jean Fabri departed for Berne to complain in the name of all the ministers of Geneva that certain, both of the ministers and also of the other subjects of Messieurs of Berne, had accused, in the person of M. Calvin, their doctrine of being heretical. To this end, Messieurs of Geneva sent a letter by Fabri to Messieurs of Berne, praying them to give our preachers an audience and to remedy the charge with which they had been falsely reproached.[11]

Maître Jean Fabri presented the letter to Messieurs of Berne and explained the purpose of his journey, but achieved nothing except that the chief magistrate advised him to return at a later date, since the majority of the Council were away, and the matter would have to be deferred until their return, when it would receive their careful attention.

[11] The text of this letter, dated 2 October 1554, is given in *Calvini Opera*, XX, coll. 425-426. The chief accusers were André Zébédée, pastor of Nyon, Jean Lange, pastor of Bursins, and Jerome Bolsec, who had been living in Thonon since being banished from Geneva.

[4 October 1554]

LETTER FROM THE PASTORS OF GENEVA TO THEIR EXCELLENCIES OF BERNE[12]

Illustrious, powerful, and most honourable seigneurs, we present our humble respects, and entreat you to excuse us for turning to you with a complaint concerning the most outrageous and immoderate opinions which are held against us in your territory, not so much with the purpose of denigrating our persons as of exposing the Gospel and the whole of Christianity to opprobrium and scorn. We remind you, messieurs, that until now we have never bothered you with our quarrels, not because we have not frequently had just occasion to bring to your attention the injustices which have been disseminated falsely against us, but because we have preferred to be silent rather than cause you any trouble or molestation. Now, however, that necessity compels us to open our mouth we trust you will receive our approach with all the more sympathy and readiness, and that you will be graciously inclined not only to hear our petition but also to remedy the evil which we have decided to bring to your notice. It is not here a question of our persons, for, if we had been unjustly censured, your law-courts would be open to us, as to everyone else, throughout your territory. But it is because those of whom we complain to you assail in particular the doctrine which we maintain — something which ought not to be dragged before the courts — that we have felt it right to have recourse to your excellencies.

It is scarcely necessary, illustrious seigneurs, to explain to you what reproach and ignominy recoils on the holy Gospel when the preachers and other subjects of the territory of Berne call the preachers of Geneva heretics. This, in your wisdom, you can see for yourselves. When there has been some dispute over doctrine it has been necessary to exercise prudence and moderation to close the mouth of the enemies of the faith, seeing how they watch and lie in wait for us; but now that God has given us the blessing of being harmoniously united with each other, those who shout and rage against us show not only that their sole intention is to cause trouble and scandal, but also that they are like saboteurs disrupting the sacred union with which God has blessed us. Your preachers are, by God's grace, of one mind, both among themselves and also with us, as you may learn from them; for if they do not assure you

---

[12] Fabri also took with him this and the following letter. This action of the pastors of Geneva was supported by a letter from Viret and the pastors of the presbytery of Lausanne to their colleagues in Berne. The letter given here is published in *Calvini Opera, XV*, coll. 250ff.

that there exists between us as peaceable a relationship of genuine brotherhood and harmony as could be desired, we shall not request any favour of your excellencies. But if they tell you — and we are certain they will — that between us there is no enmity or antagonism, this should be proof sufficient to you that those who are slandering us seek neither your honour nor your benefit and security. For our part, we can honestly testify that we have always endeavoured to be united in the truth of God with all your ministers, so that in requesting you to take our cause in hand we are inviting you to maintain the honour of God no less than your own.

The following is the matter over which we request you to take action. In a congregation of the classis of Morges, when a large number of people were present, a certain person slandered our brother M. Jean Calvin to such an extent that it is commonly heard throughout the territory that he has been condemned as a heretic; and this slander has been frequently repeated. Further, on the occasion of the wedding of the Seigneur de Cran's son,[13] Zébédée, a preacher from Nyon, declared quite openly that the doctrine which we hold, and which we are willing to seal with our blood, was a heresy worse than all the papacy and that those who proclaimed it were devils, indeed, that he would rather defend the mass. Again, a man named Jerome [Bolsec], who, as you know, was banished from the city of Geneva because of his errors, did not hesitate to call our brother Calvin a heretic and the antichrist.

Consider, illustrious seigneurs, whether we can disregard such things without being traitors to God, who has charged us, as St. Paul says [cf. Tit. 1:9], not only to teach those who are willing to learn but also to resist all slanderers. We are hopeful, therefore, that as faithful and Christian rulers you will come to our aid in this cause, by refusing to allow the Church of God to be laid waste under your protection and the Gospel to be calumniated, especially in view of the fact that by peacefully turning to you we have avoided stirring up trouble or unrest. This consideration will induce you all the more to remedy this evil in such a way that by your action God will be glorified, the scandal removed, and the audacity of those whose sole intention is to spread confusion everywhere will be suppressed. And, sustained by your equity and justice, it will be our duty more than ever to pray that God will prosper you, as indeed we entreat Him to keep you under His holy protection, and to govern you by His Holy Spirit in all righteousness

---

[13] Urbain Quisard, Sire de Crans, was related to Ami Perrin, and his castle was one of the fiercest centres of opposition to Genevan orthodoxy.

and integrity, causing the authority with which He has entrusted you to redound to His glory.

Geneva, 4 October 1554

If, illustrious seigneurs, you see fit to order a fuller investigation of this matter, we are ready to substantiate everything as it has been set down here in writing, although there will be no need of a prolonged inquiry, since the report is noised abroad everywhere.

[*4 October 1554*]

LETTER FROM THE PASTORS OF GENEVA TO THEIR COLLEAGUES OF BERNE[14]

Greetings: Our brother and colleague[15] has come to you at our command in order that he may lodge before your illustrious Council a no less just than necessary complaint concerning the unbridled effrontery of certain men who are at present defaming our most excellent brother Calvin as a heretic; nor is this taking place only in taverns and at drinking parties, which would be intolerable enough, but also in church buildings and at public assemblies. It is no new thing for them to indulge in this license, so that at the slightest prompting, and whenever the fancy takes them, they malign us, it may be without mentioning names, but yet not obscurely or secretly. For a long time we have kept silent in the hope that when their disgraceful conduct had reached saturation point, though they might not be restored to a sound mind, yet at least they would be silenced either by shame or by boredom. But now that the evil daily grows worse, and their frenzy is intensified by our silence, we feel that this affliction has been endured long enough. Moreover, in order that you may know that we would not be seeking redress had we not been compelled by urgent necessity, we shall briefly relate the things that have happened within the space of a few days.

Recently, when the brethren of the presbytery of Morges were holding their synod, one of those present called Angelus[16] not only denounced Calvin as a heretic in the presence of the whole assembly because he had expounded a passage from the fifth chapter of the epistle to the Hebrews in a manner that displeased him, but also

[14] This letter is published in *Calvini Opera*, XV, coll. 256ff.
[15] Jean Fabri (see p. 298 above).
[16] Angelus is the Latin equivalent of the French name L'Ange or Lange (see note 11, p. 298 above).

assailed us with many outrageous insults, with the result that the report rapidly spread throughout the whole region that we had been condemned as heretics by the ministers of Berne. Shortly after this there followed a no less crude incident; for when the guests invited from various places, among whom was a senator from our city, had assembled for the illustrious and lavish marriage festivities Zébédée started blustering against the providence of God — concerning which, as you know, we teach that He turns the devil and the wicked this way and that as by an unseen rein, so that His just judgments may be executed — and not only made a bitter attack on us but also raved that we were worse heretics than the papists. He even indirectly censured our Council because by its authority it provided protection for so detestable an error (as he called it) no more worthy of acceptance than the mass. He referred to that passage where the demons besought Christ to be allowed to enter into the herd of swine. You see why these men are filling the whole neighbourhood with unrest. Furthermore, encouraged by their audacity, that worthless fellow Jerome [Bolsec], now living in Thonon, does not hesitate to keep on calling Calvin a heretic and antichrist. And on the opposite bank of the lake there is another, not dissimilar, individual, Sebastian by name,[17] who not only utters the same things by word of mouth but even commits them to writing.

Now the moment has come for you to judge how disgraceful and disorderly is the disturbance which is advancing everywhere in this region, how great an occasion for ridicule is being given to the papists, indeed to what derision the sacred name of Christ is exposed. The fact is that nearly all the weak are tottering, the godly are dreadfully tormented, profane despisers scoff and in public shamelessly spue forth whatever they like against godly doctrine. On both sides quarrels are already beginning to erupt. We, to whom the thought of a violent remedy is abhorrent, consider that there will be no better course than to bring this complaint before

---

[17] Sebastian Castellio. Castellio had been won to the Reformed faith by Calvin, whom he met in Strasbourg in 1540 and who subsequently secured his appointment as rector of the college in Geneva. His criticism of some of Calvin's theological views, in particular his doctrines of Christ's descent into hell and of election, caused him to leave Geneva in 1544. His translations of the Bible into Latin (1551) and French (1555) met with disapproval because of the liberties he took. In 1553 Castellio was appointed professor of the Greek language in Basle. The following year — the year of this present letter — saw the publication of his *De Haereticis*, in which he condemned the execution of Servetus and pleaded for tolerance. He died in 1563, and it was only after this that his two polemical works *De Praedestinatione* and *Contra Libellum Calvini* were published, in 1578 and 1612 respectively.

your Council and humbly to petition them to lend their assistance for the correction of these evils, lest the situation should become worse. Since, moreover, this is a cause common to us both, it is desirable for you to take the initiative, so that you may help us with your protection in this common cause; and as this is a most just request, so we are confident that you will do what we ask both freely and gladly. For if it would be unreasonable for you, assuming we remained silent, not to take action for the cessation of these disturbances after being warned from elsewhere, is not this your duty now both because you have been approached by us and also because of the brotherly bonds which unite us in Christ? We have nothing else to ask of you, except that one of your number should be chosen to conduct our colleague before the Council so that he may obtain a ready hearing and your illustrious Council may understand that you have this matter very much at heart.

Farewell, most dear and respected brethren. May the Lord guide you by His Spirit and sustain you by His grace to the end.

Geneva, 6 October 1554[18]

Messieurs of Berne then wrote a letter[19] to our Seigneurs in which they said that they were distressed at the disputes and contentions between the ministers, and that they had tried to prevent such conflicts and controversies, and still wished to do so more than ever. They exhorted our Seigneurs to attempt the same with their ministers. Thereupon, and especially because there was no discrimination between the innocent and the guilty, the ministers of Geneva wrote again to Messieurs of Berne, and also to the ministers.[20] Copies of this correspondence are attached to this register in a file.

[18] The date given is *"pridie nonas Octobris"*, that is, 6 October, whereas the Register tells us that Fabri left for Berne on 4 October. It may be that the secretary, perhaps not yet fully accustomed to the Julian calendar, had forgotten that in October the Nones fell on the 7th and not the 5th day.

The original letter bore the following signatures:

"Your brethren and colleagues the pastors of the church of Geneva

Johannes Calvinus	Michael Copus
Abelus Poupinus	a Sancto Andrea
Franciscus Bourgoinus	Jo. Faber"
Raimondus Calvetus	

[19] For the text of this letter see *Calvini Opera*, XV, coll. 313f., 17 November 1554. Cf. the instructions of the Bernese to their French-speaking pastors, *loc. cit.*, coll. 311ff., 17 November 1554.

[20] For the text of the second letter (27 November 1554) see *Calvini Opera*, XV, coll. 319f. Cf. *ibid.*, XX, coll. 426f., Messieurs of Geneva to Messieurs of Berne (27 November 1554). The texts mentioned have not been preserved with the Register.

The ministers of Berne then wrote that because their Seigneurs had issued clear injunctions to their ministers concerning this matter, and also had banished the physician Jerome, they felt that it would be better not to bring our letter to the notice of their Seigneurs for fear lest they should trouble them unduly.[21]

When, however, Jerome was recalled by Messieurs of Berne, and his banishment cancelled, the ministers of Geneva wrote another letter to the ministers of Berne, dated 27 December 1554, which is also in the attached file.[22]

[21] Cf. the letter from Haller to Calvin (4 No. Decembris 1554), *Calvini Opera*, XV, coll. 325ff.
[22] Cf. the letter of 4 kal. Januari 1554, *loc. cit.*, coll. 362ff.

1555

[24 January 1555]

THE CONSISTORY'S AUTHORITY CONFIRMED

On Thursday 24 January the Council of 60 and the Council of Two Hundred assemble in connection with the question of the authority of the Consistory and excommunication, and at both Councils M. Jean Calvin, in the name of the Consistory, the ministers of the city also being present with him, very adequately refuted the arguments which had been advanced for the diminution or rather the demolition of the Consistory's authority, and demonstrated from passages of Holy Scripture and from the practice always found in the Church when it was in a state of purity what was the true use of excommunication, and to whom it belonged to excommunicate and to admit to communion.

Thereupon, despite every effort of Satan to overthrow so godly and useful an order, Sr. Amblard Corne, the first Syndic, announced to the ministers in full Council that God had been victorious, and that both the Council of 60 and the Council of 200 had resolved that the Consistory should retain its status and exercise its accustomed authority, in accordance with the Word of God and the ordinances previously passed.

(At about this time several brethren who desired to improve their understanding of the Scriptures requested the ministers to preach, each in turn, and expound a passage of Holy Scripture every Friday at midday. They started with the Epistle to the Romans.)[1]

[16 February 1555]

RAYMOND CHAUVET SENT TO BERNE

On 16 February M. Raymond Chauvet, minister in Geneva, was sent to Berne by his ministerial colleagues with letters both to the

---

[1] This paragraph is transcribed in the margin of the Register. It indicates a recommencement of the "congregation" held from time to time in Geneva during the ministry of Calvin.

Seigneurs and to the ministers there.[2] This was done because Zébédée, the minister at Nyon, and Lange, the minister at Bursins, after going to Berne, were boasting of having won a victory before the Senate and shouting their triumph everywhere, while they continued with ever greater intensity their slanders and calumnies against M. Calvin and the doctrine which is preached in Geneva.

On arriving in Berne, M. Raymond was told that Messieurs had written to their ministers and hoped that from now on everything would be properly controlled; but if not, then they would deal with matters in a manner which Messieurs of Geneva and their ministers would find satisfactory.

It was during these proceedings that an order was sent to the bailiffs of Berne that it was to be announced by the ministers that no person should go to receive the supper in Geneva according to the Calvinistic rites.

Syndics, 1555: Jean Lambert, Henri Aubert, Pierre Bonne, Pierre-Jean Jessé.[3]
Lieutenant: Hudriod Du Molard.

[6 March 1555]

CALVIN AND CHAUVET GO TO BERNE

All these things were reported to Messieurs, our seigneurs and superiors, and as they had to send ambassadors to Berne in connection with other matters Messieurs resolved that M. Calvin should go with them to take up the matter mentioned above. When, however, all the other ministers objected that this matter was not peculiar to M. Calvin, but affected them all in common, Messieurs agreed to send Maître Raymond with Calvin. These two set out on their journey on Wednesday 6 March, and the syndic Henri Aubert and M. Chamois[4] travelled with them.

---

[2] For the text of the first of these letters, dated 15 February 1555, see *Calvini Opera*, XV, coll. 430f.

[3] Three of these four new syndics were resolute Calvinists, a fact which was to prove decisive during the Perrin affair a few months later. Bonne resigned at the time of this affair.

[4] François Chamois was a former syndic and was Lieutenant in 1554. For the instructions given to these four ambassadors see *Calvini Opera*, XV, coll. 478ff., 5 March 1555.

[8 March 1555]

TESTIMONIAL FOR ANTOINE GRENET

On Friday 8 March the brethren granted Antoine Grenet, of Auvergne, a testimonial concerning the good quality of his life and conduct in this church. It was signed by F. Bourgoin, Michel Cop,[5] Saint-André and Jean Fabri, in the name of themselves and of those who were absent.

ANSWER TO THE ACCUSATIONS MADE AGAINST THE MINISTERS OF GENEVA

With regard to the charges made at Berne, the chief magistrate and others delegated by the Senate answered that the parties would be called together and the matter investigated in Berne on Sunday the last day of March, when all would be put right by the best and most appropriate means.[7] The chief magistrate also stated that Messieurs of Berne were writing to their bailiffs cancelling the order mentioned above, and that it was never their intention that the announcement should be published in this way.

Furthermore, the majority of the Seigneurs of Berne had been misinformed and were angry because of the calumnies of a number of malicious slanderers against M. Jean Calvin and this city. Now, however, that they had heard the true facts of the case they showed every sign of friendliness both to Calvin and to this church. Moreover, the ministers of Berne had declared in full Council and made it public that they were completely at one with us in doctrine.

[28 March 1555]

CALVIN AND CHAUVET VISIT BERNE AGAIN

In accordance with the day assigned as above, the same ambassadors who had previously been to Berne were sent again, together with M. Jean Calvin and M. Raymond Chauvet. They left on Thursday 28 March.[8]

---

[5] Michel Cop was the brother of Nicolas Cop, Rector of the University of Paris, a great friend of Calvin.

[6] For the text see *Calvini Opera*, XV, coll. 482ff.

[7] For the text of the letter, dated 13 March 1555, fixing the date of this conference, see *Calvini Opera* XV, coll. 500f.

[8] The instructions given to the ambassadors will be found in *Calvini Opera*, XV, coll. 526ff.

These ambassadors and ministers left Berne on 5 April after receiving an affirmation from Messieurs of Berne that they esteemed M. Jean Calvin as a true and faithful servant of God and his doctrine as true and godly, and that, in order to maintain the peace of the churches, they would write to their ministers in a manner that would prove satisfactory.

A few days later, Messieurs of Berne sent an injunction to their churches, dated 3 April, in which, instead of approving the doctrine of the ministers of Geneva, the Genevan doctrine was indirectly taxed with showing too much curiosity and with wishing to enter too deeply into the secrets of God, and also with being contrary to the discussions held in Lausanne.[9]

JEAN VERNOU AND JEAN LAUVERGEAT

Maître Jean Vernou and M. Jean Lauvergeat, who had been sent by the ministers of this church to the brethren who are scattered in several valleys of Piedmont, wrote a letter dated 22 April describing how the Lord was advancing His work there, as may be seen from this letter.[10] Vernou and Lauvergeat were commissioned to go and preach the Word there in response to the request of three brethren who were sent from there for this purpose.

M. JACQUES L'ANGLOIS SENT TO POITIERS

Because the brethren in Poitiers had also requested this church to send a man who would minister the Word of God to them M. Jacques L'Anglois was chosen to go to them and devote himself to this charge.[11]

[10 May 1555]

TESTIMONIAL FOR JEAN THIERSAULT

Friday 10 May. At the request of one named Jean Thierselet, otherwise called Thiersault, a native of the diocese of Meaulx-en-Brie, a hearing was given at our Congregation to certain members of this church who spoke concerning the life and conduct of

---

[9] For the text see *Calvini Opera*, coll. 547ff. (3 April 1555); cf. coll. 542ff. and Calvin's reply, coll. 550f.

[10] For the text of the letter see *Calvini Opera*, coll. 575ff. (22 April 1555).

[11] The ministry of Jacques L'Anglois at Poitiers was relatively brief. He was later pastor at Tours, Lausanne, and Lyon, where he was martyred in 1572.

Thiersault. Since they testified to his good character, he was granted a testimonial to the good repute in which he was held. The letter, dated 10 May 1555, was addressed to the brethren of Neuchâtel because he hoped to find some employment in the church there.

[26 May 1555]

CHAUVET AND MACAR GO TO BERNE

On Sunday 26 May M. Raymond Chauvet and M. Jean Macar left for Berne with letters and instructions authorizing them to make objections to Messieurs of Berne because of the scandals which were becoming increasingly serious as the result of their injunction mentioned above. Messieurs of this city wrote to the same end; and the presbyteries of Lausanne and Thonon sent similar complaints to Berne.

M. Raymond then returned to attend to the provision of witnesses, while Macar remained in Berne to watch and keep his hand on the progress of affairs there.

TUMULT IN GENEVA

In the meantime great commotion and tumult was caused in the city of Geneva by a number of seditious persons. When Ami Perrin, Balthasar Sept, François Chabod, Pierre Verne, and Jean Michalet were held suspect they fled from the city. After having been summoned by the sound of the trumpet over a period of several days, and condemned for contempt, finally, on Monday 3 June, sentence was pronounced against them with due ceremony by the Syndics in their tribunal: all five were to be taken to Champey and there beheaded, their bodies quartered, and each quarter displayed in the four most public places in the Genevan territory. In addition, Perrin, before being beheaded, was to have the hand cut off with which he had violently seized the syndical mace, and both his hand and his head were to be displayed at Champey.[12]

LABORIER AND TRIGALET FOR PIEDMONT

On Tuesday 4 June, because the ministers who had been sent to Piedmont had returned and complained that they could not fulfil the charge that had been committed to them, and also because

---

[12] By seizing the syndical mace, the symbol of executive power, Perrin had laid himself open to the charge of *lèse-majesté*.

Maître Jean Lauvergeat asked permission to pay another visit to his mother and his relatives, it was resolved that M. Jean Vernou should return to Piedmont and with him M. Antoine Laborier and M. Jean Trigalet, who willingly submitted to the decision of the church.

[6 June 1555]

RETURN OF MACAR FROM BERNE

On Thursday 6 June our brother Macar returned from Berne without having been able to achieve anything in connection with the affair for which he had remained there, but rather bringing back rough and hostile answers. He carried with him a letter from Messieurs of Berne to Messieurs of this city.[13]

IMPRISONMENT OF VERNOU, LABORIER, AND TRIGALET

On Monday 17 June a letter was brought from our brothers Jean Vernou, Antoine Laborier, and Jean Trigalet, who had left us on the previous Monday, informing us that as they were travelling they had been seized and bound by the provost of Chambéry, and that the letter which they were carrying had been taken from them. May the Lord strengthen them! Their letter was answered by our brother Calvin in the name of all.[14]

[28 June 1555]

D'AIREBAUDOUZE APPOINTED TO JUSSY

On Friday 28 June, permission having been obtained from Messieurs to elect a minister once more to fulfil preaching duties and other ministerial functions in this town, M. Pierre Airebaudouze[15] was chosen to take over in Jussy in the place of M. Nicholas des Gallars, and it was resolved that des Gallars should return to work here in the city.

---

[13] For the text of this letter see *Calvini Opera*, XV, coll. 630f. (3 June 1555).

[14] This first exchange of letters appears not to have been preserved. See next page for the text of a letter dated 1 August 1555 written from prison by Vernou, Laborier, Trigalet, and others to the Company of Pastors in Geneva. These men never reached the Piedmontese valleys, but suffered martyrdom at Chambéry.

[15] Pierre d'Airebaudouze, Baron of Anduze, was pastor in Geneva from 1555 to 1561 and in various towns in the southwest of France.

MATTEO GRIBALDI REPRIMANDED

The following Saturday, because Matteo Gribaldi, Sire de Farges,[16] had maintained and written a number of heretical opinions and had criticized the doctrine preached in this church, the Syndic of the Consistory, Pierre-Jean Jessé, and M. Jean de la Maisonneuve and the ministers assembled, and Gribaldi was summoned. He arrived accompanied by several Italians and in particular by the physician Maître François.[17] On entering he asked: "Where is Master Calvin?" and offered his hand to him. M. Jean Calvin, however, refused to take it, saying: "I will not shake hands until we are in agreement over doctrine, for we should not open these proceedings with formalities". Thereupon Gribaldi said: "Adieu, messieurs", and went off. Soon afterwards he was summoned to the city hall and reproved for his errors by M. Calvin in the presence of the Syndic and other members of the Council.

TESTIMONIAL FOR NICOLAS PASTEUR

On Friday, the 14th, the brethren assembled in the Congregation granted a testimonial to Nicolas Pasteur,[18] a native of Normandy, who had been appointed master of a school in a certain place under the jurisdiction of Neuchâtel.

[1 August 1555]

LETTER FROM LABORIER, VERNOU, TRIGALET, AND OTHERS IMPRISONED AT CHAMBERY TO THE COMPANY OF PASTORS OF GENEVA[19]

The love of God our Father and the grace of our Lord Jesus Christ be upon you always, by the imparting of the Holy Spirit.

Gentlemen and most dear brethren, we have been greatly comforted by the letters which you have kindly written us, especially in seeing by them that your customary magnanimity has supported

---

[16] Matteo Gribaldi Mofa was an Italian lawyer with anti-trinitarian tendencies.

[17] The identity of the physician "François" is uncertain.

[18] Nicolas Pasteur had been a bookseller and since 1550 had resided in Geneva.

[19] Quite a considerable correspondence between the prisoners of Chambéry and the Company of Pastors survives; cf. *Calvini Opera*, XV, *passim*. This letter, however, has remained unknown.

us despite our fault,[20] which cannot be described as small, as its effects show us all too clearly. Have we achieved anything by what we have done? Have we, by our misguided prudence, prevented what we feared from happening? Alas, no. For three or four days later, when we were still sorrowing over our fault, the news came that Satan was inflicting his fury on those whom we wished to preserve. Our grief was then redoubled; and we knew very well that this was for our humiliation, having learnt that the prudence of men cannot prevent the providence of God. We have in ourselves more than enough imperfections to keep us lowly before God; but this one is so obvious that it exceeds all the others. The Lord God has caused us to feel this most vividly so that for the rest of our lives we may be humbled by it; yet He is willing to pardon us, as we believe He has already done. We entreat you to pray God for us, since the need for prayer is greater than ever — and not so much for us as for this poor people, that God may withdraw His rod from them or may soften them, and that, if it is necessary, He may soon send upon us what He pleases. Meanwhile we shall pray for you and for them while awaiting the outcome of our case, whatever it may be that God is pleased to give us, confident that in guarding our faith, as is our duty, He will enable us to fulfil our calling.

Our brother Jean Guilhen, the bearer of this letter, will give you news of what is happening in these parts and also the answer which has been given him by the man with whom he has been negotiating. Jean Guilhen, indeed, has comforted us greatly and, as he will tell you, has conducted himself honourably in order to do so. The Lord God wishes to restore him to you — to you who sent him to us, and to him who has acquitted himself so well. May He give us grace to profit from the good counsel which He gave us. Having learnt from your letters that the letters which we sent to our Seigneurs of Geneva have been well received, we are determined to continue while we have opportunity. Please inform us if you will whether what we have written to them has

---

[20] The prisoners are alluding to their scruples of conscience over the false information which they had given to their interrogators with the object of protecting their congregations. In a previous letter, dated 25 July, they had expressed their shame at having denied knowledge of Reformed services at Balbote and Fenestrella, in the valley of Pragela, and also of a Vaudois pastor named Paul. This present letter may well be a reply to an undated letter from Calvin (*Calvini Opera*, XV, coll. 707ff.). One sentence of Calvin's: "Be assured that your prudence in answering was truly of the Spirit of God and not of the guile of this world", could have been intended to calm their scruples.

been approved or not, and attend to this matter as you are much more familiar with things than we.

May the Father of mercy fill you with His blessings in such abundance as your duties require, so that you may ever show yourselves such as you have been known to be until now. Amen.

From the cells of Chambéry, the first day of August.
Your most humble brethren and servants

Antoine Laborie
Jehan Vernou
Jean Trigalet
Bertrand Bataille
G. Tauray

We beg you to commend us to the holy prayers and good graces of Messieurs Farel and Viret, and their churches.

1556

Syndics: On Sunday 9 February Ami Curtet, known as Bottillier, Jean Chautemps, Jean de la Maisonneuve, and Pierre Migerand were elected as Syndics.

Lieutenant: Claude Dupan.

Consistory: The syndic Pierre Migerand was appointed to the Consistory sistory, together with Amblard Corne and Jean Donzel; but when Donzel was appointed *Châtelain de Chapitre*[1] Jean Pernet took his place on the Consistory.

[5 March 1556]

DEATH OF ABEL POUPIN

On Thursday 5 March 1556 M. Abel Poupin, minister in this church of Geneva, died after a long and painful illness and numerous relapses. He was buried the same day. The funeral was attended by a number of the Seigneurs, together with the ministers and a great many people.

[7 March 1556]

DEPOSITION OF JEAN FABRI

On Saturday 7 March an extraordinary session of the Consistory was held to consider a charge brought against M. Jean Fabri, a minister in this city, of adultery with the wife of a man named

---

[1] The "châtelain de Chapitre" was a functionary of the city whose duty was to administer the "lands of the Chapter", a series of villages under the Seigneury of Geneva which prior to the Reformation had belonged to the Chapter of the cathedral. Jean Donzel was later elected syndic, in 1558 and 1566.

Jean Jacquème. Both Fabri and Jacquème and his wife were instructed to appear before Messieurs on the Monday following.

On the same day M. Jean Fabri was told by the Syndics de la Maisonneuve and Migerand not to preach on the next day, while the hearing of his case before Messieurs was pending.

On the Monday following Messieurs heard the case of Fabri, after information had been given, in accordance with the order of the Consistory, by Calvin and Guillaume Chicand, who had been sent for this purpose. Fabri denied the greater part of the charge, but none the less confessed sufficient to be judged unworthy to continue as a minister. Accordingly he was deposed from the ministry by the verdict and order of Messieurs.[2]

[12 March 1556]

VISITATIONS IN THE CITY

On Thursday 12 March it was resolved in the Consistory, and afterwards approved by Messieurs, that visitations should be made throughout the city for the examination of persons, so that the Lord's supper might not be profaned, and for the exhortation of all to do their duty to God and to hear His holy Word. There was to be one minister with every two of the visitants, together with the *dizenier* of each district. As there were 25 *dizeniers*, four were assigned to each minister, since only six ministers were available for this visitation, and the 25th was assigned to the first who was to undertake it.

[April 1556]

CLAUDE BADUEL

About 8 April of the same year M. Claude Baduel[3] was elected a minister in this church, and because it was feared that he had too weak a voice for preaching in the city it was decided that he should deliver a sermon in the Madeleine, which he did on 15 April in the presence of the Syndics and the members of the Council.

---

[2] This deposition, however, did not prevent Fabri from being appointed pastor in Piedmont, his native land, in 1558.

[3] Claude Baduel was the celebrated Latinist and professor, and an avowed supporter of Calvin.

PIERRE DUC

At the same time M. Pierre Duc, a teacher in the school,[4] was also elected a minister. Subsequently, however, when it was reported that he had entered into some usurious contract, though both the ministers and Messieurs exonerated him of blame, yet, because of the recent scandal with M. Jean Fabri and to ensure that no evil suspicion should attach to the sacred ministry, and also because he was most usefully engaged in his present post, it was resolved to proceed no further with his election.

[24 April 1556]

LOUIS ENOCH

On Friday 24 April M. Louis Enoch, the principal of the college, was elected to the ministry of the Word.

[10 May 1556]

PRESENTATION OF MACAR AND ENOCH

On Sunday 10 May 1556 M. Jean Macar, minister of Russin and Dardagnes, and M. Louis Enoch were presented to the people at the morning service at 8 o'clock in St. Pierre and the afternoon service at 3 o'clock in St. Gervais.

[17 May 1556]

PRESENTATION OF BADUEL

On the following Sunday, the 17th, M. Claude Baduel was presented to the parishes of Russin and Dardagnes, in the place of Macar, who presented him.

[22 June 1556]

JEAN VIGNAULX SENT TO PIEDMONT

On 22 June 1556 Jean Vignaulx was elected to be sent to the brethren of Piedmont, who had requested that one or two more

---

[4] Pierre Duc, of St. Didier in the Dombes (Ain), held various posts in the church and the schools of Geneva between 1554 and 1562, when he was sent as pastor in the Dombes.

ministers should be provided because of the size of the flock which, by the grace of God, was growing daily.

[*30 July 1556*]

THE CONSISTORY PERMITTED TO ADMINISTER THE OATH

On Thursday 30 July the Consistory began to hear testimonies given on oath. This was the result of a complaint made to Messieurs that some persons did not scruple to lie before the Consistory, indulging in various kinds of falsification and dissimulation, and a proposal that the administration of the oath to them would have the effect of making them afraid of bearing false witness.

[*6 August 1556*]

BOINVILLE

On Thursday 6 August the Consistory agreed to the request of the wife of the Sire de Boinville[5] that the latter should be summoned by means of three fortnightly announcements to appear and answer several matters with which he was charged, and on the Sunday following, the 9th, the first announcement was made publicly from the pulpit at the 8 o'clock service, as is customary.

[*25 August 1556*]

MINISTERS SENT TO BRAZIL

On Tuesday 25 August, in consequence of the receipt of a letter requesting this church to send ministers to the new islands [Brazil], which the French had conquered, M. Pierre Richer and M. Guillaume Charretier were elected. These two were subsequently commended to the care of the Lord and sent off with a letter from this church.[6]

---

[5] Guillaume Lecointe, Sire de Boinville, resident in Geneva since 1553, had a number of troubles in 1556 when he was accused of blasphemy and other offences.

[6] The most important source of information concerning this Calvinistic expedition to Brazil is the contemporary chronicle of Jean de Léry, of which there have been several editions since the sixteenth century.

[26 August 1556]

VISIT OF CALVIN TO FRANKFURT

On the next day, which was Wednesday, Monsieur Calvin left for Frankfurt in response to a request from the French church there and several of the Seigneurs of the Council of that city that he should pay them a visit for the purpose of settling certain troubles which had arisen in that church.[7]

[5 September 1556]

MARTIN DE ARGUES SENT TO BOURGES

On Saturday 5 September, following a request from the people of Bourges, M. Martin de Argues[8] was elected to go and minister the Word of God there, and on the following Friday a letter was given him for this purpose, addressed to the faithful in that city and signed in the Congregation by the ministers of this Church.

JEAN LAUVERGEAT SENT TO PIEDMONT

A few days later in the same month M. Jean Lauvergeat was sent to Piedmont to serve as schoolmaster and minister in a village which had embraced the Gospel. This village had sent a letter asking for a minister.

[15 November 1556]

ORDINANCES CONCERNING BLASPHEMY AND ADULTERY

On Sunday 15 November the General Council was presented with good and godly ordinances, agreeable to the Word of God, respecting oaths, blasphemies, cursings, and denials of God, as well as acts of adultery. These ordinances had been passed by a large majority in the Small Council and in the Council of Two Hundred, but in the General Council the majority had considered them too rigorous, and consequently they had not been approved — to the great regret of respectable citizens, and to the great joy of those

---

[7] Calvin had been asked to act as arbiter in a dispute between Valérand Poullin, pastor of the French church in Frankfurt, and Augustin Legrand, an important merchant of that city. Cf. *Calvini Opera*, XVI, coll. 288ff.

[8] Almost all that is known of Martin de Argues is that he came from Biarritz.

who wished only for unlimited license so that they might indulge in all kinds of evil without fear of punishment.

On the same day Amblard Corne was elected Lieutenant.

ALBERT SENT TO PIEDMONT

On Friday 27 November, since a letter had been received from the brethren in Piedmont requesting that more workers should be sent because the harvest was increasing, the ministers of this church chose and sent one named M. Albert [blank], of Albigeois.[9]

[9] This person has not been identified.

1557

[1 January 1557]

DISCUSSIONS AUTHORIZED

On Friday, New Year's Day, a discussion was commenced in the presence of the ministers by a number of reputable members of this church who desired to be trained in Holy Scripture. It was resolved that the leader should follow one of the apostolic epistles, and it was decided to begin with the Epistle to the Hebrews. Philibert Grené was picked to act as leader, and the resolution of each point under discussion was assigned to M. Calvin with much edification. These discussions will be continued, God willing, and will be held on the first Friday of each month, on the understanding that only the ministers and those who wish to participate in their turn shall be present.

JEAN CHAMBELI SENT TO PIEDMONT

A letter was received from the congregations of Piedmont requesting that yet more men should be sent to minister the Word to them. Accordingly M. Jean Chambeli, of Issoudun, who previously had been tutor to the children of M. Chevalier, was chosen and sent.

MATHIEU GRANDJEAN APPOINTED SCHOOLMASTER AT THE HOSPITAL

During this same month of January Messieurs gave order that a man should be elected to serve as resident master of the school at the Hospital — a man free from the responsibilities of a wife and children, who would also be capable of preaching and conducting services, should the necessity arise through illness or incapacitation for some other reason of the ministers. M. Mathieu Grandjean, who previously had been tutor to the children of M. Germain Colladon, was elected.[1]

---

[1] Mathieu Grandjean, of La Charité in the district of Macon, was a pastor in Geneva from 1557 until his death in 1561.

A MARRIAGE DISSOLVED BECAUSE OF TOO GREAT INEQUALITY OF AGE

At about this time, by resolution of the Consistory and decree of Messieurs, the marriage contracted between the widow of Jean Achard, aged more than 70, and a servant of hers, aged about 27 or 28, was dissolved because of the too great inequality of age. The Consistory resolved further that Messieurs should be requested to make a ruling on this matter for the future.

SCHOOLMASTERS IN THE VILLAGES

Messieurs appointed schoolmasters to certain parishes under their jurisdiction for the instruction of the children, providing them with lodging and a small salary to help them to live.

[February 1557]

FEBRUARY 1557
JEAN GERARD SENT TO BLOIS

A letter was received from a certain congregation of believers in Blois requesting that someone should be sent to minister the Word of God to them. Accordingly Jean Gérard, otherwise called du Gay, of Anjou was elected.[2]

SYNDICS

On Sunday the 7th of this month Pernet de Fosses, Jean Pernet, Louis Franc, and Guillaume Chicand were elected Syndics in the General Council. May God give them the spirit of wisdom and understanding.

DE CHERPONT APPOINTED SCHOOLMASTER AT NEUCHATEL

The brethren of Neuchâtel sent a request to the ministers of this city that they should provide a good schoolmaster in place of M. Mathurin de la Brosse, who had been appointed minister at Saint-Blaise. Accordingly M. François de Cherpont, a native of Paris, was elected.[3]

---

[2] Jean Gérard was a young pastor whose health deteriorated after going to Blois; he returned to Geneva where he died in 1560.

[3] Mathurin de la Brosse, formerly a Paris physician, later became a pastor in Sens. Saint-Blaise was a village in the neighbourhood of Neuchâtel. Francois de Cherpont was later a pastor in France.

[March 1557]

MARCH 1557
VISITATIONS

At the beginning of this month Messieurs gave order that visitations should be conducted throughout the city for the purpose of inquiring into the faith, life, and conduct of each person, and that a list of their names should be made, to the encouragement of respectable citizens and the restraint of evildoers. This was to be carried out by one of the syndics, one of the ministers, one of the Consistory, a secretary, and the *dizenier* of the district which was being visited.

M. GASPARD SENT TO PARIS

On Monday the 15th Maître Gaspard,[4] minister of Neuchâtel, the husband of M. Guillaume Farel's niece, passed through on his way to Paris to assist the congregation there, which, by the grace of God, is a large one, and which has made a request for several ministers.

JEAN D'ESPOIR ASSIGNED TO ROUEN

With M. Gaspard went M. Jean d'Espoir,[5] on his way to minister the Word of the Lord in Rouen, at the request of the brethren there.

JEAN DE PONVERS ASSIGNED TO THE ISLAND OF NOIRMOUTIER

On the same day M. Jean de Ponvers, of Périgueux, left, having been appointed to the islands near La Rochelle to minister the Word of God there.

[April, May 1557]

APRIL, MAY 1557
DEATH OF SAINT-ANDRE

At this time our brother Me. Jean de Saint-André,[6] to whom the brethren had entrusted this Register, was ill, and he conducted

---

[4] Gaspard Carmel, also known as Fleuri or Fleurier, was especially reputed for his evangelistic activity in France. He died in Geneva, where he had become a pastor, in 1560.

[5] Jean d'Espoir, or de Pleurs, had previously founded the church in Angers and had officiated for some time in the church of Geneva.

[6] Jean de Saint-André had been secretary of the Company of Pastors since 1552. His place as secretary was taken by Jean Macar, who acted in this capacity for only a few months, however.

himself in his illness as he had done when in health, testifying to all who came to see him of the hope which he had of eternal life; and after having lingered for a long time he passed away, to the great sorrow of the whole church, shortly after midnight on the fifth day of May. That same day he was buried. At the funeral the Syndics and nearly all the Seigneurs were present, together with the Ministers and a large number of the populace.

CLAUDE CHEVALIER ASSIGNED TO POITIERS

In the month of April Claude Chevalier[7] was elected and sent to assist Maître Jacques Langlois, the minister of the Word of God in the church of Poitiers.

ANTOINE BACHELAR ASSIGNED TO LYON

At the end of the same month, after we had examined Maître Antoine Bachelar, of Aix-en-Provence, and heard him preach, and also had made careful inquiries concerning his life, he was sent to proclaim the Word of God to the believers in Lyon. But some two or three months later he was compelled to return, both because he had fallen ill and also because his identity was becoming known.

MARTIN TACHARD AND GIOFFREDO VARAGLIA SENT TO PIEDMONT

At the same time a letter was received from Piedmont appealing for more preachers of the Gospel. Accordingly Maître Martin Tachard[9] and an Italian named Gioffredo Varaglia da Cuni were elected and sent.

EVRARD APPOINTED TO ANVERS

In the month of May, since the believers in the town of Anvers had agreed together that they would elect as their minister whomever should be sent to them from Geneva, Maître Evrard[10] [blank] was elected and sent to preach the Word of God to them.

---

[7] Claude Chevalier, of Romette in Dauphiné (Haute-Alpes), at first officiated in the church at Poitiers and subsequently in that of Alès (Gard).

[8] Antoine Bachelar, also called Cabanes, at first officiated in the church of Lyon and subsequently in that of Nantes. The last clause of this paragraph was added at a later date.

[9] Martin Tachard, of Montauban, was later pastor in his native town until his martyrdom in 1567.

[10] The identity of this person is uncertain.

[*June, July 1557*]

JUNE - JULY 1557

MONSIEUR DE LA GARDE APPOINTED TO ANDUZE

At the beginning of June M. Guy Moranges, otherwise called Monsieur de la Garde,[11] left for Anduze to serve as pastor to the inhabitants of that region who had the knowledge of God and who are said to be very numerous. At the end of two months, however, it became necessary for him to return with the consent of the elders there, both because of his illness and also because of the severe persecution which had broken out.

ANTOINE VIVES APPOINTED TO ISSOUDUN

On 20 June, after having expounded a passage of Scripture in the presence of the brethren, Antoine Vives,[12] of Languedoc, left to become a preacher of the Gospel at Issoudun in the province of Berri.

ELECTION OF NEW MINISTERS

On Friday 4 June, after our censures had been made in the customary manner, we proceeded to the business of electing a minister in the place of Saint-André and two others for a new church which Messieurs intended to erect, called the church of Saint Germain, because the people were daily increasing in number. After having earnestly invoked the name of God, several good candidates were nominated. For the time being, however, no decision was taken, except that we should wait for Monsieur de Collonges[13] who, being too much exposed to danger in Paris where he was performing the office of pastor, had taken leave of the church in order to come here, and also that Maître Mathieu Grandjean, who about six months previously had been elected by the brethren as schoolmaster at the Hospital,[14] should preach in our presence and be examined by us.

On the following Monday Maître Mathieu expounded a passage from Acts 15 in the presence of the brethren, and it was apparent that he was too timid and as yet lacking in style. None the less,

---

[11] Guy Moranges, also called de la Garde or La Porte, is better known for his ministry in several churches of Auvergne, his native territory.

[12] Antoine Vives was martyred in 1561.

[13] François de Morel, sire de Collonges, was one of the first important leaders of the Reformed Church of France and was Moderator of the national synod of Paris of 1559.

[14] See p. 320 above.

it was decided to proceed to the examination. On being examined with a variety of questions, he was judged to be a man of good knowledge, although he was slow in making his answers.

On Friday 18 June, when the brethren from both the country and the city were assembled, it was confirmed that a minister should be elected in place of our brother Saint-André, but it was agreed to wait some time longer to see whether God would send us someone more adequate than those whose names were before us. Monsieur du Pont,[15] of Blois, was then elected, and when he came into the presence of the brethren he accepted the appointment with modesty. And, lest he should lose heart, Maître Mathieu was told that we still had to elect two ministers and that he should do all he could to equip himself.

At noon on the next day Monsieur du Pont expounded Psalm 82, which the brethren had assigned him. Then on Friday 25 June he was examined on the principal articles of our religion, and afterwards on several other occasions, and the brethren were well satisfied with him. On Thursday 1 July he delivered his first sermon in the presence of the brethren and the delegates of Messieurs, namely, the Syndic Chicand and the Seigneur Jean-François Bernard.[16] After we had offered our comments it was resolved that we should defer his presentation to Messieurs until we had listened to Monsieur de Collonges who had returned, and Maître Mathieu had also preached a sermon, so that all three could be presented together to the Seigneurie.

On Friday 2 July, when the brethren from both the country and the city were assembled, they called Monsieur de Collonges and told him that they had elected him as a minister; and on his accepting the charge he was told to study Psalm 125 so that he might expound it at noon on the next day. Recognizing that Maître Mathieu was not sufficiently stylish for preaching in the city, the brethren decided that it would be necessary to bring in one of the brethren from the country; and Maître Nicholas Colladon, who was minister at Vandoeuvres, was chosen. Then, in view of the fact that Monsieur Baduel, who was at Russin, had not only to follow a difficult road but also to cross a dangerous torrent[17] when going from one parish to another, and having regard to his frail constitution and the loss of one of his eyes, the brethren ruled

---

[15] Claude du Pont was a pastor of Geneva from 1557 until his death in 1559.

[16] Guillaume Chicand was an ardent supporter of Calvin, and Jean-François Bernard played an important role in the political life of Geneva from 1555 to 1580.

[17] The Allondon, a tributary of the right bank of the Rhone (canton of Geneva).

that he should move to Vandoeuvres and Cologny, and that Maître Mathieu should serve at Russin and Dardagny. They also sought for some way of relieving Maître Jean de Montliard who was then minister at Draillans, since he had requested this, explaining that because of his foot he was unable to carry out his duties in that place where the houses of his parishioners were so scattered and distant from each other, and could not easily travel from one village to the other to visit any who were sick. Moreover, because Messieurs had stated that they were anxious for Maître Nicolas Petit to be moved and for someone more robust to be placed at Chansy, since the parishes were a long way from each other and, besides, persons travelling to Geneva passed that way and sometimes stopped to hear the sermon, the brethren sought some way of making a change, in accordance with the reasonable wish of Messieurs. For the time being, however, they were unable to find a way of relieving de Montliard or of moving Maître Nicolas.

On Saturday 3 July Monsieur de Collonges expounded Psalm 125 and the brethren were well pleased with his acuteness and skill. They then gave him a passage from the 6th chapter of Ephesians on which to preach the following Friday, and this he did on that day in the presence of the brethren and the delegates of Messieurs, namely, the Syndic Chicand and the Seigneur Jean Donzel.

On Thursday 8 July Maître Mathieu delivered a sermon on a passage from the 2nd chapter of the First Epistle of St. Peter in the presence of the brethren and the delegates of Messieurs, namely, the Syndic Chicand, the Seigneur Jean Donzel, and the Seigneur Jean-François Bernard.

CHARLES MAUBUE APPOINTED SCHOOLMASTER OF THE HOSPITAL

At this time Maître Charles Maubué[18] was elected schoolmaster of the Hospital, and was presented to and accepted by Messieurs.

DE MONTLIARD APPOINTED TO CELIGNY AND NICOLAS PETIT TO DRAILLANS

On Friday 9 July the assembled brethren found a way of relieving de Montliard, namely, that he should return to Céligny, where he had first served as a minister. They also resolved that Maître André Le Cour should go to Chansy and Maître Nicolas Petit to Draillans.

---

[18] Charles Maubué held several posts in the church and the college of Geneva from 1557 until his death in 1566.

On Monday 12 July Monsieur de Collonges, Monsieur du Pont, and Maître Mathieu were presented to Messieurs by Monsieur Calvin, and Messieurs accepted them and approved all our arrangements, namely, that Colladon, de Collonges, and Claude du Pont should minister in the city, and that Baduel should go to Vandoeuvres, Maître Mathieu to Russin, de Montliard to Céligny, Le Cour to Chansy, and Maître Nicolas to Draillans.

COLLADON, DE COLLONGES, AND DU PONT PRESENTED IN GENEVA

On Sunday 18 July Maître Nicolas Colladon, Maître François de Morel, called de Collonges, and Maître Claude du Pont were presented by Monsieur Calvin to the people, both in the church of St. Pierre and in the church of St. Gervais, as pastors in the church of Geneva.

MATHIEU GRANDJEAN PRESENTED IN RUSSIN

On the same day Maître Mathieu Grandjean was presented to the people of Russin and Dardagny by Maître Claude Baduel. Seigneur Jean Donzel attended the presentation on behalf of Messieurs.

CLAUDE BADUEL PRESENTED AT VANDOEUVRES

On Sunday 25 July Maître Claude Baduel was presented by Maître Nicolas Colladon to Vandoeuvres and Cologny, with Seigneur Jean Donzel in attendance.

ARRANGEMENTS IN GENEVA

On Friday 23 July the brethren resolved that Calvin and de Saules[19] should preach weekly in the Madeleine, de Collonges and Colladon in St. Germain, Raymond [Chauvet] and Enoch in St. Gervais, Cop and Macar in the morning in St. Pierre, and also that Bourgoin should preach at 8 o'clock on Sundays and on Wednesdays in the Madeleine and should also conduct the catechism, and Du Pont on Sundays and Wednesdays in St. Gervais, together with the catechism.

---

[19] Nicolas des Gallars, sire de Saules (cf. note 14, p. 63 above).

[August 1557]

August 1557

ANDRE LE COUR PRESENTED AT CHANSY AND CARTIGNY

On Sunday 8 August Maître André Le Cour was presented as pastor to the people of Chansy and Cartigny by Maître Nicolas Petit, formerly minister of these parishes.

DE SAULES GOES TO PARIS

At about this time one of the leading elders of the church of Paris arrived here, expressly sent with a letter of credence to take back with him one of the ministers of the church of Geneva. In accordance with a resolution passed by us on 12 July, Monsieur de Saules left of his own free will for Paris in order to strengthen the brethren there. The day of his departure from Geneva was 16 August.[20]

TENSION BETWEEN GENEVA AND BERNE

On Friday 6 August the brethren from both country and city assembled and Monsieur Calvin informed them that Messieurs of Berne had condemned our Seigneurs and the whole city of Geneva, in the person of their procurator, to make reparation to Ami Perrin and his accomplices in respect of all expenses and damages that they had incurred, and that at the end of ten days the sentence would be carried out. From this it was abundantly clear that the persons and belongings of all citizens who entered the territory of Berne, or who had any possessions there, would be forfeit. It was agreed that, in anticipation of this danger, on the following Sunday the preachers of the city should exhort the people to humble themselves and patiently to await the help of God. This was done, and most notably by Monsieur Calvin, with the result that the whole populace remained calm; and for this reason God had pity on them and the sentence was suspended, or rather, as it seems, politely retracted.

[September 1557]

September 1557

LE GAY APPOINTED TO BEARN

On 6 September Monsieur Calvin informed the brethren that the people of Béarn were asking for a minister, and that it was

---

[20] The envoy from Paris, Nicolas du Rousseau, was captured and put to death on the return journey. Des Gallars succeeded in escaping and in reaching Paris.

also necessary to elect four others for Lyon, Piedmont, Aix, and Bourdeaux. With reference to Béarn, Maître François Le Gay was elected and left.[21]

PASQUIER BACNOT APPOINTED TO PIEDMONT

Maître Pasquier Bacnot was elected for Piedmont, and left on 14 September.

CLAUDE BOISSIERE ASSIGNED TO AIX

Maître Claude Boissière, of Tencin in the province of Dauphiné, was elected for Aix-en-Provence, and left on 22 September.

FRANCOIS LE GAY FOR BEARN

Maître François Le Gay was appointed to Béarn, and left on 14 October.

[*7 September 1557*]

LETTER FROM NICOLAS DES GALLARS, IN PARIS, TO HIS GENEVAN COLLEAGUES[22]

The letter of which a copy follows was received on 16 September 1557.

To my most dear and respected brethren and colleagues: Greetings.

I imagine that you have already heard, if only by way of rumours, of the great misfortune that our congregation suffered three days ago. Almost two hundred persons are held captive by the enemy who threaten them with all kinds of dire consequences. Among them are many distinguished individuals, both men and women; but not the least respect is shown either for their family or for their station. Coryphaeus[23] is quite impervious to all petitions: to such an extent is he under the spell of Thais and Galer-

---

[21] François Le Gay, or Dugué, of Boisnormand, was assigned to the province of Béarn where he worked at the court of Navarre as well as at Nérac (Lot-et-Garonne).

[22] This and the two following letters are concerned with the affair of the Rue Saint-Jacques in Paris. Officers of the crown had arrested and imprisoned a group of Parisian personages who were present at a secret service. This affair was to have international repercussions. Cf. *Calvini Opera*, XVI, coll. 602f.

[23] Κορύφαιος (des Gallars writes it in the Greek), the head man, designates the king, Henry II.

ites.²⁴ Indeed, they are the only ones he believes and trusts. Tell me, what action can I take in the face of this great disaster? Everywhere I am known — more so than I had expected — and it is widely reported that a new leader has been sent whose soldiers are the agents of this new tragedy. In due course you will be told more fully by others and by me how all this happened. The dangers of this war are now so great that I cannot remain here any longer. If, therefore, you think I can be of any use in our city, let me escape to you. My comrades in battle are unaware of the condition on which I was sent, since they have not received your letter. They consider me to be entirely committed and bound to them, and although I have from the beginning declared that it could not be so, yet they are unwilling to believe me. I rejoice and give thanks to Almighty God that I have been present in these troubles; for, if I have achieved nothing else, at least I have blocked many misconceived and pernicious plans, which would not only have caused the greatest offence but would also have brought upon us worse disaster and the utmost calamity. It is for this reason that I pray and beseech you to send a letter to them without delay so that, instead of making some rash move, they may submit to sound counsel. Should you delay to write, I fear it will be of little use; for it is difficult to restrain the impulse of many persons. The rest I will tell you when I am able to communicate freely with you.

I trust you are all strong in the Lord, and especially Passelius,²⁵ my kinsman, to whom I sent recently a letter to be shared with you. May the Lord rule you by His Spirit and keep you in safety for the benefit of His flock. Farewell.

From camp, 7 September 1557

                              Your most respectful N D GLSI[26]

                              On the same day, 16 September, Calvin sent a reply in the name of all the brethren, a copy of which follows.

---

[24] "Thais", a name which was commonly applied to a courtesan, designates Diane de Poitiers. "Galerites" designates Cardinal Jean Bertrand, Guardian of the Seals, who was charged with the drawing up of the case.

[25] This person has not been identified.

[26] A cryptic abbreviation for Nicolaus De Gallasio.

[16 September 1557]

LETTER FROM CALVIN TO DES GALLARS[27]

Greetings. I have delayed answering your earlier letter, both because I was anxiously awaiting news of what had happened to your companion,[28] and also because I wished to give you information about the state of affairs with us, which was then quite uncertain. I had, in fact, already started to write to you when the sad report reached us, and this in turn was followed two days later by your letter, which arrived today. Although my first reaction was one of horror and I was almost prostrated with grief, yet I lost no time in seeking a means of remedy. On Tuesday, which was the 14th, our neighbouring friends promised us their support. The day before, at the request of a number of godly men, our brother Veracius[29] had been charged with leading a new delegation. For since many supposed that the fury of the tyrant would have exhausted itself in this new calamity it seemed good to make another attempt. I had given Veracius the most careful instructions. I had also implored Beza to associate himself with us which I am sure he did; for opportunely he had left Arctopolis[30] a few days previously. As soon as I learnt of the assault of the enemy, I secretly sent messengers on swift horses to catch up with Veracius, who that night had been in Paterniacum.[31] Everybody was aroused by every means possible to give the most urgent attention to this cause. In the midst of so great a sorrow the knowledge that I have performed my duty has at least afforded some consolation. I took care to keep the report hidden from your wife, so that she might be spared anxiety while things were still uncertain. Meanwhile she is with me, and behaving herself with such self-control and composure that I could not be better pleased. It will be no small comfort to you to know that, though anxious about you, as was fitting, yet she put the common safety of the church and the glory of Christ first, rather than your life.

Now with respect to the advice for which you ask, the united judgment of your colleagues is as follows: if you leave your post during these first disturbances we fear, not without reason, that your departure will cast down the spirits of all, indeed almost drive

---

[27] This letter is published in *Calvini Opera*, XVI, coll. 627f. It was written by Calvin, on behalf of the Company, in reply to the preceding letter of 7 September.
[28] Cf. note 20, p. 328 above.
[29] That is, Jean Budé.
[30] That is, Berne.
[31] That is, Payerne (Vaud).

them to the extremes of despair. You know how the presence of a single leader can hold together a whole army. If, then, you were to withdraw, it would immediately be suspected that you were fleeing in desperation. Therefore so long as turbulent movements may in some measure be checked it is desirable that you should be close at hand, so that they may be assured by indisputable evidence that you are a partner in their perils. This proof will be a source of no little encouragement not only to them but also to all who are in sympathy with them. There is no need for me to emphasize how dear your life is to us; but if the safety of so many souls were not more dear to us, we should not be dear to you. Now most of all it is important to make every effort to ensure that what remains does not become weak, and indeed altogether collapse, since nothing would be more difficult than to reassemble the remnants when they have been completely scattered. If you see that your presence is necessary for holding things together, we beseech you most earnestly to remain for some time longer, until, with the slackening of the enemy's fury, a measure of tranquillity affords justification for your departure, or until some greater exigency forces you out. If, however, the fear of others restricts your effectiveness, or you see the way to be closed before you, it is not our wish that you should sit by in idleness; for, so long as you are there, you should especially be prompt to stir up the whole flock of Christ to follow their Master. Doubtless, also, you are aware that there are many who are waiting to seize on any word of yours which may provide an excuse for timidity. This makes the importance of your presence all the more plain. You will see what we have written to the flock.[32] You will be able to judge from the circumstances what is the best course to take. It may be, of course, that before this letter reaches you the cause for alarm will have abated, or that you have been released or have decided to remain. We feel, therefore, that nothing more is needed than to encourage you to persevere until a more opportune moment for your departure presents itself, so that the brethren may not think that they have been deserted. We would advise you, also, to do nothing without the approval of your colleagues, lest, by withdrawing in defiance of their judgment, you should be setting a harmful precedent. May the Lord guide you and them in this crisis by the spirit of wisdom, understanding, and uprightness; may He be present with you and with the cover of His wings protect, strengthen, and sustain both you and the whole church.

16 September

---

[32] See the letter that follows.

[16 September 1557]

LETTER FROM THE COMPANY OF PASTORS TO THE CHURCH IN PARIS[33]

The love of God our Father and the grace of our Lord Jesus Christ be with you always by the imparting of the Holy Spirit.

Most dear sirs and brethren, there is no need for us to tell you at greater length how saddened and distressed we are at the news of your affliction, since this follows from the bonds which unite us and also from the fact that ours is a common cause. If we had some practical means of demonstrating with what earnestness we long to ease your plight, you would have a more open proof of our concern. But, apart from assuring you of our prayers, there is little that we are able to do; though whatever action we feel may be helpful has not been overlooked. Be that as it may, however, never doubt that our God will watch over you and will hear your tears and groanings. If, indeed, we do not trust in His providence, even the slightest disturbance will be an abyss to engulf us, any puff of wind will unsettle us, and we shall be thoroughly perplexed and confused; in short, our whole life will be a puzzle — especially when Satan and his servants are given their head to torment and trouble the poor Church of God. We must always hold fast to this truth, that if God cares for all His creatures He will not abandon those who call on Him. If not a single sparrow falls to the ground without His will, His fatherly care for those who are His own children will never fail. It is true that when we see a calamity like this which could bring in its train a state of extreme desolation, we are strongly tempted to suppose that God is tardy to intervene and put things right. But it is not said without reason that God wishes to test our faith like gold in a furnace [I Pet. 1:6f.]. Although, then, He does not stretch out His hand to help us as soon as we would like, let us never waver in the assurance that every hair on our head is counted by Him. And if at times He permits the blood of those who are His to be spilt, even so He does not cease to hold their tears precious, keeping them as it were in His bottle, as David says in Psalm 56 [Ps. 56:8]. It is certain that He has only permitted what has happened as a preparation for some great thing which surpasses all our thoughts. Until now those who have been called to martyrdom have been treated as contemptible by the world, both as regards the quality of their persons and also as regards

---

[33] This letter is published in *Calvini Opera*, XVI, coll. 629ff.

their number which has never before been so great at one time. May we not believe that God has already prepared an outcome of this which will cause us doubly to rejoice and glorify Him? Be that as it may, if we are truly wise we shall subject ourselves to Him and, even if all should be thrown into confusion, calmly await the deliverance which He has promised us.

Meanwhile, most dear brethren, we urge you to practise the lesson which we have learnt from the great Master, namely, to possess our souls in patience [Lk. 21:19]. We know, indeed, how difficult it is for the flesh, but remember that when we are assailed by our enemies then it is also the hour to fight against ourselves and our passions. And do not think that it is too much to expect that you should suffer calmly like placid sheep in the face of the fury of wolves, for you have the promise that the good and faithful Shepherd who has taken us under His care will never fail us, however furious and monstrous the cruelty of our enemies may be: God is fully powerful to drive them back by whatever means He sees fit or without any means at all. Be particularly careful not to attempt anything which His Word does not permit. As we hold ourselves prompt to obey Him, so we have the assurance that He will repel these attacks or else give us strength and grace to endure them; but if ever we go beyond what He sanctions we must fear that we shall receive at last the wages of our temerity. We speak like this not because we wish to be bold to your cost, but because we are well aware that in such terrifying circumstances one can be tempted to participate in many ventures which it is difficult to keep in check. We are giving you the same advice as that by which we ourselves would wish to be governed and restrained in similar circumstances. The fact is that it would be much better for us all to be overwhelmed, rather than that the Gospel of God should be exposed to the accusation that it caused people to take up arms for the purpose of sedition and rioting. For God will always cause the ashes of His servants to bear fruit, but excessive and violent behaviour can lead only to sterility. Therefore, most dear sirs and brethren, show that you have profited in the school of Him who demands that we should sacrifice ourselves for Him, sparing no effort to maintain His cause by suffering until such time as He smashes the weapons of His enemies or wins them to His side.

Now, since you did not receive our letter authorizing our colleague to come to you — not to remain permanently with you, as this was not possible, but only to comfort and assist you for a while — we ask you again, as we did in the letter, to forgive us that we cannot meet your request more fully. He offered of his own accord to undertake this journey for the purpose of ministering to you, though on the understanding that someone else would be provided for you; and there was not one of us who did not desire to take his turn in filling his place here, stealing time as it were, not so much out of regard for the charge which we have here as through fear that you should be left unprovided for. Now that these troubles have supervened, we pray you to consider carefully whether his presence with you may not be more harmful than profitable. St. Augustine wisely held that if a flock is attacked without the pastor being specially sought for, he, as the one who should strengthen the rest, has no justification for leaving them; but that if an attempt is made to persecute the church in the person of the pastor, it is better for him to withdraw himself so that by his absence the rage of the enemies may be appeased.[34] Seeing, then, that our colleague came to you to supply a present need, while expecting that provision would be made for a more definite and permanent appointment, consider whether it would not be more expedient that such arrangement, which could inflame the fury of your enemies, should be discontinued; for we hear reports that the intention is to aggravate the troubles and afflictions with which they assail you. It is sufficient for us to have mentioned these things, for we have every confidence both in your prudence and also in your ability to anticipate future problems in the light of the necessity with which you are confronted. In any case, his departure should not result in your being scattered, for today more than ever it is necessary for you to rally under the banner, conscious of your frailty, and knowing that Satan's cunning is directed to no other end than that you should be dispersed until you disappear altogether. Stand together united, therefore, and close your ranks, calling with one mind and voice on Him who has promised to be present wherever two or three are gathered together in His name [Mt. 18:20].

Accordingly, dear sirs and brethren, after commending ourselves to your prayers, we shall for our part beseech our heavenly Father to keep you under the protection of His Son, strengthening you in invincible constancy, guiding you into all wisdom, uprightness, simplicity, humility, and constancy by His Holy Spirit, and restraining your enemies until it pleases Him to overthrow them.

16 September 1557, from our assembly

---

[34] Augustine, Letter CCXXVIII, to Honoratus.

December 1557

[December 1557]

DEATH OF MATHIEU MALESIER

On 11 December our brother Maître Mathieu Malesier, minister of the Word of God in the parish of Bossey, passed away at about 6 o'clock in the evening, to the great sorrow of all the brethren, for he had always fulfilled his office with faithfulness.

D'ESPOIR APPOINTED TO BOSSEY

On Friday 15 December, the day of our censures, Jean de Pleurs[35] was unanimously elected by the brethren as minister for Bossey in the place of our late brother, Maître Mathieu.

[35] Jean de Pleurs was also known as d'Espoir. See note 5, p. 322 above.

1558

January 1558

JEAN MACAR APPOINTED TO PARIS

On 1 January our brother Maître Jean Macar left this city to minister the Word of God in the church of Paris, for which we had elected him in the place of our brother Maître des Gallars.

On the same day, and in his company, Monsieur Seguran[1] left for Dieppe, elected by us to serve as minister there, and Maître [blank][2] left for Rouen to fulfil the same vocation, to which he also had been assigned by the brethren.

May 1558

CLAUDE BOISSIERE APPOINTED TO SAINTES

On 28 May Maître Claude Boissière, who had been at Aix-en-Provence, left there to preach the Word of God in Saintes, to which he had been appointed by the brethren.

JACQUES ROUVIERES AND LANCELOT D'ALBEAU APPOINTED TO TOURS

On the last day of May Maîtres Jacques Rouvières[3] and Lancelot

---

[1] André Seguran, of Aix-en-Provence: his ministry at Dieppe was terminated by his premature death.

[2] The name is omitted. The church in Rouen was organized in 1557 by a pastor named La Jonchée, who was soon assisted by Jacques Trouillet, also known as des Roches.

[3] Jacques Rouvières seems later to have been transferred to Bourges.

d'Albeau[4] were appointed to preach the Word of God in Tours, where they have now gone.

MINISTERS' SALARIES INCREASED

In the same month our Seigneurs and superiors gave attention to the ministers' salaries, which were scarcely excessive, and increased each by twelve measures of wheat. God be praised and thanked for this! May He multiply His blessings together with His fear on these benefactors! Amen.

APPOINTMENTS TO ISSOUDUN, BOURGES, BLOIS, AND ROMORANTIN

At the same time Guy Moranges, also known as La Garde, left this city to minister the Word of God in Issoudun in the province of Berri, to which he had been appointed by the brethren.

With him went three brethren who had been dismissed from their ministry and banished from the territory of Berne for having upheld the election of God, namely, Maître David Veran, to be pastor in Bourges, Maître Antoine Channourry, for Blois, and Maître Barthélemy Corradon, for Romorantin, to which they had been appointed by the brethren.

JUNE 1558

MARTIN TACHARD APPOINTED TO PRAGELAT

On 3 June Maître Martin Tachard, who had been appointed by the brethren, left this city to preach the Word of God in Pragelat, a post for which he had been most affectionately requested both by letter and by a man who had been sent for this purpose.

JULY 1558

CHARLES DU PLESSIS APPOINTED TO TOURS

On 6 July Maître Charles du Plessis[5] was appointed a pastor of the church of Tours, where he was to work with M*. Jacques

---

[4] Lancelot d'Albeau, of Anjou, was soon to be martyred.

[5] Charles du Plessis, or d'Albiac, was probably the brother of the poet Accasse d'Albiac. He had studied at Lausanne and was martyred in 1562 at Angers.

Rouvière in the place of Maître Lancelot d'Albeau, who was going to Montoire.

AMBROISE FAGET APPOINTED TO ORLEANS

On 13 July Ambroise Faget[6] was appointed to Orléans.

AUGUST 1558

REVOLT OF NICOLAS PETIT

On the last day of August when, in the course of our general censures, our brother Maître Nicolas Petit was admonished and reproved for having made public (while preaching in his parish of Draillans) the unfortunate prohibition issued by the Seigneurs of Berne against the preaching of God's holy election, he, instead of acknowledging the seriousness of his fault, replied most insultingly to certain members of the magistracy whom he contradicted, and spoke to us with astonishing arrogance, showing no willingness to be corrected and behaving in a manner quite unworthy of a minister of the Word of God. The brethren decided that the matter should be minuted here for future action in due course.

SEPTEMBER 1558

JEAN MACAR BROUGHT BACK FROM PARIS

On 15 September, after offering prayer to God, it was resolved by all the assembled brethren that our brother Monsieur Macar should be instructed to return and prosecute his ministry here, and in his place Maître de Morel was appointed to minister the Word of God in Paris. De Morel was one of the ministers of the Gospel in this city.

---

[6] Jean Gardepuys, otherwise known as Ambroise Faget, of Faget (Haute-Garonne), is better known for his later ministry at La Rochelle.

October 1558

APPOINTMENTS TO LYON AND POITIERS

On 3 October Maître Michel Mulot[7] left here to preach the Word of God in Lyon, to which he had been appointed by the brethren.

At the same time [blank], known as du Brueil, was appointed to Poitiers in the place of Monsieur du Gué.[8]

November 1558

LUCAS HOBE APPOINTED TO SAINT-JEAN-D'ANGELY

On 16 November, after he had expounded a passage of Scripture in the presence of the brethren, Maître Lucas Hobé,[9] a native of the district of Brexe, was appointed by them to preach the Gospel in Saint-Jean-d'Angély, and he went there immediately after his election.

MINISTERS' SALARIES CONVERTED TO MONEY

At this time our Seigneurs and superiors, impelled by some consideration, gave order that each of their ministers of the Word of God should receive the inclusive sum of three hundred small florins and should no longer be given wheat.

JACQUES CHRISTIANI APPOINTED TO ISSOUDUN

Towards the end of November Maître Jacques Christiani[10] was appointed to minister the Word of God in Issoudun in the place of Maître Guy Moranges.

---

[7] Michel Mulot was now elderly, having previously served at Montbéliard, at Neuchâtel, and in Chablais.

[8] The identities of du Breuil and du Gué (du Gay) are uncertain.

[9] Lucas Hobé, called Seelac, was of humble origin. He proceeded in fact to Sainte-Foy-la-Grande (Gironde).

[10] Jacques Christiani has not been identified. The church in Issoudun was very active.

December 1558

CHAMBELI APPOINTED TO LE-HAVRE-DE-GRACE

At the beginning of December Matître François Chambeli[11] (who previously had returned from Pragelat where he had served God and His Church for a period of twenty months) left here to preach the Word of God in Le-Havre-de-Grace, having been appointed by the brethren; and Christiani left with him.

APPOINTMENTS TO GUYENNE

On 6 December Maître François de Dureil, Lucas Hobé, and Gilles [blank] left this city to preach the Gospel in the province of Guyenne, each proceeding to the place to which he had been appointed by the brethren, namely, de Dureil to Bergerac, Hobé to Sainte-Foi, and Gilles to Bordeaux.

OTHER APPOINTMENTS

At the same time our brother Maître François de Morel left here to preach in Paris in place of our brother Monsieur Macar, who had returned to Geneva; and Maîtres [blank] Dupuis and [blank] Paumier[12] left with him for Dieppe and Caen respectively, to which they had been appointed by the brethren.

At about this time Maître Christophe, son of the physician in Vevey,[13] also left to minister the Word of God in the city of Turin, to which he had been appointed by the brethren.

THEODORE DE BEZE CALLED TO THE MINISTRY

On 15 December, the day of our censures, M. Théodore de Bèze (who previously had been appointed public professor of Greek) was unanimously appointed by the brethren to serve in the ministry of the Gospel, as a preacher as well as continuing his lectures in Holy Scripture. It was decided, further, that, pending the appointment of another professor in his place, he should continue his teaching. De Bèze agreed to this with true humility and notable modesty.

---

[11] Evidently an error for Jean Chambeli.
[12] Probably Jean Dupuis who had been schoolmaster in Jussy. Paumier later ministered at Troyes.
[13] It has been suggested that this was the son of Bernardus du Moulin, a physician of Vevey.

1559

January 1559

PIERRE VIRET INVITED TO GENEVA

On 13 January the brethren unitedly resolved that our Seigneurs be requested to write to Mᵉ. Pierre Viret in Lausanne, saying that, in token of their gratitude to him whom God had used from the very beginning for the planting of the Gospel here, they would esteem it a great blessing if, driven out by others, he should find shelter in their city. This they did in an admirable letter sent to our brother in accordance with our request.

On 23 January, after prayer had been offered, the assembled brethren unanimously appointed our brother Maître Pierre Viret to be a minister of the Word of God with them in this church.[1]

February 1559

DEATH OF JACQUES BERNARD

On 4 February our brother Maître Jacques Bernard, minister of the Word of God in Peissy, passed away at about four o'clock in the morning.[2]

---

[1] Viret did not actually arrive in Geneva before March. He had lived and preached in Geneva in 1535 and played an active role in the spread of the Reformation among the people before being put out of action by a violent and mysterious poisoning.

[2] At the time of his death Jacques Bernard was pastor of the rural parish of Peissy-Satigny. Peissy is a village near Satigny.

DEATH OF CLAUDE DU PONT

In the same month also our brother Maître Claude du Pont passed away at Saint Gervais, constant to the end in the same faith which he had preached, mourned by all the brethren because he was a man of learning and godliness.

March 1559

THEODORE DE BEZE CONFIRMED AS MINISTER

On 16 March, our day of censures, M. Théodore de Bèze was elected a minister of the holy Gospel, to officiate in the place of our late brother M. Claude du Pont.

APPOINTMENT OF JEAN MERLIN[3]

On the same day also M. Jean Merlin[4] was appointed to minister at Peissy in the place of our late brother Maître Jacques Bernard.

APPOINTMENTS TO THE COLLEGE

At the same time the brethren appointed Maître Antoine Chevalier[5] to be professor of Hebrew.

Maître François Bérauld[6] was appointed public professor of Greek.

M. Jean Tagaut[7] was appointed professor of Mathematics.

M. Jean Randon[8] was appointed professor of the first class of the college.

---

[3] Most of the men mentioned in the following paragraphs belonged to a group of pastors and professors from Lausanne and the territory of Vaud who were exiled by the Bernese government in consequence of a religious quarrel.

[4] Jean-Raymond Merlin had taught Hebrew in Lausanne and later became Coligny's chaplain. His son Pierre was also an eminent pastor and also served as Coligny's chaplain for a time.

[5] Antoine Chevalier was born at Montchamps near Caen in Normandy. He served as professor of Hebrew at Cambridge, Strasbourg, and Geneva (1559-1567).

[6] François Bérauld had taught in the colleges of Montbéliard and Lausanne, and was professor of Greek in Geneva from 1558 to 1562. He then returned to France, where he occupied similar teaching posts.

[7] Jean Tagaut was a French mathematician and poet.

[8] Jean Randon had held similar posts in the college of Lausanne.

APPOINTMENTS TO PARISHES

At about this time M. François de Saint Paul[9] was appointed to go and preach the Gospel in Poitiers, in the place of Monsieur du Brueil.

Towards the end of May Maître Jacques Chappelli was appointed to preach the Word of God at [blank];[10]

Jean Cousin[11] was appointed to Caen;
Jean Voisinet to [blank];[12]
Etienne Graignon to Surlac;[13]
Bernard Seguin to Quiers;[14]
Jacques Chappelli to Bergerac;
Hélie Valtouchet to [blank];[15]
Michel Mulot to Pons;[16]
Monsieur La Garde to Sancerre.[17]

JUNE 1559

[4 June 1559]

LETTER FROM CALVIN TO AN UNKNOWN WOMAN[18]

Copy of the answer given by Calvin to a question from a certain woman who was being ill-treated by her husband because of the Gospel.

We are not so inhuman that we have no compassion for all those who are suffering for the honour of God and for the truth of the Gospel of our Lord Jesus Christ, desiring to comfort them as much as we possibly can and according to our resources. We have a special sympathy for poor women who are evilly and roughly treated by their husbands, because of the roughness and cruelty

---

[9] François de Saint Paul had previously attacked Calvin's doctrine of predestination.
[10] Jacques Chappelli was evidently appointed to Bergerac (see below).
[11] Jean Cousin is better known for his later ministry in England.
[12] Jean Voisinet's appointment was to Poitiers, but he was soon transferred to Agen in the south-west.
[13] "Surlac" is probably the same as Sarlat (Dordogne).
[14] The identity of this person is uncertain. He should not be confused with Bernard Seguin who was martyred in 1553. Quiers is undoubtedly the same as Chieri in Piedmont.
[15] Hélie Valtouchet was sent to the church of Aigues-Mortes where he later suffered martyrdom.
[16] Mulot was transferred from Lyon to Pons (Charente-Inferieure).
[17] La Garde here is undoubtedly Guy Moranges (cf. note 11, p. 324 above).
[18] This letter is published in *Calvini Opera*, XVII, col. 539.

of the tyranny and captivity which is their lot. We do not find ourselves permitted by the Word of God, however, to advise a woman to leave her husband, except by force of necessity; and we do not understand this force to be operative when a husband behaves roughly and uses threats to his wife, nor even when he beats her, but when there is imminent peril to her life, whether from persecution by the husband or by his conspiring with the enemies of the truth, or from some other source. In the case now brought to our notice we see as yet no just reason for the wife to depart unless the danger to her should become more apparent. And so we exhort her in the name of God to bear with patience the cross which God has seen fit to place upon her; and meanwhile not to deviate from the duty which she has before God to please her husband, but to be faithful whatever happens, and to show that it is not her intention to change her position. If she feels herself weak, let her pray God to give her a strong spirit of constancy; and also let her take pains to soften her husband's heart. If she is under compulsion, then the Word of God permits her to depart from him; but in doing this she is not deserting her husband, since she will always be ready to dwell with him, provided there is no danger of death.

4 June 1559

[1559]

SUMMARY OF THE CONFESSION OF FAITH OF THE STUDENTS OF THE ACADEMY OF GENEVA[19]

The confession of faith which all scholars who wish to dwell in this church must make before the rector.

Although the confession of faith contained in the Apostles' Creed should suffice for the simplicity of Christian people, yet, because some who through their disaffection have departed from the pure and true faith have disturbed the unity and order of this church and disseminated false and erroneous opinions, in order to avoid all Satan's devices and to arm ourselves against those who would wish to lead us astray, and to show that we believe with

---

[19] The confession of faith of the students, Latin and French versions of which are in existence, is a much more developed text than that given here. It is published in *Calvini Opera*, IX, coll. 721ff. It may be that this shorter form was a first draft, which subsequently was judged to be in need of expansion.

one heart and speak with one voice, and also that we reject and detest all heresies contrary to the pure faith which until now we have held and wish to follow to the end, we have agreed on the following declaration of faith concerning the unique and simple essence of God and the distinction of the three persons.

We declare, therefore, that God the Father has begotten His Word and Wisdom, which is His only Son, from all eternity, and that the Holy Spirit has proceeded from them both, in such a way that there is but one single and simple substance of Father, Son, and Holy Spirit, and that it is with respect to the persons that the Father is distinguished from the Son.

Accordingly, we detest the error of those who say that it is simply with regard to His essence and in that He is the only and true God that the Father has begotten His Son, as though the divine majesty, sovereignty, essence, and in sum true divinity belonged only to the Father, while Jesus Christ and the Holy Spirit were Gods proceeding from Him, which results in the unity of the essence being disrupted or dispelled.

In confessing that there is but one God, however, we acknowledge that all that is attributed to His divinity and glory and essence belongs both to the Son and to the Holy Spirit when one speaks simply of God, without making a comparison between the persons; but that when comparing the persons with each other we must observe what is proper to each, making a distinction such that the Son is not the Father nor the Holy Spirit the Son.

Regarding the person of our Lord Jesus Christ, apart from the fact that from all eternity He has been begotten of God His Father and is a person distinct from Him, we hold that in the human nature which He assumed for our salvation He is also the true and natural Son of God, since He united the two natures in such a way that He is but a single Mediator, God manifested in flesh, retaining always the properties of each nature.

In making this declaration we affirm and, according to the faith which we owe to God, we promise and we bind ourselves to follow this doctrine and persevere in it without knowingly contravening it either directly or indirectly for the purpose of supporting some dissension or controversy which would destroy our harmony. And in general to close the door on all discord for the future, we declare that we wish to live and die in obedience to the doctrine of this church, and to the utmost of our power to oppose all divisions which could lead to the opposite effect.

To this we assent and agree, on pain of being held perjured and disloyal.

July 1559

APPOINTMENTS TO FRANCE

On Friday 13 July the following brethren were appointed to go and preach the holy Gospel in France:
Augustin Marlorat[20] to Paris;
Martin to Béarn;
Gilles to Nérac;
Jean Graignon to work with Gilles;
Folion[21] to Toulouse;
Prudhomme[22] to Chateauroux;
The tutor in the family of Marin Maillet[23] to Villefranche.

August 1559

FURTHER APPOINTMENTS

Monsieur Ruffy[24] was appointed to the territory of Provence, and Jean Graignon to work with him;
Maître Olivier[25] to Tarascon;
Maître Brulé[26] to Vallence;
Monsieur du Gué[27] to Nantes;
Maître Aignan, son-in-law of Perrière, to Gien.
Maître Jacques Vallier[28] was appointed and sent on the [blank] to preach the Gospel in Rouen with him who had been sent previously.

[20] Augustin Marlorat is known for his publications and his martyrdom.
[21] Nicolas Folion, called La Vallée, was originally from Picardie. He served in several churches in southern and central France. His ministry in Toulouse ended in 1561.
[22] Jacques Prudhomme was another of the pastors exiled by the Bernese.
[23] Marin Maillet was an eminent Genevan. The family tutor may well have been Jean de la Rive who served for some time as pastor of the church of Villefranche-de-Rouergue.
[24] Jacques Ruffy, or Roux, is well known particularly for the spectacular role he played in the capture of Lyon by the Protestants.
[25] Possibly Mathieu Olivier, as first pastor of Massongy, in Chablais.
[26] Probably Jean Brulé.
[27] This could well be François Boisnormand, called "Dugué" or "Le Gay" (cf. note 21, p. 329 above).
[28] Jacques Vallier had had a brilliant career in Lausanne.

At this time Maître Jean Cousin was sent to preach the Word of God in Caen.

Maître Elie was sent to Saint Gilles;
Maître Geoffroy[29] to Castres;
Maître Marlorat to Paris;
Maître Jean Graignon to Sommières;
De Rodés to [blank];
Maître Henry[30] to [blank];
Pasquier[31] to Montpellier.

The aged de Bosco[32] was sent to preach the Gospel in Dieppe.
Faget was appointed to Orléans.

[29] Geoffroy Brun.
[30] Probably Jean Henry, pastor of the church at Pau, who was in touch with the court of Navarre.
[31] Probably Pierre Pasquier.
[32] Jean, or perhaps Pierre, de Bosco, or de Bosque. Jean had been a pastor in the Bernese territory.

1560

VARIOUS APPOINTMENTS

At the same time Monsieur La Garde[1] was appointed to preach the Gospel at Uzès.

Bonquin[2] and Germain Chauveton[3] were appointed to the Ile d'Oléron and the Ile de Ré respectively.

Faget, who had returned from Orléans, was sent to La Rochelle to work with Maître Pierre Richer, who had been there for the past two years.

DEATH OF JEAN RANDON

In the month of May Maître Jean Randon, professor of the first class of the college, passed away.

THEODORE DE BEZE IN GASCOGNE

On 20 July our brother Monsieur de Bèze was sent to Gascogne to instruct the king and queen of Navarre in the Word of God, and he remained there about [blank].[4]

DEATH OF LANCELOT D'ALBEAU, MARTYR

Maître Lancelot d'Albeau was appointed to Valence, where, after faithfully preaching the Gospel, he was seized by its enemies and sealed the doctrine of the truth with his blood and his death.

---

[1] Probably Guy Moranges (cf. note 11, p. 324).

[2] Jean Bonquin, or Bouquin, was allocated to the church of Chateau-d'Oléron (Charente-Inférieure).

[3] Germain Chauveton devoted the whole of his ministry to the parish of Saint-Martin-en-Ré (Charente-Inférieure).

[4] This sentence was left uncompleted. Beza spent about three months at the court of Navarre in Nérac.

DEATH OF JEAN TAGAUT

On the last day of July our brother Monsieur Tagaut passed away to the great sorrow of the brethren and the great loss of the entire college.

CLAUDE DUMOULIN APPOINTED TO FONTENAY

On 20 June Maître Claude Dumoulin was appointed to preach the Word of God in Fontenay.[5]

DEATH OF JEAN BALDIN AND APPOINTMENT OF GASPARD CARMEL IN HIS PLACE

During the same month our brother Maître Jean Baldin, minister of Moëns and Genthod, died.[6] In his place our brother Maître Gaspard[7] was appointed, and instituted in the month of August.

VARIOUS APPOINTMENTS

At this time our brother Monsieur de Saules[8] was sent to preach the Gospel in England.

Monsieur de Collènes was appointed to Vitry;

Maître Gilles, recently returned from Bordeaux, to Montaigu;

Bachelar to Nantes, whence he had returned.

On 15 August Monsieur Ruffy was appointed to preach the Word of God in Poitiers.

Vanchet was appointed to Châtellerault;

Maître Philibert Grené[9] to Bordeaux;

The schoolmaster of Jussy[10] to Marsillargues;

Guillaume Gointrat to Châtellerault.

---

[5] Claude Dumoulin, or du Molin, was a former professor in Lausanne. The reference is to the church of Fontenay-le-Comte (Vendée).

[6] Jean Baldin, or Baldouin, had been pastor of the churches in the villages of Moens and Genthod, near Geneva, since 1548.

[7] Gaspard Carmel (cf. note 4, p. 322 above).

[8] Nicolas des Gallars, sire de Saules. His ministry at the foreigners' church in London was a brief one.

[9] Philibert Grené, called La Fromentée, was later martyred in Bordeaux.

[10] The reference might be to someone named "Lemaître", but it is more probable that the schoolmaster ("le maître") of Jussy is intended. In the latter case it is probably Bernard de Prissac, who was schoolmaster at Jussy until the end of 1559, and subsequently, from 1561 onwards, pastor of several churches in Quercy.

DEATH OF GASPARD CARMEL, FAREL'S NEPHEW, AND APPOINTMENT OF CHARLES MAUBUE TO MOENS

Our brother Maître Gaspard, minister at Moëns, passed away on [blank], and Maître Charles Maubué was appointed in his place.

CLAUDE BADUEL APPOINTED PROFESSOR

At this time our brother Maître Claude Baduel, minister at Vandoeuvres, was appointed public professor in this city in place of the late Monsieur Tagaut.

DEATH OF JEAN MACAR

On 3 September our dear brother Maître Jean Macar, minister of the Word of God in this city, was carried off by a malignant fever in the flower of his age, to the great sorrow and loss of this church, persevering to his last breath in the confession of the faith which he had consistently preached. For a period of some two years he had ministered the Word of God in the church of Paris with wonderful fruitfulness, and had even visited those imprisoned in the Conciergerie for the truth of the Gospel and had warned the authorities that they would have to face God as their judge if they condemned those who were maintaining His cause; and he persevered in the discharge of this responsible duty for a period of ten months, until he was recalled because of the need in this city.

MONSIEUR D'ANDUZE RETURNS TO GENEVA AND JEAN PINAULT GOES TO JUSSY

On the [blank] our brother Maître Pierre d' Airebaudouze,[11] minister at Jussy, was called to fulfil the same office in this city, and Maître Jean Pinault,[12] who had been teaching the children at the Hospital, was appointed and sent to minister the Word of God in Jussy.

JEAN BOULIER APPOINTED TO VANDOEUVRES

In the month of December Maître Jean Boulier, also called de la Roche, who had for some time been ministering in Lyon, was appointed by the brethren to preach the Gospel in Vandoeuvres.

---

[11] Pierre d'Airebaudouze, sire d'Anduze (cf. note 15, p. 310 above).

[12] Jean Pinault went on to become one of the most eminent of the pastors of Geneva.

1561

VARIOUS APPOINTMENTS

M. d'Anduze was lent to the church of Lyon for some time following a request for the help of one of the ministers of Geneva in their need, since, by reason of the multitude of persons daily joining that church, they had an inadequate number of ministers.

M. L'Anglois, who had been ministering in Lausanne, passed through on his way to join the ministry of the church of Lyon.

M. Jean Pereri, minister of the parishes of Neydan and Fégières, was asked for by the people of Mérindol, whose minister he had been until the great persecution laid waste their church.[1] It was resolved to grant their request, provided, as usual, Messieurs were in agreement. This they were, and M. Jean Du Perril[2] was appointed in place of Pereri by the ministers, with the approval of Messieurs.

M. Bastien L'Ouvrier was sent to be minister of Saint-Antoine in Agen, after being presented for this purpose to the Company of the ministers by M. Fraisse, minister of Eynesse.

Jean Le Clerc was appointed to the church of Miramont in Agen.

In the same year M. de Bèze was recalled from France to attend the colloquy which was to be held at Poissy. M. Martyr was also requested to attend, and M. de Bèze went to Zürich in order to obtain him from the church of Zürich.

M. Pierre Sachet was sent as minister to the church of Marsillargues which had asked, like all the other churches which have been mentioned, that they might be provided with a suitable man to fulfil the office of pastor.

---

[1] The church of Mérindol (Vaucluse) had been dispersed by the massacres of 1545.

[2] Jean du Perril remained a pastor in the church of Geneva until his death in 1598.

M. François Tenant[3] was appointed to Grateloup in Agen. He had been living in the presbytery of Neuchâtel.

M. de Nanas was appointed to Ligneul.

Monsieur d'Aignon[4] was appointed to Chaumont-en-Bassigny.

M. Jean-Raymond Merlin[5] was sent to the house of the Admiral, in Cour, who had written for a man who could teach there.

At the request of the people of Metz, the French church of Strasbourg had written to inquire whether one of the ministers of Geneva could go to the city of Metz to serve as minister there at least for some time. This request was carefully discussed, but, all things considered, it was not possible to grant it, for a variety of reasons, and not least because already several of the Company were absent.

In this same year a young man named [blank] Bordat, who had a pleasant personality and was very knowledgeable, was sent to the town of Bergerac, which had written asking for a minister.

---

[3] François Tenant had been a schoolmaster in Neuchâtel.

[4] François Bourgoin, sire d'Aignon.

[5] Jean-Raymond Merlin had taught Hebrew in Lausanne, and he served in several Genevan parishes. A large part of his time with Coligny was spent in the Admiral's principal residence, at Châtillon-sur-Loing (Loiret). (Cf. note 4, p. 343 above).

1562

FURTHER APPOINTMENTS

M. Ribittus,[1] who taught the first class in the college, and M. Bérauld, lecturer in Greek, were asked for by the church of Orleans, and the request was granted, because they complained that they had insufficient means to keep themselves and their families.

M. Guy de Moranges, also called de la Garde, had been sent to the church of Orillac, and then, when that church was scattered, had left to minister in Yssoire. In course of time the people of Orillac wished him to return to them, with the result that a quarrel arose between the two churches. In order to pacify the situation a letter was written to both churches in common.

Two brethren who were formerly canons of Autun, namely, M. de la Coudrée and M. Veriet, stated and gave proof that since the time when they had held these benefices they had devoted themselves by the grace of God to preaching the truth of the Gospel in several cures which they had held, and subsequently had been approved as pastors by the Synod of Châlons. Nevertheless, there were certain persons who did not cease to call in question their vocation, suggesting that they were intruders. For this reason they requested attestation of their status, and this was granted them.

M. André Le Cour, minister at Chancy and Cartigny, was asked by the people of Yssoire to go and minister the Gospel among them, and consent was given by Messieurs, following notification of the approval of the ministers conveyed by the mouth of M. Calvin.

M. Pierre Duc, who was minister at Russin and Dardagnon, was asked by the members of the church of Dombes to exercise the

---

[1] Jean Ribittus, or Ribit, was well known for his career as a teacher in Lausanne (see note 8, p. 212 above).

ministry of the Gospel in their territory; and this was granted in the same manner as with Le Cour.

On Friday 20 March Monsieur de la Roche, also called Boulier, was asked for by the members of the church of Lyon on the ground that he was their minister; for when he was elected a minister in the church of Geneva it was understood that he would be free to go to the church of Lyon, and when announcements were made to this effect no contrary voice had been raised; but he had been quietly presented and received at Vandoeuvres and Cologny as pastor of those churches. Accordingly it was agreed that he should return to Lyon.

CHURCHMEN FROM LYON ADMONISHED

On Friday 4 September certain members of the church of Lyon were summoned concerning whom M. Viret had complained by letter,[2] because, although some belonged to the Consistory and the others to the Council of that church, to which in consequence they had obligations in times of war as well as in times of peace, none the less they had fled through fear of war; and they were admonished in the company of the ministers, who were assembled in M. Calvin's house, that they should not have behaved like this, for their conduct was disheartening to others and placed both church and city in danger.

DE BEZE AND FRANCE

On Friday 11 September M. de Bèze returned from France where he had been for the past year, as has already been mentioned.

Several days later M. d'Andelot, who was returning from Germany to France in order to raise some cavalry, asked M. de Bèze to return with him to France. He, for various reasons, refused. M. Calvin, however, gave other reasons why he should go, although it would involve danger and it was doubtful whether there would be much fruit of it. With this the rest of the brethren were in agreement, and all exhorted de Bèze to place himself in the hands of God. He declared that he would do so.[3]

---

[2] It would seem that the letter in question was one sent by Viret to Anduze, dated 2 September 1562, the text of which is given in *Calvini Opera*, XIX, coll. 514ff. According to this letter, the fugitives mentioned came originally from Toulouse. The capture of Macon by the papists had caused them to flee from Lyon.

[3] Beza had rendered the Huguenot army placed under the command of Condé important diplomatic and administrative services.

FURTHER APPOINTMENTS

At the beginning of this same year M. Antoine Monteuil was sent to minister in Melun.

La Combe[4] was appointed minister at Romans.

M. Fulgon, a native of Montélimar,[5] was asked for by persons sent for that purpose from that church.

Maître Jean Blanchard[6] was assigned to the people of Gap.

In September a letter arrived from a number of ministers of Provence who complained of certain misappropriations of money which M. Mathieu Issotier had made when exercising his ministry in that province;[7] and as Issotier had returned from there he was summoned before the Consistory.

Valeri Crespin[8] was sent to minister at Grignan.

Gaspard de Vèze[9] was sent to the church of Manosque, and when it became impossible to continue holding services there he went to minister to the people of Sisteron.

FRICTION AMONG THE PASTORS

On Friday 19 June M. Calvin informed the assembled brethren that steps should be taken to ordain ministers both for Russin and also for the united parishes of Chancy and Cartigny, since M. André Le Cour (as has already been mentioned) had gone to minister at Yssoire, in accordance with the request of the people there, and M. Pierre Duc had gone to Dombes, also following a request from the people of that church. It would also be necessary to appoint a minister in the city.

At the time we had available M. de la Faverge,[10] M. Jean Le

---

[4] Siméon La Combe was for a long time a pastor in the parishes of the south-east of France. Romans (Drôme) was almost certainly his first parish.

[5] Jacques Fulgon had been tutor of the nephew of the printer Antoine Vincent.

[6] Jean Blanchard officiated in several parishes of the province of Dauphiné, of which he was a native.

[7] The letter from the ministers of the churches of Provence to the ministers of Geneva, dated 20 September 1562, is given in *Calvini Opera*, XIX, coll. 534ff. Mathieu Issotier ("Yssautier", "Eyssautier", "Exsaultier") was the brother-in-law of Sebastian Castellio. He appeared again before the Consistory on 31 August 1563 for having distributed Castellio's *Conseils à la France désolée*, at which time he was described as ex-minister.

[8] Valeri Crespin had formerly been a printer.

[9] Gaspard de Vèze had previously been a pastor near Lausanne. Manosque and Sisteron are in the Basses-Alpes.

[10] Gaspard de la Faverge was a pastor in Geneva for several years.

Gaigneux,[11] and M. Claude Marquis,[12] and because some of the colleagues from the country (so it had been heard) wished to be appointed to the city, it was resolved that they should all withdraw from the Company, and then that those of them whom it was felt should not for the present be considered for election should come in again. When this had been done it was unanimously agreed by the brethren of both city and country that de la Faverge should be appointed minister of Russin and Marquis of Chancy. With regard to Le Gaigneux since he had already preached some sermons in the city in a manner acceptable to the hearers, as M. Calvin reported he had heard from various persons and also from Messieurs, which, besides, several others of the brethren knew to be so, and, further, because the Company had examined him and found him suitable, it was agreed to keep him in the city. Other reasons leading to this decision were that it seemed inexpedient to move any of the brethren from the country, seeing that those among them who were suitable for service in the city had not been long in their parishes, and it was considered that frequent changes were scarcely beneficial for the poor countryfolk who are more receptive and attentive to the teaching of those to whom they are accustomed. When the result of the debate was notified to the Company all were called in again, and some of the brethren from the country, who felt that they ought to be given an appointment in the city and that Le Gaigneux should be sent to the country to begin with, expressed their discontent with the outcome of the debate and even said, one after the other (I mean these particular ones, not all), that they felt they were being discouraged and that they would never have entered the ministry if they had thought that they would be left in the country, and that they had better ways of spending their time. This the rest found very strange; yet they allowed them to have their say because M. Calvin himself, in his astonishment, kept silent. It was only when he was in his room after the departure of the Company, that he said to someone, in his distress clasping his hands and raising them on high: "What is this which I see before I die?"

ADVICE OFFERED TO CERTAIN BRETHREN

On Thursday 3 December, having heard that the brethren of V. P., etc., wished to know their mind concerning certain matters

---

[11] Jean Le Gaigneux became one of Geneva's most eminent pastors, until he was deposed in 1571 for his criticism of the city's magistrates.
[12] Claude Marquis died soon afterwards.

in dispute among themselves, the brethren considered that the brethren of V. P. ought not to place difficulties in the way of observing the concordat and treaty that had been concluded in their name with the deputies from B. in the presence of the Seigneurs there named, although the brethren of V. P. had given no express charge or instruction to their delegates to agree to such articles; for, in fact, the articles in question were not at all unreasonable having regard to the calamitous situation common to all the brethren in the kingdom of France, especially in the larger cities; and, besides, if the brethren of P. and V. refused to observe these articles the name of God and the Gospel would be exposed to many reproaches and calumnies, and it would seem that they were turning their backs on peace.

Nor did they think that these brethren should refuse to obey the châtelain; for, whatever the state of affairs, he was in authority, so that the general rule of the Apostle held good: "There is no power but of God" [Rom. 13:1]. It was certainly open to them to complain of him and to demand justice should he resort to extortion.

It was felt, further, that these brethren should not refuse to pay the ordinary duties and taxes due to the king whatever might be done with them afterwards; and even if there should be doubt concerning to whom they should be given, none the less they should always have them ready so that they could protest that they had obeyed the king, and to this same end an adequate receipt should be obtained from those to whom they were handed.

As for help and encouragement from the P. d'Alem., it would seem much better to urge and entreat them to help, with money and with every other means, the army drawn up in France for the cause of the churches, which is today in great, indeed extreme, necessity, since even the richest cities are drained dry.

They also consider that to write to Sr. B. D. A. would be superfluous, since he is doing what he can, and neither he nor the others have been able to prevent several of the chief cities of the kingdom from experiencing the great calamities of war, even to the extent of being captured and pillaged.

Moreover, the brethren exhort these brethren to bear their condition patiently as being tolerable in comparison with the disturbance to be found in so many other places and to restore the peace in so far as this may be done without offending against God. They do not say this complacently and without the strongest compassion and fellow-feeling, knowing well that for their part, according to the appearance of things, they will not escape their turn to be roughly afflicted, unless the Lord by a singular mercy should spare and preserve them.[13]

[13] The significance of the initials and abbreviations in this passage has not been fully elucidated. It may be said with certainty that "P. d'Alem." stands for "princes d'Allemagne" and "Sr. B.D.A." for "sire Baron des Adrets"; and it may be accepted that the appeal mentioned came from the churches of the Marquisate of Saluces, such as those in Pragela and the valley of Angrogne. This region was under the control of the King of France, represented by his governor for Piedmont and Saluces, the future *maréchal de Bourdillon,* who held this post from 31 May 1559 to 12 December 1562. It had escaped the ravages of war in 1562, but its proximity to the French provinces of Provence and Dauphiné, where important battles were being waged, placed it under great disabilities and perils. The initials V.P. may stand for Valleé Piédmontaise.

1563

VARIOUS APPOINTMENTS

M. Colliod, also called de Varendal,[1] was sent as minister to Languedoc.

M. de Montliard, minister of Céligny, fell ill with pleurisy and died on Wednesday 6 January. The news of this was brought the next day.

In February M. Hellin, a native of Picardie, was elected in his place, presented to Messieurs, and approved as minister of Céligny.

On 11 March Monsieur d'Anduze left for Montpellier in response to a request from there. M. des Bordes,[2] who held the position of lecturer in philosophy, was ordained to preach in the absence of Monsieur d'Anduze, and M. Scrymgeour[3] was appointed to the philosophy lectureship.

On 5 May Monsieur Viret returned from Lyon and Monsieur de Bèze also returned from France.

The church of Lyon had written to Messieurs requesting that M. Viret, who had only been lent to them, might be permanently appointed to them; and since they had not advised the Company of ministers of this, it was resolved to ask them to observe the ecclesiastical order in this matter.[4]

In the month of August a letter arrived from Bordeaux requesting that M. Des Bordes should be sent to them, since he had come to study in Geneva with a view to serving in their church. It was resolved to write requesting that he might be left here for

---

[1] Pierre Colliod, sire de Varendal, was pastor of a great number of churches in Languedoc, both before and after this date. He officiated at Pézenas (Hérault) from 1562 to 1565.

[2] Jacques des Bordes studied in Geneva from 1562 to 1566 and then returned to Bordeaux, his native city.

[3] Henry Scrymgeour (or Scrimger), eminent diplomat and learned Scot, described himself as a mediocre professor and resigned in 1568.

[4] For further information see the extracts from the registers of Geneva quoted in *Calvini Opera*, XXI, coll. 800ff.

the time being and promising that an attempt would be made to send them some other suitable man. Meanwhile Monsieur d'Anduze returned from Montpellier; but it was not for long, for a short time afterwards the Company of ministers received a request for him from the people of Nîmes and Montpellier, so that their two churches might function fruitfully. The matter was considered and it was resolved to ask Messieurs to assign him to them, but for one year only. Accordingly he left on 13 September.[5]

[5] For further details of this appointment see the texts quoted in *Calvini Opera*, XXI, coll. 796ff.

1564

THE YEAR OF CALVIN'S DEATH

The circumstances of the illness and death of M. Calvin have been published.[1]

A short time previously, because M. Merlin had not returned, although he had been informed that the church needed his presence, it was resolved by M. Calvin and the Company that M. Charles Maubué, the minister of Moëns, should come, as it were on loan, to preach in the city for the time being at 4 o'clock in the morning during the week, and that M. Gabriel Ragaue, who had been designated for the church of Tours, should go and preach for Maubué on Sundays at Moëns and Genthod,[2] and that M. Colladon should preach at 6 o'clock in St. Pierre during the week until the return of Merlin. This decision was taken because Merlin had written to say that someone else should be appointed in his place, so that the brethren might not be under extra financial obligation during his absence. This suggestion did not meet with approval, however; indeed, it was felt that it would have been inhuman to treat Merlin in such a way. But it was resolved that Ragaue should be paid for his services and that the payment should be a reasonable amount deducted from Merlin's stipend.

ARRANGEMENTS FOLLOWING CALVIN'S DEATH

On Friday 2 June, the entire Company of pastors and professors being assembled, M. de Bèze spoke of the loss which the Company had suffered through the death of that faithful servant of God and

---

[1] This is undoubtedly a reference to the numerous editions of Beza's *Vie de Calvin*.

[2] The ministry of Gabriel Ragaue in Moëns and Genthod cannot have lasted more than a few months, since D. Perrot was pastor there towards the end of 1564. The first detailed reports of this parish which we possess are those of Perrot. Ragaue was also pastor of the village of Satigny for a time.

His Church, M. Calvin, and recounted the admonitions which he had uttered some days before his death, to the effect that they should persevere and with care and courage fulfil their charge, to love each other and to watch faithfully over the Church, even when hostile men arose, and to shun all ambition.[3] He then reminded the brethren that in the preceding year they had appointed him to supply, in the Consistory and in other such duties, the absence of M. Calvin, who because of his illnesses was unable to attend as frequently as had been his custom. This charge he treated as temporary (as indeed it was) and accordingly he held it to have ceased with the death of M. Calvin.

In view of the fact that the brethren had decided to elect one from their number who would serve them in this capacity, he added that in his judgment the appointment should be temporary and should be made by a yearly election, thereby avoiding the introduction of any position of pre-eminence among those who should be their successors in the service of this church; for there was a danger lest the order maintained by the brethren today might be misinterpreted by their successors, as had happened in the ancient Church. It should be done, also, to prevent other churches, both in France and elsewhere, from falling into the same danger when ambitious or incautious men, claiming to imitate the pattern of Geneva, might wish to set up a perpetual bishop in each assembly of pastors. This, he insisted, would be neither good nor beneficial, for it could well be that he who today held the position satisfactorily would not be so suitable a year later, and one observed by experience that there were times when God increases the graces He bestows on persons, and times when He diminishes them. As for the late M. Calvin, who had been like a father in the midst of the Company and also to each of its members separately, God had implanted so many graces in him and had invested him with such authority towards the people, thereby enabling each one of us the better to discharge the duties of his ministry, that, had we been bound to make a choice every year, we could not have considered any other member of the Company — which was not to belittle the abundance of the great gifts from God which are to be found there, accompanied always with a sincerity and a conscientiousness which all can perceive. God, indeed, so blessed his conduct that in all affairs, especially those that affect our ministry, the Company had never been destitute of good and wise counsel; and as there had never

[3] The text of an exhortation, which seems to be the same as the one which the Register mentions here, is given in *Calvini Opera*, IX, coll. 891ff. Calvin's death took place on 27 May 1564.

been any suspicion of his seeking advantage for himself or his family, so also he preserved a healthy equality. Now, however, we did not know whether God willed to concentrate so many of His graces in a single one of the brethren; and, besides, it was to be feared that, should an individual again in future possess many gifts from God, in the long run he would not employ them with such prudence, moderation, and humility as Calvin had continued to do, to the honour of God and the profit of the Company. Accordingly it would be necessary for them to make a change and to appoint someone else to lead the business and the debates, and other such duties, when the brethren were assembled, as had been said.

Thereupon, after each of the brethren, pastors and professors, had expressed his opinion, it was unanimously agreed that a member of the Company should be elected annually to lead the debates, preside over the business, gather the votes, and also to speak in the presence of Messieurs, in the name of the Company, and respecting the matters which concern their common ministry. None the less, if before the end of the year the one thus chosen should fail in any way in this special charge, he could be admonished for it at one of the four censures. There was, again, no intention that he should be superior to the others, but that he should acknowledge them as his brethren and companions in the work of the Lord and the ministry of the Church. In short, he should comport himself as the brethren knew and would remember, with God's help, the late M. Calvin had comported himself, who, so far from having exercised an excessive power or authority among them, on the contrary accommodating himself to all, in so far as this was possible, did no more than shoulder the heavy burden of this responsibility in order that the task of all might be eased. Indeed, he often protested that had his motives been those of self-interest he would have wished to be relieved of it, as in fact he requested when the severity and continuation of his illnesses seemed to him to render him less capable of fulfilling the duties involved.

The brethren desired all these things to be recorded in writing and, in accordance with the proposed order, they elected de Bèze for the present, having regard to the graces which God had bestowed on him and praying God that He would increase these more and more. M. de Bèze, however, sought to excuse himself on the grounds of the magnitude of the charge and his own inadequacy. But at length he accepted it, calling upon the brethren to help him with their advice and admonition as well as with their prayers. This they promised to do; and it was proposed that appointment to this charge should be made annually at the Easter censures.[4]

[7 July 1564]

ANTOINE CHEVALIER AND CAEN

On Friday 7 July a letter was read which had been addressed to Messieurs by the church of Caen requesting that M. Antoine Chevalier[5] might return to them from Geneva. He himself requested permission to do so, asserting that his parents had written to him to say that if he returned he would recover his goods, without the deduction of four hundred écus which he had received when he left home; and he also drew attention to his poverty and the number of his children. A hearing was also given to one sent by the seigneur of Langrune who had brought this letter and stated that he was charged with taking back Chevalier and his family. The Company resolved to admonish Langrune that we found it something novel that the church of Caen should wish to despoil us in order to adorn itself, and that this was an illegitimate demand. As for Chevalier, it was decided to admonish him that he should not give priority to other considerations over the vocation which he had here, and that, with respect to the recovery of his goods, the brethren would gladly request Messieurs to grant him leave for three or four months for this purpose and to help him with a letter or such other favour as they might be disposed to give; but that in their view it was not necessary for him to leave his vocation altogether.

He then replied that he could never be made to believe that he was bound to lose his goods, and that in M. Calvin's time he had been granted this permission purely and simply for him to avail himself of it if he so wished; but although the troubles which had supervened had prevented him from making use of it, yet the same liberty had always remained in force. To this the majority of the brethren responded that they remembered well that the late M. Calvin, following their decision and in their presence, had tried to dissuade Chevalier from leaving his vocation in this church, but, on failing to achieve this, had managed to persuade him to serve until Easter (which was about the month of May) on

---

[4] Cf. *Calvini Opera*, XXI, coll. 815ff., where the full text of the transactions of 2 June 1564 is given.

[5] Antoine Chevalier was professor of Hebrew in Geneva from 1559 to 1567 (cf. note 5, p. 343 above). It was not until 1567 that he was unconditionally released to return to Caen.

the understanding that if he then wished to go he should be free to do so. They reminded him further that at the censures the following Christmas Monsieur Calvin, by resolution of the brethren, had asked Chevalier, since Easter was approaching, what he intended to do, so that this church might not remain without an instructor, and that Chevalier had replied that he would never leave it unprovided for, and would be very sorry to do so. It was pointed out, moreover, that as he had not taken advantage of this liberty by that Easter, which was the term set, (although this had been granted as the result of his importunity and without approving his intention) there was no longer any question of the arrangement still being in force. This he contested with many words and much heat.

It was finally resolved by the brethren: either that he should take three months to go and attend to his affairs, or that he should continue in his post until Easter, and that in the meantime we would make other provision, without, however, in any way approving his departure. Exasperated still further by this, he protested that he would take his case before Messieurs, which he did, making some rather strange complaints.

The following Friday, namely, the 14th, Messieurs having referred the matter back to the Company of the ministers, Chevalier stated that in order to accept the conditions proposed to him the previous Friday he would require the additional choice either of remaining, now that Easter had come and gone, or of leaving, and that in the event of his leaving he would expect his salary for three months after Easter, and would continue to lecture until the day of his departure; and there were several other conditions that he added.

The brethren in turn replied that they could hardly invite anyone to accept the post of professor of Hebrew, which was at issue, when there was uncertainty as to what Chevalier intended to do. It was thus that the matter rested, without any further discussion until another occasion arose.

[*21 July 1564*]

REQUEST FROM JERSEY

On Friday 21 July a letter from the brethren of the valley of Langrune was read in which they asked advice respecting a request from the brethren of the Isle of Jersey that they should send back to them a minister at present living in Piedmont who formerly had been pastor in Jersey, but had departed after the eclipse of the

Church of England which followed the death of the good King Edward — promising, however, that he would return to them when their church had regained a measure of liberty.

Our judgment was that the promise made by this minister was binding and should be honoured, especially as the facts were not in dispute; and, moreover, that, because according to what the brethren of Jersey reported, a number of years had passed since their minister had left them after making this promise, they should call on the name of God and offer prayer with him. It was true that this minister would have done well to make known this condition to the brethren of Piedmont when he came to them, and to inform them of the promise which he had given to the brethren of Jersey, at the time when the former were offering him an appointment in their territory; yet because Queen Mary was then reigning and there was no reason to anticipate that the churches would be restored for a long time to come, it was fair to conclude that this minister had kept quiet about his promise without intending any deception. Accordingly the brethren held to their judgment as given above.[6]

RETURN OF JEAN-RAYMOND MERLIN

On 13 August M. Merlin returned from his visit to the province of Béarn, having been sent to the Queen of Navarre there.

APPOINTMENT OF JEAN TREMBLEY

On Friday 18 August M. Trembley[7] was given an appointment in the city.

[August 1564]

OUTBREAK OF PLAGUE IN GENEVA

In the month of August the plague broke out in the city and spread from place to place. It was commonly held that it had been carried in from Lyon by means of some infected clothing belonging to someone who had been visiting Lyon. Thus does God chasten us for all our sins!

As this scourge continued to spread (though, thanks be to God, it was not very severe), the ministers discussed what measures

---

[6] The reign of Mary lasted from 1553 to 1558. She was succeeded by Elizabeth I, under whom the Reformed faith was restored in England.

[7] Jean Trembley, originally from the province of Lyonnais, undertook

should be taken for going, in accordance with their duty, to minister to the afflicted up till the moment either of death or of recovery. Some were of the opinion that we should proceed prudently, taking suitable precautions, while committing ourselves to God, and advised that each one should occupy himself in his own district with such cases as he came across, as was the custom with other types of illness, and that Messieurs should be requested to sanction this, and, further, that the people should be reminded that God is powerful to protect us and them when we severally (each following his own vocation) are active in helping those afflicted with this malady. Others, however, did not find this scheme acceptable. Some, again, while expressing their approval, considered that the scheme would not be sanctioned, and were of the opinion, therefore, that we should proceed as had been done on previous occasions since the reformation of the church when the city had been severely visited with this scourge of the plague: namely, that one of the Company of the ministers of the city should be chosen by lot to assume this charge, living in separation. It is true that those who recollected these previous occasions (such as M. Raymond and M. Cop)[8] were aware that at times different arrangements had been made, and that when someone (not M. Calvin) wished to be exempted, that is, so that the lot might not fall on him, he, acting on his own authority, had caused one who did not belong to the Company of ministers to be sent; and this would have been tolerated and concealed, had he not then been rebuked and censured, and had not God withheld His blessing from such conduct, because of the scandal which resulted from it.

The majority were in favour of casting lots, and in view of the fact that he whom God appointed in this way would have the burden of extra expenses, both for keeping and feeding and paying a servant, and also for living in separation from his family and providing a supply of medicines and such other things as are ordinarily required, it was resolved that Messieurs should be asked to make provision for this.

Several of the Company were of the opinion that M. de Bèze should be excluded from the number of those eligible, so that the lot might not fall on him. Others, however, held the contrary view, maintaining that he had been received into the ministry under the same oath and conditions as the rest; and they pointed out that the ministers in the churches of Germany and Switzerland had, in accordance with their vocation, been exposed to the same danger, including the most outstanding among them, such as M.

---

[8] Raymond Chauvet and Michel Cop.

Bullinger in Zürich, M. Bucer in Strasbourg, and M. Ecolampadius in Basle; indeed, that it was well known that even M. Calvin, when he was pastor of the French church in Strasbourg and professor of theology in the employ of Messieurs of Strasbourg, had ministered to the members of his church who were struck down when the plague visited that city, comforting and admonishing them, as in the case of any other illness — to which his brother, who had frequently accompanied him, could bear witness.

It was finally resolved, by a majority vote, that M. de Bèze should withdraw from this election and not be subjected to this danger, but at the same time that he should make it all the more his concern to have his brethren in remembrance, especially the one or ones who would be subjected to this trial. A little while after M. Raymond happened to learn that during the preceding days the Council had resolved that M. de Bèze should be officially exempted from this election by lot; and he ventured to speak to certain of Messieurs, objecting that it was not the custom for Messieurs to make decisions concerning the appointment of sermons, the visitation of the sick, and other ecclesiastical duties without having first heard the mind of the Company of ministers, and that he found it extraordinary that they should now proceed differently. He also went to speak with M. de Béze and to object that he ought only to have agreed to this in the way that was customary. He therefore requested him to put this matter right, failing which he would be compelled to take it up with Messieurs in Council, in accordance with his duty as a minister.

At length a day was fixed by the ministers on which one would be chosen by lot to undertake the duty of comforting those afflicted by the plague, and on the day appointed, after all had unitedly called on the name of God, the lot was cast in the presence of the ministerial brethren from the country parishes in the following manner: a number of slips of paper answering to the number of those from whom the choice was to be made, and each with a name written on it, were placed and mixed together in a hat, which was given to one of the country ministers to hold, keeping it shut and not so much as casting a glance at it; then another set of slips of paper, equal in number and size to the first, on which, however, with the exception of one, nothing was written, was prepared, and all were folded and rolled up and placed like the first in another hat, which likewise was given to one of those not concerned in the election to hold; when this had been done, a third brother from the country approached the one who held the first hat and without looking drew out one of the slips of paper; then he whose name was written on the paper was called and rose to draw one of the papers from the second hat; and this went on until one whose name had been called drew from the second hat the only slip with writing on it, bearing in fact some word indicating this particular charge. The person thus designated was M. Jean de Gaigneux, who, after attending to such things as were necessary, devoted himself to this work. He was lodged in La Coulouvrenière[9] with a servant, so that he could be near the plague hospital outside the city.

As it happened, before he went there, but after this election by lot had taken place, M. de Bèze announced to the Company on 21 August that Messieurs wished to spare the ministers the necessity of visiting those afflicted with the plague and had appointed two supernumeraries for this purpose, the one for visiting those who were living in the city, and the other for visiting those who were in the hospital outside the city.

Some were in favour of accepting this offer of Messieurs, maintaining that in doing so we should not be contravening our oath according to which we had promised to serve even in the time of plague, since we had offered ourselves and cast the lot, and he on whom it had fallen was ready to be occupied in this ministry.

Others, however, opposed our acceptance of the offer, pointing out that to do so would expose our ministry to ridicule in view of the fact that it had long since been public knowledge that we intended to cast lots, and in view also of the fact that the church of Lyon had set us an example in this respect, for some of the ordinary ministers there had made it their business to go and comfort those who were struck down. It was resolved therefore that we should proceed in accordance with the original decision.

On the same day M. de Bèze announced that it was the wish of Messieurs that there should be two ministers in residence at St. Gervais, as was customary, and that these ministers should be M. Des Borde and M. Trembley, while M. Enoch, because of his age, should come and live on this side.

On Friday 25 August the brethren from the country were informed of what had been discussed and decided by the Company with respect to the offer from Messieurs to relieve the ministers of the duty of going to those afflicted with the plague, and their decision was approved.

After dinner we proceeded to the Council in this connection. On the morning of the following day we received the reply of Messieurs in the Council.

[9] La Coulouvrenière was situated in a suburb between the circumference of the city and the plague hospital, at the confluence of the Rhone and the Arve.

PUNISHMENT OF GASPARD ROCCA

In this same year the ministers attended the Council in order to complain about the gunsmith Gaspard,[10] an adulterer who had been placed in the stocks, and also about another adulterer living in the Peron.[11] A short time afterwards, this gunsmith had sought admission to the supper at the Consistory of the Italian church, where, on being questioned, instead of acknowledging his fault he had denied ever having committed adultery. When Messieurs were informed of this they put him in prison, brought him to trial, and had him flogged.

[14 September 1564]

COMPLAINT AGAINST THE COUNCIL

On Thursday 14 September, following a decision taken in the Company on the preceding Tuesday and Wednesday, the ministers of the city presented themselves in the Council, where M. de Bèze complained to Messieurs about the sentence passed on Amblard du Fossal.[12]

On Tuesday 26 September M. de Bèze went with M. the Syndic Roset to Berne.[13]

[3 November 1564]

DISMISSAL OF MERLIN

On Wednesday 18 October M. Merlin preached a sermon in which he maintained that it was no part of a magistrate's duty to concern himself with ecclesiastical affairs. This met with disapproval, and after several examinations he was dismissed from the ministry on 3 November.

---

[10] Gaspard Rocca (or Rocqua), who came originally from Turin, had been a citizen of Geneva only since 17 March.

[11] A street of Geneva in the parish of the Madeleine. The identity of the person mentioned is not known.

[12] Amblard du Fossal, who had been accused of committing adultery and harbouring political refugees, was found guilty and condemned to death by the Little Council of Geneva; but this sentence was commuted to a light punishment by the Council of Two Hundred.

[13] Beza was sent to Berne by the Council "to persuade the ministers there to approve the proposed alliance, which they were blocking".

[*10 November 1564*]

APPOINTMENT OF CHARLES PERROT AND JEAN-FRANCOIS SALVART

On Friday 10 November the brethren of both city and country assembled to elect two ministers, one to take the place of M. Merlin and the other to be appointed to Peissy and the neighbouring parishes. After naming four or five persons, they unanimously agreed on M. Charles Perrot[14] and M. Salvart.[15] Perrot was called in and accepted appointment, saying that he was conscious of his own inadequacy, and telling them that he was sure his mother would not disapprove. M. Salvart, however, excused himself on the grounds that he was afraid lest his father, who was still a papist, would find in this cause for still greater irritation against him. He also stated that he had already been approached by the church of Lyon, and that there were other reasons which he was unable to disclose in the presence of all the Company. The brethren answered him that because of the king's edict he would scarcely be able to live in Lyon, since he was a stranger, but that, be that as it may, the brethren would take every care to satisfy the church of Lyon and hoped to obtain his services. Regarding the other reasons, he was given time to think over the matter and asked to come and give his reply later that same day, before the assembly of the brethren had disbanded. When he came, however, he told them that he had been unable to make up his mind, and so they gave him until the following Monday. On that day he announced that he was prepared to accept appointment.

As a test of their suitability they were both given the opening section of Isaiah 29 to expound. Perrot preached on Monday the 13th of the month, and on the next day preached on the opening section of Romans 6. On Wednesday the 15th M. Salvart preached on the passage set from Isaiah.

On Saturday the 11th of the same month a letter arrived from the church of Nevers asking the brethren to send them M. Salvart or someone else as their minister.

A letter also arrived from M. d'Estrées[16] asking that our brother M. Jean Hellin, minister of Céligny, who had gone to France to attend to certain of his affairs, should be assigned to him as his

---

[14] From 1564 onwards Charles Perrot held various offices in the church and Academy of Geneva.

[15] Jean-François Salvart, also called du Palmier, of Valle d' Aosta, was at first a student in Geneva and subsequently pastor at Nevers.

[16] Jean d'Estrées, seigneur de Valieu et de Coeuvres, was Grand Master of Artillery in the royal armies.

ordinary minister. The Prince of Condé also wrote to Messieurs and to M. de Bèze in particular; and others who wrote for the same purpose were M. Pérussel,[17] minister in the Prince's household, M. de Momméjan, minister in the town of Chauny, and M. de la Chapelle.[18]

With regard to the request from Nevers, although a decision was deferred until the following Friday, the brethren of the city none the less agreed during the week that it would be good to send M. Jean de Léry.[19]

A decision on Monsieur Hellin was deferred to the Friday following.

On that day, the 10th of the month, Perrot and Salvart were examined by M. de Bèze for a period of about two hours in the presence of all the brethren. The examination took the form of a disputation.

They were then reminded of the conditions under which ministers are appointed in this church, namely, that they should serve at times in the city, at times in country parishes, in accordance with what was decided would be good and advantageous for the welfare of the churches. At this point Salvart took the opportunity of excusing himself courteously, and his excuses, which he put forward on Friday 24 November, were accepted.

Accordingly, since both Messieurs and the Company of ministers were in agreement that Monsieur Hélin should be assigned to the Seigneur who had asked for him as a permanent appointment, consideration also being given to the fact that the Prince of Condé had written about this, M. Louis Henri was put in his place. He had been preaching in the parish of Céligny while Hélin was absent, at the invitation of Hélin and with the approval of the Company of ministers.[20]

CHARGES AGAINST AN UNNAMED PERSON

On the return of N. from Tübingen, where he had been studying for a number of years, he was summoned before the brethren because it was reported that in debates and discussions with scholars he had maintained certain opinions opposed to the doc-

---

[17] François Pérussel, or Peroceli, also called La Rivière, was pastor successively of the congregations of French refugees in London, Wesel, and Frankfurt-on-Main before becoming de Condé's chaplain.

[18] Bernard de Momméjan and François Peintre, called de la Chapelle, were also pastors attached to de Condé's suite.

[19] Jean de Léry is well known for his account of the famous Calvinist expedition to Brazil (cf. note 6, p. 316 above).

[20] Louis Henri continued as pastor of Céligny until 1571.

trine of the holy supper which our churches hold; also that he had said that Maître Sebastian Castellio was an excellent person and he had no fault to find with him; and, again, that he had brought with him into this city a song formerly composed by Jerome Bolsec, who was now a prisoner in that city for the crime of heresy. N. answered that as far as the supper was concerned he had only recited the arguments of Brenz and others, without, however, adhering to their doctrine; that as for Castellio, he denied the allegation; and as for the song, that Jerome had given it to him, but that he had not approved of it nor did he approve of it now.

After witnesses had been called, however, namely, Vincent Textor and Perrot, it was established that he had spoken of the doctrine of the supper in a manner which showed acceptance and approval of the arguments of Brenz instead of acquiescing in the truth; also, that he had sung the song in question and caused others to sing it; and, further, with regard to Castellio, that he had praised him and said that he had no fault to find with him. This he admitted, but added that he was referring to his life, not his doctrine. He declared that he was in fact prepared to draw up a confession of his faith and to sign it in order to show what he really felt, with regard both to the supper and to the other points.

It was decided to admonish N. severely and to require him to draw up the confession of his faith before the following Thursday. This, however, he failed to do, and so there was no alternative but to summon him before the Consistory.

Shortly after, he produced his confession, but because he had not done it in the form requested he was told to do it differently. This he did.[21]

DEATH OF MATURIN CORDIER

On Friday 8 September that good man Cordier died happily at a great age. He had served right to the end in his original vocation as a teacher of the children and guide of the young in all sincerity, simplicity, and diligence, according to the measure which he had received from the Lord.

[21] The identity of the mysterious "N." is unknown. As for the witnesses called against him, Vincent Textor had been a student in Geneva since 1559 and "Perrot" was perhaps one of the non-matriculated students under this name. For the Bolsec affair see above, pp. 137ff. Castellio had been converted to Protestantism by Calvin in 1540 in Strasbourg. His development of theologically liberal opinions and his condemnation of the execution of Servetus brought him into conflict with the Genevan leaders. The Württemberg Reformer Johann Brenz held Lutheran views of the real presence in the eucharist which caused controversy with the Swiss Reformers.

INDEX OF PROPER NAMES

Achard, Jean, 321
Adrets, Sire Bardon de, 359
Aignon, - - -, 347
Aignon, Sire d'; see Bourgoin, François
Ain, Girod de l', 133
Airebaudouze, Pierre d', Baron of Anduze, 310, 351, 352, 355, 360, 361
Albeau, Lancelot d', 27, 337, 339, 348
Albiac, Accasse d', 338
Albiac, Charles d'; see Plessis, Charles du.
Ambrose, 156
Amar, - - -, 11
Andelot, - - -, 355
Andernar (Andernacus); see Guenther, Johannes
Anduze, Pierre d'; see Airebaudouze, Pierre d'
Angelus; see Lange, Jean
Anglois, Jacques l', 308, 352
Arche, Michel de l', 294
Argues Martin de, 318
Arlod, Domaine d', 146, 206, 222
Arnail, Bernard, 206
Ars, Jacques des, 131, 146, 150, 153
Athanasius, 225, 268
Aubert, Henri, 150, 306
Augustine, 21, 22, 138, 156, 157, 158, 162, 168, 273, 335

Bachelar, Antoine (Cabanes), 323, 350
Bacnot, Pasquier, 329
Bade, Josse, 225
Baduel, Claude, 315, 316, 325, 327, 350
Baldin, Jean, 62, 63, 83, 84, 105, 172, 284, 350

Ballotus, Joannes, 64
Bardel, Jean, 203
Bargio, Antonio, 192
Bargio, Elizabeth, 192
Barre, Jean de la, 108
Bataille, Bertrand, 313
Beatus, Rhenanus, 229
Beney, Guillaume, 146
Benoit, Guillaume, 204
Bérault, François, 343, 354
Bergier, Jean-François, 30, 31
Bernard, Jacques, 62, 63, 83, 105, 110, 111, 171, 188, 204, 223, 284, 292, 342, 343
Bernard, Jean-François, 325, 326
Berthelier, François, 12, 293, 294
Berthelier, Philibert, 11, 12, 19, 205, 285, 286, 293, 294
Bertrand, Cardinal Jean, 330
Beveridge, Henry, 115
Bèze, Théodore de (Beza), 88, 96, 117, 150, 214, 331, 343, 349, 352, 355, 360, 362, 364, 368, 370, 371, 373
Billota, Ludovica, 64
Blaise, Michel; see Morel, Michel
Blanchard, Jean, 356
Bocard, Julien, 150
Bodin, Jean, 203, 210, 211
Boinville, Sire de; see Lecointe, Guillaume
Bois, Michel du (Silvanus, Sylvius), 66, 67
Boisnormand, François; see Gay, François Le
Boissière, Claude, 329, 337
Bolsec, Jerome, 20, 21, 22, 23, 24, 132, 137–186, 201, 202, 296, 298, 300, 302, 374
Boltz, Valentinus, 174
Bonnaz (Bonne), Philibert, 205

Bonnaz (Bonne), Pierre, 150, 205, 306
Bonne, Philibert; see Bonnaz, Philibert
Bonne, Pierre; see Bonnaz, Pierre
Bonquin, Jean, 349
Bonvalot, François, 94
Bordat, - - -, 353
Bordes, Jacques des, 360, 370
Bordes, Marguerite des, 68, 69
Bordes, Pierre des, 69
Borrhaeus, Martinus; see Cellarius, Martin
Bosco (Bosque), Jean (or Pierre?) de, 348
Boulier, Jean (de la Roche), 26, 351, 355
Bourdillon, Maréchal de, 359
Bourgogne, Jacques de, Sire de Falais, 137, 140, 141, 142, 296
Bourgoin, François, Sire d'Aignon, 15, 62, 63, 83, 84, 105, 172, 188, 189, 190, 220, 222, 284, 303, 307, 327, 353
Bourrit, Charles, 133
Bouteiller; see Curtet, Jean-Ami
Brenz, Johann, 94, 151, 157, 374
Brosse, Mathurin de la, 321
Brueil, - - -, du, 340, 344
Brulé, Jean, 347
Brun, Geoffroy, 348
Bucer, Martin, 5, 6, 369
Budé, Jean (Veracius), 331
Bullinger, Heinrich, 11, 23, 24, 115, 118, 140, 151, 157, 158, 170, 175, 369

Cabanes; see Bachelar, Antoine
Calvin, Jean, 3, 4, 5, 6, 10, 12, 16, 17, 18, 20, 21, 22, 23, 24, 25, 26, 28, 29, 30, 35, 45, 58, 62, 64, 65, 66, 68, 70, 72, 82, 83, 84, 86, 90, 93, 100, 105, 106, 107, 108, 109, 110, 111, 113, 114, 115, 118, 124, 125, 128, 131, 132, 133, 134, 138, 140, 148, 149, 150, 151, 157, 159, 163, 166, 169, 170, 171, 182, 186, 187, 188, 189, 190, 191, 196, 200, 201, 204, 205, 208, 209, 217, 218, 220, 221, 224, 225, 226, 227, 237, 239, 244, 248, 252, 253, 260, 269, 276, 277, 282, 283, 284, 286, 290, 291, 292, 295, 296, 298, 301, 302, 303, 304, 305, 306, 307, 308, 310, 311, 312, 315, 318, 319, 327, 328, 330, 331, 344, 363, 364, 365, 366, 368, 369, 374
Cany, Madame de, 193
Carmel, Gaspard (Fleuri, Fleurier), 322, 350
Castellio, Sebastian, 136, 296, 302, 356, 374
Cellarius, Martin (Borrhaeus), 95
Chabod, François, 309
Chambeli, Jean, 320, 341
Chamois, François, 131, 146, 150, 153, 294, 306
Champereau, - - -, 61
Channourry, Antoine, 338
Chapeaurouge, Etienne, 206, 220
Chapelle, François de la; see Peintre, François
Chappelli, Jacques, 344
Charles V, 4, 175
Charretier, Guillaume, 27, 28, 317
Chautemps, Jean, 83, 190, 314
Chauvet, Raymond, 62, 63, 128, 172, 218, 219, 220, 284, 295, 296, 297, 303, 305, 306, 307, 309, 327, 368, 369
Chauveton, Germain, 349
Cherpont, François de, 321
Chéry, Antoine de, 216
Chevalier, Antoine, 343, 365, 366
Chevalier, Claude, 323
Chevalier, - - -, 320
Chicand, Antoine, 83, 131, 146, 150, 153
Chicand, Guillaume, 315, 321, 325, 326
Christiani, Jacques, 340
Christopher, Duke, son of Duke Ulrich of Württemberg, 87, 94, 95, 96
Clarke, Duke of Feltre, 133
Clément, Pierre, 184
Clement of Alexandria, 273
Clerc, Jean Le, 352
Coligny, Admiral Gaspard, 27, 28, 343, 353
Collènes, - - - de, 350
Colladon, Germain, 320
Colladon, Nicolas, 220, 284, 325, 327, 362
Colliod, Pierre, Sire de Varendal, 360
Collonges, Sire de; see Morel, François de
Combe, Siméon La, 356

Condé, Louis de Bourbon, Prince of, 355, 373
Cop, Michel, 62, 63, 105, 128, 172, 218, 220, 284, 303, 307, 327, 368
Cop, Nicolas, 63, 307
Cordier, Maturin, 374
Corne, Amblard, 12, 146, 150, 208, 294, 305, 314, 319
Corradon, Barthélemy, 338
Coudrée, Jean de la, 354
Cougnier, Louis, 62, 63, 84, 105, 171, 207
Cour, André Le, 297, 326, 327, 328, 354, 355, 356
Cousin, Jean, 150, 344, 348
Cranmer, Thomas, 29, 94, 185
Crespin, Valeri, 356
Curtet, Jean-Ami (Bouteiller), 187, 314

Diane de Poitiers, 330
Donzel, Jean François Philibert, 150, 314, 326, 327
Dorsière, Pierre, 147
Doumergue, Emile, 20
Droz (Drogy), Jean, 184
Duc, Pierre, 316, 354, 256
Dufour, Alain, 30
Dumoulin, Claude, 349
Dupan, Claude, 150, 294, 314
Dupuis, Jean, 341
Durand-Charroux, 128, 129

Ecclesia, Philippe de, 13, 14, 15, 62, 63, 84, 92, 93, 105, 106, 107, 108, 109, 133, 172, 188, 189, 190, 201, 202, 203, 204, 205, 206, 209, 210, 211, 220
Edward VI, 29, 367
Elie, - - -, 348
Elizabeth I, 29, 367
Enoch, Louis, 214, 316, 327, 370
Epiphanius, 164
Erasmus, Desiderius, 143, 172
Espeville, Charles d' (cover name of Calvin), 26, 290
Espoir, Jean d'; see Pleurs, Jean de
Estrées, Jean d', 372
Eusebius, 97
Eutychianus, Pope, 252

Fabri, Christophe, 180, 184
Fabri, Jean, 15, 113, 114, 172, 188, 189, 209, 211, 218, 219, 220, 284, 298, 299, 301, 303, 307, 314, 315, 316
Fabri, Nicolas, 210
Faget, Ambroise; see Gardepuys, Jean
Falais, Sire de; see Bourgogne, Jacques de
Faloys, Claude, 133
Faloys, Nicolas, 133
Faloys, Pierre, 133
Farel, Guillaume, 4, 5, 6, 9, 20, 23, 24, 28, 64, 93, 110, 116, 124, 127, 137, 180, 183, 184, 200, 201, 292, 296, 313, 322
Farges, Sire de; see Gribaldi, Matteo
Fatio, Henri, 133
Faverge, Gaspard de la, 356, 357
Favre, Antoine, 203
Favre, François, 84
Favre, Françoise, 84
Favre, Jean-Louis, 203
Ferron, Jean, 62, 63, 83, 109, 110, 111, 112
Fleuri (Fleurier); see Carmel, Gaspard
Folion, Nicolas (La Vallée), 347
Fontaine, Nicolas de la, 223, 224
Fossal, Amblard du, 371
Fosses, Pernet de, 128, 129, 130, 206, 208, 222, 321
Fraisse, Robert, 352
Franc, Louis, 321
Francis I, 4
Francis of Mayrone, 224
Frobenius (Froben), Joannes, 229
Fromentée, Philibert La; see Grené, Philibert
Fulgon, Jacques, 356
Fumée, Adam (du Mont), 68
Fumée, Antoine, 68

Gaigneux, Jean Le, 357, 370
Gallars, Nicolas des, Sire de Saules, 27, 30, 62, 63, 83, 84, 105, 171, 190, 209, 218, 220, 221, 223, 284, 310, 327, 328, 329, 330, 331, 337, 350
Garde, Guy La; see Moranges, Guy
Gardepuys, Jean (Ambroise Faget), 339, 348, 349
Garnerius, John, 216
Gay, François Le (Boisnormand), 328, 329, 340, 347
Gay, Jean du; see Gérard, Jean

Geisshauser, Oswald; see Myconius, Oswald
George, Count, brother of Duke Ulrich of Württemberg, 87
Gérald, Jean (du Gay), 26, 321
Germanus, Guillelmus, 64
Gervaix, Amyed, 146
Gilles, - - -, 341, 347, 350
Gointrat, Guillaume, 350
Goland, Simon, 134, 135
Graffenried, Baron de, 60
Graignon, Etienne, 344
Graignon, Jean, 347, 348
Grandjean Mathieu, 320, 324, 325, 326, 327
Graverius, Hugo, 64
Grené, Philibert (La Fromentée), 320, 350
Grenet, Antoine, 85, 307
Gribaldi, Matteo, Sire de Farges, 311
Grindal, Edmund, 30
Grury, - - -, 184
Gué, du; see Gay, François Le
Guegnier, Guillaume, 132
Guenther, Johannes (Andernar or Andernacus), 141
Guilhen, Jean, 312
Gyrfalconius, Thomas, 174

Hall, Basil, 16
Haller, Johann, 100, 105, 140, 304
Hamelin, Philibert, 289
Helias, - - -, 64
Hellin, Jean, 360, 372
Henri, Louis, 373
Henry II, 329
Henry, Jean, 348
Hérault, Antoine, 134
Hilary of Poitiers, 157
Hippolytus, 164
Hobé, Lucas (Seelac), 340, 341
Hosemann, Andreas; see Osiander
Hughes, Philip Edgcumbe, 31
Hyginius, Pope, 252

Ignatius, 252, 253
Irenaeus, 164, 224, 225, 229, 244, 245, 246, 247, 257, 264, 265, 266, 277
Issotier, Mathieu, 136, 356

Jacquème, Jean, 315
Jessé, Pierre-Jean, 128, 146, 150, 306, 311
Jonchée, - - -, La, 337
Justin Martyr, 224, 225
Juvenal, 138, 144, 168

Kik, J. Marcellus, 31
Kingdon, Robert M., 27, 30

Laborier, Antoine, 27, 309, 310, 311, 313
Lambert, Jean, 296, 306
Lange (or L'Ange), Jean (Angelus), 298, 301, 306
Larche, Michel de, 146
Laud, William, 17
Lauvergeat, Jean, 308, 310, 318
Lecointe, Guillaume, Sire de Boinville, 317
Lefèvre d'Etaples, 252
Legrand, Augustin, 318
Léry, Jean de, 317, 373
Lestral, Claude de, 147, 150, 190, 204

Macar, Jean, 207, 208, 218, 220, 221, 222, 284, 309, 310, 316, 322, 327, 337, 339, 341, 351
Maillet, Marin, 347
Maisonneuve, Jean de la, 138, 147, 150, 153, 311, 314, 315
Malesier, Mathieu, 62, 63, 83, 105, 172, 188, 204, 284, 292, 336
Marcion, 233, 235, 251
Mare, - - -, de la, 61
Marlorat, Augustin, 150, 347, 348
Marot, Clément, 45
Marquis, Claude, 357
Martin, 347
Martinengo, Clese, Count of, 193
Martyr, Peter (Vermigli), 193, 352
Mary Tudor, 29, 367
Masuyer, Pierre, 66, 67
Maubué, Charles, 326, 350, 362
Meigret, Laurence, 70
Melanchthon, Philip, 20, 157, 227
Mellevaux, Nicolas de, 297
Merlin, Jean-Raymond, 343, 353, 362, 367, 371, 372
Michalet, Jean, 309
Migerand, Pierre, 314, 315
Millone, Michelle de, 68
Molard, Hudriod de, 187, 189, 306
Molrey, Jean de; see Montliard, Jean de
Momméjan, Bernard de, 373

Index of Proper Names

Mont, Adam du; see Fumée, Adam
Monteuil, Antoine, 356
Montliard, Jean de (de Molrey), 297 326, 327, 360
Morand, Jean, 66, 67,
Moranges, Guy (La Garde, also La Porte), 26, 324, 338, 340, 344, 349, 354
Morel, François de, Sire de Collonges, 324, 325, 326, 327, 339, 341
Morel, Michel, 131, 146, 150, 153
Moulin, Bernardus du, 341
Moulin, Claude de, 221, 222
Mulot, Michel, 340, 344
Myconius, Oswald (Geisshauser), 172, 174, 175, 176, 184, 185

Nanas, - - - de, 353
Nicaise, - - -, 215, 217
Ninaux, Pierre, 128, 129, 295
Novatus, 283

Oecolampadius, John, 172, 369
Oliveer, Mathieu, 347
Origen, 224, 225
Osiander (Andeas Hosemann), 185
Osias (or Ozias), Martin, 190, 203, 210
Ouvrier, Bastien L', 352

Parens, Nicolas, 172
Pasquier, Pierre, 348
Paulus, Michel, 132
Paumier, - - -, 341
Peintre, François (de la Chapelle), 373
Pelagius, 283
Pernet, Jean, 147, 150, 314, 321
Perrier (or Pereri), Jean, 62, 63, 83, 105, 172, 284, 352
Perril, Jean de, 352
Perrin, Ami, 70, 107, 187, 206, 222, 295, 300, 309
Perrot, Charles, 372, 373, 374
Perrot, D., 362
Perrotel, René, 66, 67
Persius, Marcus, 174
Pérussel (or Peroceli), François (La Rivière), 373
Petit, Nicolas, 62, 63, 84, 105, 326, 327, 328, 339
Philippin, Jean, 187, 204, 208
Philo, 265

Pinault, Jean, 351
Piotay, Jean de, 297
Plessis, Charles du (d'Albiac), 338
Pleurs, Jean de (d'Espoir), 322, 336
Polycarp, 352
Pommier, Guillaume, 66, 67
Ponsellus, Petrus, 64
Pont, Claude du, 325, 327, 343
Ponvers, Jean de, 322
Porte, Guy La; see Moranges, Guy
Poullin, Valérand, 318
Poupin, Abel, 62, 68, 83, 105, 111, 150, 171, 188, 190, 209, 218, 220, 223, 284, 292, 303, 314
Prissac, Bernard de, 350
Prosper of Aquitaine, 157
Prudhomme, Jacques, 347
Pseudo-Clement, 249, 250, 251, 277
Pseudo-Tertullian, 164

Quisard, Urbain, Sire de Crans, 300

Ragaue, Gabriel, 362
Ramel, Jean-Louis, 208
Randon, Jean, 343, 348
Ravelletus, Renatus, 64
Renée, Duchess of Ferrara, 137
Ribit, Jean, 212, 213, 214, 354
Richet, Pierre, 27, 28, 317, 349
Rigotti, - - -, 150
Rive, Girardon de la, 83
Rive, Jean de la, 347
Rivière, François La; see Pérussel, François
Rocca, Gaspard, 371
Roche, Jean de la; see Boulier, Jean
Roches, Jacques des; see Trouillet, Jacques
Rodés, - - - de, 348
Roset, Claude, 114, 201, 371
Roset, Michel, 114
Rousseau, Nicolas, 328
Rouvières, Jacques, 337, 339
Roux, Guichard, 11
Roux, Jacques; see Ruffy, Jacques
Ruffi, Pierre, 92
Ruffy (or Roux), Jacques, 347, 350
Rufinus, 250

Sabellius, 258
Sachet, Pierre, 352
Saint-André, Jean de, 62, 63, 84, 105, 137, 172, 188, 218, 220, 223, 284, 303, 322, 324, 325

Saint-Paul, François de, 150, 344
Salvert, Jean-François, 372, 373
Saules, Sire de; see Gallars, Nicolas des
Saunier, Antoine, 64, 65, 67
Schärtlin, Hans Sebastian, 175
Schärtlin, Sebastian, 175
Scrymgeour, Henry, 360
Seelac, Lucas; see Hobé, Lucas
Seguin, Bernard, 344
Seguran, André, 337
Sept, Balthasar, 309
Servetus, Michael, 17, 18, 19, 20, 137, 223-285, 290, 291, 296, 302, 374
Silvanus, Michael; see Bois, Michel du
Sixtus III, Pope, 251
Soterus, Pope, 251
Steiger, Baron, 60
Sturm, Johannes, 142
Sulzer, Simon, 60, 174, 175, 176
Sylvius, Michael; see Bois, Michel du

Tachard, Martin, 323, 338
Tagaut, Jean, 343, 349, 350
Tapétier, Nicolas, 215, 216, 217
Tauray, G., 313
Tenant, François, 353
Tertullian, 224, 225, 229, 230, 231, 232, 233, 234, 235, 236, 237, 238, 239, 240, 242, 244, 246, 249, 251, 257, 258, 265, 266, 268, 277
Textor, Vincent, 374
Thiersault (Thierselet), Jean, 308, 309
Tissot, Pierre, 106, 114, 223, 294
Tournon, Cardinal de, 20
Toussain, Pierre, 93, 94, 96, 97, 98, 183
Trembley, Jean, 367, 370
Treppereau, Louis, 62, 63, 64, 65, 67, 83, 171, 212, 213
Trigalet, Jean, 27, 309, 310, 311, 313
Troillet, Jean, 200, 201, 202, 203
Trouillet, Jacques (des Roches), 337
Truckenbrot, Jacobus, 172

Ulrich, Duke of Württemberg, 87, 94, 95

Valla, Lorenzo, 21, 143, 168, 170, 174
Vallée, Nicolas La; see Folion, Nicolas
Vallier, Jacques, 347
Valtouchet, Hélie, 344
Vanchet, - - -, 350
Vandel, Pierre, 114, 187, 189, 295, 296
Varagli, Gioffredo, 323
Varendal, Sire de; see Colliod, Pierre
Vaucher, Gustave, 31
Veracius; see Budé, Jean
Veran, David, 338
Veriet, Jean, 354
Vermigli; see Martyr, Peter
Verne, Pierre, 309
Vernou, Jean, 27, 308, 310, 311, 313
Vesalius, Andreas, 142
Vèze, Gaspard de, 356
Vignaulx, Jean, 316
Villegagnon, Nicolas de, 27
Vincent, Antoine, 356
Viret, Pierre, 4, 5, 65, 70, 93, 150, 175, 200, 201, 292, 296, 299, 313, 342, 355, 360
Vitalis, François, 211, 218, 219
Vives, Antoine, 324
Voisinet, Jean, 344
Vuissenburgus, Vuolfgangus; see Wissenburg, Wolfgang
Vulliod, André, 296

Whitgift, John, 17
Wissenburg, Wolfgang, 174

Zanchius, Jerome, 193
Zébédée, André, 298, 300, 302, 306
Zwingli, Huldreich, 11, 148, 166, 170, 172

www.ingramcontent.com/pod-product-compliance
Lightning Source LLC
Chambersburg PA
CBHW071142300426
44113CB00009B/1058